13904138

The Best Sons of the Fatherland

The Best Sons
of the Fatherland

WORKERS IN THE VANGUARD
OF SOVIET COLLECTIVIZATION

Lynne Viola

New York   Oxford
Oxford University Press
1987

Oxford University Press

Oxford   New York   Toronto
Delhi   Bombay   Calcutta   Madras   Karachi
Petaling Jaya   Singapore   Hong Kong   Tokyo
Nairobi   Dar es Salaam   Cape Town
Melbourne   Auckland
and associated companies in
Beirut   Berlin   Ibadan   Nicosia

Copyright © 1987 by Oxford University Press, Inc.

Published by Oxford University Press, Inc.,
200 Madison Avenue, New York, New York 10016

Oxford is a registered trademark of Oxford University Press.

Library of Congress Cataloging-in-Publication Data
Viola, Lynne.
The best sons of the fatherland.
Bibliography: p.   Includes index.
1. Collectivization of agriculture—Soviet Union—History.
2. Collective farms—Soviet Union—Officials and employees.
3. Soviet Union—Economic policy—1928–1932.
4. Labor and laboring classes—Soviet Union.   I. Title.
HD1492.S65V56   1987   338.7′63′0947   86-17987
ISBN 0-19-504134-8

2 4 6 8 10 9 7 5 3 1
Printed in the United States of America
on acid-free paper

To Grace and Joe

Onward 25!
    Onward 25!
Steel
    worker-thousanders.
The enemy advances,
    it's time to finish off
this band
    of priests and kulaks.
Let thousand-horse-powered
    tractors puff
In place of
    worn-out jades.
The kulak is ready—
    look, again
With a sawed-off shotgun
    burrowed away in the backwoods.
To the front, 25!
    Onward, 25!
Steel
    worker-thousanders.

—From "March of the Twenty-Five Thousand"
by Vladimir Maiakovskii

Acknowledgments

The preparation of this book has been facilitated by the generous support of the Department of History at Princeton University, which awarded me university fellowships and summer aid during my tenure as a graduate student, and by the Russian Research Center of Harvard University, which granted me a postdoctoral fellowship in 1984–85. Part of the research for the book was carried out in the Soviet Union under the auspices of the International Research and Exchange Board (IREX), which awarded me a fellowship to study in the USSR as an exchange student at Moscow State University during the 1981–82 academic year.

While in the USSR, I worked at the Lenin Library, INION, the State Historical Library, BAN, and in Soviet archives administered by the Main Archival Administration (GAU). I wish to acknowledge the most gracious assistance offered to me by the fine staffs of these institutions. I am especially indebted to the GAU, which provided me with the invaluable professional experience of working in Soviet archives, and, in particular, to L. E. Selivanova of the GAU Foreign Department. My special thanks also to my Soviet advisor, Professor V. M. Selunskaia, who aided me greatly in my work and was always kind, patient, and good-humored in her dealings with a sometimes bumbling foreigner.

The remainder of the research was conducted in the United States, primarily at Princeton University's Firestone Library, the University of Illinois at Urbana-Champaign (often through interlibrary loan), and the libraries of Harvard University. I would like to express my gratitude to these institutions and their staffs and, in particular, to Dr. Orest Pelech, formerly the Slavic bibliographer at Firestone.

Many colleagues and friends have aided me in my work. My very special thanks to the members of my dissertation committee—Cyril Black, Richard Wortman, and Stephen F. Cohen—who provided invaluable criticism and suggestions for revision. Thanks also to Sheila Fitzpatrick, who first introduced me to the study of Soviet history (and to the 25,000ers), without whose aid this book would never have reached completion; Hiroaki Kuromiya, whose own work has had a tremendous influence on me and whose criticism has been invaluable; Sally Ewing, Bill Husband, Roberta Manning, Anne Rassweiler, and Pamela Thomson Verrico, who all read parts of the book; the History Department of the State University of New York, Binghamton, which has provided me with gainful employment and an encouraging, democratic work atmosphere; Betsy Fox-Genovese and Eugene Genovese for being special; and Governor Doug Bradford, who provided some rather unique stimuli to my work. I would also like to take this opportunity to express my gratitude to Nancy Lane and Henry Krawitz of Oxford University Press, and to Libby Seaberg; their encouragement and painstaking work on my manuscript deserve special recognition. Finally, I would like to thank R. W. Davies, who has contributed immensely, albeit indirectly, to this work through his pioneering research on the early years of collectivization; he has most generously allowed me to include in my book two of the tables from his monumental study of collectivization, *The Socialist Offensive: The Collectivization of Soviet Agriculture, 1929–1930*. Charles Schlacks, Jr., allowed me to draw extensively from my previously published article on the 25,000ers in *Russian History/Histoire Russe* for use in the second chapter.

Contents

The Best Sons of the Fatherland

Introduction

This is a study of the campaign of the 25,000ers (*dvadtsatipiatitysiachniki*). The 25,000ers were members of the "vanguard" of the Soviet industrial proletariat—skilled or highly skilled cadre workers, civil war veterans, shock workers, factory activists, Communist party members—who were recruited to participate in the collectivization of Soviet agriculture and to serve as the first cadre of collective farm chairmen in the newly organized collective farm system. The recruitment of the 25,000ers was the largest and most successful of the First Five-Year Plan mobilization campaigns and was conducted against the heady backdrop of the revolutionary-heroic atmosphere of Stalin's revolution from above. The 25,000ers entered the countryside in the midst of the frenzied drive to collectivize agriculture in late January and early February 1930. Their participation in collectivization and the initial organization of the collective farms was designed to serve as a breakthrough policy to enable the regime to implement the momentous transformation of agriculture and peasant life which took place at this time. The workers' primary purposes were to represent the interests of Moscow against a rural officialdom perceived to be incompetent, socially alien, and politically suspect (and, in so doing, to transform that officialdom by way of purge and recruitment of new cadres),

3

and to reorganize peasant agriculture by bringing the industrial revolution to the countryside. In 1930 there was a 25,000er on one out of every five collective farms in the USSR as a whole and on one out of every three collective farms in the major grain-producing regions. The majority of the 25,000ers remained in the countryside until the end of the First Five-Year Plan. By that time the campaign had evolved from a crusade to a state of siege. The transformation of the campaign was a reflection and consequence of the transformation which the revolution as a whole experienced in the countryside as it confronted the realities of rural Soviet Russia. The revolution gave way to repression, and the dynamism and enthusiasm of the first phase of collectivization were replaced by consolidation and entrenchment. The story of the campaign of the 25,000ers is a study of a leading detachment among the rank-and-file cadres of the Stalin revolution and their experiences in the collectivization of Soviet agriculture.

The 25,000ers, who dwell in both relative and absolute obscurity in the West, are regarded as heroes in the Soviet Union today: heroes of the working class and heroes of the First Five-Year Plan. Aging 25,000ers are, on occasion, featured highlights on Soviet television and several have even been cast in bronze, as was the case of the former worker Ivan Andreevich Buianov, whose statue stands in the village of Gorkii.[1] Mikhail Sholokhov immortalized the workers in his novel on collectivization, *Virgin Soil Upturned*, which featured the model 25,000er Davydov, said to be based on the character of a 25,000er from Rostov.[2] The 25,000ers receive standard mention—or tribute—in Soviet textbooks and historical works in an adulatory style generally reserved for current leaders and veterans of the Great War of the Fatherland (World War II). The 25,000ers numbered among the "best sons of the fatherland."[3] In the 1950s Khrushchev held them up as models when he decided to launch a similar policy in the recruitment of the "35,000ers"; Brezhnev hailed them as "worker-revolutionaries" in a speech celebrating the fiftieth anniversary of the October Revolution.[4] Criticism of the 25,000ers, while not anathema, is unwelcome, and in a recent case it was dismissed as "self-evident ridiculousness."[5] In the Soviet Union today, the 25,000ers have achieved official historical infallibility. They serve as a reminder of a more militant time when socialism was thought to be just beyond the next construction site or Vladimir Il'ich collective farm. They have become symbols of the First Five-Year Plan revolution.

By focusing on the 25,000ers, this book attempts to investigate an important detachment from among the previously anonymous cadres who helped to implement the First Five-Year Plan revolution and who, in doing so, enacted the final chapter in the Russian Revolution. The study of the

25,000ers illustrates the workings of the revolution and, in particular, the collectivization of Soviet agriculture. First, it sheds new light on the process by which the state mobilized support and recruited cadres for collectivization. Second, by providing an on-the-scene angle of vision, it illuminates the actual process of collectivization and shows how little the center's (i.e., the central authorities') intentions corresponded to the experience of cadres at the local level. Third, this book is intended as an exploration of the perspective of the cadres in the field and their work in the countryside. It is the first—and, to date, only—work to investigate a specific group of actors from among the rank-and-file shock troops of the First Five-Year Plan revolution and to follow them in their everyday work activities as "leading cadres" in socialist construction (or the building of socialism).

In a sense, this book unearths a lost chapter in the history of the First Five-Year Plan period and collectivization. The 25,000ers (along with other groups of leading cadres of the revolution) have disappeared from view in the West both because of the traditional historiographical concentration on high politics and because of the tragic consequences which collectivization had for much of the Soviet countryside. These consequences, in particular, have served to restrict and cloud the Western field of vision, with the result that more effort is directed at fixing blame than understanding the historical process and the actors who participated in the process. Acutely aware of this problem, the late E. H. Carr observed that much of Western historiography on the Soviet Union "has been vitiated by this inability to achieve even the most elementary measure of imaginative understanding of what goes on in the mind of the other party, so that the words and actions of the other are always made to appear malign, senseless, or hypocritical. History cannot be written unless the historian can achieve some kind of contact with the mind of those about whom he is writing."[6] A basic premise of this study is that an understanding of the motivations, perceptions, and behavior of the cadres who participated in collectivization is necessary for an analysis of both the process of policy implementation and the often tragic consequences of the policies and the process.

Such a premise necessitates, first, an explanation of how the state was able to enlist the active support of factory workers in the collectivization effort. Collectivization required the recruitment of hundreds of thousands of cadres to implement policy. With its focus on the 25,000ers, this book examines the issue of how the cadres of the First Five-Year Plan revolution were recruited. How did the state mobilize support for its policies? What types of factory workers were most likely to be responsive to the state's recruitment efforts? And why did workers participate in collectivization? The story of the 25,000ers demonstrates that Stalin's revolution from above had an important base of support in the working class, and that this particular group of workers—representative of a significant portion of the Soviet working class—was prepared to work in the countryside for an extended period of time and at considerable personal sacrifice.

The premise also calls for an analysis of the ways in which the social and political profile of the 25,000ers influenced their activities in the countryside and their understanding of collectivization and collective farm work. How did their prior experience in the factory, their preconceptions of peasants, rural officials, and the countryside affect their willingness to serve on the collective farms and their approach to work? How did the atmosphere of revolutionary heroics, class war, and external threat brought about by the First Five-Year Plan revolution and enhanced by capitalist encirclement influence them in their decisions to join the 25,000ers and in their perceptions of events in rural Soviet Russia? The 25,000ers' observations of the collectivization process, their relations with rural officials, and their work on the collective farms are explored in an attempt to illuminate these issues.

The final area of investigation, which derives from the central premise of the study, is an analysis of the collectivization campaign itself, using the 25,000ers as a vehicle for analysis. The 25,000ers were sent to the countryside to represent Moscow and to take control of the chaotic and frenzied collectivization campaign. The campaign of the 25,000ers illustrates the difficulties which Moscow encountered in attempting to exert its authority on the implementation process and to control rapidly moving events. It also sheds light on the workings of rural administration and its important role in determining the shape of the collectivization drive. The campaign of the 25,000ers offers new insights into how the countryside was governed during the early period of collectivization.

This book also attempts to resurrect the mentality of the times. The immense suffering caused by collectivization, the famine of 1932–33, and the ubiquitous terror of the late 1930s have understandably served to obscure our historical recollection of the optimism, excitement, and revolutionary militancy of the First Five-Year Plan revolution. The highly charged atmosphere of the times is often dismissed as artificial, barbaric, or reflective only of the mind-set of a relatively small group of fanatics and utopian dreamers. Yet there were many ''true believers'' (to borrow Lev Kopelev's description) and to some extent it was precisely the mentality of these true believers which preconditioned the country for the events of the 1930s. This makes the mentality of the times an important area of investigation. Needless to say, only a very small part of this issue is touched upon. However, it is an aim of the study to examine the mentality of the 25,000ers as well as (more peripherally) the mind-set of the rural cadres whom the 25,000ers confronted.

Although the study of mentality is necessarily impressionistic, it is important to attempt to reconstruct the reigning spirit of the times in order to understand the ethos behind the actions. Lev Kopelev, reflecting upon his own experience as a participant in the upheavals of those times, wrote:

> With the rest of my generation, I firmly believed that the ends justified the means. Our great goal was the universal triumph of Communism, and for the sake of the goal everything was permissible—to lie, to steal, to destroy hundreds of thousands and even millions of people, all those who were hindering our work or could hinder it, everyone who stood in the way. And to hesitate or doubt about all this was to give in to "intellectual squeamishness" and "stupid liberalism," the attributes of people who "could not see the forest for the trees."[7]

Although he cast his recollection against a harsh retrospective judgment, Kopelev's point is that his generation believed in what it was doing. This book examines one group of true believers. The study of the campaign of the 25,000ers is intended to provide insight into the workings, times, and cadres of Stalin's revolution.

1

Workers to the Countryside: From Revolution to Revolution

[T]he theory of "*samotek*" [spontaneity or drift] in socialist construction is an anti-Marxist theory. The socialist city must *lead* behind it the petit-bourgeois peasant countryside not otherwise than by *planting* in the countryside collective farms and state farms and transferring the countryside onto a new socialist path.

I. V. STALIN, "K voprosam agrarnoi politiki v SSSR"

The winds of revolution swept down upon the landscape of Soviet Russia for the third and final time during the period of the First Five-Year Plan (1928–32). The concluding chapter in the history of the Russian Revolution was to be based upon the twin pillars of rapid industrialization and wholesale collectivization. It was upon these foundations that the Soviet Union was transformed into an enormous construction site for the building of socialism. An army of shock troops within the Communist party, the Komsomol, and the industrial working class was electrified by the challenge of a new revolutionary struggle. Hundreds of thousands of urban Communists and factory workers were mobilized to struggle on the fronts of industrialization and collectivization. Twenty-five thousand industrial workers were recruited to lead the massive crusade to the countryside to collectivize peasant Russia in a reenactment of the civil war tradition of sending workers to the villages to build socialism. This was the Soviet great leap forward, and the nation was consumed with building, transforming, fulfilling and overfulfilling plans, and launching offensives. Struggle became the leitmotif of an epoch and a generation. The atmosphere was charged with militancy and sustained by visions of the millenium. The revolution of the First Five-Year Plan was celebrated as the final stage on the road to socialism and the historic realization of the goals of the October Revolution of 1917.

The origins of the First Five-Year Plan revolution derived from the original contradictions of the October Revolution. In 1917 the Bolshevik party, by means of the dictatorship of the proletariat, had embarked upon the road to socialism under conditions of international isolation and socioeconomic backwardness. The Bolshevik party had come to power in a country in which the peasantry constituted over 80 percent of the total population; the industrial working class, in whose name the revolution was proclaimed, accounted for less than 2 percent of the population and was still closely tied to the peasantry from which it originated.[1] There were neither historical precedents nor theoretical ground rules to guide the Bolsheviks in this first experiment in socialist revolution. The party, based on a minority dictatorship, confronted the task of modernizing a backward, agrarian Russia in order to create the requisite socioeconomic base to support the political superstructure which came into being as a result of the October Revolution.

Simultaneously, the party faced the necessity of attempting to preserve the tenuous balance of the worker-peasant alliance (or *smychka*), which had made a working-class revolution politically viable in peasant Russia and, in light of the failure of an international socialist revolution, which was to provide the primary theoretical justification for socialism in one country in the 1920s. Based upon a political compromise and mutually contradictory socioeconomic interests, the worker-peasant alliance was never intended to be a permanent fixture in Soviet society; the socioeconomic underpinnings of the alliance were expected to erode as the proletarian dictatorship developed into a classless society. The industrialization of the country would result in a shift of the population from the countryside to the cities and the creation of a fixed, majority-class proletariat; in the countryside, small-scale peasant agriculture would be replaced by modern, large-scale collectivized agriculture.

Until that time, however, the worker-peasant alliance was potentially unstable and could easily come apart if its precarious balance were not maintained. In the not-unexpected event of Bolshevik disillusionment with the peasant ally or of an attempt to assert the primacy of the proletarian ally during the transition to socialism, the alliance was likely to dissolve at the first sign of crisis and thereby jeopardize the party's goal of socioeconomic transformation en route to socialism. Such a crisis materialized first during the period of the Russian civil war and again at the end of the 1920s. The response of the party in both of these crises was to emphasize its proletarian identity and to appeal to the working class for support and aid in resolving the state's difficulties. The experience of the Bolshevik party in the crisis of the civil war was to be a formative experience and would prefigure the behavior of the party, the working class, and the peasantry in the crisis which was to take shape at the close of the 1920s. The civil war experience would also provide the precedent and tradition for the role of the working class in the countryside during collectivization and, most notably, for the 25,000ers' campaign.

The Civil War

Civil war raged in Russia for three years, exacting a death toll of some nine million—mainly civilian—lives as a result of battle field casualties, starvation, and epidemic.[2] The civil war followed four years of destruction wrought by World War I. When the Bolsheviks came to power, they confronted a ravished economy and an almost complete breakdown of food supply to the cities. Famine stalked the land. The dire food situation was further complicated during most of 1918 and 1919 when the major grain-producing regions of the country fell into the hands of the White armies. War Communism was introduced as the Bolshevik policy of the civil war years. It featured forced grain requisitioning, extensive nationalization of large- and small-scale industry, a ban on private trade, the partial elimination of a money economy, and Red terror; in short, War Communism was an attempt to leap into socialism. For the Bolsheviks the civil war became a struggle for political survival and a struggle against famine; perhaps contrary to logic, it also came to be known as the heroic period of the Russian Revolution.

The Struggle for Grain

The struggle for grain was of overriding importance during the period of the Russian civil war. Food supply problems did not begin with the Bolshevik victory in October; they began during World War I when inflation and a manufactured-goods famine impeded the market's free play in agricultural products and served as a plague on both the house of Romanov and the Provisional Government which came into being in the wake of the February Revolution of 1917.[3] Two important factors in determining the extreme form which Bolshevik grain-procurement policy assumed in 1918–21[4] were the brutality of the civil war and, during parts of the civil war, the loss to the enemy of such rich grain-producing regions as the Ukraine, Siberia, the Kuban, and much of the Volga area. However, what distinguished the Bolshevik policy from that of preceding policies was the party's definition of the causes of the grain problem and the class orientation adopted in the implementation of grain policies.

In 1918 Lenin claimed that the rural bourgeoisie was using grain as a political weapon against Soviet power.[5] According to Lenin and his party, the kulak (or wealthy peasant—see Glossary), who accounted for approximately 14 percent of the rural population on the eve of the revolution, was hoarding his grain in an attempt to subvert Soviet power and to starve the working class and the Red army. In order to defeat the kulak enemy, Lenin called upon the working class to lead a crusade for grain. He maintained that the working class was the "leader of the poor," the "leader of the toiler" in the countryside, and the "builder of the state of the toilers." The workers were to rally their allies, the poor peasants, against the kulak. According to Lenin, the class-conscious worker was the only force which the party could rely upon in the struggle against hunger. Moreover, with its close ties to the peasantry, the working class was assumed to be the most capable force in dealing with the dark peasant masses. The working class constituted the primary social constituency of Soviet power and therefore served as the main reserve for the recruitment of cadres to implement Bolshevik grain policy.[6]

The recruitment of workers for grain requisitioning began almost immediately after the October Revolution. During the first five months following the October Revolution, factories and plants often sent brigades of workers to the countryside to gather grain for their fellow employees. It was only in May 1918, when Lenin urged the workers of Petrograd to go to the countryside to gather grain, that the detachments began to be formed on a mass scale.[7] It is estimated that between 1918 and 1921 some 250,000 urban forces participated in grain requisitioning; factory workers reportedly constituted one half of these forces.[8]

Because class war was the basis of grain requisitioning, the detachments' first task was to rally the poor peasant to the side of the working class and Soviet power. This was done by means of the Committees of Village Poor (or the *Kombedy*), which were in existence from June to November of 1918.[9] The committees had two purposes. First, they were to aid the detachments in grain requisitioning; in return for their services committee members were to receive a certain percentage of requisitioned grain. Second, they served as a counterweight to the less politically and socially reliable rural soviets, which were said to be incapable of procuring grain.[10] Industrial workers were often instrumental in the formation of the committees and provided the cadres for about one quarter of all committee chairmen.[11]

The policy of forming the Committees of Village Poor was short-lived. Class war in the villages had sharply increased rural violence. The struggle for grain was generally not restricted to a struggle against the rural bourgeoisie. The middle peasant (the vast peasant majority midway between the kulak and the poor peasant) was frequently classified as an ally of the kulak, and was officially considered to be a wavering element in the village; the food detachments' task was to see that the middle peasant wavered to the side of Soviet power by ensuring that middle peasants did not receive the same treatment as the kulak. The food detachments soon found, however, that it was no easy task to divide the village according to urban preconceptions of rural social stratification. Villages often simply banded together against the urban interventionists. As a consequence, outbreaks of violence directed against the detachments were more than an occasional phenomenon.[12] The detachments responded in kind and this led to a marked anti-middle peasant—or more accurately, antipeasant—mood among both working-class detachment participants and the party at large.[13] In response to the increasing level of rural violence, the Committees of Village Poor were disbanded and attempts were made to include the middle peasant in the alliance of workers and peasants. However, rural violence did not diminish with the abolishment of the committees but continued as long as the policy of grain requisitioning was in force. The peasants did not part willingly with their grain; nor did the food detachments limit their grain requisitioning to kulaks and surplus stocks. The detachments frequently requisitioned subsistence stocks of grain, leaving the villages without food.

Grain requisitioning left the peasantry with bitter memories and a great deal of antipathy toward townspeople and workers. Peasant violence directed against the food detachments as well as near-famine conditions in the cities gave rise to feelings of hostility toward the peasantry among many groups of industrial workers and party members. Such hostility would be difficult to eradicate in the years following the civil war. Of more immediate significance, however, the rural violence of the civil war period, which had evolved from the policies of grain requisitioning, class war, and working-class intervention in rural affairs, would lead to the breakdown of the worker-peasant alliance by 1921.

The Dictatorship of the Proletariat in the Countryside

The Bolshevik party was an urban party with little knowledge of or experience in rural affairs. When the Bolsheviks came to power in October, they had no rural base of support, for peasants accounted for only 7.6 percent of the Bolshevik party's membership.[14] Well aware of the party's isolation, Lenin attempted to win the peasantry's support by issuing the famous decree on land at the Second Congress of Soviets. This decree, which abolished private ownership and nationalized the land, served to legitimize the peasant confiscations of gentry lands and to increase further the fragmentation of land holdings. This decree was a necessary political compromise; the party's goal remained the formation of a large-scale socialized agriculture. In October it appeared that the party was content to win the support of the majority of Russia's population and then to proceed slowly to socialism, but the civil war drastically altered the original circumstances under which the Bolsheviks came to power and won the peasantry's support. With the outbreak of the civil war it soon became clear that the initial deal made with the peasantry was not enough to secure the victory of Soviet power. It was imperative that the party quickly extend its political base to the countryside. As they had in the struggle for grain, the Bolsheviks would enlist the aid of the working class to storm the countryside in an attempt to implant the organs of the dictatorship of the proletariat in the villages of rural Russia.

The attempt to build a political base in the countryside was in large part an outgrowth of the struggle for grain. The members of the food detachments played a major role in attempting to erect the foundations of Soviet power in the villages. During the initial stages of the civil war, it soon became apparent to the Bolsheviks that the rural soviets could not be relied upon to implement the policies of Soviet power. Other socialist parties—the Socialist Revolutionaries, in particular—still maintained a hold in many *volost*-level soviets; at the level of the *sel'sovet* (see Glossary), wealthier strata of the peasantry played a political role disproportionate to their numbers in the general population.[15] The Bolsheviks therefore counterposed the institution of the Committee of Village Poor to the institution of the soviet in an attempt to bolshevize the latter. In 1918–19 many soviets were purged and reelected in order to obtain a social and political profile more closely attuned to the party's needs and ideals.[16] Industrial workers frequently were promoted into the rural soviet hierarchy, and by the end of 1918, they were said to constitute approximately 50 percent of soviet instructors on the *guberniia* and *uezd* levels.[17] Nevertheless, the rural soviets were to remain extremely weak and ineffective throughout the civil war years.

The main force of Soviet power in the countryside during the civil war years was the party. A concerted effort was made to bolster the strength of the party in the countryside. From 1917 to 1921 peasant membership in the party increased from 16,700 to 185,300; however, the expansion of peasant membership was deceptive since a large part of this expansion was based on the recruitment of peasant soldiers serving in the Red army.[18] Moreover, peasant Communists were the most backward stratum in the party. Since the party was aware of this fact, there was always an element of distrust implicit in the relationship between the central organs of the party and the rural party. This distrust was evident in the 1921 party purge in which 44.7 percent of all rural Communists were excluded from the party.[19] Industrial workers, both those who were recruited explicitly for rural party work or the food detachments and those who left the hungry cities during these years, accounted for a significant percentage of the rural party. According to one Soviet scholar, workers constituted from one fifth to one third of the party in grain-producing areas in 1918.[20] The real force of the party in the countryside, however, lay in the institution of the Communist instructor or plenipotentiary (often an industrial worker), who, because of party cadre shortages, was frequently granted extraordinary powers to override local institutions in order to implement policy.[21] The rural party, during its formative period, developed a style of administration which was heavily dependent on the use of force and campaignlike lightening raids into the villages to implement policy. The party remained an isolated outpost of the proletarian dictatorship in alien territory.

The working-class assault on the village was a literal attempt to install the dictatorship of the proletariat in the countryside. This attempt reflected the party's overall relation with the working class during the civil war. At this time the party relied on the working class for victory. Workers served also as the main pool from which to recruit cadres for administrative work in order to replace the highly suspect bourgeois specialists from the tsarist regime.[22] Due both to ideological imperatives and manpower shortages, the civil war quickly turned into an era of proletarianization: the old apparatus was "crushed," following the dictates of Lenin in *State and Revolution*. Caution and compromise were abandoned as the party launched an all-out drive toward socialism.

As the party attempted the leap into socialism, its initial compromise with the peasantry on the land issue was abandoned by some elements within the party's leadership and rank and file. An ill-fated and not entirely sanctioned drive was attempted to collectivize agriculture. Between July 1918 and December 1921 the number of agricultural collectives in the RSFSR (see Glossary) climbed from 912 to 15,819.[23] Many of these collectives were organized by workers—either those in food detachments or those who had fled the hungry cities. In later years workers would be hailed as the "pioneers of collectivization" because of the civil war experience. This first attempt at collectivization met with fierce peasant opposition.[24] The party would be forced to retreat from collectivization by 1921, but the important precedent of working-class participation in collectivization would be remembered as part of the civil war's heroic legacy.

The party's attempt to implant the dictatorship of the proletariat in the countryside during the civil war somewhat resembled an attempt to artificially inseminate rural Russia with the proletarian ethos, interests, and personnel of the Bolshevik urban center. In most cases rural Russia proved to be hostile territory for the party. By the end of the civil war the isolation of the party in its urban enclaves was painfully evident.

The End of the Civil War

Soviet power emerged victorious from the civil war. The alliance of workers and peasants, upon which Soviet power was based, did not fare as well and, in fact, was in shambles by the end of the civil war. It had held together only as long as the threat of the return of the White armies and the return of the gentry landlords hung over Soviet Russia. Once this threat was dispelled, there was no longer a bond to weld together the contradictory interests of the working class and peasantry. In the countryside, agriculture was devastated, famine haunted the villages, and the peasantry rose in rebellion against grain requisitioning and Communist rule. In the cities the ranks of the radical working class of 1917 were decimated by the losses in the battles of the civil war and by the mass exodus from the starving cities. The workers who remained were hungry, exhausted, and unwilling to continue the sacrifice of lives and ideals once the wartime exigencies were over. The urban economy lay in ruins and a wave of industrial strikes swept across the cities in early 1921. The policies of War Communism had wreaked havoc in the land. The party held on to the reins of power, but in deadly isolation from the peasants and workers who had brought it to the forefront in October. Rebellion at the Kronstadt naval base was the final blow: it forced Lenin and the party to discard War Communism and to sound the alert for a general retreat.

The retreat from War Communism also signaled a retreat from the countryside. This retreat left rural Russia, though starving and socially traumatized, in much the same condition it had been in 1917. The dictatorship of the proletariat had failed to make a significant mark on the countryside. The peasantry desired nothing more than the fruits of a traditional bourgeois revolution: land and the right to sell produce on the market without interference from the state. The abolishment of the market under War Communism and the state's grain-requisitioning practices had led to a direct clash of interests between the peasantry and the dictatorship of the proletariat. The tattered peasantry emerged the victor in this contest of interests; the party was forced to retreat from its political and social programs in the countryside. The organs of the dictatorship of the proletariat in the countryside entered into a state of siege which was to last for the duration of the decade.

The lessons of the breakdown of the worker-peasant alliance would be remembered for a long time to come. The civil war experience remained alive in the mind of the party, the working class, and the peasantry throughout the 1920s. The peasantry lived with a fear of the return of War Communism and Red commissars. The party and the working class retained different, and contradictory, images of the civil war experience. For some, the civil war experience served as a constant reminder of the frailty of the worker-peasant alliance and the need to appease the peasantry in order to preserve Soviet power. For others, the experience was recalled with bitter memories as one in which the cities were held hostage by the countryside. Many lived with a dread recollection of the starvation which had gripped the cities, the brute violence of the dark peasant masses, and the power of the kulak to threaten the viability of Soviet power and the well-being of the industrial working class. The legacy of the civil war would prove to be a cornerstone of Soviet policy in the decade of the 1920s.

The civil war experience provided the party with an additional legacy that was largely symbolic but equally significant. The civil war entered into the annals of party history as the "heroic period of the Russian Revolution." Despite the suffering and chaos of the times, the civil war would be recalled by many as a period of great revolutionary enthusiasm.[25] The civil war provided the revolutionary myths and traditions which Stalin was to call upon at the end of the 1920s, on the eve of the next great leap to socialism. The civil war experience set the precedent for active working-class intervention in the countryside. It established the proletariat as the leading force in the worker-peasant alliance. Henceforth, the proletariat would be hailed as the agent of revolutionary consciousness most capable of leading the backward peasant masses onto the path of socialism. Implicit in this definition of the role of the working class was a distrust of and disillusionment with the peasantry. The civil war tradition of active working-class involvement in the countryside would center on the rural class struggle, the pioneering attempt at collectivization, the storming of the villages to implant the dictatorship of the proletariat in rural Russia, and the all-important problem of grain. As time progressed, retrospective evaluations of the civil war would often fail to discern the distinctions between policies which derived from wartime necessity and policies which derived from ideological imperative. The traditions of the civil war period would reemerge in 1929 in the last of the great Russian revolutions.

The New Economic Policy

Lenin introduced the New Economic Policy (NEP) at the Tenth Party Congress in 1921. NEP began as a retreat from the policies of War Communism; it was intended to allow for a regrouping of forces necessary to a renewed socialist offensive. The primary task of NEP was to appease the peasantry and to win back its support. Grain requisitioning was replaced by a tax in kind in agricultural produce, and the market was gradually restored as the central mechanism for the state's procurement of grain to feed the cities.

NEP was designed to foster the economic recovery of the nation. In the cities further concessions to capitalism were granted; the ban on private trade was lifted, and restrictions on small, independent businesses were eased, while the state held on to the "commanding heights" of nationalized large-scale industry, banking, and transportation. The support of the peasantry and economic recovery were prerequisites to the survival of Soviet power during the transition to socialism. When international revolution failed to materialize and it became clear that aid from the advanced nations of Western Europe would not be forthcoming, the policies of NEP assumed an added imperative.

The dictatorship of the proletariat remained the foundation of Soviet power during this period. It continued to be based upon an alliance between the working class and peasantry. That alliance had been shattered during the civil war and the dictatorship of the proletariat had become in actuality a dictatorship of the party. NEP was designed to reforge the alliance and to rebuild the social support of the state. Officially, the alliance continued to be based on the leading role of the industrial proletariat, but as the 1920s progressed, the proletariat would lose this leading role. The stature of the peasantry would be enhanced during the years of the 1920s. NEP would be based less on an alliance than on a continuing struggle between the interests of workers and peasants and between their respective advocates in the party.

Lenin and NEP

NEP began as a reflection of the political pragmatism of Lenin. By 1924, however, NEP had cast off its cloak of pragmatism and had assumed a mantle of Marxist-Leninist theoretical legitimacy. During the initial phase of NEP, Lenin was forced by circumstance to reexamine the revolutionary alliance of the working class and peasantry, as well as the problems confronting socialism in backward Russia. In the process he developed a new theoretical construct which would enable socialism to be built in peasant Russia. In his last articles Lenin provided a set of guidelines for the party to follow during the transition to socialism.

Lenin confronted the issue of Russia's preparedness for revolution in his article "Our Revolution," in which he attributed the success of the October Revolution to a combination of a peasant war and a working-class revolution. Although he admitted that social and economic conditions in Russia were not ripe for a socialist revolution, he maintained that it had been the duty of the party to seize the revolutionary movement. Quoting Napoleon, he wrote, "on s'engage et puis . . . on voit." Translated into the language of Marxism-Leninism, this meant roughly that the party in 1917 had erected the political superstructure and would afterward proceed to build the base to support that superstructure.[26] This was a variation on a theme from his earlier work "What Is to Be Done?" In that work he had written that the Social Democratic intelligentsia would inject the working class with revolutionary consciousness, thus reversing Marx by implicitly postulating that consciousness determines being. In 1923 Lenin once again struck a blow at the forces of historical determinism. During the NEP years the party and the working class were to assume the role of conscious agents of history and to construct the social and economic base of socialism from the building materials of peasant Russia. This was what was meant by "building socialism."

Lenin compiled the blueprints for building socialism in his articles "On Cooperation," "Better Fewer, but Better," and "Pages from a Diary." In order to ensure the survival of Soviet power while awaiting the outbreak of international revolution, it was necessary to win the support of the peasantry and to lead them toward the path of socialism. This would be done through the vehicle of the agricultural cooperative, which would cater to the material self-interest of the peasantry and provide a base for nascent socialism in the countryside.[27] Lenin went on to say that Soviet power could hold out until international revolution broke out, provided that certain conditions were fulfilled. These conditions included the development of the cooperative movement, rural cultural revolution, industrialization, and, above all, the preservation of the worker-peasant alliance.[28]

Despite Lenin's emphasis on maintaining the support of the peasantry, he continued to reserve the leading role in the alliance for the industrial proletariat. The alliance was not one of equal partners. In "Pages from a Diary" Lenin defined the role of the working-class ally in the alliance of the transition period. In this article he called upon the working class to expand and further develop the nascent patronage (or *shefstvo*) movement—a movement in which working-class organizations assumed patronage over rural organizations or areas and provided them with various types of practical aid. According to Lenin the working class was the best propagandist of communism among the peasantry. Under the guidance of the party, the working class was to carry the idea of socialism to the peasantry and to act as the lever of cultural revolution and socialist transformation in the countryside.[29]

Lenin wrote in 1923 that NEP was intended to last for an entire historical epoch: one to two decades at best.[30] He left the party an ambiguous legacy. On the one hand he advocated a gradual evolution toward socialism in the countryside. On the other hand he maintained that the countryside, left to its own devices, would not spontaneously enter the path of socialism, that the conscious agents of history, in the form of the party and working class, would have to take the initiative in building socialism in the countryside. Similar to the ambiguities of "What Is to Be Done?" Lenin's NEP legacy provided no answer to the problem of what to do if the peasant resisted change, resisted socialism, resisted the agents of consciousness. Nor did he provide an answer of what to do if the worker-peasant alliance became unbalanced and the working class lost its leading role. The spirit of Lenin's NEP would be dutifully followed for the greater part of the 1920s; the party would confront greater problems in its attempts to put the policies of NEP into practice. The existing base of the dictatorship of the proletariat would stubbornly resist the party's attempt to transform that base into the foundations of a socialist society.

NEP and the Peasantry

The backwardness of Russian agriculture was the main obstacle to the successful development of NEP. Russian agriculture had emerged from seven years of war in a state of virtual devastation. In 1921 famine struck the countryside, claiming over 5 million lives.[31] Russian agriculture gradually recovered to its prewar level of production, and by 1926 grain production had reached its 1913 level. Despite recovery, Russian agriculture remained painfully primitive. The three-field system of crop rotation prevailed on all but 7.2 percent of arable land in the RSFSR in 1924.[32] Russian peasants continued to farm their small land holdings in scattered strips often dispersed over great distances. The survival of the village commune, which determined the allocation of village lands, the types of crops to be sown, and the pattern and schedule of agricultural labor, perpetuated these traditional patterns of Russian agriculture. The commune was granted a new lease on life by the 1922 Land Code, which sanctioned any desirable form of land tenure. Consequently, during the 1920s over 90 percent of all land holdings were held under communal tenure.[33] The technological level of Russian agriculture hardly surpassed that of the Muscovite period. The number of tractors in the countryside was woefully inadequate. The Russian peasant continued to rely on the horse and ox as well as on traditional primitive, wooden agricultural implements.[34] And most villages dwelled in splendid isolation from town and government, living and working according to the traditions and mores of centuries past. By any standard of measurement, Russian agriculture in the mid-1920s was deplorably backward.

Despite the backwardness of Russian agriculture, grain production did increase during the 1920s, reaching its prewar level by 1926. Underlying this apparent success, however, were serious strains in the marketing of grain during the NEP years. The revolution had destroyed or greatly weakened the two main suppliers of grain for the market and export—the large gentry estates and the kulak farms. The majority of Russian peasants in the 1920s did not produce grain exclusively for the market. Their first priority was to satisfy their own needs; consequently, the state depended for marketing upon the availability of the peasant's surplus stocks of grain. Moreover, after the revolution there was less incentive for peasants to market grain. Prior to the revolution the peasants had to sell grain on the market in order to obtain the cash to pay state taxes.[35] After the revolution the main incentive for ensuring that the peasants market their surplus grain was trade in manufactured goods.

During the 1920s the expansion of the internal market in grain was intended to ensure a market for the state's manufactured goods and to provide the necessary flow of revenues to finance the state's industrial development. However, in order to ensure a net profit for industry, it was necessary to turn the terms of trade against the peasantry. This led to a situation in which the peasants were likely to withhold their grain until agricultural prices rose. This was precisely what occurred during the scissors' crisis of 1923–24. As a consequence the party was forced to raise agricultural prices. The rise in agricultural prices hindered industrial development and, by 1927, would lead to a manufactured-goods famine and a crisis in grain procurement. In the 1920s pricing policy became a major issue in the party's debates with the left opposition, led by Preobrazhenskii, urging that the terms of trade be turned against the peasantry to hasten industrial development, and the right opposition, led by Bukharin, claiming that this would lead to a complete withdrawal of the peasant from the market and, consequently, the breakdown of the worker-peasant alliance.

The left opposition objected to the orientation of NEP agricultural policy under the diumvirate of Stalin and Bukharin. In order to expand the internal market, the diumvirate required a prosperous peasantry. Bukharin went so far as to tell the kulak to enrich himself.[36] Under the diumvirate the road to socialism in the countryside was diverted onto a capitalist detour. The economic policies of NEP contradicted the political aims of the dictatorship of the proletariat. The left opposition accused the party leadership of dismissing the danger of the kulak and slighting the interests of the proletariat. And, in fact, during the 1920s there was a renewed tendency, however slight, toward social stratification in the countryside.

The problems of the backwardness of Russian agriculture acted as an obstacle to the successful development of NEP. Despite the best intentions of the party, the economic realities of rural Russia impeded the progress of socialism in the countryside. The party's only recourse was to attempt to build up the infrastructure of the dictatorship of the proletariat as a mechanism for implementing policies to foster the progress of Russian agriculture and socialism in the countryside.

The party remained the primary force of Soviet power in the countryside during the 1920s. There had been an attempt to strengthen the rural party during the years of the civil war, but the party purge of 1921 had decimated its ranks.[37] Between 1921 and 1923 little was done to strengthen the rural party; in fact, discriminatory class policies were enforced against peasant recruitment. In 1924 at the October plenum of the Central Committee of the Communist Party, Stalin and Bukharin called for, against the opposition of Zinoviev and the Leningrad party organization, improved party work in the countryside. The result was an increase in the number of peasants in the party between 1924 and 1926.[38] In addition, over 3,000 urban Communists were poured into the countryside in 1924 to strengthen the rural organs of Soviet power, including the party.[39] In 1927, however, restrictions on peasant recruitment were once again in effect. The party was to remain largely an urban organization with an extremely weak and ineffective base in the countryside.[40]

In 1926 there were 25.5 rural Communists for every ten thousand rural inhabitants as compared to 319.3 Communists per ten thousand urban inhabitants.[41] Furthermore, the percentage of rural Communists who were farmers according to occupation was extremely low. The average peasant could not afford the time away from his farm which was required for party work. Consequently, the percentage of wealthier peasants and rural officials in the party was disproportionately high.[42] The quality of rural Communists was also a major problem during the mid-1920s. Only 3.7 percent of the members of the rural party had either a higher or secondary school education; 35.4 percent were either illiterate or self-educated.[43] In addition, the rural party suffered from inexperience and low tenure. For example, in 1927 over 50 percent of rural Communists were still only candidates; almost half of the members of the rural party had joined after 1924.[44] Finally, the rural party was accused of harboring a variety of backward tendencies, ranging from religious activities to drunkenness to corruption.[45]

The civil war had left its mark on the Communist party in the countryside. There was an attitude of mutual distrust between Communists and peasants during the 1920s. Moreover, the style of party interaction with the rural population contradicted the spirit of NEP and recalled the reigning ethos of War Communism from the civil war days.[46] Rural Communists tended to be heavy-handed in their dealings with the local population. The rural party often seemed to resemble a state under siege. Rural Communists were accused of perpetuating civil war styles of command and of treating all peasants as if they were kulaks.

Soviet power made even fewer inroads into the countryside. In 1923 each *sel'sovet* serviced as many as five villages on the average; by 1929 there was only one *sel'sovet* for every 8.31 rural settlements in the RSFSR and only 1,447,928 members (for the USSR as a whole) amidst a rural population of some 125 million. The organs of Soviet power were staffed primarily by peasants, and, as they did in the rural party, wealthier peasants and officials tended to predominate—especially after 1925. Furthermore, in 1925 only 9.4 percent of all *sel'sovet* members were Communists.[47] In the mid-1920s there was an attempt by the state to strengthen the rural soviets. However, the campaign to revitalize the soviets did little to improve their authority in the countryside, and the soviets remained weak and largely inactive throughout the 1920s.[48]

The basic weakness of the soviets lay in the fact that throughout the 1920s they were overshadowed by the traditional organ of peasant authority—the village commune. The village soviets were dependent upon the commune— the real organ of rural government during the 1920s—for their budgets. Thus, the state had to depend upon a traditional peasant institution, which was a stronghold of the wealthier strata of the village, to govern the countryside.

The consequences of the state's failure to establish the infrastructure of the proletarian dictatorship in the countryside seriously undermined its efforts to follow the dictates of Lenin's last articles. This was most notably evident in the agricultural cooperative movement. Although the number of consumer cooperatives increased during the 1920s, encompassing 37.8 percent of all peasants by 1927, the cooperatives tended to attract the wealthier strata of the peasantry in numbers disproportionate to their weight in the general rural population.[49] Part of the reason for this was that there was no regulation of the cooperative movement from above; the state depended upon agricultural specialists to foster the progress of the cooperative movement. Yet most of these specialists were so-called bourgeois specialists who had worked on the Stolypin peasant reform before the revolution and who continued to promote the consolidation of peasant farms into private homesteads instead of promoting socialized agriculture.[50] In addition to having problems with the cooperative movement, the state failed to implement a serious program of agricultural investments. Most of the state's funds were poured into industry during this period; moreover, of the credit which was directed to the countryside, only 50 percent went to the cooperatives while the rest was invested in private farms.[51] By the end of the 1920s the cooperative movement was to signify an ideal for the most part, rather than a real movement.

The dictatorship of the proletariat was not a reality in rural Russia during the NEP era. Lenin's legacy remained a theoretical abstraction which was realized only in the great debates of the Soviet leaders at conferences, plenums, and congresses of the Communist party. By 1927 the peasant was no closer to socialism than he had been in 1921. The worker-peasant alliance resembled two wartime enemies retreating during a winter armistice to recoup their losses. Moreover, there were many voices in the party and the industrial working class which claimed that the interests of the proletariat were being slighted and ignored by the policies and practices of NEP. It was claimed that the leading role of the proletariat in the worker-peasant alliance was being eroded.

NEP and the Working Class

In 1923 Lenin had urged the working class to go to the countryside and lead the peasantry to socialism; the workers were to assume, in practice and not just in theory, the leading role in the worker-peasant alliance. And some workers did, in fact, make the journey to the countryside but, instead of building socialism, they more often impeded its potential for development.

The rural patronage movement was expected to provide a bridge between the working class and the peasantry during the transition to socialism. In 1926 there were over one million members in the movement. Yet, in actuality, the patronage movement had little real impact among workers, given that only some 7 percent of the million-member-strong movement were said to be active members.[52] The primary orientation of the patronage movement was cultural; the movement's activities were limited to the organization of village libraries and literacy classes and the sending of literature and newspapers to the villages. At the Fourteenth Party Congress in 1925, Molotov urged the patronage movement to become involved in practical work—aid to the rural party, soviets, and cooperatives. However, until 1929 the movement was to remain a highly ineffective instrument for social change in the countryside.[53]

Throughout the 1920s the patronage movement was criticized for its "parade-style" activities in the countryside. The most frequent activity of the worker-patrons was speech making. Although delivering speeches allowed workers to practice oratory skills that were in abeyance since 1917, the peasants gained little else. One frustrated peasant said, "We are sick of hearing about the international situation."[54] The patrons were also renowned for their dramaturgical prowess and often staged performances of revolutionary plays in the village. The peasants soon tired of this as well and urged their patrons to do something practical for them. They asked for economic aid, agricultural implements, and agronomic assistance.[55] Instead, they received well-intentioned social and cultural work. This often led to conflict. For example, during an epidemic one village called upon its patrons for medical assistance. Great was their displeasure when their patrons arrived and staged a performance of a play instead.[56] The patronage movement failed to become a mass movement of workers in the 1920s, and the patrons did little to strengthen the status of the working class in the eyes of the peasantry.

The status of the working class fared little better in the cities during the NEP era. In the 1920s factory workers—especially youth, women, and the unskilled—experienced serious economic hardship. Unemployment was endemic in the 1920s and increased dramatically as the decade progressed, largely as a result of rural overpopulation and the consequent influx of peasants to the cities in search of urban employment.[57] Industrialization failed to keep pace with the growing demand for jobs. As the urban population expanded with rural migrants, housing problems became more and more acute, thereby adding further to the problems of the industrial proletariat.[58] The economic position of the Soviet working class failed to fulfill the rising expectations of material betterment which had come about as a result of the 1917 revolution.

As the social and economic status of the working class declined during the 1920s, there was a tendency for many workers to pin the blame on NEP policy. Workers often perceived the peasantry and urban bourgeoisie as recipients of NEP favoritism. Social and economic inequalities were on the rise in the 1920s. Wage differentials between factory workers and white collar workers widened.[59] This led to increasing working-class antipathy toward bourgeois specialists. Moreover, expensive food stores, Gypsy restaurants, and gambling houses returned to the cities, thus granting NEP an aura of bourgeois decadence. Popular literature of the 1920s portrayed NEP society as decadent, bourgeois, corrupt, and littered with class aliens.[60] In addition, many workers began to resent the relatively privileged NEPmen (private traders)—especially those who traded in food produce. By 1927 the NEPmen were supplying the cities with over 50 percent of meat products, as well as other agricultural produce. As food supply problems increased in 1927–28, workers were forced to buy much of their food at speculative prices from the NEPmen.[61]

The peasant was also a target for working-class grievances. Urban unemployment, housing shortages, and food supply problems served to intensify urban-rural antagonisms, particularly towards the end of the 1920s. Many workers, especially those who had sunk deep roots into urban life, resented peasant newcomers for taking workers' jobs and blamed the peasantry for urban food problems.[62] By 1927 the proletariat was hardly in a position to view itself as the leading force in the worker-peasant alliance. And the situation was to grow far worse after 1927, when NEP entered its crisis.

THE CRISIS OF NEP

The last years of NEP ushered in a period of incessant crisis. Although Lenin's NEP legacy was accepted by the party as the main foundation for building socialism in the years 1921–27, in practice his legacy foundered on the harsh realities of peasant Russia and on the party's inability to strengthen the dictatorship of the proletariat in the countryside. The party's policy in the countryside amounted to a policy of noninterference and drift in the sphere of rural affairs. By 1927 the worker-peasant alliance was hardly a reality. The policies of NEP had been designed to avoid the dangerous and theoretically untenable possibility of a breakdown in the worker-peasant alliance. The crisis of NEP, which began with the war scare of 1927, proved that the feared breakdown had become a reality.

The 1927 war scare brought to the surface popular fears of military intervention, dormant since the days of the civil war. The nation soon came to resemble a state under siege, and parallels were drawn with the civil war era. This served to revive memories of the urban famine of the civil war. The haunting fear of a kulak grain strike swept across urban Soviet Russia as food supply problems intensified in the late 1920s. As the civil war era was recalled in the minds of Communists and many workers, so, too, was the military heroic tradition of that era recalled. The revolutionary ethos of those times was reborn. There was a marked inclination toward the acceptance of radical, maximalist solutions in dealing with the problems of Soviet Russia. Many were impatient to see the goals of October fulfilled, and the tenor of the times was reflected in two new slogans of the late 1920s which posited that there were no fortresses which a Bolshevik could not storm and that the Bolsheviks were not "vegetarians" in the realm of class relations. This set the scene for the third revolution, which would begin in 1929; the more immediate consequence of the war scare, however, was the beginning of a crisis in the state's relations with the peasantry.

In 1927–28, despite a good harvest, grain marketings declined precipitously due to low state procurement prices for grain. The kulak was accused of initiating a grain strike in order to sabotage the state's industrialization program and to undermine the dictatorship of the proletariat. The war scare had made industrialization imperative: Soviet Russia either had to build up its defense capabilities or it would be destroyed, existing as it did in the midst of capitalist encirclement. The party panicked, believing that the peasant would withdraw from the market, thereby jeopardizing industrialization by cutting off the flow of capital revenues to build up Soviet industry. The state had no grain reserves, and the urban population had grown rapidly during the 1920s, thus requiring a comparable increase in food supplies. The all important issue of grain and food to feed the cities and the Red army arose to threaten the stability of the state.

In the cities the working class was hit hard by the food supply crisis. Rationing was reintroduced as in the days of the civil war. Most workers were forced to turn to the private market in order to feed themselves and their families.[63] On the private market, prices skyrocketed and speculation ran rife.

At the state stores, workers stood for hours in queues. The food problem was a central issue in the minds of many workers.[64] The leadership, meanwhile, was not unaware of the dangers of working-class discontent fueled by the problems of food supply.[65] Many workers were already disgruntled due to what they perceived as NEP favoritism toward the peasantry and bourgeois specialists. In 1928 urban class antagonisms were further inflamed by the Shakhty trial, which charged bourgeois specialists with economic sabotage on behalf of foreign capital.

The party responded to the grain crisis by implementing extraordinary measures.[66] An aura of War Communism hung over the countryside as the practice of forced grain requisitioning was reimposed. The rural party was fiercely criticized for its timidity in the face of the kulak grain strike. Urban forces were poured into the countryside in order to implement grain requisitioning. Rural violence became an everyday phenomenon as peasants launched attacks on grain-requisitioning brigades, and the brigades responded in kind.

The grain crisis led to a new split in the party. The right opposition led by Bukharin criticized the use of extraordinary measures and accused Stalin and his supporters of reviving the practices of War Communism. The right claimed that this was leading to the dreaded breakdown in the worker-peasant alliance. The lesson which Bukharin and his allies had learned from the civil war was that it was necessary to pacify the peasantry at any cost. They proposed more moderate rates of industrialization, higher prices for agricultural products, and increases in the supply of manufactured goods to the countryside.

For Stalin and his supporters the lesson of the civil war was somewhat different. Stalin also recognized the necessity of maintaining the alliance and the support of the peasantry. Throughout most of the 1920s he had advocated policies in precisely this direction. However, in 1927–28 Stalin viewed the possibility of a breakdown in the alliance and the dangers of the grain crisis in terms of the consequences which they would have for the working class. For Stalin the lesson of the civil war was the loss of working-class support for the state in 1921. In his speeches of 1927–28 he dwelled upon the threat of urban famine and proposed the collectivization of Soviet agriculture as the ultimate solution to the problems of food supply, industrialization, and defense. Stalin and his supporters in the party would not tolerate concessions to the peasantry, and believed that the only solution to the crisis of NEP was a renewed socialist offensive on all fronts. This included, first and foremost, the collectivization of Soviet agriculture. The crisis atmosphere of the late 1920s precluded moderate approaches to socialist construction. It also called to mind the revolutionary heroic period of the civil war, thereby providing the context in which the party would once again call upon the industrial proletariat for active support in the First Five-Year Plan revolution.

Collectivization and the Onset of Revolution

Stalin placed increasing stress on collectivization from the time of his 1928 journey to Siberia. He set the tone for much of the party in his speeches of 1928–29 and specified the reasons why collectivization was a *political* necessity. Stalin laid stress on three features in particular of the current crisis—the growing danger of the kulak, the necessity of maintaining a high rate of industrialization, and the threat of a breakdown in the relations of the working class and the party if food supply problems continued.[67] Underlying these three aspects of the crisis was the threat of war, a theme with which he was especially concerned at the Central Committee plenum in July 1928. He spoke of the danger of the lack of a grain reserve in the case of war. He maintained that this could lead to a two-front war similar to the civil war, when the nation struggled against both the White armies and a peasantry reluctant to part with its grain.[68] A massive peasant rebellion sparked by grain requisitioning and linked to a foreign invasion could spell the doom of the Soviet state. At the Central Committee plenum in April 1929, he once again warned of the danger of a breakdown in party–working-class relations if the grain crisis and consequent food supply problems were not resolved. Collectivization was a political necessity. Therefore, he stated categorically that it was necessary to begin *gradually* to organize agriculture on the basis of large-scale collective farming.[69] The implicit message of his emphasis on the danger of a breakdown in the state's relations with the working class was that collectivization, as an integral part of industrialization and the resolution of food supply problems, was of immediate interest to the working class.

Although in 1928 and early 1929 Stalin stressed the importance of collectivization and even spoke of the "inevitability" of exacting a "tribute" from the peasantry, as late as April 1929 he still maintained publicly that small-scale individual peasant farms would continue to play a "dominant" role in the foreseeable future.[70] Between April and early November 1929 he maintained an intriguing silence on matters of collectivization and the countryside. In the meantime the assault on the countryside began, and collectivization became a reality in the Soviet countryside.

From 1 June to 1 October 1929 the percentage of collectivized peasant households in the USSR increased from 3.9 to 7.5. The increase was most marked in the major grain-producing regions. The Lower Volga and the North Caucasus surpassed all other regions with percentages of collectivized peasant

households of 18.1 and 19.1, respectively.[71] Although enthusiastically supported by the center, collectivization in the summer and fall of 1929 was
largely the result of campaigns launched by regional, *okrug* (see Glossary),
and district party organizations. Commenting on regional and district initiative in collectivization in this period, R. W. Davies has written that "the
central authorities were confronted 'from below' with plans which exceeded
their own expectations . . . "[72] This pattern, in fact, was to continue
throughout the initial stages of collectivization.

The high rates of collectivization achieved in the major grain regions encouraged the central authorities in Moscow to adopt more ambitious collectivization plans of their own. The Central Committee plenum of November
1929 announced a course of wholesale collectivization. This announcement,
however, was less a "decision" than an endorsement of the actions of the
provincial party organizations. According to Davies, the November plenum
"registered and announced" the shift in party policy toward wholesale collectivization rather than inaugurating it.[73] This would also be true of the
national legislation on collectivization which was based on plans formulated
by the December Politburo commission on collectivization and published on
5 January 1930. The tempos which the Politburo set for collectivization in the
January decree were indeed radical. The Lower Volga, the Middle Volga, and
the North Caucasus were to complete wholesale collectivization by the fall of
1930 or, at the latest, the spring of 1931; all remaining grain regions were to
complete their campaigns by the fall of 1931 or, at the latest, the spring of
1932.[74] However, the national legislation was grafted onto already existing
regional legislation which had announced sometimes similar, sometimes more
excessive, tempos of collectivization long before the January decree and in
many cases even before the conclusion of the Politburo commission's work.[75]
This, in fact, became something of a pattern as the regional, *okrug*, and district
party organizations pushed central policies to the limit, thereby encouraging
or necessitating revisions and refinements of central directives to keep pace
with the furious development of the campaign.

No one in the party—including Stalin, who had remained silent until
November—could have foreseen the radical turn of events which took place
in November and December; certainly no one foresaw what was to follow in
the winter 1930 collectivization campaign. The center stepped in to take
charge of the collectivization movement midway into the campaign; by this
time the campaign had already acquired a dynamic of its own. The political
atmosphere of the First Five-Year Plan period and the mounting fervor of the
provincial party organizations set the pace for the collectivization campaign.
And the campaign, developing on the heels of the grain-requisitioning drives
of 1929, had engendered massive policy violations in the countryside and a

wave of peasant discontent. The disorder, along with the sheer magnitude of the campaign, required strong leadership, which, the center argued, only the proletariat could provide. Wholesale collectivization increased the countryside's need for manpower and once again placed into focus the weakness of the infrastructure of the proletarian dictatorship in the countryside.

Cadre formation became one of the most urgent tasks of the Soviet state during collectivization. Throughout the 1920s, party and government presence in the countryside was extremely weak. As late as 1 January 1930, there were only 339,000 Communists in the countryside.[76] The countryside was in the grips of the so-called people famine. And by 1929 the range of problems which the state confronted in rural administration through the civil war and NEP periods was further complicated by a renewed emphasis on the political and social unreliability of rural officialdom. The rural party, which was hit proportionately harder than any other sector of the party in the 1929–30 purge, was accused of harboring "class aliens" and a disproportionate number of wealthy peasants.[77] The *sel'sovet*s were subject to these same accusations,[78] and both soviet and party organs were accused of resisting central policies and/or of committing serious mistakes in the implementation of policy.

The party distrusted its rural officials and bemoaned their poor qualifications and suspect class origins, attributing problems in policy implementation to these factors. Although these factors did indeed account for many problems, an equally significant problem of rural officialdom was structural. The rural administrative structure was burdensome, the line of command confused, and the demarcation of responsibility and function blurred and poorly defined. Consequently, rural policy implementation often tended either to the extreme of inertia or, as in the civil war days, to campaign-style politics. Attempting to prod rural officialdom into action was not entirely unlike the situation faced by the tsarist regime in 1914: it was a question of all or nothing—total mobilization or total inertia.

These structural problems were complicated further during the grain procurement crisis of the late 1920s. The implementation of extraordinary measures entailed a certain amount of "reconstruction" of the rural apparatus through purges, expulsions, and dismissals.[79] Many of the rural cadres in office in 1928–29 were new to their posts and inexperienced. Moreover, they had received their "preparatory training" in the civil war atmosphere of the grain-requisitioning campaigns. This pertained especially to party officials above the village level. They often began their work as plenipotentiaries with extraordinary powers to overrule local organs. This experience was formative. Village-level organs, on the other hand, had been largely superseded in their powers by higher administrative bodies and plenipotentiaries during the requisitioning campaign. The training of village-level authorities in the grain-requisitioning campaign derived either from a confrontational stance with higher authorities or from powerlessness and consequent inactivity.

Although the differences in the institutional behavior of rural officials were rooted largely in the structural mechanism of administration in the countryside, the party continued to place the greatest emphasis on the "politics" of rural officialdom rather than on its structural problems. The rural party and soviet networks were accused of "right deviationism" and "left extremism." It was generally the village-level officials (especially *sel'sovet* members) who were accused of the "right deviation in practice." Administrative personnel (especially in the party organs) above the village level were accused more often of "left extremism in practice." However, political labels could be deceptive and on occasion both the right and left labels were applied to one and the same organ over a period of time. Part of the reason for the confusion in political labeling in the countryside was that the labels generally lost their political meaning once they came to the countryside and were actually little more than descriptions of how rural cadres implemented policy. Rightists tended toward inertia or toward opposition to specific policies such as grain requisitioning and collectivization; leftists frequently tended toward a campaign style of implementation based on a disdainful attitude toward peasants and a marauding civil war style which posited that socialism could be built at gunpoint. The political problems of rural officialdom increased dramatically during the summer and fall 1929 collectivization drive and impelled the center to turn to the working class and urban party cadres for assistance in the drive.

The demand for cadres in the collectivization drive temporarily overrode any considerations about structural reforms in rural administration.[80] In the short term the solution to the cadre crisis lay in the recruitment of working-class forces for the countryside. Workers were expected to provide the type of correct, class-conscious leadership which would militate against both right and left tendencies, prevent the class enemy from exerting an influence on the rural population, and carry out the party line. Workers were viewed as more socially and politically reliable than most rural officials. In addition, the workers, as opposed to the more alien forces of officialdom, be they urban or rural, were believed to speak a "common language" with the peasants.

Workers were also considered to possess a sort of innate ability to lead and their leadership abilities were expected to be applied in rural politics and on the collective farms. It was also believed that the workers' experience in factory-level party, trade union, and other organizations, as well as their "tempering" in the class struggle and the civil war, made them suitable for a leading political role in the collectivization campaign. Moreover, their experience in factory production was considered sufficient qualification for collective farm work. The Stalin leadership claimed that it was *practical* to send workers to lead collective farms. This claim was based on the widespread expectation that agriculture would be placed on an industrial basis and that the organization of production would come to resemble that of industry. Collective farms would be similar to factories and collective farm chairmen to factory directors.

It was Stalin who formulated the theoretical basis for the role of the working class in rural socialist construction. In his speech "Year of the Great Turn," delivered in early November 1929 on the occasion of the twelfth anniversary of the October Revolution, Stalin claimed that collectivization had become a mass movement and that the reason for this resided in the entry of the middle peasant into the collective farms. Stalin believed that among the reasons for the success of the collective farm movement was the role which "advanced workers" had played in the factory brigades sent to work in the countryside in 1929. Stalin maintained that workers were the "best propagandists" of the collective farms.[81] Stalin's contention, one which was frequently echoed in the press in 1929 and 1930, derived from a similar claim made by Lenin in 1923 in his article "Pages from a Diary." Following Lenin's lead, Stalin maintained that the working class, under the party's guidance, was to serve as the agent of historical consciousness in the countryside in order to build socialism among the peasantry. The working class was to assume a role similar to the one Lenin advocated for the Social Democratic intelligentsia in "What Is to Be Done?" If the spontaneous strivings of the working class required the conscious guidance of the Social Democratic intelligentsia in 1902, then by 1929 the working class had advanced to the stature of conscious force, with the responsibility to lead the spontaneous peasantry to socialism.

Stalin's theoretical formulation of the working class's role in the countryside was most clearly stated in his speech on 27 December 1929 at the Conference of Marxist Agronomists. Based in part on the Leninist emphasis on the role of consciousness in historical development, in part on Stalin's own inclination toward a conscious approach to historical development emerging from the supremacy of revolutionary will, and in part on the response to the right opposition and its supposed trust in historical spontaneity, Stalin's speech maintained that the "socialist town must *lead* behind it the petit-bourgeois peasant countryside not otherwise than by *planting* in the countryside collective farms and state farms and transferring the countryside onto a new socialist path." Stalin intentionally emphasized the words "to plant" (*nasazhdat'*) and "to lead" (*povesti*) because he believed that the countryside, on its own and without outside conscious leadership, would inevitably follow a capitalist path of development.[82] Consistent with the general orientation of the revolution from above, it was necessary to mobilize the conscious agents of Soviet society to build socialism in the countryside. The "advanced workers" about whom Stalin had spoken a month earlier, in his November 1929 speech, would number among the agents of consciousness and, most important, would form the new vanguard of historical development in the countryside.

By the fall of 1929 the necessity of recruiting industrial workers for the countryside had assumed an added political imperative. The existing collective farm movement, still of relatively small dimensions, had come under increasing scrutiny and suspicion. In a speech delivered at the First Moscow Regional Party Conference on 14 September 1929, Molotov claimed that the class enemy, the kulak, was no longer content simply to obstruct rural socialist construction, but now had gone on the offensive. The kulak, according to Molotov, had penetrated the collective farm system and its leadership in order to subvert it from within. Molotov cited a series of collective farms which had turned against the state by speculating in grain on the private market and refusing to turn over grain surpluses to the state. He discussed the exposure of the once-model collective farm Krasyni Meliorator, which had been accused of a number of serious political violations.[83] At the same time, the press launched a similar campaign against such subversive collective farms, which now received the designation of false or kulak collective farms.[84] The lesson of the Krasyni Meliorator case was that a collective farm charter was not an automatic guarantee of reliability. Because the early collective farms had been organized spontaneously—that is, without Moscow's direct supervision or the guiding force of the party and proletariat—they were vulnerable to class alien influences. The lack of central control in the collectivization campaign spanning the summer and fall of 1929 and the problems associated with the cadre crisis had led to this. In order to ensure the reliability of the collective farms, it was necessary to purge them of kulaks and to provide them with "correct" leadership. It was no longer simply a question of leading the countryside to socialism; it was now necessary both to recruit workers to participate in the collectivization campaign *and* to recruit workers to serve in permanent positions on the collective farms.

The civil war tradition of the role of the working class in the countryside came alive in the late 1920s as workers were called upon to fulfill the historic role which Stalin and the party claimed for them in the revolution. Beginning with the soviet election campaign that ran from late 1928 through 1929, when fifty thousand factory workers were sent to the countryside, the recruitment of working-class forces for rural policy implementation became a mass phenomenon.[85] Between 1928 and June 1930 over one hundred thousand factory workers participated in one aspect or another of the implementation of state policy in the countryside.[86] The mass worker mobilizations were to continue until the spring of 1931 when an official, although not entirely effective, halt was called to mass mobilizations of workers from the factory bench for campaign work of all types.[87]

The most important mass recruitment of workers for the countryside was to be the campaign of the 25,000ers. The 25,000ers were to serve in permanent positions on the collective farms in order to ensure the reliability of the collective farm movement. The decision to recruit the 25,000ers was made at the very same time that the policy of wholesale collectivization was announced to the country at the November 1929 plenum of the Central Committee. All available forces were required for the collectivization effort. The 25,000ers would be joined by tens of thousands of urban party and government officials, Komsomol members, demobilized Red army soldiers, internal security forces (OGPU—see Glossary), and rural officials. Together they would lead the great crusade to the countryside, where the traditions, ethos, and practices of the revolutionary heroic period of the civil war would be revived. The final chapter in the Russian Revolution had begun.

Conclusion

The revolution of the First Five-Year Plan entered the annals of history as a revolution from above. Its primary end was the construction of socialism in the USSR and the means to that end were programs of centrally directed and induced industrialization and collectivization. During the First Five-Year Plan the traditions of the revolutionary heroic period of the Russian Revolution—the civil war—were revived, and the state called upon the industrial working class to man the barricades and to lead the offensive of socialist construction. As it had in the civil war, the worker-peasant alliance was to disintegrate and assume the form of an alliance between the party and the working class. The revolution from above would be implemented on the basis of an alliance between the state and certain politically and socially significant forces within the urban Communist party rank and file, the Komsomol, and the working class.

The industrial proletariat served as the core of the alliance. At this time the proletariat was glorified and the traditions of the civil war came to the fore. The working class was considered to be politically and socially reliable: it was class-conscious and disciplined and followed the correct party line. It was said that the Soviet factory worker had been schooled in revolution, civil war, and the class struggle. The leadership called upon the Soviet worker to storm the fortresses of the old order, as well as the many enclaves of inefficiency, corruption, and opposition within the party and government. Lenin's ideas on workers' control were recalled as factory workers were recruited en masse into government offices and institutions of higher education. The party, the government, the universities, and even the countryside were subjected to a process of proletarianization. The working class was not to leave a single remnant of the old order intact. Instead of relying on normal administrative channels, the leadership appealed directly to its party rank and file and the working class for support in the implementation of the revolution; the party and the state bureaucracies in both the countryside and the city were subject to a process of transformation as personnel were purged and replaced by cadres who were deemed of greater social and political reliability in the dual process of purge and promotion. Only the working class was considered capable of aiding the state in revolution from above, in the construction of socialism. However, the glory and the trust did not apply to all Soviet workers but were reserved only for certain strata of the working class—generally, the urbanized or hereditary proletariat with long years of tenure at the factory and a record of service to party and state.

The alliance which served as the basis of the revolution from above was by no means an alliance of equal partners. For the leadership, it served an important purpose: It was the fulcrum upon which policy was implemented, and it allowed the state to achieve the initial breakthroughs in the socialist transformation of the country. In the crisis atmosphere of the late 1920s, it also served the important purpose of diverting working-class grievances from the state and a range of systemic socioeconomic problems to the enemy within and the enemy without, and of mobilizing the support of the party's key social constituency in the revolution from above. Nor was the alliance strictly that of two separate, self-contained entities. Since the Lenin Levy of 1924, which was a massive draft of factory workers into the Communist party, the party had increasingly become a workers' party in composition as well as in name. The party's working-class complexion enhanced the pressures for radical change and a third revolution in light of the deteriorating social and economic position of the proletariat in the 1920s. The cement which held the alliance together therefore became a common language, a common ethos, and a shared set of perceptions, fears, and—at least in the short term—interests. The leadership appealed to the working class for political support by implementing policies of rapid industrialization, by promoting mass worker recruitments into the party, the bureaucracy, and educational institutions, by manipulating working class social and economic grievances from the NEP years, and by playing upon popular fears of a renewed intervention and famine caused by the treachery of the rural bourgeoisie. It was on this basis that certain politically vital sectors of the urban proletariat became "partners" in the alliance. They were to be joined by thousands of rank-and-file party and

Komsomol members, mobilized government officials, and militia, Red army, and internal security forces. Yet the vital fabric of the alliance was the revolutionary vigor injected into the period by the renewed emphasis on the proletarian ethos and the leading role of the proletariat in the socialist transformation of the country.

The campaign of the 25,000ers was a major symbol of the alliance and of the First Five-Year Plan revolution from above. The decision to recruit the 25,000ers was directly linked to the collectivization campaign and the cadre crisis and was based on political and ideological imperatives, which were legitimized by tradition. The center sought to exert its control through the 25,000ers. Following the collectivization drive of the summer and fall of 1929, the center had found itself at the tail of events. The rapid pace of collectivization and the cadre crisis impelled it to attempt to exert its control through its specially chosen representatives. The 25,000ers were to be employed directly on the collective farms as chairmen and administrators. As was the case in the civil war and War Communism, the party's response to the crisis of NEP and the rapidly changing situation in the countryside would assume an ad hoc, improvisational nature as the party struggled to extend its control over events and rushed detachments of its cadres, including the 25,000ers, from one front to the next, leaving them to determine how concretely the revolution would be made. The revolution from above and the campaign of the 25,000ers would largely be a series of improvisational, stopgap measures in response to one crisis or problem after another, glossed over by ideology and the myth of a monolithic, centralized party-state and carried out under the central impetus of a renewed radical atmosphere and a centrally sanctioned offensive on all fronts. Yet the campaign of the 25,000ers was not simply an issue of control or sheer expediency. The campaign revived the civil war tradition of an active role for the working class in the revolution and in the countryside, where the 25,000ers were to serve as agents of revolution from above. They were to inject consciousness into the vast spontaneity of history. The campaign of the 25,000ers was to represent in microcosm the history of the First Five-Year Plan revolution and the central role which the industrial proletariat was to assume in that revolution's implementation.

2

The Recruitment of the 25,000ers

Such an upsurge [*pod''em*] which we now observe is characteristic only of large revolutionary overturns. This is not an ordinary upsurge, but a revolutionary upsurge, especially the upsurge among workers. All questions of workers' daily life [*byt*], all questions with which the trade unions are concerned in relation to wages, etc. are now subsumed by the question of collectivization. All problems in workers' provisioning, all questions about inefficiencies, food shortages, high prices, etc., are subsumed by collectivization. All the attention of the working class is centered on collectivization. It [the working class] instinctively feels that the key to all these problems is collectivization and that the sooner this issue is resolved, the sooner all the remaining problems will be resolved . . . We presently have a real revolutionary movement in the working class for collectivization: a real revolutionary socialist campaign to the countryside for collectivization when workers gladly decline a high salary and go to the countryside. There are masses of cases of the best skilled workers refusing high salaries and going to the countryside.

A. A. ANDREEV, speech at the Third Plenum of the North Caucasus Regional Party Committee, 13 January 1930

The campaign of the 25,000ers was inaugurated by a massive recruitment drive unprecedented in scope and aim. It was the largest and most successful of the First Five-Year Plan mobilizations of workers and rank-and-file Communist party members for service on the fronts of industrialization and collectivization. In the recruitment of the 25,000ers the state called upon the working class for active support in the implementation of collectivization. The enormously successful campaign to recruit the 25,000ers demonstrated that the state had important sources of social support within the working class

36

which were to be of immense significance in the state's endeavors to carry out the ambitious plans of the First Five-Year Plan revolution.

The recruitment of the 25,000ers took place in the context of the First Five-Year Plan mobilization atmosphere. The leadership manipulated and played upon popular fears of military intervention and memories of civil war famine, rekindled by the war scare and the grain crisis of the late 1920s. The dominant motifs of the First Five-Year Plan revolution were military and the imagery was that of the Russian civil war. The working class was called upon to sacrifice for the good of the cause and the preservation of the nation. The state sought to deflect working-class grievances away from systemic problems and toward the external and internal enemies—the kulak, the bourgeois specialist, the NEPman, and the political opposition—all said to be in league with the agents of international imperialism. The economically precarious position of many workers during the NEP years, along with the heightened class tensions of the late 1920s and the perception (among workers) of NEP as a propeasant, anti-working-class policy, made the working class particularly responsive to the state's mobilization devices.

The drive to recruit the 25,000ers was strikingly similar to a military recruitment campaign in the initial stages of a patriotic war. The catchword of the times was *pod''em*, which was used to signify revolutionary elan or an upsurge of militant enthusiasm. The word *pod''em* captured the essense of the times: the sense of excitement which had caught in its grip rank-and-file party members, Komsomol members, and key sectors of the industrial proletariat during the First Five-Year Plan revolution. This sense of excitement was sparked and reinforced by the continuing news of fronts, offensives, battles, shoot-outs with kulaks, and light-cavalry raids. It was fueled by the pent-up socioeconomic grievances of the uneventful NEP years, the rhetoric of class war and revolution, and imagery from the heroic epoch of the Russian civil war. It was within an atmosphere of renewed proletarian chauvinism, Soviet patriotism, all-out class war, and memories of the civil war tradition of a workers' crusade to the countryside that the recruitment of the 25,000ers took place.

The Organization of the Recruitment Drive

The decision to recruit the 25,000ers was announced at the November 1929 plenum of the Central Committee of the Communist party.[1] In late November and early December 1929 the Central Committee's department of rural affairs held a series of meetings with representatives from the Central Council of Trade Unions, Kolkhoztsentr (see Glossary), and regional party organizations in order to outline general procedure for the planning, organization, and implementation of the campaign.[2] Kolkhoztsentr was assigned responsibility for the distribution, use, and preparation of the workers, while the Central Council of Trade Unions was entrusted with the organization of the recruitment drive.[3]

At a meeting on 3 December the Central Council of Trade Unions established a directing center to coordinate the recruitment drive throughout the country. The Central Council then worked out control figures for the recruitment of workers in consultation with the central committees of individual trade unions in Moscow and their regional affiliates.[4] The majority of the 25,000ers were to be recruited from the main industrial centers of the Soviet Union: the Ukraine (7,500), Moscow Region (6,600), Leningrad Region (4,390), the Urals (1,700), and Ivanovo-Voznesensk (1,300). The largest number of workers were to be selected from the metalworkers' union (9,300), followed, in descending order, by the textile workers' union (4,030), the railroad workers' union (3,520), and the mine workers' union (2,540). These regions and trade unions were selected according to the size of the work force per region and union and the political maturity which the state perceived among workers in these regions and unions.

According to an unpublished Central Committee directive of 19 December 1929, the main criterion for the selection of workers from among the pool of volunteers was to be "quality."[5] All the selection criteria were intended to ensure that the workers possessed "sufficient organizational-political experience," as called for by the November plenum announcement. The 25,000ers were to be selected from the "most advanced workers": they were to be "class-conscious," "politically literate," skilled, and urbanized.[6] The workers were to be active in party, Komsomol, or trade union work. Not less than 70 percent were to be members of the party or Komsomol and 15 percent were to be women. Heavy emphasis was also placed on recruitment of factory activists: members of the factory committee, party cell, union shop bureau, shock worker movement, and so forth. The 25,000ers were expected to have at least five years of work experience in the factory. They were not to be recruited from among those workers who had farms or immediate family in the village, commuted to the factory from nearby villages, or had recently arrived at the factory and still retained a peasant visage: these workers were not deemed to be politically literate or class-conscious. Also excluded were heavy drinkers, shop troublemakers, and workers who had participated in one of the party oppositional groupings of the 1920s.[7] The 25,000er was intended to be the model worker, the model activist, and the model revolutionary.

In order to ensure a high qualitative level among the recruits, a hierarchical screening procedure was instituted for the review of volunteers. In most regions a four-tiered screening process was set up for the selection of workers. After a worker had submitted a written declaration to volunteer, filled out a questionnaire, and obtained a reference from his factory party cell (if a party member) or factory committee, he was subject to review by the factory party cell and/or a general factory or shop meeting, and then by selection committees under his factory committee, the regional trade union representing his profession, and, finally, the regional council of trade unions. In many areas the selection process was continued at the preparation courses held for workers on the eve of their departure. Recruitment was intended to be highly selective.[8]

Kolkhoztsentr was in charge of formulating plans for the distribution of the 25,000ers. Ten thousand 25,000ers were targeted for districts of wholesale collectivization.[9] The workers were to be used primarily on large collective farms and in the major grain regions.[10] The majority were to be directed to the Ukraine, the Central Black Earth Region, the Middle and Lower Volgas, the North Caucasus, Siberia, Kazakhstan, Central Asia, the Urals, and Siberia (see table 1). They were to be sent to regions with which their factories had either patronage agreements or mutual production interests (such as textile-factory and flax regions) which could establish a basis for a patronage agreement.[11] Whenever possible, workers were to be sent either in groups or to the same district with other workers from their factories or regions.

Kolkhoztsentr, in collaboration with local collective farm and party organs, was also enlisted to formulate a plan for the use of the 25,000ers. The majority of workers were to be sent directly onto the collective farms to work as chairmen, members of the administration, or party cell secretaries. An additional 2,950 workers were to be sent for practical study on large state farms before assuming positions as collective farm chairmen, and another 1,530 were to be sent to work in the machine tractor stations.[12] Although there were strict orders not to use the workers in government offices or in organs above the district level, in practice they were employed throughout the rural party and government network.[13]

After the completion of the recruitment drive the workers were to receive preliminary preparation for their new duties as leading collective farm cadres. Kolkhoztsentr was charged with the overall supervision of the preparation of the workers. Each worker was required to take a course of approximately two weeks duration before setting out for the countryside; in some cases they also passed through short courses in their areas of rural employment in order to study local conditions. All course work was to be completed by mid-January so that the workers could be at their posts in time for spring sowing and the upcoming collective farm board elections.[14]

The recruitment drive was set into motion in most areas of the country within the first ten days of December. By that time the plans on recruitment

TABLE 1 *

CONTROL PLANS FOR THE REGIONAL DISTRIBUTION OF 25,000ers

REGION	25,000ers from region	25,000ers to remain in region	25,000ers sent from:							TOTALS
			Leningrad	Moscow	Ukraine	Ivanovo	N.Novgorod	Urals	Zakavkaz'e	
Northern	160	160	140							300
Leningrad**	4,390	650								650
Moscow	6,600	1,000								1,000
Ukraine	7,500	5,550								5,550
Ivanovo	1,300	400								400
Nizhegorodskii***	800	700								700
Western	400	400				900				1,300
Central Black Earth	200	200		1,850						2,050
Middle Volga	300	300		1,800						2,100
Lower Volga	500	500	1,800	200						2,500
North Caucasus	1,000	1,000			1,500					2,500
Siberia+	300	300	1,700							2,000
ZSFSR	680	650								650
Dagestan ASSR									30	30
Central Asia/Kirgiziia			100	600		300				1,000
Ural	1,700	1,200								1,200
Bashkiria ASSR	250							500		500
Far East	100	100			150					250
Crimea ASSR				250						250
Tatariia ASSR		250								250
BSSR	200	200					100			300
Kazakhstan ASSR				900	300					1,200
TOTALS	26,380	13,560	3,740	5,600	1,950	900 ++	100	500	30	26,380 +++

*TsGANKh, f. 7446, op. 12, d. 3, 1.4.

+This includes Buriat-Mongolia.

**This includes Karaliia.

++Mistake in calculation; actual total is 1,200.

***This includes Chuvash.

+++Mistake in calculation; actual total is 26,680.

quotas, selection criteria, and preparation had been formulated in most places. There were several matters, however, which were not resolved until late December or early January. These included first the issues of where individual workers would be sent and how long their duties would require them to stay in the countryside. Kolkhoztsentr was slow in formulating plans for both the use and distribution of the workers; as a consequence, these plans (especially at the *okrug* and district levels) were not finalized until after the recruitment campaign had ended. In addition, there was no ruling on how long the workers would stay in the countryside; the only decision remotely close to resolving this issue was the designation of the 25,000ers as "permanent" cadres. The precise meaning of *permanent*, however, was unclear and most likely was simply used to denote a less transitory sojourn in the countryside than that of the various rural patronage brigades. It was only on 17 January 1930 that some indication was given about the workers' stay. In a People's Commissariat of Labor decree the workers were granted special salary privileges for one year, thus indicating that a one-year minimum was initially the expected, if not official, norm.[15]

The issue of the salary of the workers was left unresolved until 29 December 1929. Throughout December the press reported numerous complaints about this delay, as well as a number of rumors about salaries for the workers. *Pravda* published several articles complaining that the issue of the 25,000ers' salary had not been resolved and that this issue was "of extreme interest to the worker-volunteers."[16] Elsewhere rumors were circulated that salary would be based on either the worker's party status and family size or the party maximum (salary) of the district of rural employment.[17] The Central Council of Trade Unions criticized the press for circulating rumors and assured workers that their salary would not suffer a decline upon their leaving the factory.[18] However, the salary issue was resolved only after the recruitment campaign was completed or was near completion in most regions.[19] By getting a worker's former enterprise to pay the difference in the worker's salary between factory and collective farm employment, the Central Council of Trade Unions managed to secure (at least on paper) the payment of the same-size salary workers had received in industrial employment. Nevertheless, the delay in resolving this issue was to cause problems in the implementation of the recruitment drive.

On 19 December 1929 the Central Committee circulated a secret directive to all party committees, informing them that the recruitment of the 25,000ers was no ordinary campaign.[20] According to the directive, the selection of nonparty workers was to be on a strictly *voluntary* basis. If necessary, however, selection committees could apply "mobilization methods" in the recruitment of party and Komsomol members. (In this specific context the

Soviet usage of the term "mobilization" [*mobilizatsiia*] was roughly equivalent to "conscription."[21]) Mobilization was intended only as a last resort. In the published and unpublished directives on the implementation of recruitment, repeated emphasis was placed on the need to maintain the voluntary nature of the campaign.[22] Further, the Central Committee urged the selection committees not to recruit workers simply on the basis of formal indicators—party status, years in production, and so forth. Party organizers were to oversee recruitment and to ensure that each volunteer was qualified to serve as a 25,000er. The directive also warned that the factories would attempt to send poor or useless workers and that the party would have to struggle against this tendency. The directive emphasized the campaign's extreme importance and accurately pinpointed one of the major trouble areas which the campaign organizers were to confront—namely, factory resistance to recruitment. The implementation of the recruitment drive was to reveal a side of Soviet politics singularly lacking centralized control and demonstrating a good deal of conflict between the center and factory officialdom. The enthusiastic response of Soviet factory workers to the recruitment drive would be met by the virulent opposition of factory officials, who endeavored to block the campaign in an effort to save *their* "most advanced workers" for the industrialization effort in the enterprises.

The Implementation of the Recruitment Drive

The recruitment campaign's leading slogan was "time does not wait."[23] In the two months following the November plenum decision on the 25,000ers, factories in the major industrial centers were busily engaged in campaign activities. Factory wall newspapers reported on worker response, and recruiting posters urging workers to enlist in the campaign went up in factories and shops all over the Soviet Union. The central and local press published stories and pictures of worker-volunteers, singing their praises and recording the previously unheralded biographies of hundreds of Soviet factory workers. An avalanche of meetings came down upon the factories, and attendance was remarkably high—75 to 80 percent for metalworkers in Leningrad factories.[24] The Leningrad Regional Council of Trade Unions called upon Moscow, the Urals, and the Donbass to enter into socialist competition for the best campaign and the highest quality of volunteers.[25] In Leningrad, where the campaign was a stunning success, recruitment was completed in less than two weeks; in most other areas the recruitment drive was over by late December or early January. Factory workers and factory officials found themselves in the thick of a campaign destined to become one of the hallmarks of the First Five-Year Plan revolution.

The Ranks of the 25,000ers

The recruitment campaign elicited an enormous response from the Soviet working class. Over 70,000 workers volunteered to go to the grain front; from these, 27,519 workers were selected to be 25,000ers.[26] The planned quotas for recruitment were fulfilled and overfulfilled. In the large industrial centers of Leningrad, Moscow, and the Ukraine, the turnout was overwhelming: 12,000 volunteers in Leningrad, 17,696 volunteers in Moscow, and 16,526 volunteers in the Ukraine.[27] The metalworkers, always the most stalwart support of the party, rose to the occasion in typically heroic dimensions: 19,034 metalworkers volunteered for roughly nine thousand places. In the larger enterprises of Leningrad and Moscow, where workers were heavily concentrated and had a tradition of political activism, volunteers poured into the factory selection committees, competing with one another for selection as a 25,000er. At the great Putilov factory in Leningrad, the roster of 25,000ers was impressive. It was headed by the chairman of the factory committee, the worker Arkhipov, and also included: the worker I. S. Balashov, a member of the Leningrad soviet and a worker with twenty-five years work experience at the bench; Foma Varaksin, a worker–newspaper correspondent; the fifty-five year-old worker S. A. Markovskii, who had been at Putilov since 1893; Elena Aleksandrovna Novikova, who had forty-three years experience at the bench and was the secretary of the cultural commission and a women's organizer; and A. I. Tuzhikov, the chairman of a shop union bureau, a hereditary proletarian, and a civil war veteran who had been awarded a watch for distinguished service in quelling the Kronstadt uprising.[28] The Putilov volunteers were joined by thousands of other worker-activists with equally prestigious credentials from the major enterprises of the Soviet Union.

Communist workers were in the forefront of the ranks of the 25,000ers. According to data based on 23,409 25,000ers, 69.9 percent were party members and 8.6 percent belonged to the Komsomol (see table 2). These percentages fulfilled and overfulfilled the party-Komsomol quota of 70 percent set by the recruitment drive organizers and distinguished the 25,000ers as an elite group: the percentage of party members among industrial workers, as a whole, was only 12.1 percent at this time and even among such workers as the shock workers the percentage was not nearly as high as that among the 25,000ers.[29] The majority of these worker-Communists were among the beneficiaries of the working-class levies into the party which had been conducted in the mid-1920s.[30] For example, the 25,000er Inzhevatkin, who had worked in the factory since the age of fourteen and had served at the fronts of the civil war, was recruited into the party in the Lenin Levy of 1924. P. F. Kononov, a construction worker since the age of fourteen, a civil war veteran, and a worker with forty-eight years at the bench, was also recruited into the party in the Lenin Levy. A. V. Gruzdev, who conducted political literacy circles at his factory, was the editor of his factory wall newspaper, and was a rural patronage activist who had led atheist propaganda campaigns in Baptist villages, was another Lenin Levy recruit and civil war veteran.[31] Proudly bearing the title and status of worker-revolutionaries, older veterans of the Communist party also joined the 25,000ers' ranks. I. V. Vasil'ev, a metalist and shock worker with thirty-three years at the bench, was a Red Guard in 1917, a member of a soviet executive committee, and a military commissar in the civil war. The 25,000er D. B. Radus, a worker with forty-two years at the bench, joined the party in 1905 and, following the 1905 revolution, was forced to emigrate to the United States, where he worked for eight years as a farmer. Ivan Kozlov, who began work at the age of fifteen and was born into a working-class family, was active in the 1917 strike movement and served as a Kremlin guard in 1919 before entering the Red army to fight at the fronts of the civil war.[32] As they had in the days of the civil war, worker-Communists were among the first to enlist in the campaign, and they served as models for the worker-25,000ers.

The overwhelming majority of the 25,000ers were urbanized cadre workers—workers with long years of experience at the bench who were either hereditary proletarians or were born in, but had severed their ties to, the countryside. Forty-eight percent of these workers had been employed in industry for more than twelve years and 39 percent had been in industry from five to twelve years (see table 2). The 25,000ers also tended to be either skilled or highly skilled workers[33] who earned considerably higher wages than the average industrial worker in 1929 and tended, on the average, to be literate and to have had some form of schooling.[34]

The 25,000ers were also factory activists. The majority had served for at least three years in some type of social or political organization in their factories. They were members of factory committees, shop union bureaus, cooperative societies, and rural patronage organizations. At the large Putilov and Krasnaia Zaria factories in Leningrad, respectively, 45 percent and 40 percent of all volunteers were factory activists.[35] The workers were also recruited in large numbers from production activists—leaders and members of production conferences and shock brigades—and foremen.[36] Many had prior experience in the countryside as members of grain-requisitioning or collectivization brigades; in Leningrad 25 percent of all 25,000ers had been

TABLE 2*

COMPOSITION OF THE 25,000ers

REGION	Numbers Selected According to Region	Sex % M	Sex % F	Age (Years) % under 22	23-29	30-39	over 40	Partiinost % VKP(b)	VLKSM	Non-Party	Labor Stazh (Yrs) % under 5	5-12	over 12
Northern	234	80.4	19.6	12.9	38.9	37.6	10.6	56.9	8.9	34.2	18.1	33.1	48.8
Leningrad	4,614	91	9	9.3	47.7	31.2	11.8	75.5	8.2	16.3	9.1	57.4	33.5
Moscow	5,565	89.8	10.2	8.9	50.5	30.4	10.2	76.2	7	16.8	13.6	30.8	55.6
Western	317	93.1	6.9	3.9	33.3	47.1	15.7	61.9	10.7	27.4	11.7	31.4	56.9
Ivanovo	1,445	87.4	12.6	9.9	48.8	31.7	9.6	83	4	13	16	45.1	38.9
Central Black Earth	284	96.9	3.1	6.6	44.8	30.9	17.7	77.9	5.6	16.5	9.9	43.1	47
Ural	251	94.9	5.1	12.8	42.3	33.8	11.1	66.2	8.7	25.1	5.5	48.3	46.2
Bashkiriia ASSR	113	93	7	10.5	48.7	30.1	10.6	71.7	9.7	18.6	10.6	41.6	47.8
Middle Volga	241	94.2	5.8	5.8	39	41.1	14.1	66.4	5.3	28.3	15.3	36.1	48.6
Lower Volga	1,012	90.3	9.7	7.6	40.5	37.3	14.6	74.1	5.4	20.5	16	38.6	45.4
Crimea ASSR	200	---- NO DATA ----		---- NO DATA ----				64	14	22	---- NO DATA ----		
North Caucasus	272	90.5	9.1	2.2	56.6	32.7	8.5	76.5	5.5	18	12.8	48.2	39
Far East	331	96.4	3.6	10.2	26.3	32.9	30.6	68.6	9.6	21.8	22	25.7	52.3
BSSR	934	89	11	9.9	43.6	34.8	11.7	81.1	7.6	11.3	8	43.6	48.4
Ukraine	7,397	96.1	3.9	---- NO DATA ----				57.6	11.3	31.1	17.1	7.1	75.8
Armenia	54	88.9	11.1	11.1	42.6	37.1	9.2	70.4	7.4	22.2	27.7	40.8	31.5
Azerbaidzhan	348	98.9	1.1	8.9	41.5	39.7	9.9	74.2	10.6	15.2	1.4	52.6	46
Uzbekistan	197	95.4	4.6	10.6	40.7	31.9	16.8	66.5	9.6	23.9	21.7	44.1	34.2
TOTALS	23,409	92.3	7.7	9.0	47.1	32.1	11.8	69.9	8.6	21.5	13	39	48

*Politicheskii i trudovoi pod"em rabochego klassa SSSR (1928-1929 gg.). Sbornik dokumentov (Moscow: Gospolitizdat, 1956), dok. 315, pp. 544-545.

members of rural patronage brigades.[37] Finally, it is important to note that a large percentage of the 25,000ers had been tempered in the school of class struggle and battle during their years of service as Red army soldiers in the heroic period of the civil war.[38]

The majority of the 25,000ers were males between the ages of twenty-three and thirty-nine years (see table 2). The organizers of the recruitment drive aimed at accepting only a minimum number of youth in order to send mature, disciplined workers to the countryside. This policy accounted for the low percentage of Komsomol members among the 25,000ers. In addition to the low percentages of youth, female workers constituted only 7.7 percent of the 25,000ers, although the percentage of female 25,000ers was higher in regions in which female labor constituted a significant proportion of the work force (see table 2). Moreover, according to biographical data on female 25,000ers, these workers appear to have represented a very small elite among the female labor force and were differentiated from their counterparts by a high degree of social and political activity, extensive production skills, and party membership.[39]

By meeting the selection criteria which had been formulated at the start of the campaign, the 25,000ers satisfied the call for the "most advanced workers." In fact, according to most indicators, the 25,000ers surpassed the standards set for selection, especially those for party-Komsomol membership, years at the bench, and social and political activity in the factory. In its recruitment drive, the state had sought the support of this sector of the working class and had succeeded beyond all expectation. The 25,000ers were skilled or highly skilled workers with long years at the bench; factory activists and party or Komsomol members; urbanized workers; and veterans of the shock workers' movement, the grain-requisitioning campaigns of the late 1920s, and the civil war. They formed a remarkable cohort of workers who had entered the factory at an early age; witnessed or participated in the 1917 revolution and civil war as idealistic teenagers or young adults; worked in industry through the 1920s; and participated in the social and political organizations within their factories, where they had risen to positions of responsibility in production, shop-level administration, the party, and union work.

The Factories and the Recruitment Drive

The Soviet press reported that the recruitment drive was an enormous success, and newspapers were filled with glowing accounts of the revolutionary upsurge in the factories. Despite the high quality of the workers and their enthusiastic response to recruitment as reported in the press and in unpublished trade union accounts, the campaign was not free of problems, for in appealing to workers for support in the campaign, the state confronted the opposition of factory administrators, factory committees, factory party cells, and trade union bureaus reluctant to part with skilled workers and factory activists. Moreover, the recruitment campaign was hindered by poor organization and the lack of clear, uniform instructions to lower level recruiting organs. Ultimately, the campaign's success was to depend on the state's ability to circumvent a resistant factory officialdom and to appeal directly to Soviet workers.

The degree of success registered in local recruitment drives varied widely and often depended upon such factors as the extent to which Stalin had established a strong base of political support in the area and the extent to which the area suffered from shortages in its skilled labor force. The campaign in Leningrad, a Stalin stronghold under Kirov (the Leningrad regional party secretary), was extremely successful. There the trade unions raised their recruitment quotas, gave the campaign high priority and maximum publicity, and met their quotas as early as 10 December 1929. The campaign's success in Leningrad was also due, in large part, to the nature of Leningrad's labor force (for example, the predominance of metalists and cadre workers there).[40] The campaign in Moscow, which until recently had been a stronghold of the right opposition under Uglanov, was the target of constant criticism for its failure to make use of the revolutionary upsurge among the Moscow workers. Factory officialdom in Moscow fiercely resisted the loss of its skilled workers. This resistance was a consequence both of shortages of skilled labor and earlier mobilizations of skilled workers from Moscow factories. In addition, the campaign in Moscow was adversely affected by the predominance of the lower-skilled, lower-paid textile workers in its labor force and by workers who, in general, had closer and more direct ties to the countryside. It should finally be noted that particular industries and regions had difficulties in implementing the campaign because of certain intrinsic problems. For example, the trade union of chemical-industry workers conducted a poor campaign because the chemical industry suffered from especially severe shortages in skilled labor at this time. Ivanovo-Voznesensk and the Western Region, like Moscow, also came in for heavy criticism for their problems in campaign implementation. Unlike Moscow, however, there was little political labeling involved in this criticism, and the problems appear to have resulted from shortages of skilled labor and the predominance in these regions' labor forces of the types of unskilled, noncadre workers who did not fit the criteria for recruitment.[41]

One of the most serious and widespread problems in the recruitment drive was the failure of the central authorities to provide sufficient leadership and organizational information on the procedure of campaign implementation. Throughout the first half of December, trade union and factory committee officials in many regions complained that they had not yet received quotas and other information on recruitment. The factory committees of the Elektrosvet and Kalinin factories in Moscow claimed that they were not informed officially about the campaign until mid-December. Reports from the Ukraine indicated that recruitment was slow precisely because so few instructions had been sent. An editorial in *Pravda* noted that many unions and factory committees were awaiting detailed instructions. The editorial warned that additional information would not be forthcoming and that the unions and factory committees were expected to demonstrate their own initiative in the campaign. In the meantime the Central Council of Trade Unions insisted that "there is a plan of work" while at the same time echoing *Pravda* by urging local organizations not "to wait for new directions." An article in *Leningradskaia pravda* mocked the indecisive local organizations, scolding, "Can't they read the newspapers?"[42]

These delays initially led to poor worker response to recruitment. Local trade union and factory officials complained that delays in determining the destinations, salary, and duration of service in the countryside were slowing down the recruitment drive. Many workers hesitated to volunteer for an assignment which could as easily land them among nomadic tribesmen in Central Asia as among peasants in their own regions. Workers were also slow to respond as long as the basic issue of salary was not determined.[43] A member of the factory committee of Ruskabel in Moscow explained that few workers had enlisted because the factory selection committee "could not answer their questions: where would the volunteers be sent to, how would their families be provided for, etc."[44] The secretary of the factory committee of Krasnyi Fakel in the Ukraine complained, "As long as we don't know the size of the salary, we cannot develop work [on recruitment]. When you tell us everything, then you can ask everything from us."[45] An article in the newspaper *Vecherniaia Moskva* expressed alarm that not all of the workers knew what was expected of them: For example, "Comrade P., in a whiny voice, will say, 'You tell me how long we will be mobilized for. They say for our whole life. But if we are to be mobilized for a year or two or three, then I will be happy to go.'"[46] The absence of the most basic information on important issues affecting the workers served to hinder the pace of the campaign in many areas until late December, when most of these issues were finally resolved.

Another major problem in recruitment was factory-level resistance to the recruitment of skilled workers. During the First Five-Year Plan period, skilled workers were in great demand. With increasingly high turnover rates and the large influx of unskilled laborers from the countryside, cadre workers (and especially the highly skilled among them) were at a premium. Factory directors, factory committees, factory party cells, and shop union bureaus often resisted the recruitment of their best workers by refusing to release volunteers or by forcing undesirable elements to volunteer.

In its 19 December directive, the Central Committee had predicted that the factories would struggle against the recruitment drive. The director of the large Moscow factory Dinamo protested against the large quota which his factory received. Moreover, all of the Dinamo volunteers were highly skilled workers. The director complained that Dinamo had already lost many skilled workers through mass promotions and earlier mobilizations; in addition, he complained that there were no replacements at the labor exchange for the type of skilled labor he needed.[47] The administration, trade union, and party cell at Factory No. 25 in Moscow also refused to fulfill their quota; Factory No. 25 claimed that the party district committee had exempted the factory from all further mobilizations due to earlier losses of skilled workers.[48] The secretary of the Vladimir Il'ich factory committee in Moscow stated point-blank that "the quota [for recruitment] is too large and we will not fulfill it."[49] The director of the Borets factory in Moscow was less direct in his protest; when his chauffeur volunteered, he complained, "And what will happen when I am called in to the trust? I will be late and because of this the program will suffer."[50]

In addition to the problem of the loss of skilled labor, there were two other factors which served to impede recruitment. The first was fear of stripping the factory of its activists. The campaign planners were aware that this would happen and the Moscow newspaper *Rabochaia Moskva* admitted that "the mobilization of 6,000 advanced proletarians [from Moscow] will to a large degree strip our enterprises, weaken the active layer [*sloi*] of workers." It added, however, that this result was expected and it would therefore be necessary to prepare a new cadre of factory activists. A later article in the same newspaper claimed that those factories which resisted the recruitment revealed their ignorance of the meaning of the campaign. The article stated that the recruitment of the 25,000ers and their replacement by a new cadre of activists from the rank-and-file workers at the bench were two integral processes,[51] and, in fact, the aim of the working-class mobilizations was precisely to replenish the suspect state and party bureaucracies with working-class forces as well as to replace the mobilized workers with new worker-activists. Nonetheless, the recruitment of the 25,000ers served to further drain the factories of their social and political activists, and as the First Five-Year Plan was to reveal, it would be no easy task to rebuild this stratum of advanced and politically active workers.[52]

The second factor which served to impede the recruitment drive was the simultaneous implementation of several other campaigns, not to mention the everyday issues of industrial production. This appears to have been especially the case in the Moscow campaign. Factory officials in Moscow often explained their tardiness in campaign implementation by claiming preoccupation with the party purge or the collective agreement campaign or in reaching planned targets of industrial production.[53] This was a time of campaigns and a race for quantity and quality in production. Many organizers had little time for the recruitment drive even if they were not opposed to the loss of their skilled workers and factory activists.

The Central Council of Trade Unions called upon its local committees to resist the efforts of "shop patriots" to withhold skilled workers. Factory organs were urged to avoid local interests and narrow pragmatism.[54] Frequently, however, factory selection committees not only continued to resist recruitment but attempted to send undesirable elements to avoid the loss of valued workers. At a meeting at the Uralseparator factory, the chairman of the shop union bureau, in a show of admirable shop patriotism, announced that there were two items on the agenda, one of which was important. The "unimportant item" concerned the recruitment drive. In regard to the campaign, he said, "Wait to enlist—the cause will go on without us. The factory needs skilled workers and only those who are not needed at the factory should go to the collective farms."[55] In Tula a worker with a bad heart was recruited. He was told by his solicitous factory selection committee, "You are ill . . . go to the collective farm—there the air is good and the work is easy."[56] Individual factories were criticized for attempting to recruit "political illiterates," workers who had been expelled from the party, Trotskyites, workers with farms, drunks, "rowdy elements," and so forth.[57] A problem which appears to have been somewhat widespread in Moscow was the tendency of factories to attempt to send unskilled youth with insufficient years of experience at the bench. The 25,000er Spiridonov later protested that his factory Krasnoe Znamia had attempted to send only unskilled youth. These attempts may also have been the result of rumors about salary which claimed that the unskilled would receive only their rural wages, and as a consequence, the factories would not be burdened with additional payments to former workers.[58]

The campaign to recruit women workers was particularly unsuccessful: only 7.7 percent of the required 15 percent were recruited. The *zhenotdel* (the party's department on women's issues) was blamed for this lack of success.[59] In general, however, it would appear that the recruitment of women was a low-priority item in most local campaigns. There is no evidence to indicate that women were especially encouraged to volunteer; on the contrary, several regional organizations revised central directives and lowered their quotas for women.[60] One consideration which was likely to have been weighed heavily by local recruiters and women workers was traditional peasant hostility to women in positions of authority. Another and perhaps more important consideration for factory recruiters was that women who fit the criteria for selection as 25,000ers were an extremely small minority among women workers as a whole. The majority of women workers did not measure up to their male counterparts in terms of skill level, years in the factory, education, or party membership. Those who did, constituted the very thin layer of female worker-activists in the factory. Factory recruiters, as they were in the case of male activists, were reluctant to strip their factories of such important workers and activists.[61]

The resistance of factory officialdom was a major obstacle to the successful implementation of the campaign. The evidence clearly indicates that this resistance was motivated primarily by the factories' unwillingness to part with scarce labor resources and worker activists. There is some evidence to suggest, however, that there may also have been elements of political resistance. The trade unions, under the leadership of Bukharin's ally Tomskii, had been opposed to the use of industrial workers in the countryside and, especially, in grain requisitioning and collectivization. Scattered evidence would suggest that such opposition may have lingered on in the trade unions well after the expulsion of Tomskii from the trade union leadership in mid-1929. In an article in the trade union newspaper *Trud*, it was reported that the Third Plenum of the Central Council of Trade Unions had revealed that "some union officials" did not understand the full import of the campaign. At this plenum, Dogadov, Tomskii's replacement, noted with a hint of disapproval that the 25,000ers would be directed to the countryside at the expense of much-needed skilled industrial cadres.[62] On the eve of the plenum, an editorial in *Trud* warned that it would be very difficult to remove so many skilled workers from industry, and a number of articles, which made a timely appearance in the press during the recruitment drive, noted that workers' brigades were often met with great hostility in the countryside and that workers were ill prepared for agricultural work.[63]

It was widely advertised at the time that the right opposition was against the recruitment of the 25,000ers. Whether this was simply the stigma attached to being opposed to the campaign or an accusation with some basis in fact is difficult to determine. It is clear, however, that the majority of such accusations were directed against the former stronghold of the right opposition—Moscow—and its trade union organization. The Moscow Regional Council of Trade Unions was reprimanded several times for its "negligence" in the campaign, and special plenipotentiaries were mobilized in Moscow to urge on local union committees in the campaign.[64] It is possible that elements of support for the right opposition lingered on among trade union and factory officials in Moscow. It is also possible, however, that the composition of Moscow's labor force disinclined recruiters to the loss of skilled, experienced workers. The Moscow party and trade union organizations, moreover, appear to have had a tradition of independence and, in fact, attempted to resist the increasing encroachments of central control in several other instances as well.[65]

The resistance of factory officialdom to the recruitment drive eventually led to the direct intervention of the party in the implementation process. According to the press, the party had entrusted the unions with this important task, and the unions had failed to live up to their role in socialist construction. The proof of this—in Moscow's case—was that the unions could not implement the campaign without the aid of the party, which intervened by sending in plenipotentiaries in early January.[66] The party intervened in other problem areas as well. Intervention resulted from local recruiters' slowness in meeting quotas and came only in late December or early January—the point at which the recruitment drive should have been completed.[67] Although direct intervention in the implementation of the recruitment drive occurred on a selective basis in late December and early January and was limited to problem regions, party intervention in the selection process was made standard practice by a Central Committee decree published on 22 January 1930. In this decree local party committees were given ultimate responsibility for the final selection of the workers from among the volunteers and were told that their first priority must be the qualitative level of the candidates.[68] Leadership of the campaign was taken away from the Central Council of Trade Unions because it was unable to control its local and factory organs. Nor could it overcome the local interests and shop patriotism of factory officialdom, which had attempted to impede the campaign at every step along the way of the implementation process.

The recruitment drive illustrated the sometimes contradictory nature of the First Five-Year Plan revolution, which aimed for the maximum in economic modernization while at the same time insisting that modernization occur within the parameters of the social and political guidelines of the proletarian dictatorship. The factories were required to increase production while releasing their best workers for participation in the numerous mobilizations of skilled workers for promotion in the bureaucracy, the purge of the state administration, enrollment in higher technical education, and work in the countryside. The consequences of these contradictory demands were frequently inconsistency, disorder, and an uneasy balance between different institutional concerns, revealing a side of Soviet politics lacking unity of purpose and divided by differing interests. In the recruitment of the 25,000ers this meant that ultimately the state had to circumvent factory officialdom and, with the aid of the party organs, appeal directly to workers over the head of resistant factory officials for support in the campaign. And the result was that, in spite of the opposition of factory officials and problems in campaign implementation, the recruitment drive was an enormous success. The response of the working class to the drive was good, with large numbers of highly qualified workers enlisting as volunteers. It is necessary next to examine the motives which led workers to volunteer for dangerous and difficult work in the countryside. It will become clear then that the Soviet working class, as a reserve for the shock troops of the Stalin revolution, was also a force of considerable importance in the arena of Soviet politics during the First Five-Year Plan period.

Workers and the Recruitment Drive

Soviet scholars generally maintain that the 25,000ers were motivated by a high degree of class consciousness and support for the party's policy of collectivization.[69] In the West there is a reflexive tendency to dismiss such a view, Western scholars traditionally attributing success in Soviet recruitments of rank-and-file cadres to coercion or appeals to self-interest.[70] The traditional views of Soviet and Western scholars may be diametrically opposed, but they are based on the similar underlying assumption that their conclusions are valid for the Soviet working class as a whole. In fact, the motivations of the 25,000ers were neither as uniform nor as clear-cut as the combined Soviet and Western literature suggests. Furthermore, the 25,000ers were representative of a politically and numerically significant group of workers—politically active cadre workers. Their primary motives in volunteering to participate in the campaign were not based on coercion or material self-interest. The 25,000ers were workers who, on one level or another, identified with the state and party and supported the program of the First Five-Year Plan revolution. If we sift through the evidence and look for nuances and patterns within the sometimes dense rhetoric of these workers' letters and statements, a picture will emerge of the complex motives which led the 25,000ers to volunteer to participate in collectivization. Before we do this sifting, however, it is necessary to consider in some detail the issues of coercion and material self-interest in order to place the volunteers' motivations in perspective.

Mobilization Methods and Administrative Pressure in Recruitment

The role played by mobilization methods, or administrative pressure, in the recruitment drive is central to an analysis of the motivations of the 25,000ers.

Interestingly enough, the use of administrative pressure was not nearly as prevalent as would be expected, given the times, the polity, and the high-pressured pace of the campaign. This is not to argue a complete absence of the use of such pressures. However, for the most part, administrative pressure tended to be exerted infrequently and to be less the result of workers' unwillingness to join the ranks than of factory officialdom's resistance to the loss of valued workers and of its attempt to force unqualified workers to enlist in the campaign.

A tendency toward the use of administrative pressure was to some extent inevitable in the high-pressured methods of campaign implementation practiced in the frenzied days of the First Five-Year Plan period. Local officials were badgered not to lose a minute in revolutionary tempos. Factories, trade unions, and entire regions were urged to enter into socialist competition for the best recruitment campaign. Recruitment quotas were established for all factories, and the ideal candidate and most eager volunteer was often a valued worker in short supply at his factory. At several enterprises in Ivanovo-Voznesensk, Moscow, and the Western Region, factory recruiters pressured unskilled workers (especially youth) and shop troublemakers to enlist in order to avoid the loss of skilled workers. The majority of such unwilling volunteers were eventually rejected by selection committees above the factory level for failing to meet the criteria necessary for recruitment.[71] The Moscow Region was criticized for resorting to the use of administrative pressure in the campaign. The Moscow trade unions and factory recruiters had begun their enlistment drive in earnest only toward the end of the campaign period. Consequently, administrative pressure was sometimes applied in order to meet recruitment goals before the campaign deadline. This led to relatively higher percentages of mobilized workers in Moscow than in other regions.[72]

The Central Committee had ordered the recruitment of workers to be on a strictly voluntary basis. This was the directive that was circulated through the trade union and party administrative network.[73] The use, if necessary, of administrative pressure was authorized only in the recruitment of party and Komsomol workers. It was hoped and indeed expected that Communist workers would voluntarily enlist. If they did not, they could be mobilized to serve in the countryside since they were under the traditional obligation to adhere to party discipline in fulfilling the tasks assigned to them by the party's Central Committee. As the following editorial in *Rabochaia Moskva* neatly summarized, the principle of party responsibility was emphasized throughout the drive:

> Underlying the need to carry out recruitment on a voluntary basis, it is essential to combine this principle together with responsibility, of course, most of all in relation to party and komsomol workers.[74]

In cases of mobilization, the worker-Communist would be persuaded to volunteer on the basis of class duty; if this failed, he would be told that he had a duty to volunteer.[75] There were, most likely, more than a few instances of factory party cells appealing to the guilty class conscience of an unobliging worker-Communist.

The evidence suggests, however, that in the majority of cases the recruitment of the 25,000ers was voluntary. Two factors appear to have worked against the widespread use of administrative pressures: the first was the generally favorable response of the workers to the campaign and the fact that a politically select stratum of workers was targeted for recruitment; the second was the party's counsel that the use of administrative pressure should always be avoided, except in the case of worker-Communists if absolutely necessary. It was not in the party's interest to recruit unwilling workers to serve on such an important front as that of collectivization. Unwilling or unqualified workers would simply disrupt the collectivization effort and desert at the first opportunity. The party was able to counter the factories' use of administrative pressure in forcing undesirables to volunteer by rejecting them once the selection process passed above the factory level. Moreover, a barrage of criticism was directed against regions in which recruiters made use of administrative pressure. In Leningrad, for example, the Vyborg district committee of the party issued an order directly forbidding the use of administrative methods in the district.[76] In the Urals the regional party committee was forced to intervene in the Nizhnyi Tagil'skii *Okrug* campaign and overrule the party *okrug* committee's decision to carry out recruitment solely on the basis of mobilization methods.[77]

The party's insistence on the voluntary principle in recruitment appears to have been generally successful. In Leningrad 90 percent of the 25,000ers were said to be volunteers;[78] statistical data for Moscow and other regions are, in the best of cases, scant and, more often, unavailable. There is, however, some archival data on the campaign in Moscow which confirms the essentially noncoercive nature of recruitment. According to progress reports on the recruitment drive among Moscow's metalworkers, only six enterprises were guilty of resorting to administrative pressure and all were harshly criticized.[79] A limited sample of campaign questionnaires from 25,000ers at the Tormoznoi and Kolomenskii factories in Moscow give a rough indication that about 25 percent of the workers were mobilized—and all but one were party members.[80] This percentage basically corresponds to other evidence on the problems in the Moscow campaign and, given the exceedingly troubled nature of Moscow's recruitment drive, can be offered as the probable high figure for the percentage of mobilized workers in the campaign as a whole. The lower figure of 10 percent for Leningrad can serve as an estimate of the percentage mobilized in a more successful local campaign. It is also more than probable that the majority of mobilized 25,000ers were mobilized Communists rather than nonparty and unqualified workers or shop troublemakers forced under administrative pressure to enlist.[81] Above all it should be emphasized that evidence for the use of coercion in the recruitment drive is highly problematic and poorly reflected in the sources. But as we shall see below, the recruitment was primarily voluntary despite instances of the use of administrative pressure in individual enterprises and local campaigns.

Material and Economic Considerations in the Recruitment Drive

Material and economic considerations played a secondary role in the recruitment of the 25,000ers. Life in the countryside at this time was dismally bleak. Consumer goods rarely made their way to the villages, and workers and other outsiders were often denied access to the cooperative stores which stocked the few dry goods which were available. And although it might be expected that food produce would be more readily available in the village than in the hungry cities, the collectivization drive was to lead to a deterioration in the availability of food in the countryside, as well as the partial substitution of barter—dependent on access to consumer goods—for a money economy on the private and black markets for agricultural produce. The cultural level was even worse than the material standard of the countryside. Newspapers arrived infrequently, if at all, and the village libraries resembled the cooperative stores in their quality and quantity. There was little material incentive for a skilled worker to leave his factory and share in the trials and tribulations of the collective farmer.

In the recruitment of the 25,000ers, the state made an attempt to offset the decline in material standards of life which the workers faced as they departed from the factories. The salary conditions and rights of the 25,000ers were published in *Pravda* on 30 December 1929 in a Council of Peoples' Commissars decree of 29 December. Workers were guaranteed the right to return to their former jobs and place of employment upon their return from the countryside. The costs of transportation were to be paid by the worker's enterprise. A worker was promised a salary *equal* to that of his former job through payment of the difference in sum between his earlier salary and the new salary of his rural assignment. The enterprises were responsible for payment of this difference in sum. In addition, 25,000ers' families remaining in the city were guaranteed the right to maintain their present living quarters without a reduction in living space and were guaranteed the continued enjoyment of all family benefits arising from the collective agreement signed by the 25,000er and his enterprise. Family members were also to have first priority for employment through the labor exchange (or employment office). Children were to have priority in gaining admission to educational institutions and in receiving student stipends.[82]

The salary guarantees and rights had a limited appeal to factory workers. In individual cases they attracted workers who were burdened by financial concerns and by having a family to clothe, feed, and house.[83] In general, however, they served more as insurance or as an attempt to guarantee former standards of living than as economic privileges. Only two clauses in the list of rights may have served as an incentive in recruitment—employment opportunities for immediate family members and educational benefits for children. Workers with unemployed wives or children of working or university age may have been attracted by these provisions since the Soviet Union still suffered from high rates of unemployment among women and youth in the fall of 1929. However, these benefits had a limited impact for two reasons: first, because quite a few wives accompanied their husbands to the countryside; and, second, because a sizeable proportion of the 25,000ers were under twenty-nine years of age (see table 2) and therefore too young to have children of working or university age. It should be noted that despite these limitations, there were several reported cases of 25,000ers who attempted to use the right of family employment to secure jobs for relatives (and not just their immediate ones). These cases reached the press because the labor exchanges protested against several attempts to register relatives beyond the immediate family.[84]

These rights may have had an appeal to unskilled workers with families. Moreover, it is possible that many workers acted under the assumption that they could live off wages in kind in the countryside while their families would be able to live off their factory wages. Although there were never any directives on wages in kind and only the worker himself could receive the wages he earned in his rural position, it was possible for those families of 25,000ers who remained in the cities to be directly paid the difference between factory and rural salary.[85] Young and unskilled workers with families, whose economic situation had, on the average, deteriorated in the last years of NEP, may indeed have been influenced to volunteer by considerations such as these. Yet young (under the age of twenty-two) and unskilled workers made up a small minority of the 25,000ers.

Skilled workers, on the other hand, had a great deal to lose if they left the factory and entered rural work. In 1929 skilled workers, while not necessarily economically secure, were still better off economically than unskilled workers or the majority of peasants earning their living by agricultural work alone. The material fortunes of these skilled workers suffered a drastic decline upon entering into rural work, a decline well documented both in the workers' letters and in archival sources. In general, skilled industrial workers received much higher wages than most rural officials. For example, the majority of the 25,000ers who were miners in Kuzbass received rural salaries two to ten times less than what they had earned in the mines. Moreover, in many cases the workers failed to receive any salary at all from cash-poor collective farms, not to mention the difference payment from hostile industrial enterprises.[86] Most workers were aware of the material standards of life they could expect once they were in the countryside. The majority of the 25,000ers were skilled or highly skilled workers and therefore had little to gain financially and much to lose by leaving the factory and entering a collective farm.

These issues were important in recruitment, however, in so far as the delay in formulating the economic rights of the volunteers served to impede the recruitment drive in many areas. In most cities recruitment was completed or near completion by the time the decree on economic rights was published. Workers were naturally reluctant to volunteer under circumstances in which they did not know what their earnings would be or how their families would be provided for.[87] In Leningrad, on the other hand, there was a well-developed network of rumors about the economic rights which the 25,000ers were expected to receive. In general the rumors turned out to be either incorrect or similar to the rights outlined in the Council of Peoples' Commissars decree but were not in any sense more of an incentive to volunteer than were the actual Council of Peoples' Commissars rights. Nevertheless, the Leningrad campaign was not hindered by workers reluctant to volunteer because of lack of information on salary and economic rights. The main role which economic considerations played in most local campaigns was a negative one. The delay in the formulation of economic provisions served only to slow down recruitment until workers could be sure of their rights.

Two other material considerations which may have played some role in recruitment were educational opportunities and chances for eventual advancement and promotion. Some 25,000ers journeyed to the countryside with expectations of future educational opportunities. Several wrote letters to their factories, expressing the hope that their rural service would entitle them to return to school upon completion of their duties.[88] A number did, in fact, gain access to higher education when the campaign was completed.[89] However, the original Council of Peoples' Commissars decree contained no provisions on educational opportunities; these provisions arose only later. As it should in the case of economic incentives, the possibility of rumor should be taken into account here, for some workers may have volunteered with expectations of future educational opportunities. Yet it is more than likely that the skilled workers who volunteered to go to the countryside could, by exerting much less effort, have secured the opportunity to study had they simply remained at the factory. The campaign took place at a time of extensive working-class recruitments into educational institutions, and these recruitments drew upon workers who were very similar in composition to the 25,000ers.

The existence of opportunities for social advancement and promotion also influenced recruitment. By 1931–32 many of the 25,000ers who remained in the countryside had entered into higher party, soviet, and collective farm administrative work.[90] A number of 25,000ers who advanced to relatively important positions in the countryside were still at their posts during the Khrushchev period. The 25,000er G. P. Litovchenko became a hero of socialist labor, was a member of the Central Committee of the Ukrainian Communist party, and was twice a deputy in the Supreme Soviet of the USSR. In the early 1960s he was still the chairman of a large collective farm. V. F. Liukshin, who began his career as a railroad worker, was also a hero of socialist labor and an important rural dignitary in the early 1960s. I. A. Buianov was twice a hero of socialist labor, received the Order of Lenin, attended the Twenty-First and Twenty-Second Congresses of the Communist party as a delegate, and was twice a deputy in the Supreme Soviet.[91] These cases, of course, represent at most a small minority of the 25,000ers. Moreover, it is not likely that the average worker in 1929 could have projected hopes for the types of careers and rewards that many workers did manage to attain by the end of the 1930s. Furthermore, work in the lower rungs of rural administration simply did not offer the same potential for career advancement as did industrial administration. To a great extent, work in rural administration on the district or village levels represented something of a demotion in terms of wages, social status, and career options for skilled industrial workers in this period.

The most notable type of reward which does seem to have been expected was simple entry into the party. A number of 25,000ers entered the party immediately after volunteering or at some point during their stay in the countryside. When the 25,000er G. Bezgin told his wife that he had volunteered, she was shocked and exclaimed, "But we have three children . . . and you're not a party member." To this he replied, "Once I go this means the party." Bezgin's stay in the party, however, was cut short in the countryside of Central Asia by a band of *basmachi* (see Glossary) who bludgeoned him to death, gouging out his eyes, and disemboweling him in good *basmachi* fashion.[92] Bezgin's fate is noted in order to point out the possible costs as well as the rewards of volunteering. A fact of greater consequence is that the roughly 30 percent of nonparty 25,000ers could have entered the party with relative ease without volunteering for the campaign to the countryside. This was a time of extensive working-class recruitment into the party. Acceptance standards were lowered, and at the height of this last major working-class levy, entire factory shops were encouraged to join the party. Nevertheless, it is clear that despite a certain lack of logic, not to mention good sense, some workers did volunteer with the reward of party membership in mind.

The salary guarantees and economic rights offered to the workers were of a tenuous nature and were intended to serve more as a safeguard of former living standards than as an incentive. Once in the countryside, the workers suffered a substantial decline in living standards. Moreover, the risks of working in the countryside far outweighed any possible benefits. In spite of this, thousands of workers volunteered, at great personal sacrifice, to serve in distant and, in many cases, culturally alien villages for an unspecified duration of time. It is necessary to look beyond considerations of material self-interest in order to understand the basic motivations of the 25,000ers.

To the Front! The Military-Patriotic Upsurge

Collectivization was proclaimed to be a new front, a war for grain. The kulak, it was said, had initiated a grain strike and was locked in deadly combat with the urban proletariat. Workers were told that collectivization was essential to the success of industrialization, the problem of food supply for the cities and the Red army, and the cultural development of the countryside. In the context of capitalist encirclement and incessant war hysteria, the survival of Soviet power was perceived to be dependent on victories on the fronts of industrialization and collectivization. Civil war memories of famine and military intervention were revived in the popular mind and a radically militant attitude pervaded large sectors of the party and industrial proletariat. The nation was said to be in deadly peril and on the eve of great transformations.

Much of this atmosphere was introduced and manipulated from above in order to aid the leadership in its struggles with political opposition and to win working-class and party rank-and-file support for the policies of the First Five-Year Plan. Nevertheless, large sectors of the industrial working class were highly receptive to the state's mobilization devices. The unemployment and economic hardships of the NEP years, the mounting impatience with the NEP retreat, and the return of the bourgeois intelligentsia to a relatively privileged position increased class tensions in the late 1920s. The introduction of rationing in peacetime, high food prices, and long food lines in the cities intensified urban-rural antagonisms.[93] The state made use of these heightened tensions, often consciously intensifying them, in order to deflect working-class grievances away from systemic problems and toward perceived internal and external enemies. Sacrifice became the order of the day; Soviet patriotism, class war, and capitalist encirclement served as the context of action. In this way the leadership succeeded in recruiting many industrial workers and rank-and-file Communists to actively support and participate in the implementation of the First Five-Year Plan revolution.

The working class from which Stalin and the Soviet leadership drew their support was not, however, an undifferentiated whole. Nor did the state perceive it as such. The profile of factory workers in 1929 differed according to region, industry, occupation, skill level, age, and degree to which a worker retained ties to the countryside. These factors all contributed in some degree to the formation both of workers' attitudes to the state and the state's relations to different working-class strata.[94] Yet despite a significant stratum of workers of peasant origin (35 to 40 percent of all workers) and workers who retained ties to the land in the form of family, home, or farm in the countryside (roughly 25 percent of workers), one half of all Soviet factory workers on the eve of the First Five-Year Plan were classified as "hereditary proletarians"—that is, they were born into working-class families—and had entered the factory prior to 1917. In addition, two thirds of all Soviet factory workers were civil war veterans.[95] It was among these workers—the hereditary proletarians, the cadre workers with long years of experience at the bench, the civil war veterans and politically active workers—that the state's First Five-Year Plan program was to have its greatest appeal. Not all Soviet workers welcomed the campaign of the 25,000ers. But those who did, tended, like the 25,000ers described earlier in this chapter, to be representative of the politically active cadre worker. These workers, who represented a good proportion of the Soviet working class in 1929, served as the social base of the Stalin revolution and responded most enthusiastically to the recruitment drive.

Reports on recruitment indicated that these sectors of the working class were responding the most enthusiastically to the campaign and that there was a revolutionary upsurge among the most advanced workers.[96] The designation revolutionary upsurge to characterize the moment was, in a sense, manipulative and intended to maintain the air of excitement which had been fueled by the state's mobilization devices. In another very real sense, however, the term was an accurate characterization of the response of many workers. Andreev, the first secretary of the North Caucasus party organization, captured the essence of the upsurge in a description of what he saw as the class-conscious response of workers to the campaign (see epigraph at head of this chapter). In a speech at the third plenum of the North Caucasus regional party committee, Andreev claimed that the working class's attention was centered on collectivization because the working class viewed collectivization as the "key" to an entire set of issues which were of central concern in workers' lives. Andreev stated that there were "masses of cases of the best skilled workers" leaving the factories for the countryside and that "all questions were subsumed by the issue of collectivization."[97] And indeed many workers did link problems of everyday life to the collectivization drive. Moreover, as was shown in the profile of the 25,000ers, the "best skilled workers" were enlisting in great numbers to join the campaign. But was this, as Andreev concluded, actually a revolutionary upsurge predicated upon the class-conscious response of the best skilled workers to the imperatives of socialist construction in the countryside?

Workers volunteered to serve in the countryside because they perceived the nation to be at war and because they believed that collectivization was necessary to the survival and cultural development of the country. The framework of the campaign—and of the times—was military-patriotic. Soviet patriotism as an expression against the perceived or real dangers of internal and external aggression (and, in the sense, a *defensive* form of patriotism) was the primary leaven of the campaign and the revolution. It provided the context for action and, significantly, the context in which many workers became receptive to the idea of collectivization. If support and participation in collectivization are to be considered manifestations of class consciousness as Andreev and other Soviet leaders concluded—and this is not necessarily the case—then it seems clear that Soviet workers arrived at this consciousness primarily by route of an aggressive and defensive form of patriotism linked to a series of domestic problems, not the least of which were the success of the First Five-Year Plan and the resolution of food supply problems. Class consciousness, within the context of a workers' state, became adherence to and active support of the party line.

The recruitment campaign was strikingly similar to a military recruitment drive in the initial stages of a patriotic war. The dominant motif which appeared in speeches and statements by and about the 25,000ers was military in character and served to evoke memories of the civil war experience. The workers were constantly reminded that they had a military obligation to fulfill not unlike that which they had fulfilled in the civil war. At a Moscow reception honoring Leningrad 25,000ers on their way to the countryside, Lenin's widow, N. Krupskaia, reminded the volunteers of Lenin's 1918 letter to the workers of Petrograd urging them to go en masse to the villages to gather grain and to aid the poor peasants in the rural class struggle. At this reception Feliks Kon, the editor of *Rabochaia gazeta*, said, "You are soldiers of revolution, storming the stronghold of capitalism."[98] Speakers at the Moscow reception in honor of 25,000ers from Ivanovo-Voznesensk compared the send-off of the workers to the departure of Red army soldiers to the front during the civil war, and the civil war heroes S. M. Budennyi and K. E. Voroshilov gave rousing farewell speeches to groups of 25,000ers in guest appearances at the train stations.[99]

The 25,000ers often drew explicit parallels with their experiences in the civil war since there were many former Red army soldiers in their ranks. Almost every public statement issued by groups of 25,000ers contained a statement indicating that they would fulfill their mission in the countryside with the same determination with which they had fulfilled their duties in the civil war. The Rostov worker F. Z. Drozd declared that it was his duty to serve Soviet power on the front of collectivization just as he had served it during the civil war. He said, "I am an old partisan. Earlier, not even stopping to think, I cast aside my family and went to defend the party and Soviet power. Now when the slogan is 'transform the North Caucasus to 100 percent collectivization in one and one half years'—I, with satisfaction, go to the countryside in order again to fulfill my duty before the party and Soviet power."[100] Echoing Drozd, the 25,000er Malanina from Elektrozavod pledged, "We will go, as in 1917, to the front. There will be battles, there will be offensives."[101] Others expressed similar sentiments. Collectivization became a duty to fulfill. Many workers believed that the country was on the verge of civil war and military intervention. The importance of the civil war parallels was most apparent in the case of the Leningrad campaign. Nowhere was civil war imagery more pervasive and nowhere did workers respond more enthusiastically to recruitment.

For many workers the military rhetoric and siegelike quality of the times brought to mind the horrors and suffering of the civil war. Associating the civil war with famine and intervention, these workers linked collectivization to the solution of food shortages as well as to the defense of the nation since rapid industrialization was perceived to be a prerequisite to defense and collectivization, a prerequisite to industrialization. Many workers stated in their pledges, as did the 25,000er I. P. Pavlov, that only collectivization would guarantee that the Soviet Union would "have a sufficient quantity of grain."[102] According to a trade union report, the volunteer Kharlov stated that one of his reasons for enlisting in the campaign was "to aid the town with the supply of bread."[103] Collectivization was linked to the success of the First Five-Year Plan—the industrialization effort, the export of grain for capital funding, and the defense of the nation. The worker Zhukov praised the policy of collectivization, stating in good-worker fashion: "It has been necessary for a long time to carry out such a firm policy, the sooner to catch up to capitalist countries."[104] When the 25,000er Durenkov, a veteran worker with thirty-nine years at the bench, was asked why he wanted to give up his job at the factory, he explained, "We did not want to abandon the shop when it was necessary to go with rifles to defend the country from the bourgeoisie but we went with the firm hope of being victorious and of returning to reconstruct industry. Before 1925, there was no smoke from the factory chimney." He went on to say that, nonetheless, industry was reconstructed and that the workers would see to it that agriculture would be reconstructed as well. It was a class duty.[105] Clearly these workers supported collectivization because they perceived, as Andreev suggested, collectivization to be the key to the solution of other problems—problems which were intrinsic to the last years of NEP and which served to recall the civil war experience.

Although most workers seem to have recalled the civil war with a sense of dread, for some workers memories of the civil war period evoked feelings of pride and past glory. This, after all, had come to be known as the heroic period of the Russian Revolution. Tired of the passivity of the NEP years and what many perceived as a propeasant, antiworker orientation, some workers greeted the opening of a new revolutionary front with a real sense of excitement. The 25,000er Khromov was a former Red partisan with a forty-one-year record of service in his factory. For Khromov, service as a 25,000er revived old feelings of youth and adventure. He wrote, "Not one, I think, of the old revolutionaries [would] envy us. Here now before me arises an image of '19 [1919], when I was in this same district, climbing along snow drifts with rifle in hand and blizzard raging, like now. I feel that I am young again . . ."[106] Khromov, an older worker, was invigorated by the opening of the revolutionary offensive. This feeling was shared by many of the younger workers among the 25,000ers who had experienced the civil war in their teens, retained a romanticized memory of those heroic times, and were impatient with the evolutionary policies of NEP.

Many 25,000ers linked the campaign to the other "fronts" of the First Five-Year Plan or to the revolutionary tradition of the working class and their factories. According to a trade union report, the worker Shirokov pledged, "Work in the collective farm is the shock front. I, a communist, consider it my responsibility to be at the advanced post of this front."[107] Workers from the Putilov and Dinamo enterprises claimed that by being in the "front ranks of the steel columns of collectivization," they were continuing the glorious tradition of their factories. Dinamo volunteers pledged, "Now when the working class is sending from its ranks hundreds of the best proletarians to work on the state and collective farms, our glorious factory, Dinamo, as always, will go into the vanguard of the cause of socialist construction."[108] In his speech to 25,000ers, Feliks Kon explicitly linked the campaign to the "movement." He said, "How far we have progressed, if after 25 years from the day when Petersburg workers led by the priest Gapon with icons and banners marched with petitions to the tsar, we are now directed under Lenin's banner and the leadership of the party of Lenin in a great campaign to reconstruct agriculture in our country."[109] By placing the campaign within the context of the revolution and the working-class movement, it became part of a larger tradition. And tradition within the context of the working class, the glorious tradition of the great factories, and the revolutionary movement was, by this time, akin to Soviet patriotism. These traditions reinforced the more general patriotic fervor and warlike mentality of the times, providing the context for the upsurge of radicalism among workers.

The campaign was a part of the cause, a part of the necessary tasks of socialism and history. Duty and responsibility were stressed in the workers' pledges. The workers frequently stated that they were not only aware of the difficulties to be expected, but that they were aware of the sacrifice which would have to be made. Many workers, like the Serp i Molot factory electrician Ganev, realized that they "would receive only an insignificant part of [their] present salary," but still pledged to go because they viewed it as their duty or class responsibility. The worker F. M. Sergi wrote, "I have worked in the factory for over 30 years and I earn good money. But in spite of this I declare myself mobilized with great satisfaction . . ."[110] L. Kaganovich, representing the Central Committee at a reception for the 25,000ers, captured this feeling in his speech when he said to the workers, "Your role is the role of the proletarian leader. There will be difficulties, there will be kulak resistance and sometimes even collective farmer resistance, but history is moving in our favor."[111]

While history moved in favor of the working class, it dealt less favorably with social groups classified under the broad heading of class enemy. A significant group among the 25,000ers, moreover, appeared anxious to hurry history along in its offensive against the kulak and seem to have volunteered precisely in order to aid history in this sphere of its socialist endeavors. At the Moscow reception for Leningrad 25,000ers, Kaganovich defined the issue of the kulak threat for the 25,000ers with remarkable and characteristic clarity in his two-hour speech. He said, "Either we destroy the kulak as a class or the kulak will grow as a class of capitalists and liquidate the dictatorship of the proletariat."[112] The 25,000er Konderev, a worker at Leningrad's Bol'shevik factory and a former Red partisan, was receptive to this warning; he declared, "I want to organize peasants in collective farms. And in relation to the kulak, I will take a brutal line. The kulaks are against the collective farm. They arm the peasants against the workers. I will show in practice that the worker is a friend of the poor and middle peasants and an irreconcilable enemy of the kulak." It should be noted that Konderev had worked in the countryside during the civil war (probably in a food detachment), and his father, described as a peasant activist, had been killed by kulaks. Konderev claimed that this was the basis of his hatred for the rural class enemy.[113] A worker from Saratov was also motivated by personal considerations. He had led an early life of poverty in the countryside and greeted the reopening of rural class warfare with satisfaction: "I escaped from the old impoverished countryside. I experienced kulak exploitation on my own hide . . . I hate that countryside and so [I] left it for the factory. When I heard that the order of the day was the elimination of the kulak as a class, I decided to return . . ."[114] There were, in fact, several documented cases of 25,000ers who had been born in rural poverty, worked as agricultural day laborers in their youth, and left for the city at the first opportunity. These workers, who had severed all ties to the villages and who had spent long years at the factory bench, quickly came to identify with the city and their factories and often looked back at the countryside and their former employers with marked hostility.[115] These were workers who were motivated to volunteer on the basis of intense grievances rooted in their past experience.

There were also, of course, a number of adventurers, "who dreamed of blazing gun fights with kulaks." The 25,000er Fedorov, for example, was to name the collective farm which he led, "Death to Kulaks."[116] Others, once in the countryside, would carry socialism to the peasantry—like the hero of Andrei Platonov's novel *Chevengur*—on the point of a bayonet. As a rule, these workers picked up their weapons only after presenting the obligatory speech on the world revolution, the international situation, or the idiocy of rural life. Other workers, like the 25,000er Cherednichenko, simply disliked peasants and would use force in their work because that it is how they believed peasants must be dealt with.[117] The food shortages and high market prices of the last years of NEP, the contribution of peasants to urban unemployment and consequent conflicts in the factories between cadre workers and peasants in the 1920s, and many workers' lingering distrust of the "dark" peasant masses from the days of the civil war and the food detachments kindled a strong antipeasant mood among some groups of industrial workers.

Antipeasant feelings, along with the belief that the rural class enemy was indeed a threat, were reinforced by reports of the murders of activists and workers while on grain-requisitioning missions in the late 1920s. The newspapers covered these stories widely, and meetings were often called in factories to discuss the latest victim of the class war. To give just one example of the nature of the publicity which these cases received, the example of an extremely graphic photo from the widely read journal *Litsom k derevne* (the December 1929 issue) is apt. The photo featured a body-length portrait of a plenipotentiary with half of his head blown off by the usual "kulak" sawed-off shotgun and his brains unraveling onto his shoulders.[118] This was a most vivid portrayal of the class struggle in action and must have had a strong effect on urban readers. Several workers volunteered, citing reasons of solidarity with such victims of the class struggle, as they came to be known.

This was the case of the worker Ivan Balashov, from the Putilov factory. Murders of workers continued to serve as a motivation even after the campaign was over. When another 25,000er from Putilov was murdered, ten of his former coworkers, including one of the oldest workers at the plant, volunteered to take his place in the countryside.[119] Once again, as in the case of the other reasons cited for volunteering, these workers arrived at their decision by way of defensive motivations. In this case it was the internal, and not the external, threat, but the result was the same.

A significant number of workers were motivated to volunteer in order to serve in a war of a very different nature. This was the war on backwardness in the countryside, a war which was an integral part of the First Five-Year Plan and the collectivization of Soviet agriculture; as such, it was considered vital to the progress and long-term success of the nation, as well as, in a limited respect, the defense of the nation. The war on backwardness was necessary to create a population of literate, politically and socially active, loyal Soviet citizens in the countryside. They, after all, would serve as the base of the Red army in addition to supplying it and the cities with food.

Many workers who volunteered for this reason had been born in the countryside but did not look back on their earlier experience with the hostility and thirst for vengence of some of the other rural-born workers. In fact, once the 25,000ers were in the countryside, one of the most widespread concerns in their letters was the pervasive backwardness which impeded their work at every step.[120] Sholokhov's famous 25,000er Davydov, the hero of *Virgin Soil Upturned*, was constantly heard discussing the "good life" which they were building for the peasant children, so that they would not have to endure the hardship and suffering of their fathers and grandfathers.[121] Many real-life 25,000ers expressed similar sentiments. The 25,000er G. V. Khalin, stated:

> I am from the peasantry myself. For a long time, I not only had to observe the life of the peasant but myself tasted all of the superstitions by which all of our old prerevolutionary peasantry was nourished.
>
> I saw that the only way for the peasantry to break out of its indigent condition was to enter the collective farm.[122]

The worker V. Kochetkov, who had eleven years experience in the factory, expressed a desire "to make our grain economically correct and cultured" and to teach the peasants "to think like us who go to the countryside to reconstruct the countryside historically on a factory basis." The worker Zhukov, having spent seventeen years at the factory bench, said, "We must declare war on the old traditions and not only increase harvests but concern ourselves with the internalization of culture into the dark peasant masses."[123] It was from this group of workers and, in particular, from those born in the countryside that many of the 25,000ers who would remain on the collective farms into the 1950s and 1960s came.

A final group of workers included in this category were workers who volunteered on the basis of past experience in rural patronage activities. This group included workers, who, like I. I. Skripko, the chairman of his plant's rural patronage cell, were from the rank-and-file activists of the patronage movement.[124] Also included were workers who volunteered in order to work in regions or villages with which their factories had held long-term patronage agreements. In many cases these workers were familiar with the peasants and areas in which they were to serve.[125]

The majority of 25,000ers identified with the state and shared its view of the importance of collectivization to the success of the First Five-Year Plan, the defense of the nation, the resolution of urban food supply problems, and the cultural development of the country. Their statements and pledges were cast largely in defensive terms and often derived either from working-class problems and tensions of the NEP period or associations drawn from the civil war days. These problems and associations, which were intensified by the military-patriotic atmosphere of the times, served to create the militant upsurge among workers and to make the goals of the First Five-Year Plan the goals of the working class. The 25,000ers spoke the language of the times, sprinkled as it was with Marxist, class, revolutionary, and civil war motifs and terminology. However, not all Soviet workers responded in this fashion. The 25,000ers were representative of a particular sector of the working class; outside this sector, Soviet workers often responded very differently to the campaign and to collectivization.

Dissident Voices

The mood of factory workers and their attitudes about collectivization were serious concerns to party and trade union officials in 1929. Press and trade union reports all note a certain amount of opposition to collectivization from a segment of the working class. Workers were reported to be "agitating" against collective farms in workers' barracks; it was reported that some workers in the North Caucasus called grain requisitioning a return to War Communism. There were also cases of workers withdrawing their savings from banks and their applications for party membership in protest over collectivization.[126] Most often, these were workers who lived in the villages and commuted to nearby factories for work or workers who returned to the villages regularly either on a seasonal basis or while on leave.[127] These workers, it was reported, agitated against collectivization when home in the villages and told their families not to pay taxes or give grain to requisitioners. According to reports in the fall of 1929 on Ukrainian villages in which metalworkers (commuters) lived, it was the commuting peasant-worker who was most vocally opposed to collectivization; this conclusion, moreover, was reported by fellow metal-workers—cadre workers.[128] Many workers who opposed collectivization and refused to enter collective farms were illegally expelled from their trade unions in late 1929 and early 1930 (until this practice was officially condemned) or simply liquidated their farms and left the countryside forever in the early months of 1930.[129] The party and the trade unions greatly feared the contagious effect such protest might have on other workers and emphasized the importance of reeducating such harmful elements.[130]

During the recruitment drive some workers voiced their opposition to collectivization and the campaign of the 25,000ers. There were workers who expressed sympathy with the plight of the peasantry and spoke out against collectivization at the general factory assemblies devoted to the recruitment drive. At the Provodnik factory the 25,000ers were labeled by some workers the "grave diggers of the kulak class"; whether "kulak class" was substituted for peasantry by the author of the report on this factory is not certain but not unlikely. Peter Il'in, a young volunteer, was stabbed by his father when he announced that he was joining the ranks; his father was reported to be elderly, a religious believer—in short, petit-bourgeois according to Soviet parlance of the day. A report from the Ukraine noted that along with the revolutionary upsurge, the campaign had rekindled the fires of the class struggle between cadre workers and peasant-workers at many factories.[131]

Although much of the opposition to the campaign derived from opposition to collectivization, there were also workers who protested in a manner similar to that of factory officialdom. These workers complained about the damage which would be done to the industrial effort by siphoning off so many skilled cadre workers from the factories and objected to sending people unfamiliar with agriculture to work on the collective farms. Such objections often emphasized the anti-working-class moods among the peasants which would contribute to the failure of the campaign. These objections were usually labeled "kulak," "kulak-provoked," or manifestations of the right opposition.[132] Almost all anticollectivization sentiment earned these labels at the time, but in the case of objections specifically against working-class recruitments, there may have been some greater element of truth involved, for these voices did reflect specific protest that was linked to the right opposition.

There were two other forms of opposition to the campaign which were less frequently voiced and which appear to have emanated mainly from types of workers who were similar to the 25,000ers in degree of skill and number of years at the bench but who differed from the 25,000ers in their low level of political activity. These forms of opposition were, first, hostility to peasants and, second, objections to leaving the factory for life in the countryside. Not all workers who were hostile to the peasantry wanted to go to the countryside to take part in the "class war." The worker Cherednichenko, who eventually was mobilized as a 25,000er, did not wish to volunteer because he was proud of his reputation as his factory's best foreman and because he neither liked nor trusted, in his words, "muzhik-buckwheat eaters."[133] Workers in Nizhnyi Tagil'skii *Okrug* in the Urals refused to volunteer. They protested: "We are skilled workers and natives of Tagila. Therefore we will not go to work on a collective farm."[134] Going to work in the countryside, after all, meant a drastic decline in living standards, cultural deprivation, and the simple but hard fact that it was necessary to uproot oneself and leave familiar surroundings for the unknown.

There were several reports of workers, probably following similar motivations, who not only did not want to go to a collective farm but objected to being asked in the first place. At a meeting of the Krasnyi Proletarii factory, the chairman of the factory committee said, "It is necessary to send the most vigilant to the collective farm." He met with the response "and why then do the factory committee members send us and not go themselves?"[135] In the Chicherin mines in the North Caucasus at a meeting of party activists, the party rank and file protested when their leaders called for volunteers, and also demanded that the leaders sign up. Here the rank and file met with success, and as a consequence, the secretaries of the mine committee and the mine's party cell became "volunteers," while the rank and file remained at the mines.[136]

A large measure of dedication and political support for the state's ambitious policies was a necessary essential in motivating workers to volunteer. And although some workers were opposed to collectivization and the campaign of the 25,000ers, the majority of workers who volunteered or who were nominated by their factory selection committees and passed reviews on the regional level supported the party's rural policies on some level. Workers who expressed disapproval or opposition to these policies were generally disqualified from selection—especially once selection passed above the enterprise level. In most regions the numbers of volunteers far exceeded quotas and, as a consequence, often as many as 50 percent of the candidates would be cut.[137]

In addition to attempts to screen out all workers who expressed disagreement with party policy, there was a conscious, if not always successful, effort to exclude unreliable workers. According to trade union and press reports, these included drunks; religious believers; illiterates; workers with insufficient years at the bench; workers who were too young, too old, infirm, or too closely tied to the countryside (i.e., recent factory arrivals or workers with strong ties to their villages); workers with a history of labor violations, party violations, or passivity in party work; and workers who lacked "vigilance," disagreed with the party line, or failed to meet the standards set in the recruitment selection criteria.[138] An additional factor which served to mitigate the effect of attempts to recruit unqualified workers was the widespread use of political labels to brand derelict recruiters; in addition to possible legal or party action, they were labeled representatives of the right opposition, Trotskyites, or kulak agents. In the context of the times, it became a political danger to allow "kulak" and "class alien" penetration of the ranks of the 25,000ers.[139] In this way working-class voices of opposition to the campaign were silenced and disregarded by the state, which chose to address itself exclusively to the politically active cadre workers. And the opposition of "unreliable workers" was drowned out by the wave of acclamation rising from the ranks of the state's chief social and political constituency within the working class.

Conclusion

The recruitment drive ended as perhaps one of the most successful Soviet campaigns of its kind. Overall, according to the statistical profile of the 25,000ers presented above, it achieved its goals and succeeded in recruiting workers who, in fact, surpassed the strict selection criteria. The drive's success can be explained by several factors. First, the original selection criteria restricted the field of recruitment to the cadre workers—workers who were expected to identify with the state's goals. Second, every attempt was made to target recruitment toward key industrial regions and industries, where the labor force measured up to the criteria set for selection. The regions and industries which had recruitment difficulties were, in general, those in which the labor force did not meet the standards for recruitment. Regional differences determined working-class response (i.e., workers closely tied to the land tended to object both to recruitment and collectivization), as well as factory reluctance to part with valued labor resources in regions suffering from skilled labor shortages. This was the case in Moscow, for example, where there was a large substratum of peasant-workers. This was also the case in the textile industry, where workers tended to have lower skill levels and fewer years at the bench, and where women workers were predominant (61.2 percent) in the work force. Where the labor force tended to be more highly skilled, more urbanized, and more politically active (in terms of party membership and participation in factory organizations), as, for example, in Leningrad and the Urals and in the metal and machine industries, the recruitment drive was relatively free from the problems which beset it in regions like Moscow and in industries like the textile industry.[140]

The highly favorable results of the recruitment drive, however, were ultimately linked to the state's success in addressing the grievances, fears, and needs of a part of its working class. The state addressed itself to those workers who had become politically active and had risen to leadership roles in their factories during the second half of the 1920s. It addressed itself to those workers who identified least with the policies of the NEP period and who had most to gain from the new, more aggressive policies of the First Five-Year Plan. The state was able to capitalize successfully on anti-NEP sentiment, urban-rural antagonisms, the growing anxiety over food supply problems, and the popular war scare. It linked the successful fulfillment of the First Five-Year Plan to the very survival of Soviet power. The evidence suggests that the primary determinant in the success of the recruitment drive and the positive response of many Soviet workers was the military-patriotic context of the times. Within this setting that sector of the working class which identified its fate with the city, with the proletariat, and with the Soviet state proved highly responsive to the leadership's mobilization devices. The campaign also found a receptive audience among smaller groups of workers, who, although culturally urbanized, had been born in the countryside and either had deep-seated resentments toward the peasantry or had a stake in the cultural development of the village. All this is not to say that there were no 25,000ers who represented the unreliable elements and adventurers among the working class as well. The vast majority who volunteered, however, did in fact represent steadfast, politically loyal workers who shared a common language and view of the world with the leadership.

The main significance of the recruitment campaign, however, resides both in the support which these workers gave to their state and party by volunteering and participating in collectivization and in the fact that material incentives and coercion played such a minimal role in recruitment. Moreover, it has become clear that the 25,000ers represented a particular stratum of the Soviet working class: the politically active cadre worker. This is extremely important for understanding the social underpinnings of the Stalin revolution. The significance of the cadre worker is not to be sought in numbers (although they did represent a good proportion of workers), but in political importance. In the face of resistant factory officials, as well as a largely hostile rural officialdom and peasantry, the leadership turned to these workers for aid in the implementation of the revolution. These workers provided the main forces for the implementation of collectivization, as well as for the mass education and affirmative-action programs of the First Five-Year Plan, the party and state bureaucracies of the later 1930s, and the enthusiasts of socialist construction. In short, they were an important part of the social base of Stalin's revolution and played a central role in the implementation of the First Five-Year Plan revolution. The campaign of the 25,000ers was to serve as a cornerstone in the construction of a new order in the Soviet countryside: the participation of the 25,000ers in collectivization and in the foundation of the collective farm system was to facilitate the state's endeavors to implement the enormous transformation of agriculture and peasant life which took place during the frenzied, heroic, and often tragic epoch of the Stalin revolution.

3

Setting the Campaign in Motion

Have no fear, gentlemen! Remember that we stand so low on the plane of organization that the very idea that we *could* rise *too* high is absurd!
V. I. LENIN, *What Is To Be Done?*

The situation will define the work.
Response of a party district committee official
to a 25,000er seeking instructions

The 25,000ers set out for the countryside in late January and early February 1930. They arrived at the height of the all-out drive to collectivize Soviet agriculture. Rural Soviet Russia was in a state of turmoil: every village was a new front, every government and party organ was a command post. Collectivization was a race against time. It was a race for quotas and percentages. It was a numbers game in which high stakes were wagered and in which equally high risks were involved. Chaos and flux characterized the situation in the winter of 1930.

The 25,000ers were unable to sink permanent moorings into the countryside during this initial phase of the campaign. Their situation, like that of all rural Soviet Russia, remained fluid until the first sounding of a retreat was heard in early March, when Stalin's famous article "Dizzyness from Success" was published. After that the workers gradually began to settle into work in the collective farm system. Until that time, however, their experience in the countryside was shaped largely by the inability of Moscow to exert its control over the frenzied collectivization drive and its consequent failure to provide the workers with any type of assistance or institutional support. The workers were left to fend for themselves, and Moscow's plans for the campaign of the 25,000ers remained, for the time being, on paper. The vastness of the tasks of the revolution, the resulting ubiquitous chaos, and the quite unprecedented nature of the 25,000ers' campaign form the backdrop of

74

what happened when planning confronted reality in the context of the First Five-Year Plan revolution. The gulf between plan and reality, which was so painfully evident in the winter of 1930, prefigured the enormous problems which the center would have in exerting its control over events in the countryside through its chosen representatives, the worker-25,000ers.

Plan and Reality

Before setting out for work in late January 1930, the 25,000ers underwent an intensive two-week program of preparatory courses designed by Kolkhoztsentr and the Central Council of Trade Unions. The course organizers experienced a number of serious problems, ranging from Kolkhoztsentr's failure to provide the necessary course materials in sufficient quantities and on time to the shortage of instructors. Additional lectures were broadcast on Moscow radio to make up for some of these deficiencies and featured such celebrities as I. A. Iakovlev, the Commissar of Agriculture; K. Ia. Bauman, the first secretary of the Moscow party organization; G. N. Kaminskii, the chairman of Kolkhoztsentr; and N. Krupskaia, Lenin's widow.[1] Most workers would later complain that the courses were poor and had not prepared them for the reality of the countryside and collectivization. At least some small percentage of the workers in Moscow never even took these initial courses because the recruitment campaign was completed so late.[2] The workers would be offered further instruction and short-term courses beginning in the summer of 1930, but, by far, their primary education would be obtained by way of basic life experience in the villages and collective farms of Soviet Russia.

The 25,000ers were intended to be at their posts in time for the start of the spring sowing campaign and for the reelections of the collective farm administrative boards.[3] By 2 February, 18,300 workers had arrived in the countryside; an additional 2,340 had joined their ranks by 9 February, bringing the total number of 25,000ers already in the countryside to 20,640.[4] The remainder completed their journey by mid-February.

The journey to the countryside was a transitional experience for many 25,000ers, containing echoes of the revolutionary enthusiasm unleashed in the urban campaign but, nonetheless, pregnant with harbingers of what was to come. The 25,000ers had left the cities in a blaze of glory. They became heroes of the revolutionary order before ever setting foot in the countryside. Their pictures, their names, their previously unheralded biographies received nationwide attention in the press. They sat as honored guests in Moscow's Hall of Columns and in other celebrated meeting places while party and trade union leaders sang their praises.[5] They were toasted at their factories, and their fellow workers issued instructions (*nakazy*) calling on them to represent the working class with honor at their new posts. They gave speeches at the train stations from which they left the cities, and were bid farewell to the accompaniment of triumphal marches and revolutionary songs. The 25,000ers were off to a new front. They were the favored sons and daughters of the First Five-Year Plan revolution.

En route to the countryside the uplifting strains of the triumphal marches continued to be heard; but as the 25,000ers moved further away from the cities, the bands grew smaller and the music less audible. On the trains the workers practiced their oratory skills, exchanged information learned in their preparatory courses, or read through their assortment of political and agricultural handbooks and pamphlets.[6] In some cases the 25,000ers continued to be honored at local receptions and at passing train stations;[7] in other cases the 25,000ers began to receive a presage of what could be expected in the very near future.

In many areas of the countryside, the praise and warm handshakes of central party and city officials were replaced by the hostility and cold stares of regional and local officials. Several detachments of 25,000ers experienced difficulties with railroad officials while en route. Train cars of 25,000ers were temporarily delayed due to more pressing transport needs. The railroads were accused of attempting to "sabotage" the safe and timely arrival of the 25,000ers.[8] Elsewhere, regional and local officials made clear to the 25,000ers precisely what the workers might expect in the countryside—minus any revolutionary heroic glossing. At a reception for 25,000ers in German Povol'zhe, a local official told the workers, "To tell you the truth, comrades, it is not soviet to go [to the villages]. Believe me . . . you cannot live in peace with the local population."[9] The revolutionary aura which surrounded the 25,000ers in the cities and continued to drift with them en route to the countryside gradually began to dissipate. The 25,000er Kossev, recalling the journey, captured the essence of the transition; he said, "They saw us off with a triumphal march, they met us with a funeral dirge."[10] With their feet planted firmly in half-reality, the 25,000ers entered the Soviet countryside.

The setting into which the 25,000ers emerged was quite different from the one which they had recently left. It was not simply a question of a change of scenery from factory smokestacks to peasant huts and the wide-open expanses of the countryside; this was not an entirely unfamiliar scene for many of the workers. Nor was it only a matter, in the case of some 25,000ers, of a transition from ethnic Russian cities to the culturally alien villages of the peoples of Central Asia, Buriatiia, or Osetiia. The difference lay in the atmosphere and order engendered by the furious pace of the ongoing collectivization drive.

The Administrative Order in the Countryside

The 25,000ers stepped into the whirlwind of the socialist transformation of the countryside. The collectivization campaign had completely transfigured the administrative order in the countryside. This transfiguration had been in the process of evolution from late 1927 and early 1928 when extraordinary measures in grain collections were first introduced; it reached its high point in January and February of 1930. The routine hierarchy of the government-party rural apparatus, never entirely routine in the Soviet context, had broken down. In its place had arisen the institutions of the plenipotentiary and the party instructor. Plenipotentiaries and instructors raced from institution to institution, from village to village, to enumerate, implement, and enforce policy. Policy assumed the aspect of administrative procedure, all of its separate and theoretically distinct aspects combined into one. In this way each level of the party and government hierarchy instituted a plenipotentiary blitzkrieg upon the next successive regional level or sometimes even over the head of the regional level immediately subordinate and directly on to the district or village level.

Administrative routine in the countryside was further upset by rapid personnel turnover, which had steadily increased throughout the late 1920s and into 1930. According to preliminary data, in the 1929–30 purge of the party, 47,753 (or 16.9 percent) rural Communists were expelled from the party; an additional 3,857 (or 10.2 percent) were removed from responsible posts.[11] Turnover rates for chairmen and secretaries of *sel' sovet*s reached alarming dimensions; in many areas there were from eight to ten different chairmen in one year.[12] The high turnover rates in the *sel' sovet*s were the result of administrative purges, arrests, and, in some cases, flight on the part of harried officials. Turnover rates for both the party and government network were compounded further by constant transfers of reliable officials from area to area in a game of troubleshooter hopscotch. The instability of rural administrative personnel was augmented when the decision was made to hold extraordinary unscheduled reelections of a large part of the *sel' sovet*s in early 1930.[13] As a consequence, according to contemporary reports, from 40 to 50 percent of all *sel' sovet*s were reelected, and as many as 82 percent of *sel' sovet* chairmen were replaced in some regions of the country.[14] In addition, all collective farm administrative boards were subject to reelection in February.[15]

Another dimension of the breakdown of normal administrative routine in the countryside was the lack of specificity in functional and legal demarcations of rights and responsibilities of rural governing organs. To a large degree, this was an old problem, stemming from conflicts and overlap between party and soviet organs. By late 1929, however, several additional factors arose which compounded these traditional problems. As late as November 1929, when *raionirovanie* (the administrative reorganization of the country into *raion*, or district, territorial units) had just been completed, the journal *Sovetskoe stroitel' stvo*, reported that with the emergence of the administrative unit of the district, the role of the *okrug* was now unclear and undefined.[16] This problem would eventually lead to the elimination of the administrative unit of the *okrug* in the summer of 1930. In the meantime, however, the regional chain of command was not clearly defined. The role of the *sel' sovet* as an administrative organ also began to lose clarity. In the fall of 1929 there was a spontaneous movement, fiercely criticized by the center, to liquidate the *sel' sovet*s in districts of wholesale collectivization. This movement partially arose because of revived revolutionary utopian ideas favoring the ''withering away'' of government. More fundamentally, however, attempts to eliminate *sel' sovet*s were related to the problem of the mutual rights and responsibilities of the *sel' sovet* and the newly emerging collective farm administrative organs. There was no clear demarcation of legal and administrative responsibilities between these two organs, and in many cases collective farm administrative boards simply and arbitrarily usurped the powers of the *sel' sovet*s and sometimes even disbanded them. Moreover, the territorial jurisdiction of the *sel' sovet*s began to dissolve when collective farms were so large that they encompassed the territories of several *sel' sovet*s.[17]

It was within this administrative context that the collectivization drive was implemented in early 1930. The drive was led by an army of government plenipotentiaries, party instructors, and district and village officials. The atmosphere was that of a military campaign. The air was charged with a sense of high excitement, revolutionary fervor, and danger. The collectivization drive subsumed the ordinary workings of the rural party and government; policy measures and administrative matters outside the sphere of collectivization were temporarily shelved.

This was the situation which the 25,000ers faced when they entered the countryside. When the workers first confronted the campaign's organizational infrastructure in the countryside, they found themselves stepping into a bottomless pit. The realities of rural Soviet Russia served to completely confound all plans for the distribution and use of the 25,000ers. Moreover, rural officials were hostile to the workers, perceiving them as a threat to their authority. Nonetheless, the 25,000ers managed to make their entry into the countryside; precisely where they surfaced or in what role is another issue.

The Organizational Infrastructure of the Campaign

Kolkhoztsentr's plans for the distribution and use of the workers had been completed well in advance of the departure date set for the 25,000ers.

Kolkhoztsentr's plans, however, were limited to control figures for the distribution and use of the workers solely on the regional level and were completely lacking in specificity. Kolkhoztsentr's affiliates on the *okrug* and district levels failed to compile their own plans for the distribution and use of the 25,000ers.[18] Kolkhoztsentr was forced to issue repeated instructions and warnings to its regional agencies in an attempt to exert them to apply pressure on their *okrug-* and district-level affiliates to prepare for the arrival of the workers.[19] In addition, Kolkhoztsentr issued reprimands to its agencies in Voronezh, Ufa, Baku, Moscow, Arkhangel'sk, Novosibirsk, and the Ukraine.[20] Despite these efforts, results were not forthcoming.

As late as 25 January 1930, when many workers had already left for the countryside, the majority of *okrug*s and districts still had no plans for the distribution of the 25,000ers. There were no plans in the Lower Volga, the Urals, the Crimea, Tatariia, and Bashkiriia; plans for the distribution of the workers in Moscow, the North Caucasus, and the Middle Volga were characterized as either highly incomplete or defective.[21] The Siberian regional party committee's commission on the 25,000ers was disclosed as a paper commission which had failed even to do preparatory work on the campaign.[22] The rural party was absorbed in a much more pressing campaign at this time—the collectivization drive—and failed to assume responsibility for the compilation of plans for the distribution and use of the 25,000ers.

The party fraction (or unit) of Kolkhoztsentr, however, continued, alternately, to implore and threaten its regional counterparts within the Kolkhoztsentr administrative network to devote their attention to the campaign of the 25,000ers in earnest. At the end of January Kolkhoztsentr issued instructions for the fourth time on the procedures to be applied in the distribution and use of the 25,000ers.[23] This followed a press report on the chairman of the Central Black Earth Region Kolkhoztsentr agency who admitted that he did not know how many 25,000ers were coming to the region, nor what to do with them when they arrived. He received a strict reprimand from Kolkhoztsentr.[24]

Once the 25,000ers entered into the jurisdiction of the *okrug-* and district-level offices of Kolkhoztsentr, the situation deteriorated further. There was little time for precise record keeping in the Soviet countryside at this time; as a consequence, Kolkhoztsentr "lost" a great many of the 25,000ers once they left the cities. In principle, Kolkhoztsentr's *okrug*-level offices were to file reports with their regional superiors three times per month on the number of 25,000ers and their type of work; the regional agencies, in turn, were to forward this information to the center according to a similar time schedule.[25] Given the prevailing chaos in the countryside, this was rather wishful thinking. In February and March of 1930 over 10,000 of the 25,000ers were not accounted for.[26] It was not until the summer of 1930 that Kolkhoztsentr was able to compile an overall account of the numbers of 25,000ers. At that time Kolkhoztsentr claimed that 27,519 25,000ers had been sent to the countryside in the winter of 1930.[27]

Kolkhoztsentr's *okrug-* and district-level agencies failed to forward information on the 25,000ers under their jurisdiction. Frequently, such information was nonexistent to begin with. This was a problem which was to plague the campaign throughout the duration of the 25,000ers' stay in the countryside. In Siberia much of the information on the 25,000ers was lost when the administrative-territorial unit of the *okrug* (initially responsible for maintaining records on the workers) was abolished in the summer of 1930. Consequently, the Siberian regional Kolkhoztsentr offices did not know how many 25,000ers were in Siberia.[28] The Urals' regional Kolkhoztsentr agency had records for only 54 percent of its 25,000ers, and in the Middle Volga (at least initially) Kolkhoztsentr organs simply kept no records at all.[29] In August 1930 a research brigade from the newspaper *Bednota* investigated the progress made in tracking 25,000ers in the Moscow Region. First the brigade visited the Moscow Regional Union of Unions of Agricultural Cooperatives whose representative was surprised by the brigade's inquiries and said, "We have no one here who ever worked with the 25,000ers." Then the brigade went to the offices of the Moscow regional Kolkhoztsentr agency. Here the brigade was told: "We have no data about the work of the 25,000ers. You know, we were reorganized. The *okrug* Kolkhoztsentr office transferred all work on the 25,000ers to the Moscow regional Kolkhoztsentr office, the Moscow regional office transferred it to the union of unions [of agricultural cooperatives] and back again . . . Since May the Moscow regional Kolkhoztsentr agency has had no contact whatsoever with the 25,000ers."[30] As late as 1930 and early 1931 Kolkhoztsentr reported that its affiliates in Uzbekistan, Tadzhikistan, Kirgiziia, Bashkiriia, and Azerbaidzhan had provided no data on 25,000ers in their regions.[31]

It should be emphasized that despite the continuing confusion in keeping records on the 25,000ers, accounting did generally improve over what it had been in the initial phase of the campaign. This is evident in Kolkhoztsentr's amazing accomplishment in the summer of 1930, when it managed to compile a table (see table 3) of regional distribution figures for the 25,000ers. By that time the 25,000ers had more or less settled into permanent positions within the rural sector. In February and most of March, however, their situation was fluid due to frequent transfers, the retention of many within the Kolkhoztsentr apparatus, and cases of failure or refusal to give the 25,000ers work. The disorder in the campaign reflected the prevailing disorder in rural administration at this time and set the scene for the first steps of the 25,000ers into the whirlwind of collectivization.

First Steps

Once in the countryside the 25,000ers passed into the jurisdiction of the regional, *okrug*, and district agencies of Kolkhoztsentr. Standing commissions were created within the regional-level agencies to provide general supervision over the distribution and use of the workers. In *okrug*s in which there were more than seventy 25,000ers, an instructor was to be appointed within the apparatus of the *okrug* Kolkhoztsentr office to take charge of all matters pertaining to the workers. At the district level the chairmen of Kolkhoztsentr agencies were held personally responsible for the 25,000ers.[32] This, at least, was the plan of organizational jurisdiction on paper in February. There was, however, a good deal of regional variation in establishing a hierarchy of supervision of the 25,000ers.[33] And, in fact, it transpired that the 25,000ers would serve within a hierarchy of multiple jurisdictions, with the result that no single organization or institution assumed direct responsibility for the workers and, instead, tended to transfer responsibility for the 25,000ers to other parallel bureaucracies or to lower regional levels of their own bureaucracy.

There had been no preparation for the arrival of the workers in the majority of regions to which 25,000ers were sent. Many workers found themselves stranded in regional and *okrug* centers with nothing to do. In letters to the Central Committee's Department of Agitation and Mass Campaigns, 25,000ers frequently complained that they were given no work.[34] In the North Caucasus many workers were given no defined post for the entire month of February; in national minority areas the workers also found themselves unemployed for an extended period of time.[35] Many regional, *okrug*, and district Kolkhoztsentr organs delayed giving the workers assignments or shifted the responsibility for the 25,000ers to other bureaucracies.

The 25,000ers who arrived in Samarkand in early February were forced to sit inactive for the entire month. The 25,000er I. I. Skripko wrote a letter of complaint to the newspaper *Izvestiia*. He said that he, along with sixty Leningrad 25,000ers and three Moscow 25,000ers, had arrived in Samarkand on 2 February. They were greeted with the usual triumphal marches and speeches and then housed in comfortable barracks, where they received relative luxury items like tea and sugar and were entertained with visits to the movies. Skripko described the situation as similar to a "resort." He complained, however, that the 25,000ers were growing tired of this resort and had exhausted their energy for giving speeches. They were supposed to be given their assignments on 8 February, but transport to the countryside was delayed until the arrival of the Ivanovo-Voznesensk 25,000ers. When this detachment finally arrived, the deployment of the 25,000ers was once again delayed so that the

TABLE 3*

RECRUITMENT AND SELECTION OF 25,000ers PER REGION ACCORDING TO CONTROL FIGURES FROM KOLKHOZTSENTR
(Dated: Not earlier than July 1930)

REGION	Control Figure for Recruitment C	A	Numbers Remaining in Region C	A	Leningrad C	A	Moscow C	A	Ukraine C	A	Ivanovo C	A	Nizhegorodskii C	A	Ural C	A	Zakavkaz'e (ZSFSR) C	A	TOTALS C	A
									Numbers Coming From These Regions:											
Northern	160	229	160	229	140	139													300	368
Leningrad & Karelia	4,390	4,399	650	651															650	651
Moscow	6,600	4,099	1,000	1,072															1,000	1,072
Ukraine	7,500	8,030	5,550	6,574															5,550	6,574
Ivanovo	1,300	1,400	400	500															400	500
Nizhegorodskii & Chuvash.ASSR	800 ***	901	700	800															700	800
Western	400	570	400	570							600	624		1					1,000	1,195
Central Black Earth	200	288	200	288		192	1,850	1,766											2,050	2,246
Middle Volga	300	no data	300	no data			1,800	432 ***										31	2,100	2,494 +++
Lower Volga	500	no data	500	no data	1,800	1,875	1,200											1	2,500 +++	1,875 ***+++
North Caucasus	1,000	663	1,000	663				263	1,500	956								49	2,500	1,931
Siberia & Buriat-Mongolia	300 ****	123	300	123	1,700	1,442 ***													2,000	1,565 ***
ZSFSR**	680	562	650	430															650	430
Dagestan ASSR																	30	no data	30	no data
Central Asia & Kirgizia***		9		9	100	100 ***	600	55 ***			300	300 ****							1,000	464
Ural	1,700	1,673	1,200	1,278															1,200	1,278
Bashkiria ASSR	117	117	117												500	395			500	512

TABLE 3* (Continued)

RECRUITMENT AND SELECTION OF 25,000ers PER REGION ACCORDING TO CONTROL FIGURES FROM KOLKHOZTSENTR
(Dated: Not earlier than July 1930)

REGION	Control Figure for Recruitment		Numbers Remaining in Region		Numbers Coming From These Regions:														TOTALS	
					Leningrad		Moscow		Ukraine		Ivanovo		Nizhegorodskii		Ural		Zakavkaz'e (ZSFSR)			
	C	A	C	A	C	A	C	A	C	A	C	A	C	A	C	A	C	A	C	A
Far East	250	346	250	346															250	346
Crimea ASSR	100	no data	100	no data					150	no data									250	no data
Tatariia ASSR		113		113			250	243										50	250	400 +++
BSSR	200	513	200	513									100	99					300	612
Kazakhstan ASSR							900	700	300	500					500	395			1,200	1,200
TOTALS	26,380	24,035	13,560	14,276	3,740	3,748	5,600 +	3,459 ++	1,950	1,456	900	924 ******	100	100 ++	500	395	30	133 ++	26,380	27,513 *****

*N. A. Ivnitskii and D. M. Ezerskii, ed., "Dvadtsatipiatitysiachniki i ikh rol' v kollektivizatsii sel'skogo khoziaistva v 1930 g.," Materialy po istorii SSSR. Dokumenty po istorii Sovetskogo obshchestva, vyp. 1 (Moscow: AN SSSR, 1955), pp. 462-463. (The table headings, "C" and "A", stand for "control figure" and "actual figure".) All notes below are from this unless indicated.
**Without Azerbaidzhan.
***Incomplete data.
****This figure is not confirmed.
*****This is a corrected figure given by editors.
******The editors increase this to 27,519 on basis of other evidence. (LV).
+This figure is incorrect. It should be 6,600 according to the sum of column. (LV).
++These figures, when added to Number Remaining in Region, should equal recruitment numbers, but do not in these cases. (LV).
+++These figures do not equal sum of their horizontal column. This may be due to incomplete or missing data. (LV).

83

workers could attend a two-week course on the Uzbek language. Skripko objected, saying, "How can one learn Uzbek in twelve days?" In despair, he asked, "How much longer must we be held in this resort?"[36]

In several areas 25,000ers were detained in the regional and *okrug* centers due to problems of transport to the villages. Mud slides and unseasonable clothing forced many Ukrainian 25,000ers to delay their journey.[37] In Kazakhstan four Moscow 25,000ers were refused transport by the *okrug* authorities and told to obtain horses and make the trip alone. Poorly provisioned and ignorant of the local language, these workers were soon forced to turn back due to bad weather. Once back in the *okrug* center they were told that their "mishap" was a "trifle" and that the *okrug* authorities would give them better horses for their next attempt. The workers, however, refused to attempt the trip due to the impassability of the roads. They were housed in barracks and remained for a month without employment.[38]

In other areas the 25,000ers managed to make it to the district centers, only to find that no one had prepared for their arrival. One 25,000er wrote, "We went to the district soviet executive committee. [We] stood in the corridor. No one talked to us, no one told us who was to go where, what the local conditions were like. After one half hour, they gave us a form indicating that we were to be sent to school to learn accounting and bookkeeping."[39] Some 25,000ers were told in the districts, "We have no vacancies for leading work on the collective farms."[40] The 25,000er Bogretsov was assigned to work on the district soviet executive committee without specific duties; he was told to lead collective farm construction "in general."[41] The 25,000er Nilenin, assigned to Rzhenskii *Okrug* in the Western Region, confronted the following situation:

> When he arrived in the district on the evening of 5 February, he had to spend the night in a kulak's house. On 6 February he went to the Section, planned to begin work immediately, and there, on the very first day of arrival, confronted a stiff wall of bureaucratism. "It was suggested to me and the other worker-collective farmer, Kokurov, to sit and 'size up' work, and so we sized the work up . . . Our patience finally broke and we issued sharp demands to the secretary of the party district committee, after which we were given a handful of old business and told—run around, get acquainted' . . ."[42]

Elsewhere the 25,000ers were handed off from one organ to another in an attempt to avoid responsibility for their use.

The 25,000er Siviakova, in the Lower Volga, described the situation which she confronted in a letter to her trade union. She wrote:

> We worked in a state farm in Khvalinskii district. We were fired suddenly and sent to Balakovskii district. We paid our own way there. At the party district committee, they said, "We don't need you, we didn't send for you, go

to Zaitsev at the district field cultivation collective farm union." We went from this institution to the [next] institution, asked Zaitsev, "Where will we sleep and how will we move our things?" [He] answered, "Rent a horse." We went back to the Vol'skii *okrug* party committee. There they said, "Comrades, go back to Leningrad or work at the cement factory." When we refused to work at the cement factory, they told us to go work at the state farm and milk cows. "If you refuse, we'll say you are deserters." This is how we are appreciated here.[43]

Other 25,000ers, in similar situations, were transferred repeatedly from one post to another. The 25,000er Fedotov was transferred seven times within two weeks.[44] The experience of the 25,000er V. Ikonnikov was documented in an article in *Trud* entitled "Diary of a 25,000er." Between mid-January and late March Ikonnikov held nine different positions.[45] Unemployment and frequent transfers were more than occasional problems for the 25,000ers, but the main problem in this initial stage of the campaign was the tendency for Kolkhoztsentr agencies to retain the workers in their offices in an attempt both to augment their small staffs and to proletarianize their personnel and therefore avoid the brunt of the administrative purge of the time.[46]

Workers were retained in Kolkhoztsentr offices above the district level in Siberia, the Urals, the Ukraine, Kirgiziia, Tatariia, Dagestan, and Buriat-Mongolia.[47] It was reported that the majority of Moscow 25,000ers were employed on the *okrug* level as of early March.[48] The Central Committee and Kolkhoztsentr had anticipated this problem earlier and had categorically ordered that not one 25,000er was to remain in the offices of Kolkhoztsentr.[49] Nevertheless, regional-, *okrug*-, and district-level officials refused to send the 25,000ers into the countryside. Instead, they attempted to solve their own cadre problems by adding the workers to their staff. When 25,000ers complained, they were told, "They sent you into our jurisdiction, so we will use you where we choose."[50] The center claimed that the Kolkhoztsentr network was attempting "to turn [the 25,000ers] into bureaucrats . . . "[51] The 25,000er Prokopov wrote in disgust, "I did not leave the factory in order to work in a chancellery."[52] It was reported at this time that over 11 percent of the workers were incorrectly employed.[53]

Incorrect employment, however, frequently went beyond the appropriation of 25,000ers by the bureaucratic network of Kolkhoztsentr. Many 25,000ers found themselves employed in menial tasks—cleaning stables, milking cows, digging ditches—or employed entirely outside the collective farm system in such varied positions as newspaper editors, librarians, movie-theater directors, etc.[54] It was clear at this stage that central planning had broken down with the arrival of the 25,000ers in the countryside.

The 25,000ers were not slow to respond to this state of affairs. The workers inundated the center with thousands of letters of complaint (addressed to the

Central Committee, Kolkhoztsentr, the trade unions, and so forth). They sent a signal to the central authorities that the provincial organizations had been totally unprepared for their arrival. They wrote about the problems of transfers, unemployment, and incorrect assignments. They also complained about material conditions: many 25,000ers were poorly provisioned, did not receive their salaries, and were not provided with housing. The 25,000ers complained that local officials greeted them "bureaucratically": they did not understand the importance of the 25,000ers and were often hostile. Finally, and most important, there were scattered reports of individual 25,000ers "deserting" their posts and returning to the factories. This, even more than the workers' letters, prompted Moscow to act.[55]

Moscow's response to the plight of the 25,000ers was twofold. It consisted, on the one hand, of a barrage of criticism and reprimands directed to regional-, *okrug-*, and district-level organs and officials and, on the other hand, of an attempt to establish a system of control to ensure that central policy regarding the 25,000ers was correctly implemented. Iurkin, the new chairman of Kolkhoztsentr, sent an angry telegram to all regional Kolkhoztsentr offices in early February. He wrote that Kolkhoztsentr had received "disgusting" information on the poor reception of 25,000ers in many areas. This, said Iurkin, was playing into the "hands of the class enemy." He told officials to employ the 25,000ers correctly, to guarantee their salary and housing, and to assure them of a comradely atmosphere in their work. He concluded with the warning that chairmen of district Kolkhoztsentr agencies would be held personally responsible if poor conditions forced the flight of even one 25,000er under their jurisdiction.[56] The Central Council of Trade Unions also came to the defense of the 25,000ers. In an order of 8 March 1930 the presidium of the Central Council called upon the Workers' and Peasants' Inspectorate to draw to responsibility Tadzhik-istan Kolkhoztsentr and to issue reprimands to trade union organs in Tadzhikistan and in Central Asia.[57] This was only the tip of an iceberg of criticism; it gained in intensity as each organization in the regional hierarchy echoed the center and attempted to pin the blame on the next lower unit in the chain of command. Moreover, the issuing of reprimands and criticism would continue unabated throughout the 25,000ers' stay in the countryside.

The attempt to establish a network of control over the campaign was a more important aspect of the center's response to the workers' plight. It was prompted by the failure of the rural organs to implement central policies and plans concerning the 25,000ers. In turn, this failure was augmented by the intense hostility of rural officials to the workers. These problems derived from a more basic problem: the breakdown of administrative routine in the countryside during the massive collectivization drive. Lacking formal lines of demarcation of functional rights and responsibilities, each branch of the regional party and government hierarchy tended, as a rule, to shift responsibility for correct policy implementation to its immediate subordinate in the regional chain of command or to shift responsibility horizontally to another organization on its own regional level. The ultimate consequence of this was that no single organization assumed ultimate responsibility in policy implementation.

In attempting to set right the problems in the campaign, Moscow failed to respond to the fundamental disorders in rural administration which had given rise to the problems in the first place. Instead the center augmented the chaos by expanding the institutional cast of characters responsible for one or another aspect of the campaign to dimensions rivaling a Cecil B. deMille production. Beginning in mid-February 1930 the central organs of the party, Kolkhoztsentr, and the trade unions began to erect a dense and overlapping system of controls and responsibilities for various aspects of the campaign. On the most general level the party, the trade unions, the Central Control Commission, and the Workers' and Peasants' Inspectorate were to serve as watchdogs over Kolkhoztsentr's implementation of the campaign. Kolkhoztsentr, however, was not the only organization responsible for the 25,000ers. In all, some nineteen different agencies were held responsible for some aspect of the campaign.[58] The 25,000ers were caught within a dense and confusing web of multiple jurisdictions.

As a consequence it was seldom clear to the workers, let alone to the concerned rural agencies, precisely who was in charge of what aspect of the campaign. For example, a 25,000er who was fired and wished to contest this action had several recourses. He might go to the party district committee, which, in principle, oversaw hiring, firing, and transfers; or he might go to one of his several employers (that is, the relevant Kolkhoztsentr agency or cooperative center for the product produced in the region) for redress; or he might take his case to a party or criminal court; or, finally, he could appeal to his factory committee, his trade union, or the press for help. These were the options, but they were far from foolproof. Multiple jurisdiction was not demarcated along functional lines; therefore, the usual pattern was for agencies to pass responsibility vertically or horizontally to another relevant organ in the chain of command. This led to a situation in which everyone was responsible but no one assumed responsibility.

For this reason many of the problems which the 25,000ers experienced in the first stage of the campaign continued throughout their stay in the countryside. The center countered each new problem with a new control. The controls, however, were largely ineffective because they did not alter the basic administrative order into which the 25,000ers emerged in late January and which was the source of the workers' plight. The center only added to the chaos.

The 25,000ers' situation, however, did change drastically after mid-March. In this case the center's intervention was coincidental rather than causal. It coincided with a much more significant policy initiative—the order sounded in March for the retreat from the collectivization onslaught. The retreat allowed for a regrouping of forces in the rural administrative order; the fluidity of rural administration subsided, and time was granted for a basic settling-in process. Moreover, as the center shifted the responsibility for the campaign's excesses to rural cadres and issued orders for a reshuffling of cadres, the 25,000ers became the beneficiaries. After the retreat the majority of the workers found permanent work—sometimes as a consequence of the purge of local cadres blamed for the excesses—and settled into a more routine existence in the countryside.

Conclusion

The experience of the 25,000ers must be set against the backdrop of collectivization and a rapidly changing countryside. Throughout their stay in the countryside, but particularly during the first phase of the campaign, the 25,000ers were held captive by the vagaries and chaos of an administrative order in the process of radical transformation. From the outset Moscow's planning for the rural component of the campaign had lacked precision; this would serve to inject an element of confusion into the implementation of the campaign before the 25,000ers ever reached the countryside. Once they were in the countryside, the plans formulated in Moscow were confounded and impeded by the realities of the prevailing order in the Soviet countryside. Moscow's response to the breakdown of the planning mechanism was a reaction which was characteristic of the period of the First Five-Year Plan revolution: the center responded to the weakness and problems of policy implementation with reprimands, a multiplication of controls, and an avalanche of decrees. Decrees and controls, however, were only as effective as the organizations and officials enlisted to implement them. As a consequence the center was stymied by the realities of the administrative order in rural Soviet Russia.

The campaign of the 25,000ers cannot be fully understood from the vantage point of central plans and decrees; it is necessary to depart from the vista of the Kremlin walls in order to grasp the practical impact of central policy making on the process of implementation. It is tempting to assume that Moscow was in full control of all facets of policy implementation at this time.

During this period Moscow exuded an aura of monolithic omnipotence and did everything in its power to represent itself with this visage. Its reprimands became ever more harsh; the network of strict controls mushroomed; and the provinces were hounded by continual central orders and decrees seeking to intervene in every imaginable aspect of life. The reprimands, controls, and decrees, however, became increasingly repetitious, attacking the same problems over and over again. This was necessary because the dense network of controls designed for the countryside during collectivization were erected in a bed of sand and were quite often simply impossible to enforce. The center was both all-powerful and completely helpless. It was confounded in its every step by the realities of fortress storming in rural Soviet Russia. In its rapid drive to collectivize agriculture, the center had unleashed a storm upon the countryside; it could not as easily rein in the forces as it had unleashed them.

The collectivization drive, more than any other single component of the times, determined the setting into which the 25,000ers had made their initial foray into the countryside. The chaos of the collectivization drive in winter 1930 prevented the majority of 25,000ers from assuming posts of responsibility in the Soviet countryside. Only after a partial retreat was sounded, would the 25,000ers settle into a more routine existence. Despite the fluidity of their situation, however, the 25,000ers were witness to the dizzying tempos of the collectivization drive and many even ascended to the heights of the drive's dizzying crescendos. The collectivization drive of winter 1930 was to be central to the fate of the 25,000ers and the further evolution of their campaign.

4

The Drive to Collectivize
Soviet Agriculture: Winter 1930

And he went round all the yards, all the huts, he did. He quite wore out Tit, the elder, and Tit even fell on to his knees . . . and said: "Good master, have mercy on me! If I've done something wrong in your eyes, then I'd rather you ordered me to be flogged!" The next day, again before it was light, he got up and ordered all the peasants there are here to come to an assembly . . . He came out on to the porch, greeted us and started talking. Talk, he did, talk and talk. The strange thing was we didn't understand what he was saying though he seemed to be talking Russian. "Everything," he said, "is wrong, you're doing everything the wrong way. I'm going to lead," he said, "in a different way, though I don't want at all to have to force you. But," he said, "you're my peasants. You fulfill all your obligations," he said. "If you fulfill them, fine; if you don't I shan't leave a stone unturned." But God knows what he wanted done!

"Well," he said, "now you've understood me. Go back to your homes. My way's going to start from tomorrow." So we went home. We walked back to the village. We looked at each other and looked at each other—and wandered back to our huts.

Ivan Turgenev, Hunting Sketches

He who is against the collective farm is a friend of Chamberlain.

Collectivization slogan of a district soviet executive committee
in the Crimea

The collectivization drive of the winter of 1930 was characterized as "spontaneous." *Spontaneous*, in this context, was not intended as a synonym for *voluntary*. It was meant to denote the process by which collectivization was implemented in the period of January through March 1930. This process was characterized by a deficit in organization and order, a revolutionary impulsiveness tempered by neither law nor legality, and, perhaps most of all, "teleological planning"[1] based on constant upward revisions of numerical indicators as plans were passed down the hierarchical chain of regional command. Central control, in the traditional sense, was nonexistent or ineffective; control, central or otherwise, seemingly so pervasive in Stalinist collectivization, is simply a misnomer for the arbitrary coercion which prevailed at the time.

The spontaneity of collectivization manifested itself in the forms which collectivization and collective farms assumed in this early period. Collectivization frequently consisted of a meeting; a show of peasant hands; a signature or *X* on an application to join a collective; and the arrest, exile, relocation, or harrassment and expropriation of local kulaks and troublemakers. The collective farms were often tantamount to the old Soviet countryside plus a collective farm charter and minus all those falling into the category of kulak. The degree to which socialization had occurred on the farms varied widely and, in its most extreme forms, ranged from total socialization of all and sundry to "paper socialization," by which the objects of socialization were maintained by former owners in lieu of collective storage or shelter space. In many regions of the country wholesale collectivization occurred in concert with a wholesale closing of churches and the desecration of religious objects. Livestock was slaughtered or sold en masse. Markets were closed, and a brisk but risky black-market speculative trade took root in their stead. Peasants rioted and a wave of violence spread across the land.

Collectivization quickly assumed a dynamic of its own, achieved largely as a result of the initiative of rural cadres. The center was in peril of losing control of the campaign. This was recognized and admitted at the time, although not always and everywhere. Collectivization was not intended to manifest itself in the form in which it did in the first months of 1930. Collectivization was meant to be a revolution which would undermine the old order, modernize agriculture, institute a reliable method of grain collection, stimulate a cultural revolution, and build a new social and administrative base in the countryside. The reality of the situation was that the early drive had only partially and not always effectively served to accomplish collectivization's preparatory task—the destruction of the old order and the uprooting of its foundations. It had not succeeded in constructing anything new; moreover, its destructive force put in jeopardy the very possibility of such construction. Chaos and disorder were ubiquitous and the center's main objective was to attempt to exert its control over the implementation of policy in the countryside. This was the aim of the 25,000ers' campaign. The tasks of the 25,000ers were organization and construction. The workers were looked upon as the bearers of consciousness who would inject this class attribute into the spontaneity of the countryside.[2] The ratio of conscious to spontaneous forces, however, was not auspiciously inclined in their favor during the frenzied collectivization drive of the winter of 1930. The 25,000ers, according to a retrospective description, were just a "drop in the ocean."[3]

The Winter Campaign and the Race for Percentages

On 5 January 1930 the Central Committee of the Communist party issued the decree "On the Tempos of Collectivization and Measures of State Aid to Collective Farm Construction."[4] On paper the decree marked a major turning point in the party's peasant policy and exuded a radicalism unprecedented in the Bolshevik past. The decree set the tempos for the wholesale collectivization of the country.[5] It also designated the artel as the basic form of collective farm, with the noteworthy qualification that the artel (see Glossary), which was based on partial socialization of property and collective production, was transitional to the higher form of collective farm, the *kommuna* (see Glossary), which featured complete socialization of property and production. Finally, in passing it noted that the party's new policy toward the kulak was its "elimination as a class," or "dekulakization."

The decree concluded with a warning against an artificial "administrative" approach to collectivization:

> The Central Committee in all seriousness warns the party organizations against any sort of decreeing of the collective farm movement from above which could create the danger of substituting games in collectivization for genuine socialist competition in the organization of collective farms.[6]

This was an empty warning in two respects. First, the warning was lacking in realism if not sincerity because the Central Committee failed to provide clear, precise guidelines and rules for the campaign, so that the drive's only restricting boundaries were those defined according to the whim of the provincial party organizations. Second, the warning proved to be ineffective because it, like the decree itself, came as an afterthought to the collectivization drive, which had been underway, with variations according to regions and tempos, since the summer of 1929.

Wholesale Collectivization

The decree on collectivization rang hollow. In many ways it was a paper decision which, in failing to provide a voice of moderation, served only to endorse and press forward ongoing regional collectivization drives. By the time the decree was issued, the major grain regions had already passed legislation on collectivization tempos, in many cases surpassing the excessive tempos set by the center.[7] Between October and January—that is, *prior* to the central decree (see table 4)—these regions had undergone their primary quantum leaps in collectivization according to percentage rates. The central decree had its greatest impact on secondary grain- and grain-deficit areas, which made the greatest leap forward in percentages of collectivized households in January and February.[8] The highest February percentage-point leaps occurred in the Moscow Region and the Central Black Earth Region, which also came in for the heaviest criticism among the territories of the RSFSR for excesses in collectivization once the final balance sheet was drawn at the Sixteenth Party Congress.[9]

It is difficult to determine with any great analytical precision exactly how these percentages were arrived at in the collectivization drive. Doubtless, the major determinants were human. Nevertheless, a certain pattern of tempos or planning does emerge in the collectivization campaign. Many regional party committees set much higher rates of collectivization than those established by the center in January 1930. In some cases these rates were set before the

TABLE   4*

PERCENTAGES OF COLLECTIVIZED HOUSEHOLDS
IN THE RSFSR (June 1929-March 1930)

REGION	June 1 1929	Oct. 1 1929	Jan. 1 1930	Feb. 1 1930	March 1 1930
RSFSR (as a whole)	3.7	7.3	20.1	34.7	58.6
Western	1.0	1.8	5.2	12.6	41.2
Moscow	1.8	3.3	14.3	37.1	74.2
Ivanovo	1.0	1.5	4.9	10.2	30.7
Central Black Earth	3.2	5.9	40.5	51.0	83.3
Ural	5.2	9.9	38.9	52.1	75.6
Middle Volga	3.9	8.9	41.7	51.8	60.3
Lower Volga	5.9	18.1	56–70**	61.1	70.1
North Caucasus	7.3	19.1	48.1	62.7	79.4
Siberia	4.6	6.8	5***	18.8	47.0

*Derived from R. W. Davies, The Socialist Offensive. The Collectivization of Soviet Agriculture, 1929-1930 (Cambridge, MA: Harvard University Press, 1980), p. 442 (Table 17).
**See Davies' explanatory notes, p. 443.
***See Davies' explanatory notes, p. 443, in which he questions the accuracy of this figure given the larger percentage of October 1 and suggests that this may have been a clerical error. It may be, however, that the October figure rather than the January was in error on the basis of statistics from Khlebotsentr which gives a percentage of 4.8 (rather than 6.8) for October. (It should be noted that statistics tend to vary according to the agency compiling them and, therefore, we cannot hope for absolute accuracy.) See TsGANKh, f. 4108, op. 16, d. 48, 1.83.

January decree; in other cases, after.[10] In turn, the *okrug* party committees, followed by the district party committees, would subject the regional rates to further upward revisions. This was not a uniform process, nor did it occur in all parts of the country. Nevertheless, it occurred often enough to provide evidence of a certain logic implicit in the teleological planning and atmosphere of the times. The Central Black Earth Region, for example, was scheduled to complete collectivization by the fall of 1931 or, at the latest, the spring of 1932. Many party *okrug* committees in this region called for the completion of the drive within two to three months; the district committees often followed suit and accelerated the time period to two to three weeks.[11] Siberia was to complete collectivization according to a similar time schedule. The Siberian party regional committee, however, made plans to complete collectivization in 1930. Many Siberian district committees, in turn, set time frameworks of two months for the campaign's completion.[12] Regional party committees in the Lower Volga, North Caucasus, and Moscow also set higher tempos for collectivization in their regions than those set by the Central Committee.[13]

The tendency to fulfill and overfulfill central plans for collectivization reached its most dizzying heights on the *okrug* and district levels. It was at these regional levels that any semblance to planning completely disappeared. Many *okrug* and district committees attempted to complete the drive in periods ranging from several months to several weeks. The slogan of the day of the Vesegonskii District soviet executive committee in Crimea was "collectivize the district in 24 hours."[14] At the Sixteenth Party Congress, L. M. Kaganovich claimed that the districts were often completely ignorant of Central Committee and regional party committee directives on collectivization and simply followed the lead of the *okrug* party committees, which called for the completion of collectivization by spring.[15] The *okrug*s were responsible for setting the pace of collectivization in their territories; the regional committees did not provide them with specific percentages but rather limited their role to setting a general pace for the entire region.[16] The *okrug* and district committees were certainly under pressure to keep pace with regional plans in order to avoid the accusation of right deviationism. At a certain point in the race for percentages, however, the tempos obtained or planned in the campaign by the *okrug* and district committees reached such a pace that it was no longer possible to explain the haste in the collectivization drive by fears of being branded a right deviationist. The process, and along with it, many rural cadres, had simply gotten out of hand. Planning had succumbed to teleology; the central authorities in Moscow, only half-cognizant of the consequences, had unleashed a floodgate.

The Campaign to Eliminate the Kulak as a Class

The campaign to eliminate the kulak as a class followed a similar pattern as that of the collectivization drive, of an unraveling of plans from the top down. Central legislation on the kulaks, however, developed much more slowly than the legislation on collectivization. In addition, the legislation on the kulaks, unlike that on collectivization, appears to have been intended to temper regional and local initiative for it was issued simultaneously and, in retrospect, paradoxically with the first of a series of strict central warnings against policy violations in collectivization and dekulakization that would lead eventually to Stalin's 2 March article "Dizzyness from Success" and the 14 March Central Committee decree "On the Struggle with Violations of the Party Line in the Collective Farm Movement."[17] The new policy on the kulaks, their elimination as a class, was announced publicly by Stalin in his speech at the Conference of Marxist Agronomists on 27 December 1929.[18] The policy assumed legislative coloration in the 5 January decree on the tempos of collectivization.[19] This, however, was little more than a statement of intention; more concrete plans for the elimination of the kulak as a class did not appear until the end of January.

The December Politburo commission on collectivization had included a subcommission on kulak policy chaired by K. Ia. Bauman, the secretary of the Moscow regional party committee. The deliberations of the Bauman subcommission, however, proved inconclusive partly due to Stalin's objections to several of its draft proposals and partly due to serious disagreements among subcommission members which, according to M. M. Khataevich, the Middle Volga first party secretary, hindered the decision-making process.[20] Consequently, a new Politburo commission, chaired by Molotov, was appointed on 15 January to draw up the plans for the implementation of kulak policy. The commission concluded its deliberations on 26 January and submitted its draft project to the Politburo for review. The work of the Molotov commission served as the basis for the central legislation on the elimination of the kulak as a class.[21]

The charter documents on the elimination of the kulak as a class were issued in late January and early February 1930.[22] A differential approach was suggested in the implementation of policy based on three categories of kulaks, ranging from "counterrevolutionary activists" to the relatively harmless, and imposing penalties ranging from execution and imprisonment to exile and expropriation.[23] The general number of those subject to these measures was not to exceed 3 to 5 percent of farms in the grain-producing regions and 2 to 3 percent in grain-deficit areas.[24] The implementation of measures applicable to the first two categories of kulaks was to be 50 percent complete by 15 April and finalized by the end of May.[25]

Like the 5 January decree on collectivization, this legislation was tacked on to existing regional legislation. Decisions to eliminate the kulak as a class had already been taken prior to the central legislation in the Middle Volga (20 January), Lower Volga (24 January), Central Black Earth Region (27 January), Ukraine (28 January), and North Caucasus (29 January).[26] Moreover, on the basis of a patchwork of regional decisions, local initiative, and scattered legislative acts, dekulakization in varied forms had been underway since the summer of 1929.[27] The first step toward dekulakization—the decision not to admit the kulak onto the collective farm (taken centrally in November 1929)—had been taken prior to the fall of 1929 by regional authorities in Siberia, the Lower Volga, North Caucasus, and Central Black Earth Region.[28] A Central Executive Committee-Council of People's Commissars RSFSR decree of June 1929, widening the rights of local soviets and in effect legalizing the extraordinary measures implemented under the Ural-Siberian method of 1928, served as the legal basis for criminal prosecution, expropriation, or exile of kulaks in many areas.[29] By the end of 1929 and early 1930, articles 60, 61, 79, and 169 of the RSFSR criminal code which allowed for the arrest, imprisonment, expropriation, or exile of individuals for nonpayment of taxes were applied on an extensive scale in many areas to peasants unable to pay the inordinately high taxes levied on their farms.[30] Finally, on 16 January 1930, the Central Executive Committee and the Council of People's Commissars of the USSR issued the decree "On Measures of Struggle with the Rapacious Destruction of Livestock." This decree was issued in response to the wholesale waves of slaughters and sales of livestock which occurred in this period as peasants attempted to avoid classification as a kulak. The decree entitled district soviet executive committees to arrest, expropriate, and exile kulaks guilty of the destruction of livestock.[31] By mid-January these scattered legislative acts and regional decisions had made dekulakization a legal possibility; it still remained, however, for these laws to be extended throughout the country and this was possible either on the basis of regional initiative or as a result of a central decree which would transform scattered legislative acts into a concrete and defined policy.

The regions acted first in the campaign to eliminate the kulak as a class and in so doing forced the hand of the center in this issue. Dekulakization began on local and regional initiative in late 1929 and early 1930, largely in grain-producing areas such as the Lower Volga, Middle Volga, and Siberia.[32] The 5 January decree on collectivization, which made the new policy toward the kulaks official, provided encouragement for the actions and initiative of local and regional authorities. In the Lower Volga, mostly in response to the wholesale destruction of livestock, dekulakization began on a wide scale in January; by the end of January, 40 to 60 percent of kulak farms had been eliminated in the Lower Volga.[33] In Siberia mass exiles of kulaks began with a 5 December 1929 decree of the Siberian regional party committee; in addition, as was the case elsewhere, de facto dekulakization measures were applied to those who slaughtered or sold their livestock. By early February 26 percent of kulak farms in Eastern Siberia had been expropriated.[34] Nation-wide, the drive against the kulaks would reach its quantitative peak in February when the central legislation was in place; the major grain regions had led the campaign to eliminate the kulak as a class prior to this and, consequently, provided a practical basis for the central legislation as well as a model of how not to implement dekulakization.

The central legislation on the elimination of the kulak as a class was based on local experience; the warnings against policy violations in dekulakization which accompanied the legislation were also based on local experience. On 30 January the Central Committee dispatched, along with its decree on the kulaks, telegrams to all party organs warning against implementing the policy of the elimination of the kulak as a class in areas in which wholesale collectivization had not been developed and was not intended to be. This, according to the warning, was not only a violation of policy, but also led to the neglect of the central task of collectivization. The Central Committee wrote:

> Information has been received from the local level indicating that in a series of areas organizations have neglected the collectivization campaign and have focused all their attention on dekulakization. The C.C. [Central Committee] explains that such a policy is radically incorrect. The C.C. indicates that the policy of the party is not naked dekulakization, but the development of the collective farm movement, the result and part of which is dekulakization. The C.C. demands that dekulakization not occur outside of the growth of the collective farm movement in order that the center of attention is transferred to the construction of new collective farms based on the actual mass movement of the poor and middle peasants. The C.C. reminds that only this formula will guarantee the correct implementation of the policy of the party.[35]

Following the dispatch of this telegram, the warning not to implement dekulakization without wholesale collectivization, that dekulakization was a secondary and composite part of collectivization and not an independent policy, was echoed throughout the press in editorials and articles in the early days of February 1930 in what appears to have been a centralized and well-coordinated press campaign.[36] Stalin lent his authority to this campaign to channel the energies of provincial authorities into collectivization rather than into sheer repressive mayhem in his "Answer to the Sverdlov Comrades'' (9 February), in which he stated categorically that dekulakization was to be implemented *only* in conjunction with wholesale collectivization.[37] Following this, the Commissariat of Justice (15 February) drew up a draft law forbidding the implementation of dekulakization in areas not scheduled for wholesale collectivization.[38] These actions were taken in response to reports of the excesses committed in the countryside, indications of which began to appear in the press in the first half of February.[39]

It is something of a paradox that the central legislation on the new kulak policy and the strict warnings issued by the Central Committee to the provinces appeared simultaneously. It is even more of a paradox that as the Central Committee's warnings and reprimands concerning the excesses increased, so too did the drive against the kulaks; this drive reached a high point in the month of February. Perhaps the warnings issued by the Central Committee were simply a mask of duplicity. Certainly the Stalin faction could not be accused of liberalism toward the kulak. Liberalism in any form was foreign to Stalin and his comrades in the Politburo, but the goal of achieving strict centralized control was not, and therein lies a possible solution to the riddle of the paradox just described. Moscow was not unaware of the consequences of encouraging local initiative in so delicate a matter as dekulakization. The legislation of late January and early February was intended to enable the center to gain control of this process, to subject the regional and local authorities to some measure of standardized procedure and control.

News of the excesses, random violence, and increasing peasant unrest in the countryside forced Moscow to take the initiative in the form of central legislation on the tasks and methods of the elimination of the kulak as a class. Moscow need not have intervened legislatively, for the basic legislation— admittedly of a patchwork quality—was already in place and in the process of being applied in many areas. Stalin's speech at the Conference of Marxist Agronomists and the 5 January decree on collectivization had provided the necessary official endorsement for regional and local authorities. Moscow intervened because the campaign of repression against the kulak had gone out of control, threatening state stability with the possibility of a major social collision. The situation was aptly described by a rural Communist in January 1930, before the central legislation was enacted, when he told the American Anna Louise Strong that ''having no guidance in law, the left-wing elements among our local comrades do what is right in their own eyes . . . which is anarchy. We expect government decrees soon; then there will be more order.''[40]

The government decrees were accompanied by warnings and censure. On 30 January Stalin and Molotov sent a telegram of censure to the party bureau of Central Asia with a strict warning to adhere to central policy.[41] On the following day a Central Committee telegram was sent to the regional party secretary, Khataevich (Middle Volga), in response to his party committee's decision of 20 January to exile the most dangerous kulaks in the region in *two weeks*. Khataevich was warned: "Your haste in the kulak issue has nothing in common with party policy. Your responsibility is to carry out party decisions exactly." The Middle Volga party committee soon afterward reversed its decision.[42] On 4 February the Central Committee overruled the decision of the Moscow regional party committee of 30 January pertaining to the exile of an inordinately large number of kulaks in an area not intended for wholesale collectivization.[43] The Central Committee also dispatched telegrams to S. A. Bergavinov and the Northern regional party committee (7 February), A. A. Andreev and the North Caucasus party committee (8 February), and a series of other party organs. The telegrams carried warnings to adhere to central policy and to avoid excesses in policy implementation.[44]

The response from the regional party committees to these warnings was still rather ineffective in the first half of February and led to no substantive improvement. In the Lower Volga the first party secretary, B. P. Sheboldaev, ordered authorities in Khoper *Okrug* to review carefully their lists of dekulakized households and issued telegrams to all *okrug* party committees with warnings not to apply repression to middle peasants.[45] In the Middle Volga (8 February) and Western Siberia (12 February), warnings not to implement dekulakization in areas outside of wholesale collectivization and not to allow the middle peasant to be affected by dekulakization were incorporated into revised regional soviet executive committee decrees on the elimination of the kulaks. The legislation of the Siberian soviet executive committee called attention to the "most flagrant violations" of the class line which had been committed in the dekulakization of middle peasants; it ordered the return of all expropriated property to middle peasants who had been subject to dekulakization.[46] In the revised dekulakization decree of the North Caucasus regional soviet executive committee, the chairmen of *okrug* and district soviet executive committees were warned that they would be held personally responsible for any cases of repression against middle peasants.[47] Despite these attempts to temper the extremes of the campaign, the excesses and violence continued unabated through the month of February.

As in the case of the collectivization drive, the race for percentages and high tempos in the campaign to eliminate the kulaks as a class whirled down around an ever-widening spiral as plans and practice were passed down from one level of the regional command to the next. In many areas legality was little more than one of many items on the first five-year plans of local party committees, something which would, as I. M. Vareikis (Central Black Earth first party secretary) put it at the Sixteenth Party Congress, "come with time.''[48] In the Moscow Region dekulakization occurred on a haphazard basis according to the whim of district party and soviet organs—as one Soviet historian described it, it occurred *"po-svoemu"* (in this context, haphazardly), according to locality.[49] In the Central Black Earth Region, where by the end of February an estimated 10–15 percent of the peasant population was dekulakized in certain districts, issues were decided "at one's own risk."[50] Here, Vareikis contravened central policy by encouraging dekulakization outside of areas of wholesale collectivization. In a pamphlet dated 13 February 1930 he wrote, "It would be a political mistake to set aside the implementation of practical measures in relation to the kulak in districts which today are still not districts of wholesale collectivization."[51] Central policy was also contravened in Siberia, where the regional party committee called for the expropriation of all kulaks *regardless* of the level of collectivization.[52] In most regions of the country *okrug-* and district-level authorities were allowed to set their own numerical quotas for the number of peasant households to be dekulakized.[53] Partly as a consequence of this, partly as a consequence of the subordinate status of legality in the countryside, and partly as an inevitable outcome of an excessive policy and the failure to define just who the kulak was, in such areas as Khoper *Okrug* in the Lower Volga, dekulakization reached 10–11 percent of all peasant households and 25 percent in individual districts.[54]

By the second half of February the center's efforts to control the flood which it had unleashed in the countryside became much more visible.[55] Representatives of the Central Committee and the People's Commissariat of Agriculture were sent to the countryside to gather more information on the campaign. A series of three high-level meetings were held under the auspices of the Central Committee—a meeting with representatives from the national minority areas (11 February); a meeting with representatives of the grain-deficit areas (21 February); and finally, on 24 February, a meeting to discuss the excesses accompanying collectivization and the need to provide further directives on the campaign. The first meeting resulted in the appearance of two Central Committee decrees (20 February and 25 February) censuring the haste and extremes of the campaign in national minority areas.[56] The other Central Committee meetings led to the decision to call a halt to the collectivization drive. The first indication that something new was in the air was the public announcement on 28 February of a Commissariat of Agriculture meeting which discussed the excesses in collectivization and the need to punish those guilty of illegal repression; the Commissariat of Agriculture then decided to publish a decree against the excesses and signed it on 1 March, a day before Stalin's famous article appeared.[57] Stalin's "Dizzyness from Success," written at the request of the Central Committee and dated 2 March,

called for a halt to the excesses and policy violations which, according to
Stalin, had occurred due to the "dizzyness" experienced by local cadres in
their successes in the collectivization campaign.[58] The dizzyness, however,
continued in most areas until the curtain was finally brought down with the
Central Committee decree of 14 March, "On the Struggle with Violations of
the Party Line in the Collective Farm Movement."[59]

The development of the collectivization and dekulakization campaigns
yielded tragic consequences in the first months of 1930. Moscow had
unleashed a force which quickly exceeded the boundaries of any and all
control. An excessive policy necessarily breeds new excesses. Beyond this,
there was a definite process to be observed in the frenzy and violence of the
drive. Lacking the constraints of legality, precision, an orderly hierarchy, and
an orderly world, plans tended to unravel downward around an ever-widening
regional spiral once they had left Moscow. Unlimited powers were entrusted
to highly limited functionaries to implement a campaign which had no
precedent on paper nor in the imagination, a campaign which was at best risky,
and at worst tantamount to social apocalypse. The omnipotent Moscow was
capable of designing a policy intended to uproot and overturn the foundations
of the Soviet countryside in disregard to the costs involved; it was neither
capable of controlling the storm thus unleashed nor able to foresee the real
consequences of its design.

This was the setting into which the 25,000ers emerged about midway into
the collectivization campaign. That they were expected to inject their
proletarian consciousness into all this appears as rather a fantastic pipedream,
but prediction in the best of times is no easy task and these were not the best
of times. The tidal wave of collectivization swept headlong through the Soviet
countryside, consuming everything in its midst; the 25,000ers who managed
to make it to the district centers and the villages proved no exception and were
swept along with the unyielding tide of socialist construction.

The 25,000ers in the Whirlwind of Collectivization

The implementation of the collectivization drive was structured along military
lines. Headquarters were created on the regional, *okrug*, and district levels to
lead the campaign and consisted of representatives from the party, soviet, and
other relevant agencies. Headquarter leadership was provided through a
mixture of telegrammed orders, which arrived in overwhelming numbers, and
the plenipotentiary system.[60] The main force for the implementation of the
campaign was the district-level headquarters, from which the army of urban

plenipotentiaries, estimated to be one hundred thousand strong, operated.[61] The plenipotentiaries, who were granted extraordinary powers to overrule inert or uncooperative local authorities, generally began their work by holding meetings with the village party and Komsomol forces, former Red partisans, and poor peasants in an attempt to solicit support for their activities. At some point in their visit, a general meeting of the village population was called to vote upon a collective farm charter. It was at this time that the peasants were called upon to put their signatures on a collective farm entry form and to elect a collective farm administrative board. Worker-25,000ers were often elected *in absentia.*[62] Dekulakization was carried out with the aid of the OGPU (see Glossary) and, in principle, was to occur simultaneously with collectivization. In fact, dekulakization often occurred first as a method of ridding the village of opponents of collectivization. The drive was carried out in a minimum of time as the district organs raced for percentages and the plenipotentiaries hopscotched from village to village building socialism on the run.

The majority of the 25,000ers were witness to or participants in the collectivization campaign in the first months of 1930. Before their departure the workers had been requested "to systematically inform [the central authorities] about work and local conditions" and to report any violations in collective farm construction. During this initial period of their campaign the 25,000ers wrote over five thousand letters to the Central Committee's Department of Agitation and Mass Campaigns in addition to hundreds of letters to their trade unions, factories, and the local and central press.[63] In their accounts, the workers provided an insider's view of the campaign. Their accounts were by no means uniform; the workers' responses to the events they witnessed were as varied as the original motivations which led them to join the ranks of the 25,000ers. Moreover, the accounts do not provide a complete picture of the campaign, but rather a glimpse into the view from the field. Nevertheless, it is possible to piece together several very important trends in the campaign, or, at least, the workers' perceptions of these trends, through an examination of the letters and reports of the 25,000ers.

The View from the Field

Upon entry into the countryside, many 25,000ers found themselves stranded in regional and *okrug* centers and behind desks in Soviet offices. However, a significant number managed to make their way to the village. These included workers who were stopped at the district level and, managing to avoid conscription as white-collar workers, were detached to the villages as instructors, plenipotentiaries, or members of collectivization or dekulakization brigades. Also included were those workers who received assignments on the collective farms. A part of this group found themselves presiding over "paper collective farms"—that is, collective farms in name only—and, consequently, were forced into the role of de facto collectivizers; others within this group found the situation on their farms not entirely satisfactory because of power conflicts with local officials or the destructive interference of district plenipotentiaries. The 25,000ers' response to events was sometimes determined by their official roles; at other times their response was determined by their position as outsiders and representatives of the center.

Regardless of their position, the 25,000ers were unanimous in their criticism of district-level organs participating in collectivization. Almost all 25,000ers were, to one extent or another, under the jurisdiction of the district party, soviet, or Kolkhoztsentr organs and therefore were in close communication with these offices. The workers claimed that it was the district organs which were responsible for the race for percentages in collectivization. The 25,000er Zakharov, working in the Western Region, said that the district organs had done no agitational work among the peasantry and that, as a result, the "masses" were not prepared for collectivization. According to Zakharov the districts all competed for percentages: "There they do not aim for quality, but race after quantity." This, said Zakharov, was what he had learned in the countryside.[64] The 25,000ers M. V. Bogdanov and I. K. Matveev worked on collectivization in Siberia. When they arrived, they complained about the use of force and the drive to create *kommunas*. They claimed that the district organs argued about some sort of "special Siberian conditions" which dictated haste and coercion.[65] In the Urals the 25,000er Filippov reported to Kolkhoztsentr that the district organs demanded that the entire district be transformed into two artels and one *kommuna*; he claimed that the district organs had forced the pace of collectivization artificially to 100 percent by 15 January. According to Filippov a part of the 25,000ers went along with the incorrect policy in fear of receiving party reprimands from the district; those who challenged the district were cursed, threatened, or fired.[66]

The 25,000ers who were employed on collective farms also condemned the district organs, but from a different perspective. These workers were responsible for making the farms function. There arose, consequently, a schism between "collectivizers," who claimed their work was collectivization and not farming, and the collective farm cadres who would remain to pick up the pieces after the plenipotentiaries and instructors left.[67] In his autobiographical notes the 25,000er K. Onipko wrote that the district organs urged him to agitate for 100 percent collectivization and 100 percent socialization of livestock. Using his common sense, not to mention a degree of political savvy, Onipko did indeed agitate for 100 percent socialization of livestock, but because there were as yet no common barns for the animals, he entrusted the "socialized" livestock to the safekeeping of the former owners.[68] This was a common recourse of collective farm chairmen in this period. An equally widespread problem confronted by 25,000ers in collective farms was the problem of collecting seed for spring sowing. A 25,000er from the Putilov factory said of the district organs: "Having collectivized, they forgot about . . . seed. Soon it will be necessary to go into the fields and there will be no seed. Sowing is threatened."[69] The 25,000er Lukakhina was ordered by the party district committee to gather the seed for sowing or else, but was given no indication of how this was to be done.[70] In other cases the plenipotentiaries solved the problem of seed by collectivizing it as part of policy; 25,000ers who protested this, according to several sources, were transferred, fired, or expelled from the party.[71] The 25,000er Chernutskaia, recalling the dizzying month of February, described how plenipotentiaries arrived in her semicollectivized farm and ordered full collectivization in twenty-four hours. She said that after their departure, it took her days to pick up the pieces.[72] The sentiments of Chernutskaia aptly reflected those of many 25,000ers who also were left to "pick up the pieces" after the destructive interference of district cadres.

The 25,000ers' critique of the district organs confirms, to a great extent, several of the trends depicted earlier in this chapter. The district organs were the most important actors in the practical implementation of collectivization. They adhered to no planned objective apart from the race for ever-climbing percentages. Moreover, as the 25,000ers indicate, the district organs were only interested in percentages and disregarded the consequences which their actions had on the actual management and performance of the farms. The 25,000ers' perceptions of the district organs were determined, however, not only by practice, but by several other important factors. The 25,000ers who were employed in the collective farms came into an inevitable conflict of interests with district officials. In addition, it was in the 25,000ers' interest to point the finger of blame at the district organs. This absolved the workers of responsibility, often settled scores revolving around power conflicts, and eventually led to a certain measure of "job security" for the workers. This is not to argue that the district organs were not central actors in the "race for percentages," but simply to note that some benefit accrued to those who said as much.

In addition to their harsh criticism of the district organs, the 25,000ers provided detailed accounts of the collectivization campaign. Their descriptions of the actual process of collectivization were as varied as the villages which they entered. There were, however, several important themes which emerged over and over again in their accounts. The first was the "class war." The kulak, variously defined, was a real and present danger to the 25,000ers and was not simply a socioeconomic category confronted in newspapers and party primers. The second constant appearing in 25,000ers' reports was the fairly universal resistance encountered from peasant women. The final points of agreement in the accounts were the presence in the majority of villages of local activists upon whom the 25,000ers counted for support and the widespread existence of "paper collective farms."

The 25,000ers based their class analysis of the peasantry less on rigorous socioeconomic determinants than on subjective evaluations of which individuals were most likely to gun down, axe, or disembowel a worker. Several scores of 25,000ers were beaten or murdered during this period and after, often in a most brutal fashion. The 25,000er Shivchuk, in Buriat-Mongolia, wrote to his trade union requesting a weapon. He often had to walk twelve versts (one verst = .66 miles) at night, unarmed, between the various sectors of his farm. He wrote that without a weapon, his life was in danger.[73] The 25,000er F. M. Dobroliubov, working in the Western Region, was brutally beaten on his way home from a party meeting ten versts away. His wife described what happened. On his way home at 11 P.M., Dobroliubov was approached by three men who asked him for matches. He was knocked unconscious, tied, gagged, and carried three versts off the road. Here he was beaten and left for dead. He was discovered the next day, unconscious, but alive with his money and documents untouched.[74]

The worker Zamiatin, who was not a 25,000er but one of the workers recruited from the city soviets to work in the *sel'sovet*s, described the situation faced by the 25,000er V. Klinov. Zamiatin said that the approach to Klinov's village resembled an armed camp; on his way he saw a sign nailed to a bridge which read: "Vas'ka [Klinov]—you scum, get out. We will break your legs." When he arrived, Zamiatin found the village alive with rumors of the approach of a band of riders who were coming to kill all the Communists and collective farmers. In this village dekulakization had already been implemented but, as happened elsewhere, the kulaks were not yet removed from the village. This, according to Zamiatin, had led to the crisis state which existed. With the arrival of Zamiatin, Klinov set about preparing for the exile of the kulaks. He began by removing the church bell which traditionally served as a tocsin to sound the village alarm in time of emergency and which often proved incendiary during dekulakization if not removed. The heads of kulak farms were exiled, and, according to Zamiatin, all went well until a few days later when one of the exiled kulaks returned to announce that the other kulaks would soon be coming back to seek vengence. This led to the decision to exile the families of the exiled kulaks. The announcement of this decision led to an uproar. In an attempt to forestall this action, the peasant women blocked the entrances of the huts of the kulak families. The affair ended in a pitchfork battle and the calling in of the militia.[75]

According to the 25,000ers the kulak was everywhere, and he was not only a physical threat but one of the primary obstacles to the fulfillment of the workers' duties. If a 25,000er was fortunate enough to escape the consequences of what were described as kulak-inspired fires, riots, "bullets from corners," livestock massacres, and sabotage, it was virtually impossible not to confront the vast rumor mill which hung over the villages in those days and which was attributed to the inspiration and creativity of kulaks or *podkulachniki* (kulak agents). Old women asked the 25,000er Berson if they would have to sleep under the notorious common blanket once they were on the collective farm and whether it was not true, as they had been told, that joining the collective farm meant signing oneself over to the anti-Christ.[76] The 25,000ers also confronted such rumors as "children will go hungry on the collective farm," "Soviet power will exist only until February," "they will cut off the women's hair and stamp their foreheads," and so on.[77] Throughout the countryside it was heralded that the reign of anti-Christ on earth had begun. Based on an apocalyptic mind-set and on reasoning unchanged from the days of the schism, the rumors confounded the activities of the 25,000ers at every step.

The workers generally attributed such rumors to the omnipresent *podkulachnik*. The vehicles for the spread of rumors, as well as the emergence of resistance, however, were said to be the village women. Firsthand accounts of collectivization are consistent in their emphasis on peasant women-initiated resistance. In most Russian and Ukrainian villages peasant women (especially older women) were the most vocal opponents to collectivization, dekulakization, and the socialization of livestock. Women often blocked the carting away of a village's grain and the exile of kulak neighbors and were responsible for the epidemic of women's riots (*bab'i bunty*) which swept the countryside at this time. It is very likely that there was a certain political sagacity to the widespread wave of female resistance and that such resistance was not based simply on an inherent radical tradition among women derived from standing in queues. In his memoirs General Grigorenko offered a reasonable explanation for the women's riots. He believed them to be a kind of tactic. The women would initiate opposition to the collective farm and the men would remain on the sidelines until the local activists began to attempt to quell the disorder. At that point the peasant men could safely enter the fray as chivalrous defenders of wives, mothers, and sisters, rather than as antisoviet *podkulachniki*.[78]

This explanation is consistent with other available evidence. According to a report of a worker brigade in Tambov (Central Black Earth Region), the men did not go to the worker-organized meetings but sent their female relatives instead. When asked why they did not attend the meetings, they replied, "They [the women] are equal now, as they decide so we will agree . . . ."[79] In this way it was easy for a peasant to claim that he had not joined the collective farm because his wife would not let him. The 25,000er Gruzdev was told by one peasant, "My wife does not want to socialize our cow, so I cannot do this."[80] One peasant man explained the power of the women in the following manner: "We dared not speak at meetings. If we said anything that the organizers didn't like, they abused us, called us *koolaks*, and even threatened to put us in prison . . . We let the women do the talking . . . If the organizer tried to stop them they made such a din that he had to call off the meeting."[81] Peasant men were more vulnerable to repression than women. Rarely if ever was a peasant woman described as a kulak or *podkulachnik*; she may have been under the influence of such shady characters but her behavior was generally attributed to nonrational motivations and simple political naïveté if not stupidity. For these reasons peasant women were able to get away with a great deal more than their male counterparts in resisting collectivization.[82]

Another theme stressed in the reports of the 25,000ers concerning the implementation of collectivization was the support offered by village activists. The workers who arrived in a village to implement collectivization began by calling together the local activists—party and Komsomol members and poor peasants—for a meeting. This would be the first in an avalanche of meetings which descended upon the villages. The 25,000er Shirokov wrote that on some days there were two to three meetings and that some meetings would last from five to eight hours.[83] Most often, the first meetings were held in an attempt to gather the support of the perceived "socially and politically progressive" elements of the village. The 25,000ers reported that among those who supported the cause there appeared most often former Red army men, Komsomol youth, local party forces, and what they defined as poor peasants.[84] The *sel'sovet* rarely if ever was of any use in the campaign during this period and more often than not served as an obstacle to policy implementation.[85] Based on existing groups of activists or, in other cases, those created by the workers, the 25,000ers began their work.

The primary aim of the 25,000ers' work was to direct and strengthen the collective farms; the workers were to be organizers and not agitators. They had not been intended specifically for the purpose of implementing collectivization. They entered into that role as a result of the tendency of district-level organs to shanghai them into service as plenipotentiaries on their way to the villages. However, even those who managed to make their way to the collective farms were not always successful in assuming the role which the center had intended for them. Among these 25,000ers many became collectivizers by default. Worker-25,000ers repeatedly complained that they had been assigned to nonexistent collective farms, paper collective farms. The 25,000er Alekhin arrived in the Central Black Earth Region to find that he had been assigned to a paper collective farm; all that existed of the farm, all that had ever existed was the farm's charter.[86] His experience was not uncommon among 25,000ers.[87]

Other 25,000ers arrived in the villages to find something resembling a collective farm, yet entirely lacking in the socialist attributes expected by the workers. The 25,000er Berson was dismayed to find that the local activists were more interested in Lenin's mausoleum than questions of socialized agriculture. After hearing that Lenin was embalmed and accessible in Moscow, the socially progressive elements of the village remarked to Berson: "Oi, it would be so interesting to see what he looks like there."[88] The most common problem experienced by the workers, however, was that dekulakization had not been carried out by the local activists on the farms to which they were assigned. The 25,000ers claimed that not only were the farms full of kulaks, but the farm administrative boards were in class enemy hands, as well. Therefore, 25,000ers who had the authority to do so, set about purging the farms and reelecting administrative boards. The 25,000ers most able to do this were those who were in the company or proximity of other 25,000ers from their factories or cities of recruitment. The 25,000ers were often told that so-called kulaks were on the farms because they were good workers, had large families, or were simply related to the socially and politically progressive forces of the farm. The workers also confronted collective farms which were administered by family cliques and run along the principles of nepotism. The administrative boards of these farms, in addition to the "kulak-run" farms, were generally purged or reelected when a 25,000er was in a position of strength.

All collective farm boards were theoretically subject to reelection in February 1930. The timing of the elections was to coincide with the arrival of the 25,000ers. Many 25,000ers, however, had not yet been assigned to collective farms or were not in a position to ensure that elections be held. In many cases, they came into conflict with the existing farm administration, which did everything in its power to rid itself of the "proletarian upstarts." In these cases the 25,000ers were forced to fight an uphill struggle at least until mid-March when the retreat was sounded and many local leaders were discredited and replaced.[89]

The Excesses

Before the March retreat and especially during February, the central and regional authorities were inundated with letters and reports describing the excesses committed in collectivization and dekulakization. It was precisely this type of information which had prompted the Politburo to enact central legislation on dekulakization. The central legislation, however, not only failed to stem the tide, but actually served to increase the excesses of dekulakization as the campaign spread to new areas. The 25,000ers' letters were filled with descriptions of the lawlessness and policy violations committed in these months. According to Soviet sources, the 25,000ers were instrumental in signaling the center about the excesses in the field; whether or not this indeed was the case, their letters provided detailed accounts of the extremes of the time.[90] Moreover, the 25,000ers laid the finger of blame on the district-level officials and lower-level cadres, thus anticipating, if not perhaps providing impetus for, Moscow's conclusion of March 1930 that lower-ranking rural cadres—especially from the *okrug* and district levels—were the main force behind the race for percentages and the excesses of the campaign.

Many 25,000ers were no strangers to violence and bloodshed, having lived through and/or participated in the tumultuous years of revolution and civil war. In addition, a significant percentage were intimately acquainted with the kind of rural violence so typical of the isolated and backward peasantry which existed in Soviet Russia at the time. What appears to have made the greatest impression upon the workers was not simply the violence, but rather the illegality and *grubost'* (crudeness) which characterized the work of rural cadres and served as one of the primary underlying causes of the violence.

Many 25,000ers were appalled at the way in which rural cadres campaigned for collectivization. In Chernigov the 25,000er Makovskaia described a "bureaucratic" attitude to the peasantry: she said the officials spoke to the peasants about collectivization "with revolver in hand." The 25,000er Zborovskii was told that 100 percent collectivization had been achieved in the village to which he was assigned. He soon found out that it was achieved according to the following formula devised by the *sel'sovet* chairman: "Approach and enlist. And he who does not enlist, this means, that [he] is our enemy and that we will not let him live, we will give him the worst land . . . "[91] The Leningrad worker Dmitrieva wrote her trade union an outraged letter on the treatment meted out to the peasants:

> I, a worker of Krasnyi treugol'nik [enterprise], came to my own native village and am very surprised by what has been done . . . The local communists call themselves tsar and god . . . when the peasants signed up to join the collective farm one of them [the local Communists] said, "what do you think . . . you will walk around in chrome leather boots . . . " The peasants said— "where are you leading us, what do you want us poor to do, to dress in bask sandals [*lapti*]?"

Dmitrieva wrote that if a peasant attempted to speak at a meeting, he would immediately be told to shut up: "Nu ty, zakroisia." She wrote that the village activists and "local intelligentsia" (the schoolteacher in this case) abused their privileges and kept all the manufactured goods which came the way of the village for themselves. When the peasants complained that all were supposed to be equal, the schoolteacher said, "Why cast pearls upon swine, the cultured people should make use [of the privileges] . . . " Dmitrieva attempted to encourage the peasants to protest, but they were afraid and she was powerless to act without their support. She was denied the right to participate in local party sessions and therefore wrote to her trade union for help as a last resort.[92]

Dmitrieva was not an exception even though she was assigned to her native village. Many 25,000ers—especially those not able to quickly rise in the local power structure—found themselves in the role of the defenders of the peasants' rights. In some cases the peasants simply attempted to use the workers to undermine abusive local officials; in other cases the workers attempted to use the peasants to undermine their competition in local power struggles. Regardless of the ultimate purpose, the grievances cited by peasants and workers in these cases were sincere and based on the harsh reality of the times. The 25,000er I. I. Skripko was mobbed by peasants with complaints about collectivization and officials when he arrived at a collective farm. Reflecting a certain logic and concept of procedure current at the time, the peasants asked Skripko, "If we are allowed to leave the collective farm, can they arrest us for not entering?" Skripko complained about the situation to the party district committee; when the collective farm fell apart several days later, the district committee attempted to blame Skripko.[93] Many 25,000ers were fired or expelled from the party in this period for protesting against the actions of district officials.[94]

The 25,000ers pinned the blame for the excesses of collectivization mainly on the district-level authorities. They also blamed the district authorities for the excesses of dekulakization. The conclusion of the 25,000ers received confirmation in official reports. A report on Rzhev *Okrug* in the Western Region, condemned the district plenipotentiaries for the excesses and then indicated that the 25,000ers, on the other hand, had made a good impression on the author of the report.[95] This conclusion was echoed in an extremely revealing and frank report on Buriat-Mongolia. Here excesses were widespread and had led to two large peasant uprisings. In one village arrests were made during the night. People were herded into a barn and shots were fired over their heads. One terrified woman fled into the forest and was shot. In another village gold earrings were pulled from their owners' heads, and attempts were made to take the gold from people's teeth. In yet another village a peasant described as a middle peasant was seared with an iron and had his mustache torn from his face.[96] Buriat-Mongolia should not be considered typical in this regard. The excesses here were manifested in a much more extreme fashion than in most other areas of the country (excluding Central Asia) because of its nationality problem (antagonistic Russian settlers and Buriats were mistakenly forced to join the same collectives) and the extremely low qualifications of local cadres. Nevertheless, the main blame for excesses here, as elsewhere, was attributed to the district-level authorities.

Although condemnation for the excesses of the campaign was directed mainly at lower-level cadres, the 25,000ers were not all faultless models of proletarian virtue. There were reports—*always cited as exceptions*—of 25,000ers who had been swept along in the tide of excesses and had violated party policy. Given the lateness of the 25,000ers' arrival and the insecurity of their positions in this period, it is most probable that 25,000ers played only a minor role in the excesses and that most workers did, in fact, attempt to curb the extremes of the rural cadres. There were excesses among 25,000ers, nevertheless. The excesses of these 25,000ers were based upon an overzeal-ous and dangerously naive approach to building socialism in the countryside. The 25,000er Gorbunevskii, in the Crimea, announced on 1 March that his collective farm would become a *kommuna* and that all of the peasant children would be socialized. When the parents of the soon-to-be-socialized children heard of this, they began a massive slaughter of their also soon-to-be-socialized livestock, fortunately sparing their children.[97] The 25,000er Larman demonstrated rather a poor understanding of the voluntary principle in collectivization and the meaning of local peasant initiative. He proudly described his part in the organization of a collective farm: ''The other day, I organized, myself, on my own initiative—that is, according to the will of the people themselves, a new collective farm, [called] 'Volunteer.' ''[98] Other 25,000ers behaved in the same high-handed manner that had so alarmed Dmitrieva. The 25,000er Bulavin forced peasants onto the collective farm with a revolver; he was later fired and brought to court on criminal charges.[99] The 25,000er Vasil'ev told the peasants, ''The C.C. [Central Committee] . . . and com[rade] Kalinin sent me to you. You peasants have nothing in your brains. We were sent to you to pick them.''[100]

A number of 25,000ers were guilty of violating the law in ways not always directly related to collectivization. A 25,000er in the Western Region took expropriated kitchen utensils for himself at the time of dekulakization. He offered to pay for them when pressure was exerted on him to return them.[101] Other workers were accused of embezzling collective farm funds, appropri-ating deficit goods, and failing to distribute manufactured goods to the peasants.[102] By far the most common infractions committed by 25,000ers were related to standards of behavior. This was a serious issue, since the 25,000ers as outsiders and city people in insular, backward villages were suspect to begin with and consequently subject to minute scrutiny by the community. Once a worker discredited himself, he was incapable of exercising authority in the village. The collective farm chairman, the 25,000er Voev, was the target of criticism for his involvement in drinking bouts and for gathering a "harem" of village girls around him. The Leningrad 25,000er Iur'eva, en route to her village assignment, stopped off in the district center and was said to have had affairs with several local citizens. It was reported that this sparked off a wave of rumors about the "bad morals of the Leningrader." The 25,000er Krylov took off for the district center on a collective farm horse for an all-night drinking bout. He returned the next day on foot at 6:00 A.M., announcing his return by firing off his revolver under the window of the *sel'sovet* building. His biggest crime, in the eyes of the villagers, was that he had lost a farm horse which was badly needed for field work. Voev and Iur'eva received party reprimands, while the more serious case of Krylov was referred to the party control commission.[103]

The 25,000ers were sometimes accused by district and local cadres of being responsible for the excesses of the campaign. It was said that the 25,000ers could get away with anything and that it was they who had "taught" the local cadres how to commit excesses. An official in the Lower Volga said, "If they had not come, there would not have been excesses."[104] Although some of these accusations may have been correct, they certainly oversimplify the causal factor in the wave of excesses. In part, district and local cadres were just as eager to pin the blame on the 25,000ers and to avoid responsibility as the 25,000ers had been to point the finger of blame at them. But it must be emphasized above all that the excesses were rooted in the collectivization drive and that this had already been long underway before the 25,000ers made their relatively late entry into the countryside. The excesses were an integral part of an excessive policy, the implementation of which was entrusted to inexperienced and poorly prepared cadres, whose qualifications hardly matched the great tasks of the day.

Toward Retreat

The excesses had led to such a state of affairs in the countryside that the use of the word *excesses* to describe the situation assumes an ironic and tragically understated quality. Numerical percentages of collectivized peasant households were indeed large, but the percentages often belied the actual situation, which was sometimes nothing more than high percentages of paper collectivization. The percentages of dekulakized households, equally large, did not belie the truth. The plan of dekulakization was fulfilled and overfulfilled in record time. Hundreds of thousands of peasants were dislocated at this time, sometimes through flight to the cities, but generally (and not of their own free will) as a result of resettlement in distant underpopulated areas of the country or at one of the period's vast construction sites. The excesses also manifested themselves in the formation of giant collective farms covering entire districts, widespread attempts to push for the *kommuna* form of collective (especially in Siberia and the Urals), and the compulsive tendency to socialize all and sundry. Markets were closed and wholesale collectivization led to a wholesale attack on religion; this attack included the socialist transformation of churches into clubs and reading huts, the burning of icons, and the persecution and arrest of village priests.

The winter collectivization campaign sparked a wave of violence in the countryside which appeared to threaten the social stability of the state. It was not a civil war, for the sides were too unevenly matched; nor was there any real organization behind the opposition of peasants besides episodic intradistrict linkups of rebels. Only in Central Asia did resistance to collectivization resemble something like a civil war. In general, opposition was manifested in elemental and spontaneous outbursts of peasant rebelliousness. This entailed much senseless violence and, of course, led inevitably to an escalation of violence on both sides according to the human dialectics of the times. Peasants destroyed or illegally sold their livestock en masse. The market was glutted with meat for a short time, never to be repeated on such a scale. Prices and herds of marketable livestock dropped precipitously and Budennyi, at the Sixteenth Party Congress, coined the slogan of the "elimination of the horse as a class" to describe the process.[105] The violence was a by-product of the collectivization campaign and was shaped by the traditional peasant approach to radical politics. It was derived from an excessive policy and was predicated on the lawlessness, *grubost'*, and level of political and administrative competence of the cadres of collectivization.

It was probably the violence and fear of a massive peasant rebellion, more than any other single factor, which led the center to issue the call to retreat in March. The Central Committee requested Stalin to write a condemnation of the excesses in an article which took the form of his landmark "Dizzyness from Success" and which was soon supplemented by a Central Committee decree along similar lines. Stalin later claimed that this was not a retreat, for it was not a change in policy like the introduction of NEP in 1921. Rather it was a retreat only in the sense that it was a retreat from the excesses, a struggle against those guilty of violating the essentially correct policy of the Central Committee.[106] Although in April Stalin said, "I have in mind not only local officials, but also individual *oblastniki* [regional party committee members], as well as individual members of the C.C.,"[107] the basic thrust of his criticism was aimed at cadres on the *okrug* and district levels. These cadres were to be held responsible for the excesses and were subject to dismissal, according to the Central Committee decree, if they did not hurriedly reform their ways.[108] In large part, this was the center's Machiavellian attempt to find a scapegoat for peasant grievances.

It was, however, only partially an exercise in scapegoating since, to a large extent, the center perceived the excesses and problems of the campaign precisely as they were depicted in policy statements and called the retreat in order to exert its control over the rural cadres and the implementation of central policy. This is evident in an important and highly revealing circular letter issued by the North Caucasus regional committee on 18 February 1930 to all party committees on the *okrug*, district, and village levels. The letter discussed the "mistakes" committed in collectivization.[109] This letter was to be discussed at *closed* party meetings; therefore, it is safe to conclude that the propagandistic, scapegoating effect of Stalin's article and the Central Committee decree was not intended here. This letter was an early attempt to gain control of the collectivization campaign and the cadres in the field. It was claimed that the party line had been misunderstood in the countryside, that "political mistakes" had been made, and that policy was being violated in the implementation process. And who was it who was responsible for this? As would later be the case, it was the *okrug*, district, and sometimes local party and soviet officials who were blamed. This document is significant because the North Caucasus regional committee's reading of the excesses and responsibility for them was similar to the center's but without any propagandistic intent and, consequently, may be viewed as a statement of real perceptions. It is significant because it reveals certain underlying assumptions which played a large role in the center's policy response to the excesses and which were held by the 25,000ers in the field as well.

The primary assumption behind the observations and policy statements, in which lower-level cadres were blamed for the excesses, was that central policy had been correct and realistic. This assumption made it almost inevitable that lower-level rural cadres would be blamed for problems in policy implementation, for if the initial policy had been correct, then surely it must have been the cadres, who were inept or criminal in going about their jobs. The cadres' first weakness had been what was diplomatically labeled "dizzyness," or drunkenness from the successes registered in the drive. For proof, the center, along with the 25,000ers, simply had to point to the race for percentages and the overfulfillment of planned quotas in dekulakization. The cadres' second weakness revolved around the problem of leadership, and this problem provides a basic thread linking the conclusions of the center, of the North Caucasus regional party committee, and of the 25,000ers.

According to most reports which attributed the excesses to lower-level cadres, the cadres had failed to do their jobs correctly, had implemented policy incorrectly, and had displayed more communist conceit than reliance on the "initiative of the masses." The rural cadres were criticized for a failure of leadership. Had they learned how to lead, they could have prevented the resistance of the women, which, according to current opinion, was not political but emanated from irrational female hysteria. The cadres could have mobilized the local activists for support in policy implementation. They could, therefore, have isolated the kulaks instead of providing them with an enlarged base of support. The center was, with infrequent exceptions, unwilling to admit any "dizzyness" of its own. Contemporary literary depictions of the implementation of collectivization like Sholokhov's *Virgin Soil Upturned* and V. Kirshon's *Khleb* were built on the same assumptions and ended with the moral that good leadership is the best prevention against excesses and the best route to successful policy implementation. The pervasive assumption that collectivization was feasible and that it was possible to build a base of local support and thus isolate the kulak was a major determinant of the shape which the center's March policies assumed.

In addition, the pattern of blame which evolved at this time was largely built into the system. Lines of responsibility and administrative authority were not clearly demarcated in the provincial party and government hierarchy. The districts were granted a good deal of initiative in setting their own pace and quotas of collectivization. Moreover, the implementation of policy by the plenipotentiary system led to a situation in which no one assumed responsibility for actions. The failure to establish control and administrative order in rural party and government practices led to a situation in which no one at all assumed responsibility. Each successive rung of the regional hierarchy was given enough rope to hang itself. In this way the campaign and responsibility for its implementation evolved downward along the regional hierarchy until the buck finally stopped at the district level, which was most intimately involved in the everyday aspects of the campaign. In a sense, then, it is easy to see how the burden of blame for the failures of an excessive central policy ultimately and inevitably came to rest with those most directly responsible for its execution.

This is not to deny a certain conscious attempt at scapegoating by the center. The center was not unaware of the usefulness of scapegoating and did attempt to capitalize on a Soviet-style naive monarchism which held that "the Central Committee is good and the lower-level cadres are bad." The peasants, themselves, may have provided the inspiration for this in their frequent attacks on local officials and in the widespread tendency to petition incoming workers and the center against the injustices and excesses of rural cadres, as if things would improve if the "tsar only knew" how policy was being violated in his domain. And, in fact, Stalin became a temporary folk hero with the appearance of his "Dizzyness from Success," as peasants, naively or otherwise, pitted him against rural officials who were dared to defy Comrade Stalin by continuing in their old ways.

The scapegoating intentions of the March retreat are the elements most emphasized in the Western literature on collectivization. Surely they were an important aspect of policy in March. To deny, however, the prevalent assumptions about collectivization so widespread at the time and reflected in the 25,000ers' accounts, or the very process of blame built into a system devoid of clear lines of demarcation of function and responsibility, is simply to invert the traditional peasant myth and replace it with an equally naive formulation placing all blame on the center and exonerating lower-level cadres believed either to be working under continual coercion or forgiven for they "knew not what they did." Moreover, to view the retreat as an act of total cynicism would be to deny the very real fact that rural cadres had indeed become "dizzy from success," and, despite the central impetus of the campaign, had carried the campaign beyond the control of the center. It was, after all, precisely this "spontaneity" of rural officialdom which served as a major factor in the decision to recruit the 25,000ers. In this sense Stalin's article could be viewed as the culmination of central attempts to gain control of collectivization dating from the January legislation on dekulakization.

In all probability there is enough blame to be shared equally and democratically by all concerned. The main point of this discussion of the effects of the March retreat and the process of blame for the excesses is not to determine where guilt resides, but rather to provide a basis for understanding the consequences of pointing the finger of blame at the lower-level cadres and for understanding the extent to which the center had lost control of the collectivization drive. For the 25,000ers the primary consequence of the March retreat would be an increase in "job security," an enhanced status vis-à-vis rural officials and peasants, and the opportunity finally to fulfill the tasks which had been assigned to them by the Central Committee. Before March the 25,000ers were unable to inject that much-needed "proletarian consciousness" into the campaign; after March they would finally be able to play a role in exerting central control over collectivization and the countryside. The March retreat discredited many rural officials and enhanced the authority of the 25,000ers, who were exempted from blame in the excesses and heralded as the force which would correct the excesses and policy violations. Beginning in March the 25,000ers would cease to be de facto collectivizers and would gradually enter into work as leadership forces in the collective farm system.

Conclusion

After March 1930 the 25,000ers ceased to play the role of collectivizers and began to serve the function originally intended of them. Their further involvement in collectivization, per se, was fairly limited. They were, of course, expected to be persistent in reversing the exodus, which began with the March retreat, of peasants from the collective farms. In this capacity the 25,000ers are often given credit for inspiring the organization of the collective farmers' first initiative brigades, which were used to recruit individual peasants onto existing farms. The workers would also be called upon to participate in the second Day of Collectivization, which took place in the fall of 1930 in the midst of the renewed collectivization campaign.[110] However, the majority of the 25,000ers would not play a role in the implementation of the campaign, as they had in the earlier collectivization drive. Their main work was within the young collective farm system.[111]

After the March retreat and by the summer of 1930, the overwhelming majority of 25,000ers had moved into collective farm work. From among the original group of 27,519, approximately 22,000 workers remained in the countryside by the summer of 1930. Of these, Kolkhoztsentr estimated that 19,581 were employed on collective farms. An additional 1,530 (mostly metalworkers) were employed in the machine tractor station system. The majority (78.6 percent) of those on collective farms served as chairmen or members of collective farm boards; on large collective farms they often served as directors of individual farm sectors.[112] In the summer of 1930 a 25,000er was employed on one out of every five collective farms in the USSR as a whole and on approximately one out of every three collective farms in the major grain regions (see table 5). Most of the 25,000ers worked on artels, and large collective farms serviced by a machine tractor station tended to have priority in receiving 25,000ers, as did the relatively few *kommunas* still in existence in the summer of 1930 (see table 6).

From the original 25,000ers roughly 5,000 workers had left the ranks by the summer of 1930. The workers who left did so for a variety of reasons. Death and illness played a role in the decline in numbers in this period; this appears to have been the case especially in Central Asia, where ethnic Russians were unprepared for the sometimes hostile climatic conditions, not to mention hostile tribesmen, *basmachi*, and *mullahs* (see Glossary). Many workers— probably the largest percentage—were simply ordered back to the factories. This occurred when workers were deemed unsuitable for "leadership work" on the collective farms, when workers discredited themselves in the early excesses, or when workers were chased out of villages by angry peasants after the retreat. A third group of workers left of their own free will. These

TABLE 5*

PERCENTAGE OF COLLECTIVE FARMS WITH 25,000ers (1930-1931)

REGION	1930	1931: OLD	NEW	ALL FARMS
Northern	11.9	6.6	.5	3
Kareliia	20.2	8.2	3.3	4.9
Leningrad	20.9	2.7	.4	.9
Western	27	13.2	1	3.2
Moscow	17.3	12.5	2.1	4.5
Ivanovo	15.9	9.6	1.4	3
Nizhegorodskii	9.4	6.7	.7	2.9
Ural	12.8	8.3	1.5	5.3
Bashkiriia ASSR	6.2	4.1	.6	2.5
Tatariia ASSR	8.6	7.7	1	4.2
Middle Volga	29.6	21.5	4.3	14.3
Central Black Earth	17.5	9.5	1.1	4.1
North Caucasus	40.3	20.7	2.8	16.2
Lower Volga	56.9	31.3	13.6	29.4
Dagestan ASSR	1.5	1.1	--	.4
Crimea ASSR	20.7	17.8	1.3	5.3
Kazakhstan ASSR	13.2	12.6	1.8	9.6
Western Siberia	17.7**	10.5	1	5.1
Eastern Siberia	17.7**	10.2	.8	5.3
Buriat-Mongolia	11.1	--	--	2.5
Far East	17.3	9.7	2.1	7.2
Ukraine	29.4	21.3	3.4	12.7
BSSR	16.7	11.4	1	5.6
ZSFSR	8.5	15	6.1	11
RSFSR	18.8	12	1.3	5.7
SSSR	18.8	14.3	1.5	7.4

*Data for 1930 is from Kolkhozy v 1930 g. Itogi raportov kolkhozov XVI s"ezdu VKP (b) (Moscow: Ogiz, 1931), pp. 224-235. Data for 1931 is from Kolkhozy vesnoi 1931 goda (Moscow-Leningrad, 1932), pp. 137-141. "Old collective farms" are those collective farms which were organized between the summer of 1929 and the spring of 1930, while "new collective farms" are those collective farms which were organized after fall 1930. Among all collective farms in the USSR, 46.2% were "old" and 53.8% were "new."

**This figure is for all Siberia and predated the administrative division of the region.

so-called deserters were as yet a relatively small group among the 25,000ers.[113]

The 25,000ers who deserted from the ranks were harshly criticized by their comrades, trade unions, and factory organizations. Most of them returned because they were demoralized by what they had confronted in the countryside. An older cadre worker who returned to the city reported with disgust, "There are too many injustices, it is not collectivism, it is pillage." Another 25,000er, who wrote a letter of complaint to the newspaper *Rabochaia gazeta*, said, "I, and Shagurin also, are not fit for such work as the socialist transformation of agriculture. I strongly curse both the [party] bureau and factory committee for sending us. We need help . . . "[114] The desertions were

TABLE 6*

DISTRIBUTION OF 25,000ers ACCORDING TO FARM TYPES (Spring 1930)**

REGION	PERCENTAGE OF FARMS WITH 25,000ers:				
	KOMMUNA	ARTEL	TOZ	MTS-SERVICED	NO MTS
Leningrad	54.9 (149)	18.4 (329)	2.2 (4)	30.5 (46)	20.3 (436)
Western	54.9 (235)	24.4 (612)	3.3 (4)	28.0 (32)	27.0 (819)
Moscow	51.9 (141)	16.4 (547)	3.1 (10)	17.3 (84)	17.4 (614)
Ivanovo	34.1 (16)	16.5 (256)	4.5 (8)	19.1 (9)	15.8 (271)
Nizhegorodskii	26.2 (154)	8.2 (435)	4.2 (23)	16.7 (13)	9.3 (599)
Ural	18.8 (230)	12.0 (680)	1.2 (2)	26.5 (133)	11.7 (779)
Middle Volga***	31.1 (70)	30.8 (1,089)	15.8 (49)	34.7 (256)	28.6 (952)
Central Black Earth***	29.9 (93)	18.0 (764)	7.3 (70)	30.5 (261)	14.9 (666)
North Caucasus***	27.6 (147)	44.8 (1,870)	6.4 (18)	49.1 (728)	36.9 (1,307)
Lower Volga***	34.8 (47)	58.7 (1,607)	27.6 (12)	69.3 (553)	53.5 (1,113)
Crimea ASSR	62.9 (39)	20.9 (193)	1.5 (1)	25.3 (55)	19.8 (178)
Kazakhstan ASSR	45.1 (74)	13.2 (628)	1.5 (9)	25.5 (113)	12.2 (598)
Siberia	37.7 (1,000)	9.8 (387)	1.1 (9)	39.1 (168)	16.6 (1,228)
Far East	23.0 (123)	15.8 (159)	– (–)	16.7 (13)	17.2 (269)
Ukraine***	63.1 (914)	27.0 (3,383)	12.8 (1,249)	39.4 (1,669)	19.9 (3,877)
BSSR	31.0 (31)	16.4 (520)	– (–)	20.3 (48)	16.5 (503)
ZSFSR	11.4 (5)	9.9 (253)	3.5 (23)	13.6 (100)	7.0 (181)
Uzbekistan SSR	27.8 (5)	7.2 (264)	1.5 (7)	9.9 (165)	6.9 (111)
Basic Grain Regions***	46.9 (796)	35.9 (5,589)	13.1 (708)	39.7 (2,546)	26.7 (4,547)
Producing Areas***	34.2 (1,672)	17.6 (4,104)	10.0 (679)	30.9 (1,232)	16.4 (5,223)
Consumer Areas***	33.8 (1,161)	13.8 (4,739)	3.2 (120)	15.5 (706)	14.1 (5,314)
RSFSR***	32.2 (2,674)	18.5 (10,012)	4.3 (228)	33.3 (2,502)	17.3 (10,412)
USSR***	35.8 (3,629)	19.0 (14,432)	9.4 (1,507)	29.0 (4,484)	17.1 (15,084)

*Derived from Kolkhozy v 1930 g. Itogi raportov kolkhozov XVI s"ezdu VKP (b) (Moscow: Ogiz, 1931), pp. 224-235.

**Data not given for regions with less than 200 25,000ers. Absolute numbers of 25,000ers follow in parentheses.

***The data for these regions is incomplete based on total absolute number of 25,000ers.
Number of 25,000ers not accounted for: M. Volga (1); C. Bl. E. (5); N. Caucasus (2); L. Volga (2); Ukraine (1); Grain (2); Producing (7); Consumer (4); RSFSR (12); USSR (13).

119

relatively few at this time and were harshly condemned. At the same time it is clear that the center understood what sort of conditions had prompted the desertions and consequently began efforts to improve the workers' lot.

With relatively minor exceptions the ranks of the 25,000ers held strong through the period of the mad drive to collectivize Soviet agriculture in the winter of 1930. They witnessed and participated in the destructive phase of the rural revolution and managed to wait out the storm until they could begin their work. With the signal to retreat, a period of relative calm set in during which the 25,000ers were able to take up their posts as collective farm leaders in earnest. Their work would be centered on attempts to cement the proletarian dictatorship in the countryside, to transform the Russian peasantry into collective farmers, and to introduce the ethos and organization of the factory into the collective farms.

5

The 25,000ers and the Cadres
of Collectivization: The Offensive
on Rural Officialdom

You say that article ["Dizzyness from Success"] is one in the eye for
me? No, it's not one in the eye, it's one in the heart! Right through and
out the other side! And my head wasn't dizzy when we were building up
the collective farms; it's dizzy now, after that article . . . And I've been
drinking because this article of Stalin's has smacked through me like a
bullet, and I'm bleeding my heart out . . . How did I agitate for the
collective farm? I'll tell you. One or two of our dirty dogs, though they're
counted as middle peasants, I told straight out, "You won't join the
collective farm! You're against Soviet power, eh? You fought against us
in 'nineteen . . . Well, don't expect any peace from me. I'll land you such
a smacker, you rat, that it'll make all the devils in hell feel sick!" Did I
say that? I did! And I even banged my revolver on the table . . . And I
swung to the left over the chickens not because of Trotsky, but because
I was in a hurry to see the World Revolution.

MAKAR NAGULNOV, secretary of the Gremyachy Log party cell
in Sholokhov's *Virgin Soil Upturned*

They [the 25,000ers] must become the nearest and most active helpers of
the party in the cause of socialist reconstruction of agriculture, lead the
collective farm movement, help the peasants . . . They must be the
leaders in the struggle with bureaucratism and distortions of the class
line, in the struggle with the appearance of the right deviation in practical
work in the lower party, soviet, and cooperative organs.

Address of the Moscow Regional Council of Trade Unions
to a group of 25,000ers in late 1929

Moscow's call for an end to the excesses of the collectivization campaign had
far-reaching consequences. It led, on the one hand, to a precipitous decline in
the percentage of collectivized peasant households. Collective farmers re-

121

verted en masse to individual peasant proprietors. Stalin claimed that this regression was "entirely normal" and even a "healthy" phenomenon. According to him, those who had left the farms were nothing but dead weight on the movement; they were the "deal souls" of collectivization, the "harmful" or "class alien" elements, and the "waverers."[1] Once rid of them, the collective farm movement would be able to undergo a period of consolidation. This was, in a very real sense, a retreat—if not from policy, then at least from the mad chaos of the winter campaign. On the other hand the decisions of March ushered in a new offensive and one of a different nature. This was the offensive on the cadres who had led the implementation of the winter collectivization campaign.

The offensive on the cadres came from above and from below. The unintended consequence of the March retreat had been to spark an escalation in rural violence. Anti-collective farm disturbances increased in March and April as the wrath of yesterday's collective farmers was targeted upon rural cadres who had played an active role in collectivization. The Central Committee proved to be the peasantry's unlikely ally in this assault when it further undermined the cadres' authority by accusing them of policy violations, left excesses, or the shortsighted dizzyness which appears to have reached epidemic proportions in those times. Cadres who were unwilling or unable to admit their mistakes and who refused to maintain sobriety were to be removed from their posts and subject to disciplinary measures.[2] The 25,000ers who, as a group, escaped the barrage of official censure unscathed, were called upon to take the lead in correcting the mistakes which had occurred in the campaign.[3] This would allow them an important instrument of leverage in their attempts to consolidate their position in the countryside.

The assault on cadres was the first stage in the attempt to transform the rural party and government into organs of "proletarian dictatorship," which they were in name only. The restructuring of the apparatus was, according to Stalin, an integral part of the Bolshevik offensive.[4] In order to exert its control over policy implementation, the center had to circumvent normal administrative networks. As representatives of the center, the 25,000ers were to lead in this phase of rural socialist construction. Their task was to transform the organs of the party and government into bastions of political reliability and social support for the state. The means to this transformation was the purge of existing officialdom, which had been underway since mid-1929, and the replacement of purged officials by politically and socially reliable cadres. The workers' objective was to recruit and promote "proven collective farmers" in order to create a new social base for the state in the countryside. This attempt to create a proletarian stronghold in the countryside served as the framework for the 25,000ers' work on the collective farms. Their work as collective farm managers and their attempts to "build socialism" in the countryside were linked ultimately to their successes and failures in dealing with rural officials and securing a foothold in rural officialdom.

Exodus, Retreat, and Betrayal

The mass exodus from the collective farms began in March 1930 and continued with variations according to region and rate up until the second wave of collectivization in the fall (see table 7). The percentage of collectivized households fell from 57.6 percent on 10 March to 21.8 percent on 1 October, with the greatest percentage decline occurring during the spring months.[5] The precipitous decline in percentages did not represent as drastic a change as these numbers suggest. A large part of the exodus was from paper collective farms. On a practical level, leaving a collective farm at this time was frequently similar to joining a collective farm. A signature and a form were often all that was necessary with the striking difference that in the case of leaving, it was the peasants who did the shouting rather than the officials and it was the peasants who carried off the livestock. This is not to say that the exodus was inconsequential. Its real consequences, however, had little to do with "exodus," per se, for no one actually left the scene (apart from those who left under the kulak label). The real consequence of the exodus lie in the protest which the March turnabout had given rise to: protest against collectivization, collective farms, the socialization of livestock, commissars, Communists, and local officials. Peasants rebelled and they did so in the belief that they had the sanction and support of Stalin and the Central Committee—or, at least, this is how they attempted to legitimize their protest. A statement made by peasants in Siberia was typical: "We don't believe in the plenipotentiaries and [party] cells now. We only believe the press and Stalin . . . "[6]

The floodgates of protest did not cave in immediately after the publication of Stalin's article, but began only in the second half of March following the announcement of the Central Committee decree condemning the excesses.[7] Nevertheless—perhaps due to a time factor in the dissemination of news in the countryside, perhaps due to a natural process of acceleration of passions, or perhaps due to some long repressed and slowly surfacing innate naive monarchism—Stalin rather ironically became the hero of the day. Or at least he was hero to all but the now silent right opposition and the cadres who felt the brunt of such heroism. Two rising stars of those days who were fortunate enough to sit out the campaign in the relative safety of institutions of higher education, Nikita Khrushchev and Petro Grigorenko, later recalled having viewed Stalin's article as a "masterpiece," as the "foresight of a genius."[8]

TABLE 7*

PERCENTAGES OF COLLECTIVIZED HOUSEHOLDS IN THE RSFSR (March–October 1930)

REGION	March 1**	March 10	April 1	May 1	June 1	July 1	Aug. 1	Sept. 1	Oct. 1+
RSFSR (as a whole)	58.6	-	38.4	25.3	22.4	20.5	20.3	20.0	20.4
Western	41.2	37.4	15.7	8.2	7.4	7.4	6.5	7.2	7.2
Moscow	74.2	58.1	12.5	7.5	7.3	7.3	7.1	7.1	7.4
Ivanovo	30.7	32.9 ++	9.5	5.9	5.5	5.4	5.4	5.4	5.6
Central Black Earth	83.3	81.5 ++	39.6	18.2	16.0	15.4	15.3	15.0	15.8
Ural	75.6	70.6 ++	57.8	31.9	29.1	27.0	27.8	26.9	27.0
Middle Volga	60.3	57.2 ++	43.8	30.1	27.0	27.0	27.0	24.3	24.4
Lower Volga	70.1	68.6 ++	54.0	41.4	39.4	36.1	35.4	36.1	37.9
North Caucasus	79.4	79.3 ++	67.0	63.2	58.0	50.2	53.1	51.1	52.4
Siberia	47.0	50.8	43.0	25.6	22.4	21.4	20.1	21.6	21.6

*Derived from R. W. Davies, The Socialist Offensive. The Collectivization of Soviet Agriculture, 1929–1930 (Cambridge, MA: Harvard University Press, 1980), pp. 442–443 (Table 17). Percentages for March 10 are from M. L. Bogdenko, "Kolkhoznoe stroitel'stvo vesnoi i letom 1930 g.," Istoricheskie zapiski, vol. 76 (1965), p. 31.

**Note the percentages given by Bogdenko for March 1: Ivanovo (33.8); Cen. Bl. E. (81.8); Ural (68.8); M. Volga (56.4); L. Volga (67.8); and N. Caucasus (76.8). According to the Bogdenko figures, in most areas, percentages of collectivized households continued to rise until March 10, with the exception of Moscow.

+From October, the percentages of collectivized households steadily increased.

++Compare these figures with the Bogdenko March 1 percentages.

124

The peasants seemed to have been similarly disposed toward adulation. Stalin's article was passed from hand to hand and his name resounded through the countryside. Peasants rode miles to obtain a copy of the article and paid as much as fifteen rubles for a newspaper containing the article. In one village an elderly peasant man ran through the square, article in hand, shouting "liberation!"[9]

Rural officials and local activists reacted somewhat differently to the article. In some places the article was confiscated, withheld from distribution at the post, refused publication in local newspapers, or unofficially banned as illegal reading material.[10] It was reported that "underground readings" of Stalin's article took place clandestinely in peasant huts.[11] Stalin did not remain in the underground for long, however. By mid-March, with the additional reinforcement of the Central Committee decree against excesses, the peasants began to rally openly and rather vigorously against the excesses and rural cadres. Stalin and the Central Committee were rapidly and unwittingly pushed into the vanguard of a mass wave of peasant rebellion.

Anti-collective farm demonstrations were widespread in the spring of 1930. The majority of such disturbances were local and appear to have taken the form of village riots, often led by women. With the exception of large-scale revolts in Central Asia, the available sources would seem to indicate that the disturbances were put down relatively easily, generally with the aid of the rural militia and armed civilian officials. There is scant evidence with which to judge the degree of Red army involvement in crushing anti-collective farm resistance, but it appears that in most cases the revolts were suppressed by local forces (including OGPU forces) or fizzled out on their own with the collapse of the collective farm.[12]

Soviet sources have provided evidence on several relatively large revolts which took place in the RSFSR in March. The first was in the Riazan area and appears in some ways typical, for, like many similar disturbances, it began locally and then set off a chain reaction of local revolts as word reached neighboring villages of the initial disturbance. In this case the rebels cut down telegraph and telephone wires, cutting off all communication between their village and Riazan. As news of the revolt spread, the region's collective farms toppled one after another like dominoes in a row.[13] The second large revolt for which there is published evidence took place in Uch-Pristanskii District, Biiskii *Okrug*, in the Altai region of Siberia. The revolt began on 10 March with the arrest and execution of what the sources label "a large part" of the Communists and Komsomols of the district committee. The rebels, said to be three hundred strong, then went on to seize the "arsenal" at the local militia office and to free all prisoners (probably those arrested as kulaks) held at the district center. The rebel band, which led an uprising covering one fourth of the district, had plans to seize all of the district centers of Siberia. The revolt was suppressed relatively quickly, but this incident is notable for the degree of organization and geographical breadth of the rebel activities.[14]

The majority of disturbances, however, seem to have been local. From the evidence at our disposal it does not appear that the riots followed any standard pattern apart from spontaneous violence. The only frequent common denominators in the riots that easily come to mind are peasant seizures of socialized livestock—an action which often served to spark the violence, since, with an eye to the coming sowing campaign, the local cadres generally attempted to prevent this—the sounding of the tocsin (the church bell), and the leading role, at least initially, of the village women. A riot which occurred in the village Lebedevka in Kursk at the Budennyi collective farm appears to have been typical. A 25,000er by the name of Dobychin (serving as a plenipotentiary on collectivization) arrived at the farm on 7 March. Dobychin called a meeting and was greeted with cries of "we do not want a collective farm" and "you want to derail the muzhik." Dobychin responded: "We will not hold such [types on the farm], good riddance . . . Sleep it off and you'll see that we will let the poor peasant derail he who made you drunk and sent you here." Dobychin's tact led to a general uproar and an assault on the 25,000er by the "women activists." The women approached the stage where he stood with one Praskov'ia Avdiushenko in the lead. She said to Dobychin, "Ah well, come nearer to us." With this, Praskov'ia grabbed the worker by his coat and dragged him off the stage. Dobychin somehow managed to escape, but the unrest continued and even escalated when the church watchman's wife began to sound the tocsin. With this, the peasants seized their recently socialized livestock and prepared a collective declaration requesting permission to quit the farm. This disturbance, like many others, was not suppressed, but simply ended with the collapse of the farm.[15]

The response of rural cadres to the disturbances varied. The only apparent common denominator was panic and this was not an unreasonable response. Some officials simply ran away or were chased out of villages by pitchfork-wielding peasants. In most of these cases the officials had so discredited themselves that they could never return and work effectively again. Others attempted to persuade yesterday's collective farmers not to leave the farms or tried to limit the damage by refusing to return a part of the recently socialized property (usually the draft animals needed for field work). By far, however, the most common response was to go the way of one or another extreme: Either to resist all suggestions of a retreat and continue to behave as "god and tsar" or to sink into complete demoralization based on a sense of betrayal by Stalin and the Central Committee, which appeared to many to be perpetuating a modern variation on the theme of "the tsar is good but the local officials are bad."

Most rural cadres were crushed by the March decisions. They were under attack from above and from below. If they managed to escape a peasant's axe, it might only be to end up under the no less sharp, but at least less physically damaging, axe of the party control commission, district procurator, or some other traveling investigative organ mobilized by any of a multitude of possible Soviet Sergeant Prishibeyev-style institutions. This state of affairs was largely responsible for what R. W. Davies has described as the "crisis in the party" in the period of March through July in 1930. Moscow's refusal to share the blame for the excesses of collectivization and its abnegation of responsibility for the cadres who were now under attack led to widespread discontent among rural officials.[16]

The first type of discontent fueled by Moscow's actions was labeled right deviationism and, later, Mamaevshchina after the author (Mamaev) of a critical article accusing the Central Committee of shortsightedness in the campaign and, consequently, responsibility for the excesses.[17] The basic issue was "who was dizzy?" The answer, of course, was that the Central Committee was dizzy, it had not taken into account the realities of the rural situation and the feasibility of the campaign. The March decisions and the scapegoating were, therefore, tantamount to the old formula of "the tsar is good but the local officials are bad."[18] Many cadres also railed against the Central Committee and Stalin, blaming them for the excesses.[19] A Dnepropetrovsk worker who took part in collectivization (as a brigade worker) summarized this sentiment:

> Comrade Stalin! I, a rank-and-file worker and reader of the newspaper "Pravda," follow the newspaper articles all the time! Is he who failed to shut out the noise and cries created around collectivization . . . guilty? All of us, the lower [activists] and the press overlooked this basic issue about leadership of the collective farms, but c[omrade] Stalin, incorrectly slept like a bogatyr [legendary warrior-hero] during this time and heard nothing and did not see our mistakes and therefore it is also necessary to straighten you out. But now c[omrade] Stalin heaps all the blame on the locals, but defends himself and the leadership.[20]

Although widespread opposition among rural cadres to the scapegoating effects of March played an important role in the crisis of the rural party, this was not the only or even the most important response of the cadres of collectivization.

With the publication of Stalin's article and the Central Committee decree, word began to spread throughout the countryside that the party was in retreat.[21] Many cadres could not believe what they read. The Red partisans who had led collectivization in one Ukrainian village were indignant: "What is the center kidding us?" They refused to "retreat" and accused the center of "playing into the hands of the kulak."[22] The *sel'sovet* chairman of one village, a civil war veteran, opposed the center's accusations and confiscated all copies of Stalin's article. Commenting on the article, he said, "And in regard to the voluntary principle, here I disagree with com[rade] Stalin . . . I disagree when com[rade] Stalin says that 'one cannot plant collective farms by force.' In my opinion, the voluntary principle doesn't work, force is necessary."[23] These cadres knew that the inevitable result of the March decisions would be an exodus from the farms. More important, however, the majority of them believed that they were waging a war in the countryside and that without the use of force the war would be lost. They believed that their cause was just. They were unwilling to admit that there had existed any so-called dizzyness, that their successes in the race for percentages had turned into excesses or policy violations. These cadres had, by and large, been schooled in the emergency measures of the grain crisis and many were veterans of the civil war. Relatively new to their posts, they had often replaced those party and government officials who had been dismissed in the purge which swept rural officialdom in the attempt to push through the extraordinary measures first taken in 1927–28. They tended to be Communist party members and most often served as plenipotentiaries operating out of district- or *okrug*-level agencies or as members of village party cells. They had been trained in dizzyness. They had not reneged on the revolution in the countryside; according to these cadres, it was the center which had panicked and compromised itself before the kulak and the right deviation. They saw the Central Committee racing in headlong ignominious retreat and, consequently, refused to capitulate.

Moscow had slammed on the brakes to halt the madness of the winter campaign, but it was like braking on a slippery surface. Things continued as before for several more months. There was an uproar in the party over the March decisions. There were objections to the undermining of the local cadres and to the "retreat" of the center. Stalin admitted as much at the Sixteenth Party Congress when he said, "There are people in our party who think that it was not necessary to rebuff the 'left' *zagibshchiki* [those who commit excesses] . . . They think that it was not necessary to offend our cadres and protest their exaggerations even if these exaggerations led to mistakes."[24] The negative political repercussions of the March decisions were serious enough for Stalin to argue against apparent accusations that his "Dizzy" article was an act of his own volition: "Some think that the article, 'Dizzyness from Success,' was the result of the personal initiative of Stalin. This, of course, is nonsense . . . This was the deep reflection of the C.C.'' He went on to further "implicate" the Central Committee by linking his article to the March decree: "And when the depth and size of the mistakes became clear, the C.C. was not slow to strike out at mistakes with all the force of its authority, having published its celebrated decree of 15 [*sic*] March 1930.''[25]

The duel between the center and the rural cadres continued into the summer. Stalin repeatedly emphasized that the party had not made a Brest-Litovsk- or a NEP-like retreat.[26] The center insisted that policy had not changed: wholesale collectivization remained the basic item on the party's agenda. Those cadres who resisted the Central Committee were, according to Stalin, playing into the hands of the right opposition. Stalin said that the leftists did nothing but discredit the center by reflecting party policy in a distorted light.[27] The "deviations" in the rural party, however, should not be misconstrued as manifestations of the political ideas of the right or left oppositions. They were instead rooted in methods of policy implementation and, following the retreat, often meant either opposition to scapegoating (right) or opposition to retreat (left). The debate in the party over the undermining of rural cadres and the issue of retreat continued until the Sixteenth Party Congress early in the summer of 1930. In the interval the Central Committee did not limit itself to a simple strategy of persuasion toward the cadres of collectivization.

The center took a more active part in attempting to catch on to the reins of its runaway rural apparatus by pursuing the traditional path of calls for party discipline and the corresponding rewards for failure to act according to this long-standing Bolshevik virtue. The March decree stipulated that cadres who refused to struggle against excesses were to be fired.[28] Similar directives were issued by the regional authorities.[29] The success of the party's efforts may be judged by the fact that the Central Committee was forced to repeat these directives in a letter of 2 April.[30] It is difficult to present a complete picture of the shake-up of the rural party due to the fact that overall statistics are not available and partial regional statistics exist only for certain areas. Nonetheless, a preliminary idea of the shake-up's results is possible on the basis of existing data. In Balashovskii *Okrug* in the Lower Volga one entire district party committee was dissolved, several party secretaries were fired, and 92 officials were subject to some form of disciplinary measure. According to evidence reported by a local official to the American Anna Louise Strong, 108 officials in Khoperskii *Okrug*, Lower Volga, were fired at this time.[31] In Siberia, according to data on fifteen *okrug*s, 14 district party committees were dissolved, 1,147 party members were subject to some form of disciplinary action, 330 party members were expelled, and 1,056 officials were prosecuted in criminal court. In Novosibirsk alone 58 party members were expelled; 157

received reprimands; and 18 party cell secretaries, 7 *sel'sovet* chairmen, 45 district plenipotentiaries, and 39 "others" were fired.[32] In Kazakhstan, in two *okrug*s alone, 5 district party committees were dissolved, 100 officials were arrested, and 300 received reprimands.[33] The Shklovskii district party committee in Mogilevskii *Okrug*, Belorussia, which had viewed Stalin's article as a "mistake," was dissolved. In Viazemskii *Okrug*, Western Region, the secretary of the *okrug* party committee, the chairman of the *okrug* party control commission, and the editor of the local newspaper were all fired. In Far East Region the secretaries of district party committees in Shchelkovskii, Gubinskii, Altynskii, Botlikhskii, and Kazibekskii districts were fired, and several other officials were sent to criminal court.[34] The Soviet dissident historian Roy Medvedev considers the repression of local officials to have assumed "mass" dimensions at this time.[35] It is difficult to determine the accuracy of this claim according to available sources. Nonetheless, it seems clear that for at least the spring of 1930 the Central Committee had its work cut out for it in its efforts to bring the provincial apparatus under control. This was most evident in the case of the Moscow regional party organization which had fiercely resisted the March actions and which was used by the center as an example of the political consequences accruing from recalcitrance in accepting central decisions.

Moscow Region, a grain-consuming area, was designated to complete collectivization in 1933. The Moscow regional party committee was divided, however, over tempos. Many *okrug* party committee secretaries called for increased tempos at the January (1930) plenum of the Moscow party committee; the *okrug* committees of Riazan, Tver, and Tula made plans to complete collectivization by the spring of 1930. In February, in response to the radicalism of many cadres and the successes of the race for percentages, Bauman, the first secretary of the Moscow regional party committee, gave the go-ahead for the region to complete 100 percent collectivization by spring of 1930.[36]

The Moscow party organization led the all-union race for percentages in the winter campaign, second to none in terms of quantum leaps between February and March. On 1 October 1929 only 3.2 percent of peasant households were collectivized in the Moscow Region; on 1 February 1930 the percentage had reached 36.5, and by 1 March it had soared to 73 percent. The subsequent exodus was equally dizzying: by 1 May only 7.3 percent of households remained on the farms.[37] The seriousness of the situation can be judged by the fact that the center was forced to intervene in the Moscow party organization's internal affairs twice before the March retreat. On 4 February the Central Committee overruled a Moscow decision pertaining to the exile of an inordinately large number of kulaks. Moscow was also singled out for censure in Stalin's "Answer to the Sverdlov Comrades" (9 February), where he condemned the Moscow party's policy regarding the elimination of the NEPmen as a class.[38]

The Moscow party organization refused to accept the March retreat. It was reported that sections of the lower party rank and file had accused the center of retreating and several district committees refused to publish Stalin's article in their newspaper organs.[39] At the same time the Moscow regional party leadership refused to take the blame for excesses, which some saw as an inevitable outcome of the rural revolution because of the wavering nature of the middle peasant majority, and which others believed derived from central policy. As a result the Moscow party organization refused to recant at the third plenum of its organization in late March.[40] Moscow was therefore targeted for attack.

Stalin selected Moscow, along with the Central Black Earth Region and several non-Russian areas, for criticism in his "Answer to the Collective Farmer Comrades" (3 April).[41] This led to Bauman's removal from his post as regional party secretary, although not his disgrace, as he retained his membership in the Central Committee and his candidate membership in the Politburo. Bauman was replaced by Kaganovich, who proceeded to carry out a purge of the Moscow organization. On Kaganovich's initiative 153 senior officials from the *okrug* and district levels of the party were fired, and 74 others were transferred.[42] The attack on Moscow was concluded at the Sixteenth Party Congress, at which Moscow was targeted for some of the heaviest criticism to be directed toward a region in the RSFSR for committing excesses.[43]

The Moscow party organization served as an example. It was only in April—that is, at the time of the crackdown in the Moscow party organization and of the second central directive (the letter of 2 April) calling for the punishment of those guilty of excesses—that the other regional party organizations began to "admit" their mistakes and to initiate a spring-cleaning of their organizations.[44] This was the first stage in the attempt to gain control of the situation in the countryside. Condemnation and punishment, however, were not enough to remedy the volatile situation in the villages.

Along with its attempts to rein in the cadres, the center made an effort to placate the peasantry. The mass exile of kulaks was temporarily halted at the end of March.[45] A new charter for the artel collective farm was published and a series of privileges (i.e., tax concessions and credit) for collective farmers were announced.[46] Along with these concessions, commissions were established to review complaints from peasants who had been unjustly dekulakized.[47] These measures had the effect of reinforcing the positive image of Stalin and the Central Committee which had held sway from early March, but they did little to bolster the organs of the proletarian dictatorship in the countryside. With the cadres discredited, it was necessary for the center to complement its good image with a practical base. Local authority had to be rebuilt.

The Struggle Against Excesses

The 25,000ers played a large part in the center's attempt to rebuild local authority. Simultaneously with its attack on rural cadres, the center began to bolster the position of the 25,000ers. The 25,000ers were called upon to correct the mistakes committed in collectivization.[48] They were also called upon to serve as the eyes and ears of the center in observing the activities of local organs and in reporting policy violations.[49] Further, while rural cadres were being subjected to daily press attacks, the 25,000ers were praised for their discipline, restraint, and "class-conscious" approach to work. It was repeatedly emphasized that those 25,000ers who had committed excesses were exceptions.[50] It was claimed that the 25,000ers were the main force in the struggle against excesses; they had signaled the center about local policy violations and, it was said, collective farms with 25,000ers had lower rates of exodus.[51] Finally, the center let loose a flood of orders with instructions to rural officials to secure the 25,000ers in their posts, to improve their material conditions, and to cease the criminal bureaucratic treatment of the workers.[52]

The center's reliance on the 25,000ers was an integral part of its attempts to rein in the rural cadres and to gain control of policy implementation. The 25,000ers were to represent Moscow, and, with their ascribed proletarian virtue of discipline and loyalty, they were to bring consciousness to the spontaneity of rural affairs—that is, they were to take part in introducing order and a semblance of administrative efficiency into local Soviet power. This is not to say, however, that all 25,000ers behaved according to their official image: Some responded to the March decisions in ways hardly distinguishable from other rural cadres. Image and reality did not always go hand in hand.

There were 25,000ers who did not welcome the March decisions. Unlike the reactions of other rural cadres, their reaction did not, for the most part, derive from resentment toward the scapegoating, for the 25,000ers were not scapegoated; quite the contrary, they benefited from the decisions. Workers who believed that there was any "dizzyness"—whether from above or from below—simply joined the ranks of the deserters, who were relatively few at this point. Some workers did, however, object to the effects which the March decisions had on collective farm organization. These objections were rather mild and made only by workers who were already collective farm managers at this time. When his collective farm disintegrated in March, one 25,000er explained the problem as follows:

The article of com[rade] Stalin played a big role in this [exodus]; here it must be said that the local organs were completely unprepared for this as a result of which the kulak "agitprop" managed to use it [the article] significantly better than we . . . it seems to me that it should have been written earlier so that it could have served as a clear charter for the organization of collective farms . . . [53]

Other 25,000ers complained that their farms had fallen apart. One worker said that "with the appearance of Stalin's article, everyone began to demand the dissolution of the collective farm . . . at the meeting, I said: 'Who wants to leave?' That evening almost everyone submitted declarations [to leave], only the [farm's] charter and I remained in the collective farm . . . "[54] Another worker had a similar experience and wrote the Central Committee: "I was appointed chairman of a collective farm, but now I am no longer chairman because the collective farm fell apart and I am a chairman without a collective farm."[55]

A much more serious objection was raised by those 25,000ers who considered the March decisions a retreat, a compromise with the class enemy, or simply practical foolishness. The Moscow 25,000er V. M. Murchenko was disturbed by Stalin's article. He wrote to his trade union to say that he believed that it was correct to organize collective farms by force. According to Murchenko, afterwards the peasants would realize that it had been for their own good.[56] Other 25,000ers attempted to prevent an exodus from their farms by forcibly holding the peasants to their collective farm membership agreements. Following the appearance of Stalin's article the 25,000er Cherednichenko returned livestock only to those collective farmers whom he deemed "not conscious." He refused to let anyone else quit the farm. This led to a seizure of the stables and granary by the collective farm women. They demanded the return of their animals and seed while the men stood silently, some with pitchfork in hand. A riot ensued. Cherednichenko was chased out of the village and OGPU forces were called in to suppress the riot. The peasants later claimed that they were "not against Soviet power, but only against the commissar-*peregibshchik*" (see Glossary). Cherednichenko was transferred.[57] This was the plight of other 25,000ers, who, regardless of manifestations of dizzyness, were generally retained in the collective farm system. A decree of 8 March 1930 ordered the transfer to another collective farm or different work of those 25,000ers whose farms had collapsed.[58] This is not surprising in light of the central perceptions both of the "steadfast" 25,000ers and of their role as much-needed cadres to represent the interests of the center in the countryside.

Although some 25,000ers objected to the March decisions, it was in the interests of most to welcome them, and, in fact, it appears that this was most often the case. Even before the March turnabout many workers had begun to write letters with news of the excesses to their factory committees, union organizations, and party cells and to the Central Committee and Kolkhoztsentr. According to a Soviet secondary source, 25,000ers in Khoperskii *Okrug*, Lower Volga, "bombed" their factory committee at Serp i Molot (in Moscow) with letters describing the excesses and violations in dekulakization. The 25,000er M. I. Ivanov, working in the Penza area, wrote to the newspaper *Rabochaia gazeta* in February 1930 of his doubts about the actions of local authorities. He wrote that middle peasants had been dekulakized, but that he was powerless to struggle against these excesses, given the tenuousness of his own position.[59]

The Moscow AMO worker Baryshev, who worked in Novo-Annenskii District, Lower Volga, wrote to E. M. Iaroslavskii at the Central Control Commission, requesting directions on "how to retreat." When he arrived on the collective farm, he saw that conditions were not good. Many middle peasants and even poor peasants had been dekulakized, a *kommuna* had been set up, and the mood of the local population was not encouraging. At a meeting of the district party committee he suggested that some of the livestock be returned to the peasants. Under the influence of a representative of the *okrug* party committee, the district committee rejected his suggestion. He wrote to Iaroslavskii to find out how the retreat should be carried out given the resistance of the party organs.[60] Elsewhere the 25,000ers confronted similar situations, and it was not unusual for a 25,000er to take the initiative in forcing through a discussion of Stalin's article at a party or collective farm meeting.[61]

In Central Asia the Moscow 25,000er Inzhevatkin repeatedly wrote to his factory committee and others about the excesses. Ignorant of the local language, Inzhevatkin was helpless. He reported that, owing to the indiscriminate excesses in collectivization, the local situation was extremely dangerous. On discovering that the peasants were arming, he went to the OGPU for aid, and the militia sent him fifteen people. He returned to find that a revolt had erupted on the machine tractor station, and attempts had been made to liberate the arrested kulaks. Several activists were murdered. Several days following this incident, speakers were attacked at celebrations in honor of International Women's Day in a series of districts. On the day after the festivities a crowd of two hundred demanded to be released from the neighboring collective farm. The local activists were forced to flee into a nearby hut. The crowd surrounded the hut and demanded six 25,000ers as hostages. The besieged activists refused, and shouts of "kill the communists," "down with Soviet power," and "down with the collective farm" ensued. Finally the activists agreed to grant a part of the crowd's requests, and with this agreement, strangely enough, the crowd left peacefully, giving the activists just enough time to call in outside aid to suppress the revolt. Inzhevatkin was powerless to do anything but write letters to his factory, his comrades, and his wife about the chaos of the situation. Shortly after writing a letter to his wife indicating that things had improved but that earlier he had expected to be murdered at any time, Inzhevatkin was attacked and killed by a band of thirty *basmachi* on 12 May 1930.[62]

Other 25,000ers were in a better position to fight against the excesses. A Siberian inspection brigade reported that there were lower rates of exodus from collective farms with 25,000ers.[63] The Leningrad 25,000er Spiridonov reported from Siberia that he and his fellow Leningraders "have stood firm before the lower organizations . . . in order that the issue of the *kommuna* be removed . . . the peasants are not yet ready."[64] The 25,000er Naumov, assigned to the large collective farm Interntrud in Ershovskii District, Lower Volga, fought against the excesses of the local cadres by forming an alliance with disgruntled peasants. When he arrived on the farm, the collective farmers approached him to solicit his aid against the local authorities. Naumov, who became the head of a collective farm sector, soon discovered that the farm was wracked by constant bickering and that nepotism was entrenched in the workings of the administration. The collective farmers told him that the party members had taken dekulakized property for themselves, that the *sel'sovet* chairman had appointed himself to his position, and that, in general, all of the activists were "squabblers and drunkards" who accused everyone of being a *podkulachnik*. When Naumov attempted to intercede on behalf of the peasants, he encountered the "persecution" of the party cell, which initiated a wall newspaper campaign against him and attempted to have him fired. The collective farmers threatened to riot if Naumov left. The party cell secretary, sensing trouble, decided to call in an investigative commission, which he had assumed would quickly side with the powers that be. The peasants, however, came to the commission meeting en masse to support Naumov and denounce the local cadres. Following the meeting part of the local party organization quickly skipped town and the rest were shortly removed by decisions of the *okrug* party committee secretary and the regional party control commission. Naumov's experience in the struggle against excesses and the mutually advantageous alliance with rank-and-file collective farmers were not uncommon among 25,000ers.[65]

The majority of 25,000ers held strong in their commitment to the center during the winter campaign and subsequent retreat. Before beginning their work the 25,000ers, unlike most, had been warned about excesses both by Iakovlev, the Commissar of Agriculture, and in their preparatory courses. They had been warned against using force in collectivization and had been told that only the artel was acceptable in the organization of collective farms; they were not to force through the organization of *kommuna*s and were not to socialize anything but general arable land and marketable and draft animals.[66] Therefore, the 25,000ers entered work with a better idea than most other cadres of what was and what was not acceptable to Moscow. That the workers were, indeed, more responsive to the center's dictates than were most rural cadres and that they demonstrated responsibility to the Central Committee and not to some Bolshevik god of class war is apparent in the frequent use of 25,000ers as troubleshooters to save disintegrating collective farms, to correct excesses, and to explain the center's March decisions to collective and individual farmers.[67] Moreover, the workers could only gain by aligning themselves with central policy in their struggle to gain authority in their new posts. The center was to continue to rely on the 25,000ers to represent its interests throughout their stay; they were to represent the center against the various extremes manifested in the unwieldy rural apparatus.

Therefore, the center gave the 25,000ers its unconditional support in the offensive against the cadres of collectivization. Such support was predicated both on the belief that the 25,000ers did indeed fit the ideal image drawn of them in the press and that they would adhere to the party line in the socialist reconstruction of the countryside. Given these assumptions, the 25,000ers' first task was to help to rebuild local authority. It was their job to step into the maelstrom of Bolshevik fortress storming and to pick up the pieces strewn about by the warriors of the winter campaign. First, however, the 25,000ers had to gain a foothold in the rural power structure and in order to do this, they would be forced to enter into a power struggle with the cadres of collectivization.

The Stiff Wall of Bureaucratism

The 25,000ers launched their offensive on rural officialdom in the aftermath of the March decisions. This was to be the beginning of a revolutionary transformation of the rural apparatus. The deadweight of the old administrative order in the countryside was to be uprooted, and new, "progressive" social forces were to be promoted into the administration in its stead. With the benefit of hindsight this revolutionary transformation could be viewed as simply one more stage in the permanent purge of rural officialdom, which had begun in the late 1920s and was continuing in varying degrees throughout the Stalin years. It was, however, much more than a simple administrative measure designed to reorder the rural apparatus. This revolution was an integral part of the First Five-Year Plan revolution. It consisted of the attempt to do away forever with the old administrative flotsam of years past and to create in its stead an administrative apparatus staffed by the state's new social constituency in the countryside. The ethos and language of this revolution in the countryside were very similar to that which transpired simultaneously in the urban centers; the actual process and results were rather different. It was the 25,000ers who were expected to lead this revolution.

The 25,000ers' initial confrontation with rural officialdom proved that the reconstruction of the apparatus would be no simple task. Before they could reconstruct, purge, and transform, they first had to establish a niche for themselves in the rural order by consolidating their positions, whether in the district-level administration, the *sel'sovets*, the collective farms, or some combination of offices. This in itself proved to be a major undertaking. For the first months of their stay in the countryside, the 25,000ers were forced to engage in a struggle for power.

Upon arrival in the countryside, the 25,000ers encountered a "stiff wall of bureaucracy," the press loudly proclaimed. The workers were subjected to endless transfers, incorrect job assignments, and unemployment during the first months of their campaign. They quickly learned that officials on the district level had no time for them and that officials on the village level wanted no part of them. The workers were left to fend for themselves. Quite apart from questions of power, the impact which this had on the 25,000ers often began in the material realm.

In many cases the workers' first struggles with local cadres began over housing. Given the housing shortages in the villages, not to mention shortages of building materials, this was a real problem. Workers were frequently forced to seek accommodations with local collective farmers, to pay high rents, or even to sleep in fields and barns. The 25,000er Shishkarev sought the aid of local officials in finding housing and was told: "We are not your nanny—look for yourself." The 25,000er G. I. Bocharov spent his first two months living wherever he was offered a space for the night before he finally found a two-meter room which he secured for a fifteen-ruble monthly rent.[68]

Local officials frequently failed to pay the workers and blocked their access to village cooperative stores. According to one 25,000er, all of the workers' requests to local organs and the district party about provisioning "fell on deaf ears."[69] In some areas the workers were faced with abject poverty. A group of 25,000ers in the Western Region addressed the following letter, dated February 1930, to the *okrug* party committee:

> We workers have been sent to the Western Region . . . to work in the collective farms. But our conditions of life do not allow us to work as we should. They put us on collective farms which have only been established for a month or less. They sent us to leading work on collective farms where there

were supposed to be funds and said you will be paid from the collective farm funds. But this didn't happen. They put most of us 16 people in such conditions that we beg for help . . . Those of us arriving at small collective farms are given neither money nor food, we are received worse than beggars, [there is] no housing . . .

In view of all these conditions, work is not progressing. We live and we do not know what will be next, how we will eat . . .

The local organizations take a mean attitude to this and do not themselves know how we will live, nor do they take any measures.

Under such conditions of life . . . it is impossible to work and there is only one way out. To work any more is impossible and to live in such conditions is impossible. We must escape home and then see.

We ask the *okrug* party committee to give us an answer and to tell us a way out.[70]

These types of conditions were responsible for the flight of 25,000ers among the first wave of deserters.

Hostile officials who were unsuccessful in starving workers out often made use of more direct methods, of which the most frequently employed tactic was repeated transfer. Other common practices were assignment of workers to menial tasks or outright refusal to assign a worker at all. In one case a village official rid his collective farm of a 25,000er by ordering the worker to pay an entry fee to join the farm; the worker had no money and was forced to return to his factory. In non-Russian areas local officials refused to provide Russian-speaking 25,000ers with interpreters, or they provided interpreters who intentionally misinterpreted the workers' speeches.[71]

Local officials complained that the 25,000ers were simply in the way. Officials most often lamented the uselessness of the campaign, complaining that the workers knew nothing of agricultural or local conditions. The 25,000er Kukushkin was told: "What do you understand about the work of a collective farm? You workers don't know about peasant life." When the 25,000er Kozlov attempted to complain about policy matters, he was told: "Your business is to keep silent. You know only the factory and you don't know agriculture." Elsewhere officials taunted the workers: "Here come the masters, let's see how they will work" and "And what—are we worse than the Leningraders?"[72] One 25,000er wrote:

Everyone says that such an attitude from the side of the district VKP (b) committee secretary, respected comrade Tokarev, is absolutely unacceptable. Relations are not comradely, but bureaucratic. You go to him for some sort of advice and he gives you none . . . In other words, to put it briefly, we here do not see those . . . [trade union] decrees where it is stated that a good comradely atmosphere must be created for the workers.[73]

The most common attitude of officials was concisely articulated by a district soviet executive official who told the 25,000ers: "Go to the devil. We do not need you. Go back to the city."[74]

In many cases, hostility toward the 25,000ers was not unfounded. Most workers were ignorant of agriculture. Moreover, the workers were often an administrative and financial burden on the districts and new collective farms. This was especially true for small farms, which simply did not have any cash for wage payments and could barely afford to pay the workers in kind before the harvest was in. However, the main source of the conflict between officials and 25,000ers revolved around the issue of power. The 25,000ers were a threat to the authority of rural officials.

Most 25,000ers entered the countryside confident of their superiority as Soviet workers. They were ready to take over the helm of the rural order from cadres whom they perceived as socially and politically inferior. A Moscow 25,000er, assigned to the Central Black Earth Region, loudly proclaimed, " . . . we will transform the soviets into real organs of dictatorship." The 25,000er Khromov stated, "It is necessary to act decisively . . . to reelect the *sel' sovets*, to strengthen the [party] cells . . . This is shock work."[75]

The 25,000ers frequently stated their intentions of introducing the skills of "criticism and self-criticism"—traditional party purge niceties—into rural administration. Rural officials objected to the use of these skills, viewing the 25,000ers not as self-critical Bolsheviks, but as careerists anxious to launch intrigues against them.[76] One 25,000er was told in response to his criticism: "If you don't like our rules, go back to where you came from." The 25,000er Kudriavtsev wrote: "There are 25 of us Leningraders in Kur'inskii District [Siberia]. They consider us all opportunists because we ruthlessly criticize individual good-for-nothings in the district organs who fear 'critics like fire.' "[77] Many officials did indeed fear the 25,000ers and their criticism, seeing the workers as rivals in a struggle for power. As one 25,000er wrote:

They met us . . . disrespectfully. It appears that the local officials are afraid of us.

The local officials do not like criticism, they do not like it when they are told about their mistakes. They think that only they have the right to criticize. We bring from the enterprises . . . a consciousness of the great importance of self-criticism. It is our usual weapon.[78]

In some areas, the officials so feared the workers that the 25,000ers were warned not to say that they were 25,000ers.[79] A 25,000er from the Krasnoe

Sormovo factory assigned to work in Belorussia confronted the following situation:

> When I arrived, they suggested that I work in the administration of the dairy-livestock cooperative union as a deputy chairman. I was received poorly. The chairman . . . comrade Stashkevich, gave me no practical help. He did not care about familiarizing me better with the work. In addition, he did not trust me: he gave orders to the employees not to give me papers to sign while he was away.

> They interfere with my work and are trying to fire me. After long travails, I was sent in a brigade to a district to implement collectivization. The chairman of the district soviet executive committee, com[rade] Adamchuk, not only did not help me in my work, but did not even want to talk to me knowing that I am a 25,000er . . .[80]

The mistrust of the officials was not unjustified. The 25,000ers entered the countryside as representatives of Moscow, the Central Committee, and the working class. They had de facto plenipotentiary powers in many cases; in power struggles with local and district officials they were assured the support of regional and central authorities in the long term. The arrival of the workers coincided with the February reelections of the collective farm administrative boards, the extraordinary elections of *sel'sovets*, and the ongoing purge of the party. These circumstances provided the 25,000ers with a legal, institutional weapon against their rivals if their "usual weapon" of criticism was not sufficient. Of course, not all 25,000ers were in a position to oust their rivals immediately. Those who were able to do this were generally workers who managed to form alliances with disgruntled collective farmers, or workers who were assigned to the same areas as other 25,000ers, allowing them to act in concert. Most 25,000ers, however, were forced to wait until the March decisions to make effective use of their "usual weapon" and the powers granted them by the center.

Following the March decisions rural officials were subjected not only to the onslaught of criticism from the center but also had to fend off the attacks of the 25,000ers who viewed their role as aiding the center to correct the mistakes of the locals. Rural cadres displayed no greater discipline in responding to the proletarian plenipotentiaries than to the center's seemingly sudden policy reversal. They looked upon the 25,000ers as upstarts and green recruits. Village officials objected to the workers' aims to come and behave like commissars after they—the village officials—had had to attempt to keep order during the chaotic winter months and had ended up by discrediting themselves. District officials tended to see the workers as "panic-mongers" or as urban commissars arriving only to hand out orders and demagogic proclamations.[81] They all feared the wave of purges which had followed in the wake of Stalin's article, and the workers saw themselves as leaders in this newest struggle. The officials whom the 25,000ers confronted were, after all, the cadres of collectivization, the cadres who, for better or worse, enthusiastically or under duress, had carried out the winter campaign. Moreover, this was not their first campaign. Their rough and ready ways, their tendency to use "administrative measures" were predicated upon their earlier, formative, experience in the grain-requisitioning campaigns. Whether so-called revolutionary maximalists and left *peregibshchik*s (see Glossary) or bureaucrats and right deviationists, their actions and reactions were based on what they had learned about the harsh realities of governing the countryside. They had reached some point of understanding of those realities and were not about to declare their guilt willingly and hand over power to the heroic neophytes from Putilov, AMO, and Serp i Molot.

The 25,000ers, on the other hand, perceived their tasks with the eyes of factory workers. At least initially, their view was closer to that of Moscow than to that of rural officials and rural realities. They viewed rural officials as crude, undisciplined, often corrupt, and, in not a few cases, as agents or representatives of socially dangerous class aliens. Many workers were appalled by the behavior of rural cadres and the way they handled the local population. In the eyes of some workers such crude methods were alien to the revolution. The 25,000ers, moreover, were often the direct targets of the officials' crude ways. The 25,000er Kovaleva was slapped in public by a village official; the local authorities looked the other way at what was probably a not uncommon occurrence. Many 25,000ers stressed the uncomradely, bureaucratic, or crude relations which the officials directed toward them. Others stressed the officials' low cultural level. The 25,000er Chudakov complained that he had to deal with officials who knew nothing of the party line. In other cases workers reported that officials were backward or drunkards.[82] Most often, however, uncooperative or hostile officials were described according to the political trends of the times either as right deviationists or left *peregibshchik*s, as kulaks or *podkulachniki*, and so on.

In response to the intrusion of the 25,000ers, especially after the March decisions, rural officialdom launched a short counteroffensive against the workers which paralleled its attempt to resist the March retreat and which brought down upon it the wrath of the center. The counteroffensive ended, for the most part, in the summer of 1930, although rural officials would, to varying degrees, continue to make life difficult for the workers throughout their stay. Like the 25,000ers, rural cadres made good use of the popular political epithets of the day, labeling workers right deviationists or left *peregibshchik*s. The 25,000er Strushko protested the grain-requisition quota levied on his farm, and for this the district party expelled him from the party and sent him to court. The 25,000er Solov'ev also protested an unfair levy and was accused of right deviationism, expelled from the party, and fired.[83] Workers who attempted to convene a local meeting with other 25,000ers to discuss their problems were condemned as a *gruppirovka* (grouping) within the party and disciplined accordingly.[84] In many areas 25,000ers were transferred or expelled from the party by district party committees without the permission of the regional party committee. According to one Soviet historian the reason for this treatment was often the protests lodged by 25,000ers against local officials for the excesses of the winter campaign.[85] In the Crimea up to 30 percent of the 25,000ers were arrested or tried in court.[86] Expulsions, firings, arrests, and transfers were a common recourse of officials during the counteroffensive and, to a lesser extent, afterwards.[87]

The most common recourse of rural officials were more subtle forms of persecution. Workers were denied access to local cooperative stores or forced to live several miles away from their place of work, necessitating nighttime journeys fraught with the danger of ambush.[88] There were also cases of 25,000ers who were denied the right to participate in local and district party meetings. The 25,000er Alferova asked the local comrades repeatedly for the date of the next party meeting; all the party members refused to tell her until the day following the meeting when they asked her: "Why weren't you there?"[89] Local authorities, who either intercepted the mail or routinely censored it, prevented several workers from sending letters to higher party organs or their unions and factory committees.[90] In Northern Osetiia in the North Caucasus, one collective farm conducted all its correspondence and official work in the Osetian language to block 25,000ers from participation. The regional party committee was forced to intervene with a ruling that 25,000ers must be informed of at least the substance of all important matters.[91] Elsewhere, officials resorted to spreading rumors about the workers by word of mouth or in wall newspapers accusing them of drunkenness, hooliganism, or some other transgression.[92]

The persecution of 25,000ers by local and district officials often led to serious consequences. Many workers wrote to higher party organs, their union or factories, or party control commissions, threatening to quit if support against officials was not forthcoming. Some workers simply left of their own volition. There were also reports of workers who chose suicide as a way out. Of the seven known cases of suicide, five were in some way connected to poor relations with officials.[93] The 25,000er Krotov wrote a letter to the Central Committee disclosing the excesses of the district committee. The district sought its revenge by assigning Krotov to work as a rank-and-file collective farmer in the fields. When Krotov asked for a transfer, the district committee accused him of "all sorts of crimes" and threatened him with a bad reference (*kharakteristika*) if he left. This led Krotov to attempt (unsuccessfully) suicide. As a result of his suicide attempt, Krotov was condemned for anti-*partiinost'* (roughly, behavior contrary to that expected of a Communist) and was issued a party reprimand. The real responsibility for the suicide attempt, however, was laid at the door of the district and collective farm officials, who were dealt with by the *okrug* party committee. The chairmen of the district soviet executive committee and the collective farm, along with the secretary of the collective farm party cell, were expelled from the party and brought to court, while the secretary of the district party received a reprimand.[94] The lesson derived from the suicides and attempted suicides was that local officials were behaving in a "criminal" fashion toward 25,000ers.

The center became increasingly aware of this situation following the March decisions. The fear was voiced that if the problems of the 25,000ers continued, the center would be in peril of losing the workers in mass desertions. In May there began an avalanche of central condemnation and reprimands directed at rural officials accused of responsibility for the plight of the 25,000ers.[95] Although not all of the 25,000ers' problems were due to the "stiff wall of bureaucratism" erected by rural officialdom, rural officials were forced to take the blame for all of them. Between May and August 1930 as many as twelve different decrees and directives were issued concerning the problems of the 25,000ers, and having special reference to the responsibility of rural officials.[96] The Workers' and Peasants' Inspectorate and the Central Committee's Department of Agitation and Mass Campaigns were called upon to investigate the conditions of the 25,000ers.[97] Simultaneously with the inspection tours, short course conferences of 25,000ers were convened in many areas on the district or *okrug* level to give the workers a chance to voice their complaints, exchange information, and receive positive affirmation for their endeavors.[98] The final form which the center's measures assumed consisted of a barrage of reprimands and sterner penalties directed against rural officials and a further increase in the already dense network of controls set up to oversee the life and work of the 25,000ers.

The problems which the 25,000ers faced were alleviated somewhat after the midsummer of 1930 but never completely overcome. The intervention of central and regional authorities, however, did serve to give most workers that necessary measure of leverage against their rivals, which, along with the March offensive on cadres, allowed the workers to begin to move into positions of authority. With the center's support the 25,000ers found that they could enter the struggle for power in earnest.

The Struggle for Power

The 25,000ers came to power in the wake of the March retreat. As local and district officials were purged, demoted, or fired for their part in the excesses, the 25,000ers, who were often actively involved in punishing the transgressors, became the beneficiaries of this offensive against the cadres of collectivization. For those workers who solidified their position at this time, the path was relatively easy. For other 25,000ers, the struggle had just begun, and in some cases would continue well beyond the summer of 1930. In these cases the struggle would be eased by the center's *unconditional* support, the punishment of those who persecuted 25,000ers, and the intervention of central and regional authorities into local affairs in order to decide power struggles in favor of the 25,000ers. In addition, the workers' trade unions and the press would act as ombudsmen, intervening arbitrarily into the affairs of other institutions to aid 25,000ers in need.

Arrests, dismissals, and party expulsions of rural officials assumed epidemic proportions throughout the 1930s and particularly during the years of collectivization. The 25,000ers were not exempt from this wave of mass repression. However, the repression directed against 25,000ers was distinguished by two important factors. First, it was an integral part of the power struggle with local officials and therefore just another tactic used by officials to attempt to be rid of 25,000ers. Second, the 25,000ers could depend upon the support of the center in seeking justice, for although the center did sometimes overturn cases against other rural officials, it never did so with the same consistency exerted in cases against 25,000ers. In the Central Black Earth Region, for example, the regional party control commission reversed fifteen of sixteen party expulsions and confirmed only nineteen of seventy party reprimands aimed at 25,000ers by district party committees. In addition, a decree issued by the presidium of the Central Black Earth regional party control commission and the Workers' and Peasants' Inspectorate claimed that the majority of court cases involving 25,000ers were unfounded or based on very minor offenses.[99] In Western Siberia the regional courts overturned one third of all cases against 25,000ers, while in the Middle Volga over one half of all cases were dismissed.[100] Rural officials soon found that it was no easy task to get rid of a 25,000er by way of party tribunal or civil court.

For example, the 25,000er V. G. Omel'ianenko, who was the chairman of the collective farm Smychka in the Lower Volga, wrote to the central committee of the chemical-industry-workers' trade union for help. Writing in preliminary detention, Omel'ianenko said that he had been accused of sabotage and mismanagement, adding that "this doesn't quite smell proletarian." The district party committee had accused him of falsifying the number of members on his farm in order to lower the grain-requisitioning quota. He denied this and claimed that the collective farmers even supported him:

> The people are going to protest—this is the first time they have defended me—but they see how I work day and night next to them—they don't understand what happened and I will be calm only when requisitioning is over and we can distribute the harvest—then our revenues will be clear.

> If I didn't have a family, I would have run off or the devil knows what I would have done, but besides this I am a communist and must stand firm before all difficulties.

The union intervened in this case with protests to Kolkhoztsentr, the Lower Volga regional party committee, and the procurator.[101]

The case of Kashtel'ianov was similar to that of Omel'ianenko, although it is not at all clear (nor was it clear to his trade union) precisely why this worker was in trouble. It does appear, however, that Kashtel'ianov was probably guilty of excesses of some kind in the collectivization campaign. He wrote to the central committee of the leather workers' trade union:

> I should write much more, but there is no time and no energy . . . I have worked 6–7 months in the countryside. I already know the difficulties of such work, the responsibilities and that risk which puts a strain on all work. However, this is not what I am considering. Two sudden attempts on my life from kulaks, the progressive development of my illness and other things which forced other comrades to flee from the difficulties will not stop me, on the contrary—my soul races there where there are difficulties and where I can be of most use.

After laying it on a bit thick, Kashtel'ianov finally got to the main point. He wrote: "For all this . . . I was expelled from the party and sent to court . . . Help me." He ended his letter in the same tone as he had begun it:

> I am an honorable worker, [I] went to work with an open mind. I, like other comrades, made political mistakes; I admit this. But I am not a criminal. I am a victim of the class struggle, I was slandered. I am a victim of the delusions of the district officials who don't want to admit their own mistakes but thrust them on me . . . I am desperate . . . help, help me! . . . The circle is narrowing. There is no support . . . children, I have children.

He was a worker, a Communist, a father, and even a victim of the class struggle. These factors, in addition to his status as a 25,000er, set the trade union into action. It quickly dispatched letters to the Central Control Commission requesting intervention and assurance that the rural party organs would be "attentive" in this case and to Kashtel'ianov's factory committee requesting a copy of his reference and the factory committee's intervention into his case.[102] It seems clear from this case that central organizations, which were willing and able to aid 25,000ers, did so with little regard to the nature of the conflict or the actual source of guilt.

A 25,000er had only to appeal to a regional or central party or party control commission organ (and sometimes *okrug-* and district-level organs, as well) in order to best a local opponent, purge him and his supporters, and take over the reins of control. When the 25,000er P. I. Meizinger complained of the hostility and excesses of the local party in the area where he worked in the Lower Volga, the regional party committee intervened and carried out a purge of Meizinger's enemies in the district party committee.[103] In another case the 25,000er Ivan Okunev was reported to have argued with the local party cell. He complained, why, on the one hand, did they criticize him when, on the other hand, they gave him absolutely no help in his work. To this, the party cell secretary had replied that workers need no aid, that power is in their hands, and that the workers hold all the cards anyway. Not appreciating the secretary's wit, the 25,000er called him a fool and, as a consequence, the witty secretary expelled Okunev (illegally) from the party. Okunev, a humorless sort, quickly complained to higher party authorities, and within a short time he replaced the party secretary, who, in turn, was expelled (legally) from the party.[104]

The most common type of conflict involving the intervention of higher authorities took place between newly arrived workers and the collective farm chairmen with whom they were expected to work or whom they were expected to replace. Sometimes the conflicts were over power, at other times, policy issues. There were many reports of conflicts between arriving 25,000ers and former collective chairmen.[105] More often than not, however, the reports were of conflicts between 25,000ers and currently presiding chairmen. The 25,000er Belkin was appointed to serve as deputy chairman of a collective farm under the direction of the experienced chairman, Comrade Sytov. Sytov ran a model farm but was very unpopular among the collective farmers. According to Belkin, Sytov managed the farm as if it were his own personal estate and was fond of saying, "Kolkhoz—eto ia!" ("The collective farm—c'est moi!"). Belkin, on the other hand, soon won popularity among the peasants and, with this, the animosity of Sytov. Fearful of Belkin's possible encroachment on his power, Sytov fired the 25,000er. The district party control commission quickly intervened, reinstated Belkin, and disciplined Sytov, the collective farm Sun King.[106]

The 25,000ers Shatilov and Ozizov also came into conflict with their chairmen. Shatilov arrived ready to purge the farm when the chairman objected, arguing that the farm could not afford the loss of any laborers. Shatilov went over the chairman's head to the district party committee, which, to Shatilov's chagrin, agreed with the chairman. Following this, Shatilov appealed to the *okrug* party committee, which not only supported Shatilov, but fired the chairman and appointed Shatilov in his stead. Ozizov came into conflict with his chairman when the latter rejected the 25,000er's suggestion that a barn be built for the socialized livestock. Ozizov went to the district party committee, which supported him, aided him in the purge of the farm's administration, and disciplined the chairman.[107]

It is clear from the cases cited here that the support which the central and regional authorities gave the 25,000ers was often unconditional and without regard to actual circumstances. Whether this was due to the official image of the 25,000ers as model leaders, to a perception of the workers as *svoi* (one's own) proletarian forces, or to simple distrust of and disregard for existing officialdom, outside support allowed many 25,000ers a chance to purge rivals and build their own power base. Of course, in many cases the situation was not quite so clear-cut, and not a few 25,000ers failed to gain any real authority as circumstances in the countryside were often more chaotic than what has been depicted here. Nonetheless, the cloud of dust left in the trail of the winter collectivization campaign began to settle slowly throughout the summer of 1930, and by that time the majority of 25,000ers had established themselves on the collective farms and in the *sel'sovet*s and the rural party.

The Proletarianization of Rural Officialdom

The very presence of the 25,000ers meant that the center's call for the "proletarianization" of the rural apparatus was, for the first time in Soviet history, a possibility. The 25,000ers, moreover, were joined by some seven thousand city soviet delegates (mostly factory workers), who were recruited in February 1930 to work in the *sel'sovet*s, while in the meantime the bureaucracies of Kolkhoztsentr and the People's Commissariat of Agriculture were subjected to an administrative purge and intensive efforts to proletarianize their offices.[108] However, despite hopes that the campaign of the 25,000ers would be only the beginning of a general working-class movement to the countryside, there were no further exclusively working-class recruitments for permanent rural work of the dimensions of the campaign of the 25,000ers.

Nonetheless, the 25,000ers made their presence felt in the countryside. There was a 25,000er on one out of every five collective farms in the USSR as a whole and in approximately one out of every three farms in the major grain-producing regions (see table 5). Approximately one half (47 percent) of the growth experienced by the rural party between January and April of 1930 as it increased in numbers from 339,201 to 377,717 was due to the influx of the 25,000ers, some 18,000 of whom were Communists.[109] Communist 25,000ers were generally elected to become party cell secretaries on the collective farms and often were members of district and *okrug* party committees. On many collective farms there was no party cell until a 25,000er arrived.[110] The 25,000ers also accounted for some part of the personnel change in the district-level Kolkhoztsentr agencies.[111] Finally, many 25,000ers were elected to serve on *sel'sovets*, whose percentage of chairmen of working-class origin (not necessarily 25,000er) increased in 1930 from 2 to 12 percent.[112]

Although an important force in the proletarianization of rural officialdom, the impact of the 25,000ers themselves on the social physiognomy of the rural party and government was still slight. There remained only some twenty-seven thousand 25,000ers amidst a sea of rural offices numbering into the hundreds of thousands. The workers, however, were able to use their influence in two other important areas, which probably had more of a long-term impact than did the actual presence of the 25,000ers. These areas were the purges of the rural apparatus and the widespread recruitment of new forces to replace purged officials, and the attempt to build a new base of social and political support in the countryside.

It is difficult to measure statistically the role which the 25,000ers had in the dual process of purge and new recruitments which was used to transform the rural apparatus at this time. The picture presented here is somewhat impressionistic and dependent upon claims made by Soviet scholars and statements of individual 25,000ers. It is clear, however, that the 25,000ers were intended by the center to promote these processes. Editorials stressed the workers' importance in strengthening the rural party and *sel'sovets* and in creating new cadres from collective farmers.[113] Following the March decisions and especially the Sixteenth Party Congress, the main task of the 25,000ers was said more and more to be the promotion of collective farmers, especially middle peasants (whose social support as the most numerous group in the countryside was vital to the state) and shock workers, to collective farm administration, the party and Komsomol, and the *sel'sovets*. This was also the message most stressed in the repreparation courses through which many 25,000ers passed in summer 1930.[114]

The 25,000ers were expected "to change the face of all rural organs."[115] Indeed, they played a large role in the purge of the cadres of collectivization. This was, in some ways, a continuation of the purge which the party as a whole was subject to in 1929 and 1930 and which depleted the rural party of 15 percent of its membership. The purge, however, was only one part of the strategy used in attempting to transform the party. The other part was the extensive recruitment of new members. In the cities the Central Committee aimed at creating a party in which workers from the bench formed at least 50 percent of its composition; in the countryside the recruitment of poor peasants and migrant laborers was stressed.[116] The 25,000ers took part in party purges in 1930 and actively recruited new members to the party from among the local activists upon whom the workers depended while managing the collective farms.[117]

The 25,000ers were expected to influence the change in personnel in the collective farm administrative boards and *sel'sovets* in the same way. By the summer of 1930 78.6 percent of the 25,000ers had entered office on the farms, a fact which attests to the eventual successes which 25,000ers had in purging rivals and former administrators.[118] In addition, the 25,000ers were said to have been responsible for the training of many collective farm cadres of various skill levels either through the organization of production conferences, as was done in the factories at the time, or through the sending of proven collective farmers or their children to short courses and specialized schools.[119] And although the role of the 25,000ers should not be exaggerated here, in fact an entire revolution in rural education took place during the First Five-Year Plan period as several million peasants passed through various types of courses and schools.[120]

The 25,000ers' arrival also coincided with the unscheduled reelections of *sel'sovets* called for in January in order to purge those organs which had been accused of hindering socialist construction and of harboring class enemies. The 25,000ers participated in these elections or led somewhat arbitrary purges of *sel'sovets*. The 25,000ers had been told to strengthen the *sel'sovets*, not to find substitutes for them (either through plenipotentiary rule or shifting functions to the collective farms), and if a *sel'sovet* worked poorly, the workers were to reelect it or purge it, replacing the old officials with loyal cadres.[121]

It is difficult to determine the impact which the 25,000ers had on the early-1930 unscheduled elections despite the boasts of 25,000ers like Vagner, who claimed that he began work in three different districts by first getting rid "of all the rot from the local soviet apparatus."[122] There is some evidence for their role in the regular elections of the winter of 1930–31. At that time, Kolkhoztsentr called upon the 25,000ers to use their authority to influence the local population in the elections and to "unmask" aliens and right deviationists in the soviets.[123] Iu. S. Kukushkin, the leading Soviet historian of the *sel'sovets*, claims that at this time the overwhelming majority of 25,000ers were elected to *sel'sovets*. According to Kukushkin, the percentage of *sel'sovet* chairmen who were industrial workers increased after this election, especially in the major grain regions.[124]

The 25,000ers' role in the proletarianization of the rural apparatus through purge and recruitments was an extension of the social and political policies of the cultural revolution of the First Five-Year Plan in the cities. Purge and recruitment of working-class forces in the urban government apparatus, industry, and higher education had broad ramifications in the creation of a base of social support for the state in later years, as well as providing a response to the grievances and aspirations of workers who claimed that the role of the working class had been slighted during NEP.[125] The results which these policies had in the countryside were somewhat different.

Viewed within this larger context of First Five-Year Plan social and political aims as a whole, the 25,000ers' work in transforming rural officialdom fell far short of success. For almost every policy designed to aid in the building of a new social and political base in the countryside, there was a traditional, inherent counterforce to nullify its effect. In the cadre-deficient countryside, administrative purges only served to exacerbate the problem of personnel turnover which was a scourge in all offices and all skills throughout the 1930s. The mass training and promotion of peasants did, indeed, generally serve as an avenue of social mobility, but in the context of the culturally and technologically backward Soviet countryside, social mobility most often meant leaving the countryside for work or school in the cities. While older rural cadres—the class aliens, right deviationists, left *peregibshchik*s, and so on—appear to have been effectively purged, it is impossible to speak of the formation in their stead of any permanent class of rural officials to have arisen out of the transformation of this period. Rural officialdom was to remain in flux due to high turnover rates and an almost permanent purge throughout the 1930s.[126]

The 25,000ers were too small a force "to change the face of all rural organs" singlehandedly. They, themselves, were limited in this attempt by the constraints of backwardness. A countryside deficient in cadres meant that the 25,000ers were sometimes transferred from post to post to work as troubleshooters wherever the need was greatest. This limited their ability to settle into work and develop a real proficiency in what they did. Moreover, because trustworthy cadres were at such a premium in the countryside, many 25,000ers would be rapidly pushed up the ladder of the regional hierarchy through promotions.

Although in the long term, the offensive on rural officialdom and the attempt to build a new social base for the state encountered numerous obstacles, in the short term, the offensive yielded promising results for most 25,000ers. After many travails the workers managed to come out on top in the cadre struggle. The cadres of collectivization, who had jumped the tracks in the winter campaign, had been restrained or removed, and the 25,000ers had entered into office on the collective farms. Once in a position of authority, they used that authority to promote their supporters and to build a base of local support. At long last the 25,000ers had achieved a measure of stability. If their interaction with rural officials, their victories in the power struggle, and their part in bridling the cadres of collectivization were important objectives in the campaign, then so too were the ways in which the 25,000ers were to use their newfound authority in their everyday work: how they managed the collective farms, how they interacted with collective farmers, and how they worked as officials.

6

The 25,000ers at Work on the Collective Farms

Comrades, I am a worker from the Red Putilov Works in Leningrad. I have been sent to you, here, by our Communist Party and the working class to help you organize a collective farm and destroy the kulaks as our common blood-sucker. I won't say much. You must all unite together on a collective farm . . . Why must you join the collective farm? Because, well—because you just can't go on living as you are now!

> The 25,000er Davydov in Sholokhov's *Virgin Soil Upturned*

The chairman isn't just a property manager. He has to keep up with scientific advances, and he mustn't ever lose touch with the membership. But every little thing is a problem, a headache. Nails for the building work, and roofing, and shoes for the horses . . . You look at a chairman sometimes, and he isn't rightly a chairman at all . . . a supply agent is all he is. Running around day and night to all kinds of supply boards and offices, hunting for the things he needs, buying, begging, bartering—you could institute proceedings against him.

> VALENTIN OVECHKIN, *Collective Farm Sidelights*

The spring of 1930 has entered the annals of Soviet history as the "first spring": It was the first test of collectivized agriculture. It followed in the wake of the winter collectivization campaign and ushered in, at long last, the constructive phase of the socialist transformation of the countryside. Although built upon a foundation of havoc, devastation, and paper girders, the first spring was nevertheless viewed by the party as a victory for the new order in the countryside. The spring sowing produced a record harvest and thereby served in part to mask the profound structural faults of collectivized agriculture. While the unsteady foundation upon which the spring of 1930 was

152

based would not fail to exact a heavy toll in 1932–33 and later years, for the time being the first spring was celebrated as a Bolshevik triumph.

The first spring was based not only upon the unsteady foundation of the winter collectivization campaign, but also upon a foundation of constantly shifting experimentation. This was the formative period in the evolution of the collective farm system and was predicated upon a trial-and-error approach to building socialism in the countryside. It was in a very real sense a continuation of the disorder and confusion of winter now channeled onto a constructive path, but nonetheless still groping and fluid, owing to the center's failure to provide full clarity on issues of organization and administration within the collective farms. The center issued varied, frequent, and sometimes contradictory guidelines on organizational questions, while the new collective farm administrators, attempting to make sense of the center's signals, listened, learned, and improvised. The collective farms became experimental laboratories for the study and practical application of various approaches to collective farm organization. Many of the most basic features and problems of collectivized agriculture which persist to the present arose from the experimentation conducted in these early laboratories of rural socialist construction.

The reigning ethos pervading the experimentation on the collective farms in 1930 was that of the industrial utopia. The collective farm was compared to the factory, and the principles of management, organization of labor, and labor remuneration which were applied in the collective farms, particularly in the winter of 1929–30, were borrowed wholesale from the industrial enterprises. It was precisely this all-pervasive industrial ethos which was instrumental in giving rise to the basic organizational framework of the collective farm system. Yet although the basic framework remained in place for decades after its initial construction, the industrial ethos barely survived the first spring. It is perhaps for this reason that this short chapter in Soviet socialist construction and Bolshevik utopianism has largely passed unnoticed in the Western literature on collectivization. It is difficult, however, to understand the evolution of collectivized agriculture without some consideration of the guiding principles of its formative stage. Moreover, once this long-discarded chapter in collectivization is brought back to life, it becomes clear that collectivization was much more than simply a struggle for grain. Collectivization was many things to many people, but at least to some—including many 25,000ers—it was a revolution, an attempt to destroy forever the boundaries and age-old antagonisms which divided city and countryside, an attempt to root out, by force if necessary, what Marxists deemed to be the "idiocy of rural life."

In their capacity as collective farm chairmen and administrators, the 25,000ers were intended to serve in the vanguard of this revolution; they were the pioneers of the young collective farm movement. Throughout 1930 and 1931, they struggled to cope effectively with their new and demanding work. They focused their attention on creating productive collective farms and collective farmers, and their activities were shaped both by the many different directives emanating from the center and by their own past experience as factory workers. Perhaps the ultimate determinant of their activities, however, was the Russian peasant, and in order to transform the peasant into a collective farmer, it was necessary for the 25,000ers to introduce a revolution in the traditional, nonindustrial work habits of the village, a revolution not unlike that which occurs in all countries undergoing the early stages of industrialization. The difference in this case was that the peasant had not come to the factory, but the factory to the peasant. This served to alter significantly the balance of forces in the battle of modernity and tradition.

25,000ers and Collective Farmers

The relationship between the 25,000ers as collective farm leaders and peasants as collective farm members was a central factor in determining the success of the campaign of the 25,000ers. The 25,000ers were outsiders coming into isolated, closed peasant communities. Moreover, they had come to lead, and most peasants were not sure just what this entailed. The workers faced a difficult struggle and would have to prove themselves in order to be accepted in the villages. The success of the 25,000ers' endeavors in doing this depended on both the peasants' and the workers' attitudes.

The 25,000ers' entry into the countryside had been accompanied by fanfare in the city and rumors in the countryside. Rumors about collectivization then raged like wildfire through the countryside. At the same time there were tales of the return of the Whites and the landlords; the coming of anti-Christ, Polish pans, and the Chinese; and the arrival of commissars, Communists, and gendarmes. Some said that the women and children would be socialized; others talked about the government taking the women's hair for export or the stamping of foreheads for identification at the time of the Second Coming or the White victory. Hunger and famine were prophesized and many gloomily forecast apocalypse, the return of serfdom, or a more devastating sequel to War Communism.

News of the 25,000ers' coming set off a new round of rumors, but 25,000er-specific rumors were basically variations of the themes on which the collectivization rumors were based: apocalypse; the return of the old order;

War Communism; and broadly, the national issue (ranging from invasion to fears of Russification in non-Russian territories). The 25,000ers called the rumor mill the "kulak agitprop" (agitation and propaganda committee) and often claimed that it was more effective and efficient than the party's own agitprop work. The 25,000ers were called, at various times, the new landlords, the party's *svoi* (own) commissars, Soviet gendarmes, pans, or simply, Bolsheviks or Communists, neither of which was overly complimentary.[1] In national areas it was said that the 25,000ers were coming to Russify the local population.[2] These rumors made the rounds of the villages on the eve of the 25,000ers' arrival and, consequently, it was unlikely that many peasants would await the workers with bread and salt on the village square.

Once the 25,000ers actually confronted the peasants, rumors were likely to turn into complaints or grievances centering around the imposition of the new leader from the outside. In one village peasants complained, "They send workers to us and they guarantee their salaries from the enterprises, but why don't they send us to run production at the factories?"[3] Feelings like this were common. Many peasants felt that the working class was a privileged group in society and they resented its members coming to lead peasants in affairs of which they knew little or nothing. A collective farmer complained, "And are there no good managers [*khoziaiev*] among the peasants themselves? There are, but they are denied leadership and replaced by 25,000ers . . . "[4] On one collective farm the peasants asked the 25,000ers difficult technical questions at meetings to embarrass them, and the 25,000er Maiorov was mocked with the question; "What, did you come to teach us how to drink?"[5]

If on most collective farms the peasants were critical of the workers' agricultural inexperience, on other collective farms the peasants often either did not understand what the workers had come for or simply disliked workers, per se. Many collective farmers had never heard about the campaign of the 25,000ers. Putilov 25,000ers in one village were welcomed by puzzled peasants who placed a bottle of moonshine on the table for the workers and assumed that they had come to requisition grain.[6] When the 25,000er Bolichenko and his comrades arrived on a collective farm, the peasants asked, "What will these workers do here? Why did they come?"[7] Rumors surrounded the arrival of the 25,000er Ivan Safonov. People said that he was not really a worker. At a meeting of the collective farm the peasants demanded, "Show us your hands," to see if Ivan was really a factory worker.[8] The Putilov 25,000er A. S. Rybakov was sent to a cossack village. During his first day there an old cossack looked at him scornfully and said that in 1905 they, the cossacks, had used the knout (*nagaika*) on such as he. The cossack complained, "Here, you see, they sent us a mutineer from Putilov."[9] In national minority areas the arrival of ethnic Russian 25,000ers often stirred up national resentment, and throughout the country female 25,000ers met with distrust and hostility from all sides.[10]

The collective farmers had ample reasons for their resentments. The farms had to pay a part of the worker's salary, admit him to the cooperative store, and provide him with housing. Smaller collective farms found this a heavy burden to bear. If this were not trying enough, the collective farmers had to elect the 25,000ers to the administration of the collective farms. Although the 25,000ers were not supposed to be "appointed" but elected, in the few cases when 25,000ers were not elected, dissent was labeled "kulak" or "kulak-provoked," and in at least one case, a party district committee plenipotentiary intervened to safeguard the democratic process.[11]

Working in an atmosphere of distrust and resentment, the 25,000ers had all eyes fixed upon them. For this reason a worker had to be especially careful about his moral conduct and behavior. Transgressions were punished severely, for if a worker went against the accepted moral code of a village, he lost all authority in his attempts to administer a farm. In *Virgin Soil Upturned* Sholokhov gives a fictional version of a warning given to 25,000ers on the eve of their departure for the villages:

> The authority of the working class—the vanguard of the Revolution—must be maintained at the highest level in the villages. You must conduct yourselves, comrades, with the greatest care. I don't mean only in big things, even in the small matters of everyday life you must be on the look-out. In a village you can have a drink for a kopek that'll cost you a hundred political rubles for the gossip it causes.[12]

And there were 25,000ers who spent many hundreds of "political rubles." The 25,000er Gavrilova, chairwoman of a commune, was punished for bad conduct. On May Day she went into town and got so drunk that she had to be brought back to the village stretched across the back of a horse. On her return she was expected to open the commune's ceremonies celebrating the holiday. Precisely how she accomplished this was not indicated, but the peasants were impressed enough to remark that "in all these twelve years this is the first time we greeted the first of May this way."[13] The 25,000er Lomanov, who was sent back to his factory, got drunk systematically (i.e., rather often) and was seen walking naked in the streets.[14] Workers guilty of such transgressions had either to be removed or transferred, for such behavior understandably served to destroy a worker's credibility as a collective farm leader.

If a 25,000er survived the kulak agitprop, overcame the peasants' resentment, and succeeded in conducting himself properly, the biggest test of all followed as the worker attempted to fulfill his duties as an administrator. Here the burden of responsibility for the worker's status lay almost entirely on how well he performed his tasks and got others to perform theirs. The workers first had to overcome the peasants' distrust, centering on their inexperience in farming. Then the 25,000ers' most important task was to establish at least a semblance of order in the management of the farms. A major concern of most peasants was whether the farm would be well run, whether the livestock would be properly tended, and whether there would be a harvest. A disorganized farm could easily give rise to discontent.[15] Finally, the workers had to show restraint and patience in imposing their organizational ideas—or those of the center—in order to avoid engendering the wrath of the peasants.

There were a number of conditions under which a 25,000er could, from the outset, secure a good working relation with collective farmers. Some 25,000ers wrote that they had impressed the peasants by arriving in the villages with their families. This meant that the worker was not simply another plenipotentiary or roving commissar, but that he had left the city and had come to live side by side with the peasants. Given the hardships of the times and the vast difference in the standard of living between city and countryside, settling in a village with wife and children often served to create a bond between workers and peasants. Other 25,000ers found themselves in villages from which their factories recruited seasonal labor. In these cases, the 25,000ers often were familiar with the area and the people.[16] This was also the case when 25,000ers were sent to villages and districts over which their factories had assumed patronage. Workers who could aid the collective farmers through patronage or informal relations with their factories could often prove an asset to the peasants. Factories which fulfilled their patronage obligations sent a variety of manufactured goods to and provided different types of services for the farms on which their 25,000ers worked. The larger and more important factories sent agricultural equipment, scrap metal, building materials, tools and spare parts, generators, books, newspaper subscriptions, tobacco, and other materials unobtainable in the countryside. Many factories also sent worker brigades to aid in repair work, sowing, or harvesting. Most of the factory services came in response to workers' letters—often after a trade union, party cell, or newspaper had applied pressure on the factory to fulfill its obligations. It should finally be noted that many 25,000ers brought important skills to the collective farms. Many were skilled mechanics and therefore provided much-needed services in the repair of peasant inventory and agricultural equipment.[17]

In many parts of the country the 25,000ers were welcome to the collective farms after the preceding months of chaos. Whether it was a matter of replacing an unpopular official or of bringing order and permanency to a collective farm administration, the 25,000ers were, at least, not plenipotentiaries and were there to organize and not to agitate. And in this capacity the

25,000ers often served the role of a sort of buffer between the farm and the higher authorities—generally those at the district level. Collective farm chairmen, as Merle Fainsod pointed out, were often caught in the middle between the demands of the farm and farmers and the demands of the district-level organs.[18] The 25,000ers were no exception, and their difficulties with the district organs are well documented. Not a few 25,000ers, caught in this unpleasant triangle, found themselves speaking out for the collective farmers. The workers' main concerns here tended to be problems of supplies and food. The 25,000er Bagdasarov complained at a meeting of 25,000ers in Azerbaidzhan that his collective farmers had to buy bread on the private market. Why, he asked, did not the cooperative store provide this? The 25,000er Ivan Komissarov, noted food shortages on his collective farm and complained that grain-requisitioning quotas were "taken from the air." The 25,000er Zakharov, who was a delegate to the second conference of the Western regional party committee in June 1930, stated that the collective farmers received nothing from the cooperative stores and requested the conference to concern itself with supplying the farms with specialists and agricultural equipment.[19] The 25,000ers Iarochik and Krasavin found themselves in trouble for actions which appear to have served the interests of their farms. Iarochik borrowed a horse from the local fire brigade for a village teacher's trip to town and was accused of abusing his authority; Krasavin, a fifty-two-year-old worker and party member, refused to take measures to punish farms which failed to fulfill grain-requisition quotas, and was also accused of abusing his office.[20]

The 25,000ers, it was said, had proved a success on the collective farms because they spoke a common language with the collective farmers.[21] That this was in fact true in many instances is apparent from cases of peasant protest over decisions to remove or transfer 25,000ers. On a number of collective farms collective farmers threatened to resign if their 25,000er was removed.[22] A worker who could call upon his factory for practical aid or who, on the basis of his status as a 25,000er, could intercede for the farmers with higher authorities and successfully oppose district-level organs was a definite asset on many collective farms. Moreover, many 25,000ers, as workers and, in some cases, as workers with roots in the countryside, did indeed have a far greater capacity to speak a common language with the peasants than did mobilized officials and specialists. Collective farmers accorded respect and authority to these 25,000ers and to those 25,000ers who managed successfully to organize production on the collective farms.

The establishment of good relations between 25,000ers and collective farmers did not depend only on winning the peasants' respect through good leadership. There were 25,000ers who had to fight an uphill struggle with their own ideas about peasants and to overcome a certain feeling of class superiority. Among the 25,000ers there were, as a history of the Putilov factory put it, a number of daredevils who "thought to take the muzhik by the throat."[23] Some workers had gone to the countryside with very negative feelings about the peasantry, based on memories of civil war famine, high food prices, class resentment over the "kulak grain strike," or a childhood of poverty and want in the village. The workers had been warned to work without proletarian conceit.[24] Work in the countryside, however, was difficult, and even Sholokhov's model 25,000er Davydov soon found himself adopting the rough-and-ready civil war style of the collective farm party cell secretary and local *peregibshchik* Nagulnov.[25]

The obstinacy of tradition and the staying power of rural backwardness had firmly implanted an attitude in the state that led to a "for your own good" approach to change in the countryside, a sort of cultural imperialism. If need be, the peasantry would be dragged by the hair to culture and progress. This attitude was imparted to many 25,000ers who had to deal firsthand with rural backwardness and who, like Sholokhov's Davydov, might have yelled out while being beaten by peasant women, "But it's for you, curse you . . . it's for you we're doing all this. And you're killing me."[26]

Some 25,000ers were led to despair by these problems. One worker wrote, "There is no support at all. I wanted to raise labor discipline and they threatened me. I don't know what to do. The [party] cell secretary is a drunk and always threatens me."[27] The 25,000er Balabanov wrote a rather hopeless letter about his collective farm. He claimed that on his farm the main enemy was vodka. Every Thursday he lost his labor force when everyone went off to the bazaar and got drunk.[28] Many workers blamed vodka and moonshine for their problems or the peasants' obstinacy. Others noted that nepotism was a source of many problems on the farms and that it was difficult to oppose large and powerful family networks which were entrenched in collective farm administrations.[29] Frequently, however, difficulties on the farms or with the farmers were explained, as can be expected, with reference to the class war. When problems arose, the 25,000ers, like the Communist party above, often attributed them to class aliens, kulaks, and *podkulachniki.*[30]

The "class approach" to the analysis of collective farm problems was reinforced for workers when they heard news of violence aimed at other 25,000ers. According to the leading Soviet historian of the 25,000ers, about fifty workers were killed or seriously wounded in the countryside.[31] This cannot be documented, but the figure appears to be an underestimation. The majority of documented cases of murdered 25,000ers, it should be noted, were workers assigned to national minority regions. Many more 25,000ers were the targets of beatings, threat letters, and arson.[32] All of this served as a form of free instruction in the lessons of the class war.

An overrigorous application of the class approach or the for your own good approach to collective farm work served only to lead most 25,000ers and collective farmers to an impasse. Perhaps the most successful workers were those who relied neither on force nor too much on their ideas of Marxist sociology. For the most part these were workers who had a sense of the meaning of backwardness. Balabanov, for example, who had attributed his farm's problems to vodka, showed an understanding of the situation he faced and even saw progress when the peasants ceased to yell, "Down with anti-Christ," when he spoke at collective farm meetings. He wrote that 90 percent of the peasants were illiterate so that "one cannot blame them for their lack of consciousness." He went on to say that the village library consisted of some *Pravda*s from 1925, three issues of *Bednota* from 1927, and a few books.[33]

The 25,000ers who were most successful in their work and in their relations with the peasants were those who least of all challenged peasant tradition within the framework of collectivized agriculture. And there were some highly successful 25,000ers. Many of the country's model collective farms were led by 25,000ers, and it was often claimed that collective farms with 25,000ers were better than collective farms without. A number of collective farms led by 25,000ers received awards in national or regional competitions, and many 25,000ers were decorated with orders and medals, including the Order of Lenin.[34] Above all, it should be noted once again, the year 1930 proved to be a great success for socialized agriculture because of the triumphant first spring and the bountiful harvest which followed; and the 25,000ers basked in the glow of these successes.

The jubilation of the first spring, however, cast a deceptive shadow upon the weaknesses and deficiencies of collectivized agriculture. The 25,000ers confronted many serious problems in their work which had a deciding influence not only on the fate of their campaign but on the fate of collectivized agriculture in general. In their attempts to lead the revolution in the countryside, the 25,000ers were to clash head-on with two of the main standard-bearers of rural Russia: tradition and backwardness.

"To the People"—First Five-Year Plan Style

The campaign of the 25,000ers was compared to the "to the people" movement of the 1870s when hundreds of young intelligentsia radicals flocked to the countryside to bring socialism to the peasants. The essential difference between the movement of the 1870s and the 25,000ers' movement, it was said, was that in 1929 and 1930 the peasantry was at long last ready to accept the idea of socialism, which the working class carried to the countryside.[35] This was far from the only difference, for the idea of socialism which was to be brought to the countryside had undergone a significant transfiguration. If the idea of socialism in the 1870s resembled at least in essence similar ideas then current in Western Europe, the First Five-Year Plan idea of socialism, as it pertained to the countryside, was based firmly on the idea of the revolution from above.

The 25,000ers were repeatedly told that they were not agitators but organizers. They were not to agitate for the idea of socialism with the usual speeches on Marxism, the world revolution, and the international situation, but were to promote the idea of socialism by organizing the collective farm and demonstrating the practical advantages of life and labor in the collective. The peasantry, it was believed, could not organize collective farming alone. It did not have the experience necessary to organize large-scale production and collective labor. Factory workers, on the other hand, were believed to be sufficiently experienced in large-scale socialist production to carry over their experience to the farms. For this reason, among others, the idea of socialism had to be brought to the countryside from the socialist town by the "conscious" forces of Soviet society. The idea of socialism had become, in practice, the collective farm.

The 25,000ers were instructed to "transfer the proletarian experience to the collective farms." It was widely maintained at this time that socialist agriculture would be similar to factory production in industry: the collective farms were to be agriculture factories.[36] What this meant in practice varied widely and the "proletarian experience," broadly defined, could mean anything from the imposition of the eight-hour workday in agriculture to the installation of factory whistles to replace the imprecise and technologically inferior village roosters. According to the information provided to 25,000ers, however, the proletarian experience included the organization of piecework, wage scales, labor discipline, production conferences, shock work, and socialist competition.[37] The 25,000ers were intended to bring an entirely new mode of life and labor to the countryside. The potential consequences of bringing the factory to the peasant were immense, for it entailed a destruction of traditional ways in farming and led to a direct confrontation between two very different cultures.

The formative period in the evolution of collectivized Soviet agriculture was shaped, to a large extent, by this clash of cultures, which was grafted onto the much deeper initial contradiction of the proletarian dictatorship in peasant Russia. These contradictions necessarily set constraints on the organization of the collective farms. The 25,000ers worked under these constraints at all times. Among the influences and pressures which acted upon the 25,000ers, three were of central importance in determining their actions and shaping their work: the instructions and demands issued by higher government and party authorities; their own prior experience as factory workers; and a recognition of their surroundings, which often led them to compromise with and adapt to traditional peasant modes of life and labor. This amalgam of influences set the course for a demonstration of the peasants' readiness to accept the idea of socialism.

The majority of 25,000ers discovered that the idea of socialism in the countryside was as yet a paper concept when they arrived on the collective farms. Most workers were forced to begin from an organizational ground zero. The majority of collective farms were in a state of complete disorder. Even on "older" collective farms (those organized before the winter of 1929–30), it was not uncommon for a 25,000er to discover that no one knew the collective farm's borders or that the borders were disputed by neighboring collectives. Nor was it uncommon to see collective farmland still organized in the traditional strips. If that were not problem enough, the 25,000ers were likely to discover that agricultural tools and machinery were in need of wholesale repairs, spare parts for damaged inventory were nonexistent, no mechanics or blacksmiths were available for repair work, and there was neither sufficient fodder nor shelter for what remained of the collective farm's livestock, which by that time was often weak or diseased. To make matters worse, with the possible exception of a small group of local activists, the collective farm population was unlikely to be overly enthusiastic about building socialism while the trauma of the winter campaign was still fresh in its mind. Only 2 percent of all collective farms had agronomic assistance at this time, so the workers could not turn to a specialist for advice.[38] Finally, the center had failed to provide clear guidelines and directions and would itself remain undecided on many important organizational issues throughout 1930.

The 25,000ers complained that they could not find answers to even the most basic organizational questions in their rudimentary instructions and collective farm primers. Especially in the first months, they were left to fend for themselves, with only the possible aid and support of local activists and friendly farmers. Here is how one 25,000er reacted to the general situation:

> Preliminary preparation gave us nothing. In a five-day course we were stuffed with lectures on how to create a collective farm, [they] said a few words about party policy, [and] mentioned agronomy. When we arrived . . . the center of attention was the issue of internal collective farm construction, the organization of labor on the collective farm, etc. In Moscow, not a word was said on this and we have to work this out on our own . . . [39]

This was a typical reaction to a common experience. The 25,000ers had been told not to await instructions from Moscow. They were told to be "Leninists."[40] Yet they had to start somewhere, and given that Lenin had never worked on a collective farm, it was not enough simply to be a Leninist. Therefore, they began by basing their activities on what was most familiar to them, their factory experience.

The main organizational issue which the 25,000ers confronted was, loosely defined, the issue of labor discipline. The 25,000ers first confronted the absence of any sense of order or discipline at meetings of the collective farm assembly, the village soviet, and even the various groups of local activists. This problem transcended the meetings and pervaded almost every aspect of work and life on the farms. It was a complex and serious problem for both the workers and the efficient organization of the collective farms.

The 25,000ers often described collective farm meetings as little more than the old village gathering with new names. Similar to the village gathering, at the early collective farm meetings everyone talked at once, agendas were nonexistent or were wishful thinking, peasant digressions (wittingly or otherwise) constantly led discussion away from the issue at hand into the realm of gossip, personal problems, or old stories, and the air was thick with the odor of cheap tobacco. The meetings often turned into shouting matches and could easily end in a bloody brawl. This, in fact, was usually inevitable if alcohol had been consumed prior to a meeting. This all-pervasive lack of order was often the reason why meetings were held day after day for hours at a time. Workers who were wise to these problems or who feared violence chose the alternative route to the masses of hut-to-hut chats with the peasants.

The frustration of attempting to lead meetings on the collective farms was captured by Sholokhov in a speech given by the 25,000er Davydov. Losing all patience with what were actually the more "progressive" elements of the Gremyachy Log Collective Farm, Davydov agonized at a meeting:

> Who carries on at a meeting like you do! What are you bawling for? Everyone should speak in turn and the rest keep quiet! You can't act here like a lot of bandits! Think what you're doing! . . . You ought to learn from the working class how to conduct a meeting properly. At our works we hold meetings in the shop, or the club, and they're very orderly, that's a fact! When one man speaks, the rest listen, but you all shout at once and no one can make out anything![41]

This was a typical reaction of 25,000ers to the chaos of collective farm meetings. Another worker, this one not from fiction, echoed the basic thrust of Davydov's sentiments:

> Generally at meetings of the soviet there is a racket, turmoil. More than once, I've seen the same thing in other communes. But here already it is

changing. [Now] there is an agenda and a real chairman to lead the meeting. This is predicated upon urban, proletarian, restrained training, calm and firmness . . . [42]

Whether or not proletarian "calm and firmness" could indeed be injected into collective farm meetings, some sort of order was absolutely imperative to the effective management of collectivized agriculture for the meetings were essential to the dissemination of information, job assignments, and, ironically, conflict resolution.

The peasants objected to the imposition of outside standards of order and behavior at their meetings. They were used to their own ways and clearly enjoyed their meetings as something more than simply a business or political forum. With the arrival of Communists, workers, and all types of commissars, however, they were no longer allowed to have their say and were frequently rudely interrupted by outsiders who saw in their speeches the products of wandering minds. Sholokhov's Grandpa Shchukar, although exaggerated and a bit too perfect as a loyal but backward poor peasant, presents a good example of the standard "village gathering style" in his many speeches and outbursts in *Virgin Soil Upturned*. He, too, objected to being interrupted and, in a probably untypically restrained manner, told off the collective farm party secretary:

> Last day, Makar, old chap, you talked about the World Revolution from midday till sunset. Boring it was, I must say—same old thing all the time. Why, I curled up on the bench and had a nap in the middle of it, but I didn't dare to interrupt you, and now you're interrupting me. [43]

Why, moreover, should a peasant tolerate interruptions from a factory worker who, as one peasant said of a 25,000er, probably, "couldn't tell the difference between a sheep and a dog"?[44]

In addition to procedural pandemonium at meetings, the 25,000ers had to confront the problems of old tensions, long-standing quarrels, and plain everyday bickering which existed between families and neighbors in the tightly knit peasant communities. These tensions were likely to surface at meetings or in field work if old enemies ended up in the same brigade. More likely than not, the workers probably often confused family and community conflicts with class struggle and it is not unlikely that peasants made use of class language to attack old enemies in an attempt to win over a powerful supporter to their side. Turning once again to Sholokhov, the comment of a Gremyachy Log peasant may provide an idea of how potentially disruptive this problem was to labor in the collective:

> I'll speak for myself, dear citizens. There was me and my own brother Pyotr, now, we used to live together. But we couldn't get on! Either the women would

be flying at each other so you couldn't prick 'em apart with a hayfork, or Pyotr
and me would be at it. And now you want to have the whole village in one nest!
Everything will be upside down in no time. As soon as we go out to the fields,
there's bound to be a fight. Ivan's overdoing it with my oxen, I've forgotten to
look after his horses. Why we'll be needing a squad of militia living with us all
the time. Everybody will be spitting blood.[45]

Collective labor and, with it, labor discipline had suddenly become a
necessary item, and in lieu of a permanent "squad of militia" to maintain
order, 25,000er–collective farm leaders confronted this problem by turning to
their experience in industry.

The very first item on the agenda of labor discipline was gathering the
collective farm work force each morning. Many workers installed factorylike
whistles, bells, or horns to turn out the work force.[46] From what little
evidence there is concerning peasant response to this, it appears that peasants
either were hostile or regarded these innovations with a sort of mocking
derision. The American journalist Maurice Hindus reported upon one peasant
woman's opinion of a newly installed bell. Responding to someone's quoting
of an agitator who described future life on the collective farm as a
"paradise," she elaborated:

> Paradise, of course . . . living by the bell. Did you see . . . the bell they have
> fixed up [on the collective farm]? They just live by it. They get up by it, eat by
> it, sleep by it, fight by it, and if anything should ever happen to that bell, they'd
> be more at a loss than little chickens which suddenly lose the old hen . . . I
> certainly don't like bells . . . what a life in the kolhoz [sic; collective farm],
> always under someone's orders![47]

Waking the work force and getting it to start work on time was a daily
problem. This was not the factory: there was no factory siren to announce the
beginning of the work day—except when a worker installed one—and most
peasants had neither clocks nor watches. The collective farm chairman, the
25,000er Pichugin, carefully defined each collective farmer's assignment
each night in consultation with the farmers. Each evening, without fail, the
farmers would agree, and each morning, without fail, no one would show up
for work. Pichugin was forced to go hut to hut in the mornings to round up
his workers.[48] Other 25,000ers confronted the same problem in addition to
losing laborers frequently throughout the day as collective farmers wandered
off from their work for one reason or another. As one 25,000er put it, the
peasants were simply in the habit of leaving to go home or to stop and chat
whenever they felt like it.[49]

The 25,000ers reported that collective farmers objected to fixed work
assignments and to working according to an imposed schedule.[50] They

explained that the farmers were not used to this, but used to working independently. They worked according to nature's schedule, began work with the rooster's crow, and were used to being their own master. The 25,000ers' attempts to introduce a factory regimen on the farms clashed with traditional work habits. Hindus managed once again to capture the peasants' viewpoint on this issue as he listened to a dissatisfied peasant discuss the collective farm:

> We are not learned; we are not wise. But a little self-respect we have, and we like the feeling of independence. Today we feel like lying down, and we lie down; the next day we feel like going to town, and we go to town. We do as we please. But in the *kolkhoz*, brother, it is do-as-you-are-told, like a horse— go this way and that, and don't dare turn off the road or you get it hard, a stroke or two of the whip . . . [51]

The peasants were unwilling to accept a factorylike routine on the collective farm. As one of Sholokhov's peasants put it: "Our work's different, you know, it's not like standing by a machine in a factory. There you just do your eight hours and off you go . . . "[52]

As difficult as it was for many 25,000ers even to assemble the work force and begin the day's labor, all of this was only preliminary to the real task. Once the collective farmers had begun work, 25,000er–collective farm leaders had to ensure that the work actually got done, that no one left the job, and that the inventory was taken care of. This raised a whole series of new and more complex organizational issues not the least important of which were forms of labor remuneration and nonremunerative work incentives. It was necessary to create incentives for peasants to work the land of the collective farm and this proved to be no easy task. In this sphere of their endeavors the 25,000ers responded with ad hoc solutions based on a mixture of what the government ordered or suggested, the 25,000ers' factory experience, and the peasants' own demands.

The question of the form of labor remuneration to be adopted on the collective farms was left unresolved by the state throughout 1930. In his discussion of this question R. W. Davies has commented: "Perhaps the most remarkable feature of the spring of 1930 is that sowing took place quite successfully in the kolkhozy even though collective farmers were working on credit for an unknown amount of payment, often not knowing even the system by which they would be paid."[53] Indeed this was remarkable, and, it should be added, the issue was not ultimately resolved by the state until March 1931, when, at the Sixth Congress of Soviets, payment in piecework accounted for according to the labor-day system was officially sanctioned.[54] Yet although the center hedged on this issue, first advocating one form of remuneration and then another, collective farm chairmen could not take the same liberties and maintain their authority. Collective farm chairmen had to be able to offer at least the suggestion of an incentive to their labor and therefore were forced to adopt some definite form of labor remuneration. In doing so, they served the purpose of testing various approaches to this question.

The 25,000ers approached the issue of labor remuneration with no precise guidelines in mind. In the workers' preparatory courses, no one system was advocated; instead, the program offered descriptions of several different systems, including piecework, payment "per eater" (payment based on number of family members), and payment according to work ability.[55] Yet any 25,000er who paid attention to the press and, in particular, to the model collective farm charters published in February and March 1930 could not but help noticing a decided inclination in favor of piecework.[56] Still, there were conflicting signals in the press. The advocates of transferring the factory experience wholesale to the collective farms, especially in the first months of 1930, proposed the introduction of differential wage scales and regular salaries.[57] In addition, many continued to discuss payment "per eater" positively, and this system was rather highly evaluated at an April 1930 Kolkhoztsentr meeting.[58] As late as the Sixteenth Party Congress, Iakovlev, the Commissar of Agriculture, stated, "we do not need to decree each step of the collective farmer" and left the issue of remuneration—albeit *after* grain deliveries to the state—to the discretion of the collective farms.[59] Although the issue remained confused and undecided, piecework and the labor day emerged as strongly preferred systems by the late spring and early summer of 1930.[60]

The question of labor remuneration was a major issue in many of the letters written by 25,000ers. The majority of workers indicated that they either favored or made use of a piecework system. This preference came easier to them in part because of their factory experience, but it is clear that they also were influenced by the signals from the center, which favored piecework and the labor day. The system of piecework was viewed as the best means for providing incentives to the collective farmers to produce more and better. Advocates of piecework, including many 25,000ers, believed that the traditional "per-eater" system—sometimes described as wage leveling, as in the factories—provided no incentives for laborers to increase or improve the quantity and quality of production. Moreover, some workers complained that "per-eater" payment on the collective farm was detrimental because it led to a situation where no one wanted to perform the more difficult or laborious tasks.[61]

The collective farmers almost uniformly objected to the imposition of the piecework system. According to the 25,000er Pokrovskaia, the peasants viewed differentials in payment of this kind as a "violation of the equality of all before the mir [village commune]."[62] Other workers reported the same, indicating that the collective farmers demanded to be paid according to the number of "eaters" in a family or, less frequently, according to ability.[63] Piecework and the labor day were a complete break with peasant tradition. Many 25,000ers simply accepted the status quo and established a "per-eater" payment system on the farms. In fact, according to Davies, this system predominated through 1930.[64] Less than one quarter of all collective farms in 1930 had introduced piecework, and according to Iakovlev, about one half of all collective farms had absolutely no labor or salary norms by June 1930.[65] Nonetheless, the groundwork for the establishment of the labor-day system was laid in 1930, and the 25,000ers, making use of their factory experience, played no small role in this endeavor.

This was perhaps the most difficult issue which the workers faced in their first year of work, and there is little evidence that they resolved the problems of labor remuneration much more successfully than the central authorities did. Some workers contrived extremely elaborate wage-scale systems and most got bogged down in the sheer complexity of organizing piecework. Piecework on a large collective farm entailed an elaborate accounting system and a quick glance at published descriptions of piecework systems from the 1930s will indicate just how complex a system it was.[66] Most workers had to do their own accounting, and they were poorly prepared for this. Less than half of all collective farms had accountants in the spring of 1930.[67] Moreover, piecework rates were based on an unknown quantity of value—the yield from the future harvest—and therefore were a mixture of prediction and hope. Because the issue of remuneration was so complex and still hazy, the majority of 25,000ers had to employ a variety of additional nonremunerative work incentives in order to manage the collective farms and farmers effectively.

The 25,000ers relied on their factory experience in developing incentives for improving the collective farmers' labor performance. They provided bonuses (usually hard to obtain manufactured goods) for good workers and introduced a number of honorific incentives such as wall newspapers and red boards of honor to celebrate especially productive farmers. In addition, once spring sowing was over, the 25,000ers were often able to reward outstanding laborers by sending them to courses or school or by promoting them within the collective farm. The workers also had recourse to various forms of punishment in cases of lagging labor norms. Among those most frequently cited and based on factory experience were the introduction of labor books, black boards of opprobrium, awards like the banner of the tortoise for laggards, and the institution of comrade courts to allow for the judgment, reprimand, and lectures of inadequate workers by their peers.[68]

The 25,000ers also introduced the brigade system into field work.[69] This served a number of purposes. The brigades could be pitted one against another in socialist competition as one way of increasing tempos. Moreover, since collective farm fields were often spread out over many miles and distant from the collective farm offices, collective farmers slept and ate in the fields to avoid losing time during peak work periods. A brigade leader, in lieu of a collective farm chairman who could not be everywhere at once, was assigned to direct and supervise the work of a part of the farm's work force. Brigade leaders had the responsibility of assembling the crews in the mornings, supervising their work, and making sure inventory was protected. The Putilov 25,000er Ivan Smirnov used this system and, at first, met the resistance of the peasants when he proposed organizing brigades:

> The people were used to working alone, and here it was being suggested to them to work together. At first, they said all this supervision is not necessary but when [I] showed [them], [they] agreed . . . [we] organized a brigade and the issue of inventory arose. It is essential to establish responsibility for taking care of it in the brigade. This was clear to me from the factory. If there was no responsibility for an instrument, the workers left it any old place . . . The same thing went on on the collective farm . . . Before beginning work, the whole brigade wasted two hours searching for yesterday's scattered tools . . . [70]

Smirnov, clearly exceptional, recognized that he faced a struggle with traditional peasant modes of work and behavior. As a former member of Putilov's factory committee, he had probably dealt with similar problems in Leningrad with the attempt to train the many new workers coming to the city from the countryside. Most workers, however, seem to have confronted this all-pervasive problem less self-consciously and more like the 25,000er Chudinov, who wrote that the main task was "to overcome . . . the petit-bourgeois psychology of the peasant so that each collective farmer will look at the artel as a worker looks at the socialist factory."[71]

In the language of the times, Chudinov was really discussing the problem with which this chapter section began, the problem of labor discipline. As has been shown, the 25,000ers dealt with this problem and the more general problems of labor remuneration and incentives in response to directives from above and by borrowing from their prior industrial experience. In addition, as in the case of 25,000ers who made use of the per-eater system of labor remuneration, some adaptation to traditional ways was also involved. Similar adaptation to standard peasant practice was necessary in other areas of the workers' endeavors, as well.

The peasants without fail made their voices heard on most organizational questions, and the workers generally had to listen if they wanted to get anything done. At times, workers adopted peasant practices in response both to the peasants' will and, more important, the simple practicality of an issue.

For example, this was the case in the use of the per-eater system. It was also the case in the resurrection of a much-transformed system of elders which the 25,000er Konev instituted on his farm. Konev appointed elders (*starosta*s) from those peasants who were most capable but no longer physically able to do hard work. The elders were set up within each separate branch of Konev's large farm to act as a form of "quality controller" and to look out for laggards.[72] Another 25,000er, in light of peasant opposition to class categorizations, made the conscious decision not to organize a group of poor peasants so as not to antagonize the other collective farmers; instead he relied on a general meeting of all the collective farmers, possibly based on the old village gathering.[73]

In other cases peasants attempted to hoodwink 25,000ers into maintaining the old ways. This happened several times when peasants either insisted on maintaining the old strips or suggested dividing consolidated collective farm land back into strips.[74] One Putilov 25,000er wrote to his factory with the impressive news that the peasants had suggested dividing each field into individual strips to be worked independently.[75] The Putilov worker resisted the innovation, but his letter went a long way in showing that tradition dies hard in the Russian countryside. In fact—and this was especially the case on collective farms which were not mechanized—the collective farm grainfields would often remain in strips due to the absence of land surveyors or, if consolidated, would be redivided into sections. In this way each section would be the sole responsibility of an individual brigade, and it would be marked off with pegs or stakes. The sectioning of fields was a practice which had advocates among peasants, collective farm chairmen, and at least one regional party organization and harkened back to an earlier tradition.[76]

Another area in which 25,000ers often were forced to resolve problems by compromise was the area of socialized livestock. This was one of the most sensitive issues in the organization of collective farms and it often served as the spark which inflamed villages in riots. Most collective farms lacked sufficient fodder and shelter to care for socialized livestock. Moreover, the peasants did not trust others to take care of their animals as they themselves would. When the 25,000er Koller announced that he was to take charge of his farm's livestock, the collective farmers refused and told him that first he must take courses.[77] Many other 25,000ers took what appears to have been the common way out in this period and socialized livestock on paper, but, in lieu of adequate shelter, left farm animals to the care of their former owners. In this way the animals were taken care of and continued to live with their masters in winter in the warmth of the peasant huts. Needless to say, this solution was neither feasible nor necessary on those collective farms which specialized in livestock breeding.

Horses and other work animals were generally an exception to the rule of paper socialization. The March 1930 model collective farm charter instructed collective farms to socialize all work animals because they were needed in the everyday operation of the farms. And most collective farm leaders, including the 25,000ers, did not leave draft animals in the care of former owners for fear that the animals, if not sold or slaughtered, might succumb to the same problems of labor discipline as their masters. It was not an easy task to socialize horses, however, and this almost always led to major upheavals. This was especially the case in cossack villages, where a horse was a cossack's pride. The experience of the 25,000er D. A. Ivanov, the chairman of a cossack collective farm, is interesting in this regard. When it came time to discuss the socialization of the horses, Ivanov called the cossacks together for a meeting. Not surprisingly, the cossacks did not receive Ivanov's suggestions warmly and were rather vocally opposed to the idea of socializing their horses. They argued that no one would take proper care of someone else's horse, or, at least, that the care would not be the same as that provided by a horse's real master. At some point in the discussion, the meeting went out of control and entered a state of pandemonium. By the time Ivanov regained control of the meeting, he had arrived at a most innovative solution to the problem of socializing the horses. Ivanov proposed that instead of socializing the horses, the village should sell them all and buy new horses. Then the collective farm could socialize the new horses, and in this way, no one would lose because one's own horse would not be socialized. The novelty of the idea caught the cossacks' fancy, and they all agreed to Ivanov's solution.[78] Needless to say, Ivanov's was an exceptional case. This episode does show, however, how one 25,000er was able to observe and understand peasant sensibilities and adapt his work accordingly.

There were other 25,000ers who did not share Ivanov's good sense and patience. Some of them showed little understanding of peasant ways or the needs of agriculture and erred in the direction of the "overfactoryization" of collectivized farming. The 25,000er Larman introduced the uninterrupted workweek (continuous production with one fifth of the laborers having a free day every fifth day). The 25,000er Golubev, who, it was claimed, thought he was a factory director, introduced the eight-hour day into field work. He himself refused to work overtime and closed the collective farm office each day at the end of his shift. He was condemned for this excess soon after its introduction.[79] These factory practices were not only entirely inapplicable to agriculture, but were sometimes quite harmful—during the busy seasons, for example, when farmers raced time and weather, and every hour of work counted.

On the other hand, there were instances of the application of factory practices which, although seemingly incongruent in agriculture, proved useful in many cases. The production conferences, for example, were introduced on the farms at this time and remained an enduring feature of the system long after the 25,000ers had left the countryside. As in the case of industry, they were used as a forum for the exchange of information and experience. Many 25,000ers made use of them to improve their own competency in agriculture. The conferences were also used as a training session for younger and inexperienced farmers as well as a center for gleaning the wheat from the chaff, that is, for selecting the best and most experienced collective farmers for promotion or study.[80] The 25,000ers also introduced collective farmers to shock work and socialist competition. These practices served the purpose of enhancing labor discipline as well as productivity and motivation and seem to have been most acceptable to activists and youth.[81] These practices too became an enduring, if not universally beloved, feature of the collective farm system.

The 25,000ers' approach to the problems of collective farm management in 1930 was shaped by what they read in the press and were instructed by superiors, their prior factory experience, and what they saw of and were told by the collective farmers. Many of the problems which they confronted, such as labor discipline and labor incentives, would persist in collectivized agriculture long after the 25,000ers were gone. In addition, many of the organizational forms with which they experimented, such as piecework, socialist competition, and the production conference, would eventually be endorsed as officially accepted approaches to collective farm organization and so would also persist beyond the 25,000ers' stay in the countryside. The problems which the 25,000ers confronted in attempting to bring the factory to the farm and to overcome traditional modes of life and labor would, in many ways, be more enduring than the successes which they achieved. The reason for this was that the 25,000ers were forced to confront a very basic reality of Russian life. This was the all-pervasive cultural and technological backwardness of the countryside which had for years blocked any and all efforts at reform and modernization.

The Ramifications of Rural Backwardness

Collectivization was, among other things, a war on backwardness. The cultural and technological backwardness of the countryside presented a threat more real and more serious than all of the country's NEPmen, kulaks, and class aliens combined. Poverty, illiteracy, and a chronic predisposition to periodic famine characterized much of the rural landscape. In addition, the countryside suffered from an endemic "goods famine," as well as a "people famine" or deficit in trained cadres and specialists for the rural sector. During the years of collectivization, the state trained hundreds of thousands of collective farmers and poured millions of rubles worth of agricultural equipment and supplies into the countryside in an attempt to create the cultural and technological base necessary to keep pace with the speeding superstructure of collectivization. As had happened so often in the Soviet past, however, the superstructure far outdistanced its base in the collectivization of agriculture.

It did not take long for the 25,000ers to discover the meaning of rural poverty and backwardness. It was common for workers to find that, on collective farms with tractors and other complex machinery, the collective farmers did not know how to take care of the equipment. Consequently, one of the first tasks workers faced was the repair of agricultural inventory—damaged by age, misuse, or negligence—and the search for spare parts. Workers who were mechanics generally did their own repair work and often improvised in lieu of spare parts; in these cases collective farms with 25,000ers had a real advantage over other farms.[82] Another common problem reported by 25,000ers was fodder shortages, especially in regions specializing in livestock. In many areas this problem was extremely severe and had led to mass slaughters of livestock.[83] The workers also wrote that construction material was unavailable for building barns, silos, and other necessary buildings.[84] Finally, the 25,000ers noted shortages in a variety of secondary materials, ranging from paper and ink to political and technical literature and from tobacco and sugar to radios and generators.[85]

The 25,000ers spent a good deal of time attempting to track down supplies. This often led them into conflict with district officials who were either indifferent to their plight or too busy with their own work to aid collective farm chairmen. As a consequence, many workers appealed for assistance to their factories, and if that failed, to union organizations and the press. Most of the workers were on collective farms or in districts which were under the patronage of their factories. Not all the factory patrons provided aid, but when a 25,000er was able to solicit help from his factory, collective farms and collective farmers found themselves in a relatively privileged position.

Another problem which 25,000ers encountered soon after beginning work was the absence of skilled workers, accountants, bookkeepers, agricultural specialists, and other people with specialized training. Workers frequently complained about this problem in their letters. The absence of accountants was a serious problem. Many workers had to do their own accounting, and in light of their unpreparedness for such work, this hindered basic record keeping and the organization of piecework systems on the farms. The absence of agronomists and land surveyors presented problems of equal gravity.[86] The state made vigorous efforts at this time to mobilize urban specialists for rural work, but demand greatly exceeded supply, and the people famine remained a serious problem.

The 25,000ers dealt with the people famine in several ways. The first way was to train the peasants or make use of their expertise. At the Sixteenth Party Congress the training and promotion of collective farmers was designated the number-one mission of the 25,000ers.[87] The 25,000ers sent many farmers to courses or trained them on the job and in the production conferences.[88] Moreover, many 25,000ers found themselves directly involved in the cultural revolution as leaders of schools for the liquidation of illiteracy, and of political and agricultural study circles.[89] Following the March retreat, the 25,000ers were also told to "make use of" the middle peasant in collective farm administration. The workers were no longer required to lean exclusively on the farms' poor peasants but could bring in more competent husbandrymen from a wider field of selection.[90]

However, the main way in which the 25,000ers dealt with the people famine was by their assuming the role of the needed specialist or trained cadre. Many workers found themselves occupying several positions in the farms. Because of the dearth of trained people, as well as the state's narrow social base in the countryside, a pattern of multiple-office holding emerged at this time, similar to that of the prerevolutionary Russian countryside and gentry officeholders.[91] Workers often served as bookkeeper and accountant in addition to their positions on the collective farm boards. The 25,000er Lazarovich was collective farm agronomist, bookkeeper, political education instructor, and party cell secretary. He later commented, "There was no area where I did not participate." The 25,000er Kaliberd was the chairman of the farm audit committee; director of the mill, the brick factory, and the dairy; and secretary of the party cell. The 25,000er Kovaleev simultaneously occupied twenty-four different posts.[92] Most workers, regardless of the specific cadre situation, found themselves simultaneously on the administrative board of the collective farm, a member of the local soviet, a member (usually secretary) of the party or Komsomol cell, and quite often, a member of the party district committee. In Buriat-Mongolia, 35 to 40 percent of all 25,000ers were reported to have from four to nine formal positions each.[93]

This was an intolerably large workload and most 25,000ers wrote, as did the worker A. A. Merkulov, "I get up at 4:00 to 5:00 A.M. and go to bed at 11:00 to 12:00 P.M. and sometimes later."[94] Several 25,000ers, who felt completely unprepared for their work, wrote letters asking to be relieved or provided with additional training. The 25,000er Pavel Uleskov from Krasnyi Treugol'nik wrote:

I request [that you] remove me from this work for the following reason. I am completely illiterate, self-educated to the point that I can't work anything out—I don't think that you can have correct leadership where there is an illiterate leader. I can't figure out the forms, circulars, decrees—therefore I cannot implement anything.[95]

The 25,000er Ekaterina Parshikova, who was in Kazakhstan and did not ask to be relieved, responded to the same problem as Uleskov with, "Poor me . . . I myself an only semiliterate."[96] When Ivan Komissarov wrote his trade union that he did not always feel qualified in his work and needed a better education, his union responded, "You write about your low educational level—look at the people around you and you will see that you are very literate in comparison."[97] This was true, but of little consolation.

The 25,000ers frequently complained that the district party and government organs should provide them with aid, given their heavy burdens of responsibility. However, as the workers were quick to point out, the district organs rarely aided them but instead only sent circulars which, according to one worker, "no one could read."[98] The collective farms were inundated with all manner of circulars, decrees, and paperwork at this time and one of the major complaints of both collective farm leaders and higher officials was the widespread practice of the district organs to "rule by circular." This too was a function of the rural people famine. The workers said that the circulars were difficult to make sense of; they were long and tended to be written in complex, formal, bureaucratic language. Moreover, the circulars came en masse. At the second conference of the Western regional party committee, a representative of the Workers' and Peasants' Inspectorate claimed that the lower rural organs received up to forty circulars per day. He went on to say that these did not aid workers who were unfamiliar with agriculture but only served as a new form of torture.[99] A report from early 1931 on the subject of rule by circular indicated that the collective farms received an average of seven to ten circulars or orders per day.[100] One 25,000er wrote that from the beginning of July through the first half of August 1930, his farm had received 480 circulars, while the workers Margolin and Bobkov wrote that in just one day they had received 45 circulars.[101] The 25,000er Beshniakov complained, "While the factories don't write us at all, the districts flood us with paper, they send kilograms of circulars."[102]

In addition to practicing the all-pervasive rule by circular, the district organs added injury to insult by including threats along with all the circulars. Margolin and Bobkov claimed that they constantly received circulars demanding fulfillment of some campaign or another in twenty-four hours or forty-eight hours or else to expect the prospect of arrest, reprimand, or party expulsion.[103] The 25,000ers Utianov and Logashev provided the best description of rule by circular, the inattention of the district organs, and their constant threats:

> We had hardly succeeded in checking into everything and figuring it all out when already they began to bombard us with all kinds of circulars, directives, orders, reminders. Each paper they sent us always contained threats and reprimands for the failure of the former administration to send some sort of information or other. We already received one strict reprimand with a warning for something we didn't even know about. Before arriving on the collective farm, we were in [factory] production for a long time and none of us ever received any official documents. And here right away they begin with reprimands. We went to Novouzensk, stopped by the district executive committee and Kolkhoztsentr office in order to discuss our work conditions . . . But here they met us right off before we even stepped in the door with the cry, "We will put you on trial. We will condemn you."[104]

This type of treatment by the district organs was an everyday occurrence for the 25,000ers.

Official neglect and rule by circular often led 25,000ers into insoluble problems. The situation faced by the 25,000er Pavlov in the Western Region was not unique. Pavlov said that his collective farm was constantly ordered by the various livestock cooperative centers "to solve the meat problem." He said that his farm was aided in this endeavor by the receipt of thousands of circulars. He asked, "Is this how to solve a problem?" Pavlov reported that the farm had first attempted to solve the meat problem by developing rabbit breeding but the rabbit-breeding livestock center refused to give them even two pairs of rabbits. Then, he continued, they decided to try poultry breeding but the concerned cooperative center would not provide them with an incubator. They also thought to breed pigs, but although they were promised aid in the form of a specialist, no aid was forthcoming. Pavlov's conclusion was that the district organs were good only for circulars and promises.[105]

Similar problems led to near tragic results in the case of the 25,000er Khaliuzov. Khaliuzov, a Communist and metalworker, was the chairman of a dwarf (i.e., a very small) collective farm. The farm consisted of eleven families, and among these there were, in all, fourteen people of working age (ten women and four men). Khaliuzov had arrived to find the collective farm in complete disorder and totally lacking in labor discipline. The families constantly quarreled and no one listened to his directions. In the midst of these circumstances Khaliuzov received an order to increase the farm's sown acreage four times. When Khaliuzov informed the collective farmers, they at first refused but finally agreed and worked along with Khaliuzov in the fields until they obtained the expansion in sown acreage. After this, Khaliuzov fell ill from exhaustion and was hospitalized for a week. As was not uncommon for absent collective farm chairmen, he returned to find much of his work undone. The farmers had had a huge quarrel, and two families had quit the farm (taking with them two of the working-age men) to return to the Central Black Earth Region whence they had come earlier. The quarrels continued, and each day, according to Khaliuzov, there was a scene. Tired and ill, Khaliuzov asked the party district committee to replace him or send aid but was refused. His farmers, meanwhile, decided at the end of September to stop work until they were provided with boots. Khaliuzov promised to obtain boots and set off for town in search of these scarce items. He not only failed to find any boots but returned to find that no one had done any work in his absence. That evening he attempted suicide. Unfortunately he failed in this as well as in his other activities but at least managed to receive an official leave and a stay in the hospital. Although suicide was an antiparty act and Khaliuzov's attempt was condemned, the district officials were held responsible for the 25,000er's suicide attempt.[106] Work on the collective farm in 1930 could prove fatal.

Conclusion

Collectivization was intended to bring the industrial revolution to the countryside. It was meant to destroy forever traditional modes of peasant life and labor and to erect in their places modern units of agricultural production modeled along industrial lines. The collective farm was to become a factory. It was for this reason (among others) that workers had been sent to lead the farms. The peasant was to be weaned from his so-called small property-holder instincts and taught to relate to production like an industrial worker in a factory. In other words the industrial revolution had been sent to the countryside, and the vehicle for this was the campaign of the 25,000ers.

The industrial revolution failed to take root in rural Soviet Russia. The peasant was not ready for the idea of socialism in this form. Nor were twenty-five thousand workers a sufficient force to cope with this herculean endeavor. The 25,000ers attempted to introduce industrial methods in the organization of labor and in labor remuneration on the farms and expected peasants to learn to behave like factory workers. However, the workers soon learned that tradition dies hard in the countryside. The obstinacy of tradition doomed the rural industrial revolution and left standing in its stead within the farms only the pale reminder of its spent force in the form of piecework and the labor day, socialist competition and shock work, brigades, production conferences, and so on. The basic structure of the present-day collective farm system was erected at this time, but the initial revolutionary impetus to the collectivization drive failed the test of rural reality and did not survive the years of the First Five-Year Plan. By 1932 the state had reached a stalemate—anticipated during the First Five-Year Plan years in the practical work of collective farm cadres—and would be forced to accept a socialized agriculture which combined elements of the new and the old. The labor day would remain, but the peasants would be granted the right to farm small private plots of land and to sell the produce on the free market; the peasants would become collective farmers, but their primary identity would be the peasant household; the small and scattered strips of the peasants would be consolidated—albeit at a slower rate than anticipated by the state—but the average collective farm would not become a large-scale enterprise until the 1950s.

The countryside was not ready for the idea of socialism in the form which it assumed in the hands of the 25,000ers. Collectivization and the idea of socialism as superstructure had far outrun their base. There were too few building blocks for the construction of socialism in the backward countryside, and, although a cliché, it would not be incorrect to say that this was anticipated in the contradictions inherent in the original revolutionary establishment of a proletarian dictatorship in agrarian Russia in 1917. The failure of the effort was implicit in the scheme. Building socialism remained, intrinsically, an act of revolutionary voluntarism rooted in the Russian revolutionary and Bolshevik traditions.

Nevertheless, the year 1930 marked the birth of the collective farm system and laid the foundation for its further evolution. The 25,000ers served as midwives at the birth of a new system and were long remembered as the pioneers of collective farming for their work in the construction of many of the country's first collective farms. They represented the original revolutionary impulse of the urge to collectivize the countryside. This was the inspiration behind their campaign. They had gone to the people with the idea of socialism. In most cases, however, the peasant was not ready to receive the worker and his factory ways. This determined the further course of collectivized agriculture, which now left its radical-utopian path and entered a purely administrative-organizational direction. It also determined the further fate of the campaign of the 25,000ers, for if the peasant was not prepared to receive the worker, then what was the response of the worker coming face-to-face with the reality of rural Soviet Russia? How did the reality of a backward, traditional countryside affect the momentum of a campaign which was based largely on revolutionary ardor and ideals?

7

The Denouement of the Campaign

We 25,000ers are not a little force. The reason we are Bol'sheviks is to overcome all sorts of "trifles." There are no conditions under which we will not be victorious, but for this we must struggle—must struggle, clench our teeth as we did on the front . . .

The 25,000er Mikhailov

The situation in the countryside now could be compared to that of a fisherman who is on a small boat in the middle of a lake without oars— the banks are far away.

The 25,000er Khodakov, a deserter

The village greets with distrust and hostility those who attempt to introduce into its life something of themselves, something new, and it rapidly expels and rejects them from its midst. But more frequently it is the innovators who clash with the unconquerable conservatism of the village and themselves decide to leave.

Maxim Gorky, *On the Russian Countryside*

The First All-Union Rally of 25,000ers was held on 2 February 1931. The purpose of the rally was to honor the 25,000ers as heroes and pioneers of the collective farm system. The rally was also a celebration of the first anniversary of the campaign. In order to renew their commitment to the cause, the delegates to the rally swore a solemn pledge to remain at their posts until the end of the First Five-Year Plan.[1] The All-Union Rally was one of two major landmarks in the campaign of the 25,000ers in the year 1931.

The other landmark, accompanied by no fanfare and little press attention, was a Central Committee decree of 23 December 1931. This decree, issued on the eve of the end of the First Five-Year Plan and at the expiration of the

25,000ers' pledge, instructed the regional and district organs of the party and government not to retain those 25,000ers who wished to return to the factories. Remaining 25,000ers were to be secured for "leading cadre work" through promotions and opportunities to study.[2] The campaign of the 25,000ers was symbolically accomplished by early 1931 when the rally was held and officially concluded at the end of the same year with the issue of the Central Committee decree.

The proximity in time of the conclusion of the campaign and the end of the First Five-Year Plan was not a coincidence. To understand the denouement of the campaign, it is necessary to place it within the framework of the First Five-Year Plan revolution. The revolution gradually began to dissipate in 1931. In part this was a result of the very considerable achievements of the First Five-Year Plan. The industrialization of the nation had made great strides and over half of all peasant households were collectivized. However, the loss of revolutionary momentum, especially in the countryside, was also conditioned by the enormity of the tasks and the harsh realities of modernizing a backward country. The disorder of collectivization, the costs of the revolution (human and material), and the insurmountable barriers to the idea of socialism in rural Soviet Russia tempered and transformed the revolutionary impetus, idealism, and ultraradicalism of socialist transformation in the countryside. The state now turned its efforts to consolidation and a more gradual approach to building socialism. In the countryside the forces of the state more nearly followed a policy of entrenchment as a result of the bitter legacy of collectivization. The denouement of the campaign of the 25,000ers was similar to that of the First Five-Year Plan revolution in the countryside. The campaign did not and could not continue beyond the end of the revolution because it was predicated on and sustained by the militant radicalism of the First Five-Year Plan epoch.

The experience of the 25,000ers was indicative of the experience of the cadres of the Stalin revolution. The campaign underwent a metamorphosis from crusade to state of siege. The aftermath of the early militant revolutionary phase of collectivization was entrenchment. Collectivization changed from an offensive to a defensive action. The 25,000ers ceased to be revolutionary crusaders; most became victim to the civil war mentality which had played such an important role in the recruitment campaign and the general atmosphere of the revolution. Their siegelike existence in the countryside served to reinforce their loyalties to class and party. The hardening of their convictions—and their lives—led to a warlike mentality which perceived enemies and sabotage to be omnipresent. This transformation, or, perhaps simply, evolution, of conviction and mentality was not surprising given the harsh realities of the times and the mobilization atmosphere which had consumed the nation for so many years. Yet perhaps the central determinants of this transformation were the simple problems of everyday life in the countryside and the workers' sense of isolation from class, factory, and comrades. The 25,000ers found it difficult to adapt to rural life. As cadre workers, they were urbanized and, by and large, not suited to the village. As "worker-revolutionaries," they were not prepared for day-to-day administration or compromise with what they perceived as the forces of "spontaneity." The end of the campaign coincided with the end of an era, the end of the revolution. Most 25,000ers, having accomplished their task of laying the base of the collective farm system, would maintain their loyalty to class and party but, unable to adapt to new conditions, would return to the factory at the end of the campaign.

Life in the Country

Life in the countryside during the period of collectivization was difficult according to any form of measurement. Falling standards of living, the reigning disorder of everyday life on the collective farms, arbitrary repression, rapid industrialization, and an enormous expansion in factory jobs enhanced the lure of the city more than ever before and transformed the countryside into a human sieve. Between 1926 and 1939, the number of rural inhabitants who moved to the cities was 18.7 million. Approximately half of them left the countryside in the years 1930 to 1932. The overwhelming majority of people (83 percent or 7.5 million) who left during the years of collectivization were of working age. As the young and able-bodied left the village, the countryside experienced a decline in the number of its working-age inhabitants, and between 1929 and 1932 their numbers fell from 61 to 54.5 million. Besides the low standard of material life, the villages lacked cultural facilities and any sort of outlet for a new and transitional generation growing up between tradition and modernity. More often than not, the newly educated and technically trained rural cadres of this period took their recently acquired skills to the city, where employment opportunities were readily available and the standard of living was at a more satisfactory level.[3]

The 25,000ers had entered the countryside against the tide of this enormous migration. In doing so they had to struggle with the same forces which had impelled the flow outward from the countryside. Almost immediately upon their arrival the 25,000ers experienced a drastic decline in their standard of living. The central authorities had anticipated this problem and, in order to partially offset it, had issued legislation calling for the workers' former enterprises to make up the differential in salary between that received on the collective farm and in the former job. Initially intended for one year, payment of the difference was extended for a second year in the early fall of 1930 and then for a third year in late 1931.[4]

Payment of the salary difference proved to be a difficult undertaking. The factories frequently resisted payment, claiming that they could not afford to keep the workers on their payroll. In some instances factories fired 25,000ers or decreased their salaries to offset the costs of payment. Many factories simply refused to pay it. In the Ukraine only two out of forty-three 25,000ers in the Tul'chinskii *Okrug* ever received payment, and in the Kharkov area ninety-one 25,000ers never received any money from their factories. In Petrovskii District of Luganskii *Okrug*, as many as 30 percent of the 25,000ers never received payment of the salary difference.[5] One factory committee official in the Ukraine explained: "In the . . . decree it is said that one must pay the difference, but nothing is said there that it is necessary to send it. You see, we are acting according to the law."[6] The factories were repeatedly warned not to withhold payment of the difference, and an avalanche of decrees to this effect were issued throughout the period of the 25,000ers' stay in the countryside.[7] Despite this, most 25,000ers continued having difficulties with the payment of the salary differential throughout 1930 and 1931. Moreover, when the factories were willing to send the difference payments, they were often hindered in their efforts by the failure of the Kolkhoztsentr system to provide them with the addresses of their 25,000ers.

The factories' failures in this sphere placed an additional burden on the collective farm system. Theoretically the collective farm system was expected to provide both the salary difference if the factories were late and the regular salary which the worker earned at his rural post.[8] In fact, the collective farm system was no more enthusiastic about paying workers' salaries than were the factories. And like most responsibilities, this one devolved upon the lowest level of the system: assigning responsibility to the collective farm system actually meant asking the collective farms to support the 25,000ers. The collective farms, however, were generally not in a position to do this, for most lacked the cash and often even the in-kind payments necessary to pay the workers. Many farms requested the factories to pay the full salary because they could not afford the workers. Consequently, many, if not most, 25,000ers faced continual difficulties receiving even their meager collective farm salaries.[9]

Although the issue of salary was a central concern to many 25,000ers, it was not necessarily the most important, and certainly not the only, determinant of their rural standard of living. Access to the local cooperative store and, through it, to scarce food items and consumer goods was of major importance. The cooperatives, however, proved little more able and willing to provision the workers than did the factories and farms. Many cooperatives refused to supply the workers because they were not members of the cooperative society. A 25,000er in the Donbass discovered that the local cooperative forbade the sale of produce to workers, with the reasoning that "for outsiders there is no produce."[10] In cases where the cooperatives proved less hostile, the workers found that the stores were poorly stocked and lacking in all sorts of essentials.

The 25,000ers also experienced difficulties in procuring housing and clothing. Many workers were forced to find their own housing, seek shelter with accommodating collective farmers, pay high rents, or sleep in barns and offices.[11] The situation with clothing was little better and probably worse. The 25,000er N. I. Nepogodin, in a letter to the central committee of his trade union in October 1931, wrote that his two children had neither shoes nor clothes. The children of 25,000ers in the Western Region ran around without shoes in all sorts of weather, and the 25,000er Petrov in Kazakhstan reported that he and the other 25,000ers "walk around half-dressed." One needy and disgruntled 25,000er wrote to the central committee of the leather workers' trade union that "to go without boots is simply an embarrassment for a leather worker."[12]

The 25,000ers were supposed to be provisioned according to industrial norms, not local standards.[13] Yet despite the order not to provision the workers according to local standards, it was the local cooperative organs which were to be responsible for provisioning. Local means were not sufficient for these purposes. Moreover, local hostility and official resentment toward the supposedly privileged workers often made it unlikely from the outset that the workers would even be provisioned according to local standards. An inspection tour of one district in which 25,000ers were encountering difficulties reported that the documentation on the 25,000ers for purposes of provisioning was "stored" in the lavatory of the district party committee.[14] Complaints from the 25,000ers on the problems of provisioning continued throughout their stay; the issuing of orders, instructions, and circular letters on provisioning—each a reminder of or reprimand for nonfulfillment of an earlier order—also continued, as the party, the collective farm system, and the cooperative network all struggled (with varying degrees of enthusiasm) to enforce the unenforceable.[15]

The 25,000ers were left largely on their own and were forced to make do the best they could. Workers who had brought their families with them suffered the greatest privations. A report on a group of six 25,000ers on a collective farm in the Western Region indicated that they and their families lived under horrible conditions. They received nothing from the cooperatives but sugar, and the children were starving. The author of the report wrote that the family of the 25,000er Efremov lived on rotten meat. He concluded by saying "I could not watch this" and by warning that these conditions could lead to desertions. Workers in other areas, especially national minority areas, faced similar privations. The 25,000er Korostylev wrote from Kazakhstan: "It is bad to have your family here since they give you two puds [approximately seventy-two pounds] of flour and 1 pud of wheat—this is of course not enough. There have been many times when they've given us nothing. Frost is approaching –40 degrees, yet there are no clothes and they give us nothing." The 25,000er Ivan Kommissarov was forced to send his family back to Moscow because conditions were so bad.[16]

If 25,000ers with families fared poorly, this did not mean that a worker who was single or who had left his family in the city did much better. One 25,000er compared the living situation to the year 1919, while another 25,000er wrote that he lived "by some sort of miracle." In Moldavia the 25,000er Tulin wrote, "We are supplied in such a way that we cannot work any longer. If this keeps up, by spring we will have to go to a sanatorium or the grave." A report in the newspaper *Bednota* indicated that in a series of places 25,000ers were "almost starving," while a Kolkhoztsentr report on 25,000ers in national areas indicated that many 25,000ers had lost their health forever as a result of the horrible living conditions.[17]

Many 25,000ers were forced to trade on the private or black market to survive. Ivan Kommissarov reported that he could obtain consumer goods by trading butter, eggs, or wool but that, unfortunately, he did not have access to these barter items. Workers who were forced to buy on the private market soon found themselves in a worse position than the one at which they had begun. Prices were high, and many workers ended by selling all their belongings. A report on 25,000ers in Uzbekistan indicated that in one district the 25,000ers had sold all their belongings and were now "almost begging alms." Material conditions were worst for 25,000ers in national areas and grain-consuming areas. Workers in grain-producing areas and in areas with a large number of 25,000ers fared relatively better. For example, the AMO 25,000ers in Novo-Annenskii were able to create a closed distributor store for supplies; this must be attributed largely to their location, the strength of their numbers, and their close ties with AMO.[18] The majority of 25,000ers, however, had to make do with what was available locally, taking each day as it came and living much the same as, if not worse than, the local population.

The 25,000ers' response to material deprivation and hardship was by no means uniform. The same conditions that led many workers to desert led others to a reaffirmation of their attitudes concerning party and class responsibilities. It seems clear, however, that many desertions were caused precisely by the kinds of material considerations described above. A report from a March 1930 meeting of the Shuiskii *Okrug* party committee, Western Region, concluded that official neglect and difficult living conditions had led to a mood of "demoralization" among the 25,000ers and that mood had, in turn, caused a number of early desertions. The 25,000er N. I. Nepogodin, who had his two children with him, threatened in a letter of 2 October 1931 to leave if his family did not receive material help.[19] The 25,000er Beloshin, wrote:

> The conditions of our lives are too bad. Our many addresses to the local organs and the district committee on giving us produce fall on deaf ears. They told us that there are no produce reserves in our district. Up to this time, there have been no measures taken to provision us and on this ground there is a wavering and striving to return from here to the enterprises.[20]

The 25,000er Ivan Kommissarov, complaining about poor material conditions, wrote in desperation: "We are not convicts," while the worker Ivan Golovkin stated that the 25,000ers' material conditions "should not be in our socialist society."[21] It should be noted, however, that in spite of material difficulties and a great many complaints targeting these problems, most 25,000ers, including Kommissarov and Golovkin, complained rather than quit and, in the most extreme cases, asked permission to leave instead of deserting.

Some 25,000ers were not only not demoralized by the poor material conditions of the countryside, but seemed to have been strengthened by them. The 25,000er G. I. Bocharov wrote to the central committee of the leather workers' trade union about his life. He wrote that the cooperatives refused to supply him with consumer goods. Work was hard, but, he continued, "It is nothing, [we] will hold out." The 25,000er S. G. Kuleshov wrote in a letter of May 1930 that he had no bread, meat, milk, or tea, but that this mattered little for he "was used to" all sorts of deprivations, having spent eight years in the army and having fought through the duration of the civil war.[22] A Leningrad 25,000er described the conditions which he and his comrades lived under and noted that they had resisted demoralization:

> We work day and night. We do not have a five-day work week nor a day of rest . . . We, comrades, do not complain about the difficulties of work. Several comrades live in housing which is worse than in '19 [1919]. We eat one dish of peas and a piece of bread a day. In spite of this, among us, none have been frightened off.[23]

Many 25,000ers not only managed to endure the privations but did so with a sense of commitment. In fact, it seems that the 25,000ers often viewed material hardship as an inevitable part of "front-line" duty. This is clear from their frequent references to their civil war experience.

Material difficulties were not the workers' only problems. They had to live side by side with an often highly disgruntled peasantry poised on the brink of violent outburst for weeks at a time. They worked with frequently hostile officials who viewed them as rivals, incompetent city people, or a financial burden, and who made use of the least occasion to order the transfer, arrest, or party expulsion of a 25,000er. To one degree or another, these problems continued throughout the workers' stay, though on a slightly lesser scale than in the first half of 1930, and were little improved despite arrests of "class alien" officials, who by mistreating 25,000ers were "playing into the hands of the right deviation," and despite an avalanche of paper warnings, reprimands, and decrees demanding changes in the workers' situation. Collectivization, the weak administrative infrastructure of Soviet power in the countryside, and various defects in the original plans of the campaign served as the context for the workers' problems. The 25,000ers lived and worked under siegelike conditions. The demoralized and the disheartened left, while the others, conscious of their duties, dug in and continued to serve in the isolation of a hostile terrain. The 25,000ers felt, however, increasingly cut off from the revolution, the working class, and the factory.

The 25,000ers and the Factory

The 25,000ers had left the city and the factory behind and were now submerged in the life of the village. This caused tremendous problems for many 25,000ers, and it was to the factories that these workers turned for support. The factories were the only link which the workers had to their former lives. The factories were expected to maintain contact with the 25,000ers. They were to become the workers' lifeline to the cities and the working class. In their attempts to maintain this lifeline, the 25,000ers most eloquently (from the historian's viewpoint) expressed their plight. Their continuing struggle to keep open the lifeline to the factory sheds interesting light on the workers' rural experience and reveals that one of the most serious problems which the 25,000ers perceived in their situation was the fear of being "cut off" (*otryvat'sia*) from the factory, the working class, and the city.

The central authorities also saw a potential threat in the workers becoming cut off from the cities and, from the time of the recruitment campaign, discussed the need to maintain contact between the 25,000ers and their factories.[24] The 25,000ers were entering into the territory of not only the kulak and class enemy but of the great "spontaneous petit-bourgeois" peasantry. The fear that the 25,000ers would be contaminated by this vast contagion was one of the primary motivations behind the plans to establish permanent contacts with the factories. Once the 25,000ers had arrived in the countryside and had begun work, "mistakes" committed by 25,000ers, as well as desertions, would often be blamed on the factories' failures to maintain contact and, consequently, the workers' contamination by petit-bourgeois influences.[25] In the midst of perceived class enemies, it was essential to support the 25,000ers in their difficult and demanding work.

Unfortunately, few concrete steps were taken to maintain such contacts until news began to arrive in February and March of 1930 of the 25,000ers' desperate situation and struggles with rural officialdom. As early as January 1930, Kolkhoztsentr had announced the organization of a consultation bureau which would provide answers to any questions from 25,000ers within twenty-four hours; it also directed its regional offices to set up similar bureaus. However, given Kolkhoztsentr's staff shortages and the limited number of personnel assigned to work on the 25,000ers' campaign, these decisions were to remain, according to a newspaper report, "paper decisions."[26] It was only in March that the Central Council of Trade Unions began to take steps to establish contact with the 25,000ers through the factories. In a decree of 8 March the Central Council instructed the chairmen of factory committees to organize permanent bureaus of contact with the 25,000ers under the factory committees.[27]

The attempts to maintain contacts with the 25,000ers at the factories ran into difficulties from the outset. By May 1930 the Central Committee and the Central Council of Trade Unions were already issuing reprimands and condemnation of individual factories and the factories in general for failure to establish contact with the 25,000ers.[28] The trade union newspaper *Trud* began a rather vociferous campaign against derelict factories, a campaign which lasted throughout 1930. *Trud* accused the factory committees and trade unions of "liquidationist tendencies" vis-à-vis their responsibilities for the 25,000ers, "playing into the hands of the class enemy," "trade unionism," and most frequently "right deviationism."[29]

Rare were the factories which received praise for good communications with their 25,000ers. The AMO, Dinamo, Serp i Molot, and Vladimir Il'ich factories and the Babaev plant (after initial censure) were among the very few to be praised for their efforts.[30] More common were reports of factories which had no contacts with their 25,000ers. It was reported that many factory committees either had no idea where their 25,000ers were or had lost their addresses. The Red October factory filed away 25,000ers' letters and forgot them, while the secretary of the Babaev plant's factory committee reported that indeed they had received letters but were no longer aware of their whereabouts. The secretary of the Ruskabel' factory committee refused to publish the 25,000ers' letters in the wall newspaper, treating them instead as "strictly secret" documents.[31]

The majority of factory committees not only ignored the 25,000ers' letters but resented the demands made upon them to establish contacts. As one factory committee representative said, "We have no time, we are busy with other things." The chairman of a mine committee explained to one 25,000er who presented his complaints in person, "There is no time to answer your letters because of our overload of production questions." Echoing the original complaints of factory officialdom during the recruitment campaign, the secretary of a factory party cell in the Ukraine stated boldly, "I have no time to be concerned at meetings with such nonsense as reading letters of 25,000ers and, in general, you know, as I see it, to hell with all these mobilizations."[32]

The factories' shortcomings in maintaining contacts with the 25,000ers often placed the families of 25,000ers who had remained in the cities in serious material difficulties. The families of 25,000ers were entitled to remain in their housing, to seek immediate employment if in need, and to enjoy the rights included in the workers' collective agreements with the factories. Reports began to filter in, however, that the factories were refusing to fulfill their obligations. Representatives of one factory said, "We are not a labor exchange . . . we have nothing to offer 25,000ers and their families."[33] Cases were reported of evictions of 25,000ers' families from their homes; the families of 25,000ers who remained in the cities also had difficulties obtaining the salary differential payment from the factories and, according to one report, rations cards were taken away from some families.[34] When the 25,000er A. Petrova was recruited, her factory committee and trade union representative promised that her child would be taken care of while she was away. However, the factory failed to take steps to admit the child to a day-care center. Consequently, the child was left with a fifteen-year-old brother who had to quit school to take care of him. Petrova wrote, "I consider such relations of the factory organization to the family of a comrade sent to collective farm construction inadmissible."[35]

In its 25 July 1930 issue *Trud* presented a series of articles on the neglect of 25,000ers' families who remained in the cities. The 25,000er Kuz'min's family, it was reported, did not receive the salary differential and, as a consequence, his 3 1/2-year-old son died. The 25,000er Kaverin wrote to *Trud*, "Having sent us, the 25,000ers, to work on the collective farms, the Osvobozhdennyi Trud plant has completely ceased to be interested in us. Instead of concern for our families, the plant committee and cell make them nervous, driving them to distraction." Kaverin went on to explain that his wife and the wives of several of his comrades went to the plant to talk to the party cell secretary, one Filiaev, about their husbands. They wished to know whether they could send letters to their husbands and also asked how long the men would be away. Filiaev, showing great sensitivity, replied, "Maybe for five years, maybe forever." The women appeared disconcerted in response to this, so Filiaev felt compelled to elaborate: "No one sent them, they went voluntarily. And apparently they have gone forever. We don't need them. We can make do without them . . . Don't wait for them now, go look for other husbands. They, I am sure, have already found someone for themselves." Kaverin was naturally upset by the news of Filiaev's paternal counsel and wrote to *Trud* for aid.[36]

The newspapers, especially those catering to working-class audiences, proved to be the 25,000ers' main champions in challenging the factories to maintain contacts with the workers and in exposing cases of neglect and "criminal silence" toward 25,000ers. The Central Committee, which continued to criticize the factories for poor contacts, encouraged the press to publicize the workers' plight, while the 25,000ers themselves often wrote the central press requesting its intervention with the factories.[37] *Trud* published a special "black board" for which 25,000ers were encouraged to nominate especially derelict factories and called a meeting in mid-October with the central committees of the trade unions and factory representatives to discuss the issue.[38]

The factories were no more willing to maintain contact with the 25,000ers than they had been to recruit the workers. However, the workers still continued to write letters to their comrades at the factories, the factory committees, the factory party cells, and their trade unions. On the basis of their written sentiments, the workers appear to have been much more disturbed by their increasing alienation from the factory and city than by their material situation. For the majority the factory remained a central feature in their world. Their expressions of neglect, insult, and grievance vis-à-vis contact with the factories are most significant in providing insights into the workers' experience in the countryside.

The 25,000ers feared being cut off from their factories and class. Although many were not complete strangers to rural life, this was not their life. They were products of the city, the factory, the Soviet proletariat. They perceived the countryside much the same as their party did and feared the possibility of "petit-bourgeois contamination." They expressed their feelings and described their experience with reference to Marxist categories and ample use of class language. In this sense, they revealed their class origins, as well as their party and political sympathies. In another equally real sense, however, the workers were simply expressing the plight of the urbanized individual isolated in the backwardness of rural Soviet Russia. It was to the factories that they turned for aid in attempting to diminish this isolation, and it was the factories which they condemned—not the party which sent them—for enhancing their isolation by failing to maintain contact.

The 25,000ers expressed their grievances toward the factories in the manner of a sense of betrayal. Most felt the factories owed them at least an occasional letter, given the workers' long years at the bench, and their service as 25,000ers. The 25,000ers Formovskii and Mal'kevich expressed this in a letter to their factory:

> What happened to all the glorious promises of support and contacts? What happened to the ardent speeches with which you bid us farewell to work on the collective farm? You have forgotten about us . . . Not one letter, not even a hint of the wish to establish contacts with us to aid us in our hard work . . . [39]

These sentiments were expressed repeatedly in letters written by 25,000ers. For example, the following is from a letter by a 25,000er published in *Metallist* under the bold headline "Criminal Silence": "How am I to understand your silence? When we left, you promised to write, and now at such a difficult time, I have nothing from you."[40] The same sense of betrayal can be seen in this letter by the 25,000er Samechkin:

> When we were promoted to collective farm work in the countryside, the trade union and factory organs assured us that they would maintain strong contacts and help us in our work. But what did we see in fact? [We] sent 3 letters to the Moscow regional department of the leather workers' union—2 months have passed and no answer.[41]

Finally, an excerpt from a letter by the 25,000er Kenig to his factory committee presents some idea of *why* the workers felt such a sense of betrayal. Kenig wrote, "I wrote you already several times and also the district committee of metalists, but I received no answer. I am very sorry that at our send-off much was said but deeds are few. I would like very much to correspond with the factory where I worked so long and which I am used to as my native home [*rodina*]."[42] The factory was "home," or *rodina*, to the 25,000ers; it formed the essential and central component of their everyday life and work experience while they were a part of life in the city.

The extent to which the factory and the city were home to these workers becomes even clearer in those workers' statements which touch on the difficulties of life in the countryside. The Moscow 25,000er A. A. Merkulov wrote that he received the newspapers *Trud* and *Za kollektivizatsiiu* and a trade union paper from his union but found little time in his busy schedule to read. He described the poverty and backwardness of his collective farm. According to Merkulov, there was no club, no library, no radio. Religion was very strong, and the collective farm youth were "drunkards and hooligans." Half of the *sel'sovet* members even refused to join the collective farm. Merkulov pleaded for some sort of contact with his factory. Other 25,000ers framed their grievances similarly, complaining that they were cut off from urban life, had no contacts with their factories, and in many cases, did not even receive newspapers.[43]

Life was especially difficult for Russian 25,000ers in national minority areas and here, perhaps more than elsewhere, contacts with the factories were an urgent necessity. The Leningrad 25,000er A.P. Tikhonovskii from the Zheliabov plant wrote of the difficulties of life in Central Asia. He described the vast cultural differences which he encountered in everyday life. He expressed surprise that here everyone, now including the 25,000ers, sat on the floor instead of on chairs, that the houses lacked windows, and that everyone slept in a row. He complained that the only food was dry flat wafers and currants and that "they have no idea about bread here." There were no knives or forks according to Tikhonovskii and, as in the villages of Russia, everyone ate from one bowl. He concluded by saying that it would be a great pleasure to receive news from Russia since newspapers arrived only every ten days.[44] The 25,000ers in these areas were subject to the most difficult conditions and often ended their letters with the same plea as the 25,000er Kochnev who wrote, from Uzbekistan, "[We] need moral comradely support now."[45]

The 25,000ers were surrounded by poverty and backwardness. The enthusiasm and militancy which had surrounded them in the cities had long receded into the past, revived only sporadically and somewhat artificially by the receipt of newspapers and letters and the convocation of an occasional conference of 25,000ers. In this atmosphere the 25,000ers pleaded for leadership and moral support from their factories. Rural officialdom offered them no aid, and many lacked the comradely support groups necessary to maintain their determination. The 25,000er Rumiantsev complained that the factory organs were acting "bureaucratically", "They sent us and forgot us." Moreover, he added, "by the way, now in the countryside more than ever we need support, like air, like bread."[46] The Minsk 25,000er Okunev explained why such support was so important:

> I am trying not to let down the workers who sent me to the countryside. The trouble is that I'm completely isolated from life: mail arrives twice a week, [there are] no books and not much in the way of newspapers. It wouldn't be so bad if you, that is the factory committee and party cell, sometimes wrote me and advised me on work. What sort of news from the plant? . . . How is socialist competition? This is very interesting to me.[47]

The 25,000er, Mal'kov, further explained, "The factories must understand that we don't simply need correspondence. We need leadership. [We] need fast direct answers to our daily urgent questions. This is one of the essential conditions for the success of our work. This is why we dwell on this."[48] Despite these pleas for contacts, most factories continued to ignore their 25,000ers.

The workers inundated the central authorities and the press with complaints about the factories' "criminal silence." A number of 25,000ers visited their factories while on leave from collective farm work in order to attempt to renew contacts. In most cases they were harshly rebuffed. One 25,000er went to his factory to visit his former comrades only to be unceremoniously booted out by the factory's director. The 25,000er Strastina, whose letters were ignored by her factory committee, visited her factory and was refused the right to present a report on her work at a workers' meeting.[49] The 25,000ers were desperate for some sort of contact with their previous life as workers, desperate to avoid total submersion and isolation in the Soviet countryside.

Yet the 25,000ers' campaign, in spite of all its troubles, did not founder. The workers, in the main, did not succumb to the feared "petit-bourgeois contagion" of the countryside. This is, perhaps, most evident in the very inability of the 25,000ers to merge with their rural surroundings, to cast off their proletarian identity, and to forget about the factory which no longer remembered its workers. Moreover, for many, it was not the harsh and unfamiliar setting and material deprivations alone which caused their greatest hostility and hardship, but the sense of betrayal which they felt from their former factories. The workers did not condemn the party and state which sent them to live and work in such rural blight but instead attacked the factories for endangering the campaign and for failing to support them. The original bonds between Moscow and the 25,000ers were, for the most part, not broken off. The 25,000ers remained committed to their class and party. Their original class and political commitments were reinforced by their isolation and the difficult straits in which they found themselves. The campaign did not founder because, in the end, its success, like that of the recruitment drive, did not and, in fact, could not, depend on material incentives to maintain its force. Nor could it depend on any kind of coercion or on punishment for desertion, for the country was vast and the highways of the First Five-Year Plan were teeming with people on the move, on the run, or simply out for adventure. The campaign had no other basis of support but the original motivations of the workers whose enthusiasm, determination, patriotism, or class hostility had compelled them to join the ranks of the 25,000ers. The workers' response to deprivation and isolation was a hardening of convictions and a realization that they represented one of the last outposts of the party and the proletariat in the countryside.

Bolstering the Campaign

The center's response to the plight of the 25,000ers set off a paper avalanche upon the country's regions, districts, and villages. In decrees of 21 May 1930,

6 August 1930, and 23 December 1931, the Central Committee led the campaign to remedy the problems of the workers. The decrees stressed the problems of salary, housing, food and consumer goods, and relations with local officials and the factories.[50] The Central Committee was aided in these endeavors by the Central Council of Trade Unions and Kolkhoztsentr, which each parrotted the instructions of the party in a series of important decrees and directives.[51] These decrees and directives were followed by similar instructions issued by an army of agencies and commissariats involved in various aspects of the administration of the campaign. This was rule by circular par excellence and exemplified the paper implementation of policy so widespread in the Russian countryside from time immemorial.

There was an inverse ratio, moreover, between the amount of paper devoted to a particular problem and the effectiveness of implementing a solution to the problem. Time and again the same instructions were issued, the same problems noted, with the only changes in each successive decree or directive being the extension of reprimands and threats to an ever-increasing cast of institutional actors called upon to assume responsibility for the campaign. Rule by circular and multiple jurisdictions over the 25,000ers made it unlikely that their material situation would be drastically altered. Some of the workers' problems may be attributed to the rural administrative infrastructure, which was understaffed and overworked, unprepared, and often antagonistic to the workers. Rural administration was suited to inertia or blitzkrieg campaigns but was little able to perform the routine and mundane tasks of day-to-day government. The center could not enforce its decrees and directives because it was forced to rely on the very same apparatus which was responsible for a large part of the workers' problems in the first place. The all-powerful state was in a very real sense helpless to support its own cadres. It was the victim of ideology, utopia, and mythmaking; once come to the countryside, it was held captive by the social and economic conditions which the revolution had defied in 1917 and against which it had struggled ever since to overcome.

Although it could not improve the material conditions of the 25,000ers, the center was able to aid the workers by other means largely unrelated to the countryside's administrative structure. The press published workers' letters, exposed problems, and served as an outlet for workers' grievances. The central committees of the workers' trade unions served much the same purpose as the press, although without the publicity aspect. Both the press and the trade unions played the role of ombudsmen and, in many cases, managed to secure aid for individual 25,000ers.

The Central Committee also organized mass inspection tours of the 25,000ers as well as workers' conferences on the district and *okrug* levels.

Inspections took place in the late spring and early summer of 1930 in most parts of the country.[52] Their main effect was to stimulate renewed press attention on the 25,000ers, thus bringing them back into the limelight after a period of relative silence between February and April. The press attention served to maintain the heroic images of the campaign, to glorify individual workers, and to reinforce the goals and militant ethos of the recruitment campaign. The inspections were repeated several times in 1930 and 1931.

In most cases the inspection tours ended in the convocation of conferences of 25,000ers. Usually the conferences took place on the district or *okrug* level and, on occasion, in the offices of a newspaper like *Bednota* or in the workers' home city during a summer break.[53] These conferences led to further publicity for the workers and their accompanying glorification. The conferences also provided a forum for the workers to exchange experience and information in order to renew, in a manner of speaking, their vows to the revolution, the party, and the class struggle, and to regain contact with other workers in order to reaffirm their class solidarity.[54]

The conferences were officially intended as repreparation courses. As early as December 1929, when it was clear that the short preparation courses for the 25,000ers would be insufficient, plans had been made to regroup and retrain the workers after the completion of spring sowing. However, following spring sowing the courses were delayed in many areas until the winter of 1930–31, when two-week course conferences were held for all 25,000ers.[55]

The primary result of the inspections, conferences, and courses was to bolster the workers' authority and to reinforce their original militancy. Although the paper intervention of the center could not alter the workers' material conditions, it was possible to reaffirm the importance of the campaign, the workers' sense of mission, and the center's continued trust in the workers. In addition to these means the state had other more substantive rewards to offer to its loyal supporters in order to attempt to offset the damaging effects of cultural and material deprivation.

The glorification of the 25,000ers, which was mainly confined to the press and the conferences, on occasion also took the form of presenting workers with various types of medals and awards. A number of 25,000ers were awarded Orders of Lenin and other honorary distinctions.[56] Many more 25,000ers, however, received another type of honor, which was much more tangible than an honorarium in its payment for services rendered. These workers were offered the opportunity to study or they were promoted in the bureaucracy.

The 25,000ers were granted their first study opportunity by a Central Committee decree of 6 August 1930, which granted those 25,000ers who had "proven themselves" first priority for study in short courses, agricultural institutes, or soviet-party schools.[57] A Kolkhoztsentr circular of 7 October

1930 confirmed this commitment by calling upon its regional apparatus to single out the best 25,000ers and to send them to study in order to secure them for promotion within the Kolkhoztsentr bureaucracy.[58] Further steps in this direction were taken in a Central Committee decree of 23 December 1931 stipulating that one thousand 25,000ers were slated for advanced study in agricultural institutes and colleges.[59]

In addition to offering study opportunities, the central authorities endeavored to renew their commitment to the campaign by promoting the workers directly into more responsible posts in the rural party, soviet, and collective farm system. At the time of the regional party conferences held on the eve of the Sixteenth Party Congress in June 1930, a number of 25,000ers were elected to serve as delegates to the conferences and as members of the regional committees of the party in the territories where they served.[60] The 25,000er L. I. Litvak was elected to serve as a delegate to the Sixteenth Party Congress.[61] When the *okrug* was eliminated in August 1930, and district branches of Kolkhoztsentr were organized or expanded throughout the country, it was suggested that 25,000ers, in particular, be used to staff the district branches.[62] According to the leading Soviet historian of the 25,000ers, in 1931 and 1932 the remaining 25,000ers began to move away from collective farm work into leading cadre work in the rural party and government.[63] In addition, in early January 1931 Kolkhoztsentr organized, within its own apparatus, a promotion program of 25,000ers leading to the promotion of 2,362 workers into the district and regional branches of Kolkhoztsentr.[64] The programs in further education and promotion both had as their main aim the preservation of the 25,000ers as leading cadres in the rural administrative system.

All of these measures were implemented in order to bolster the campaign of the 25,000ers. Whether viewed as co-optation, practical necessity related to cadre shortages, or the desire to staff the rural administration with trusted cadres, these measures reflected the fact that the 25,000ers were still viewed as a significant force and as valued cadres greatly needed by the system. The primary effect of these measures was symbolic: they reaffirmed the party's commitments to the workers and the importance of the campaign. The center could not change the material conditions of the workers' lives nor could it force the factories to maintain contacts with 25,000ers. It could, however, continue to emphasize the vanguard role of the 25,000ers as the center's representatives in the countryside. This served to bolster the workers' sense of mission and helped to sustain them as the campaign came increasingly to resemble an isolated outpost in enemy territory. The 25,000ers remained firm in their commitment to the party. Under siege their ranks held strong for the duration of the campaign. By the time of the December 1931 Central

Committee decree, which officially concluded the campaign, the party could claim that the 25,000ers had accomplished their mission.

The Ranks of the 25,000ers: Desertion and Duty

The original detachment of 27,519 25,000ers had fallen in numbers from 22,000 in the summer of 1930 to approximately 18,000 in 1931, on the eve of the end of the campaign. Data on the number of 25,000ers employed directly within the Kolkhoztsentr system in the spring of 1931 ranges from 14,068 to 15,030. If, in the spring of 1930, the 25,000ers were represented on 19 percent of all collective farms, then by the following year this force had fallen to a percentage of 7.4 of all collective farms, although it should be noted that a relatively large percentage (14.3) of older collective farms (organized before the spring of 1930) still had 25,000ers on their administrative boards and that the number of collective farms in general had increased (to 190,111), while the number of 25,000ers had not, thus making it inevitable that the percentage would drop. And in the major grain regions 25,000ers were still to be found on one fifth to one third of the older collective farms (see table 5).[65] These statistics, moreover, represent only those 25,000ers who were still employed within the collective farm system. Soviet scholars have estimated, taking into account 25,000ers employed in other branches of rural work, that approximately 18,000 remained in the countryside in the spring of 1931.[66] After approximately two years of work almost 10,000 (or 36 percent) 25,000ers had left the ranks, whether through desertion, arrest or purge, official permission, promotion, enrollment in school, illness, or death. The turnover rate, or more accurately, the departure rate, for the 25,000ers was relatively low when compared to turnover rates for industrial labor or other rural cadres during the First Five-Year Plan.[67] The ranks of the 25,000ers held strong through the upheavals and chaos of 1930 and 1931.

According to Soviet scholars, the 25,000ers who successfully completed their tour of duty tended to be from three overlapping groups of workers. The first group consisted of 25,000ers who were members of the Communist party. The second group was made up of workers who had been recruited in highly successful campaigns and from areas which included large numbers of political activists, cadre workers, and metalworkers. The departure rate for Leningrad 25,000ers, for example, was only 15.3 percent compared to 36 percent for all 25,000ers. A final category of 25,000er likely to serve for the duration of the campaign consisted of workers employed directly on collective farms, as opposed to those workers who found themselves employed on the higher rungs of the rural bureaucracy.[68] Although it is not possible to verify the accuracy of these Soviet claims, it is indeed probable that they are accurate, first, because they tend to confirm the impression given by the recruitment campaign, indicating that the workers most likely to volunteer were also those most likely to stay, and, second, because the data is predictable: the groups most likely to remain in the countryside were the groups which formed the majority of the 25,000ers in the first place.

Hard, statistical evidence is not available and most probably is nonexistent for the 25,000ers who did not remain for the duration of their term of service. It is, however, possible to evaluate the experience of these 25,000ers, as well as those who remained, from another perspective. This is to return once again to the workers themselves, in order to construct a coherent, though impressionistic, picture of their experience and of the reasons leading 25,000ers to join the ranks of the deserters or to remain for the campaign's duration.

The most widespread causes for the departures of 25,000ers included material and cultural difficulties, isolation from the city and factory, peasant hostility and resistance to change, and conflicts with rural officials. Approximately one half of the ten thousand departures occurred by the summer of 1930—that is, during the most difficult period of the campaign. These departures were sometimes linked to conflict with peasants and involvement in the excesses of the period, but, given that the majority of the 25,000ers were effectively excluded from power for most of this time, it was far more likely that a 25,000er's departure was a result of the actions of rural officials who made liberal use of dismissal, arrest, and purge to hasten the departure of 25,000ers.

The district organs of the party played a key role in the departures of 25,000ers in both 1930 and 1931. This conclusion is supported by data from the Central Black Earth Region from the early fall of 1930 based on seventy-seven districts with a total of 675 workers. In this region 199 workers left the countryside. The majority (56.8 percent) left as a result of district party committee decisions which determined that the workers were either not suited for work or poorly prepared; a smaller percentage (24.6) left as a result of what were described as "violations."[69] Data from the Leningrad Region shows that the district party committees continued to play an important role in the departures throughout 1931. According to data from August 1931 and based on 227 departures from among 651 workers in the Leningrad Region, the largest number of departures was based upon actions taken at the district level (78); departures based on desertions (33), violations (33), and illness (54) also accounted for a significant proportion of the total.[70] Here, as in the case of the Central Black Earth departures, departures resulting from violations must be treated with caution because of the central role which the often hostile district party officials had in defining violations and in the hiring and firing of 25,000ers. However, it is clear that a very large percentage of the departures were due to purely administrative decisions rather than simple desertion.

Violations should not be discounted entirely as a factor because they most certainly played a role in the early departures linked to the winter of 1930 collectivization drive. There were 25,000ers who committed excesses and were fired, arrested, or sent back to their factories in the spring of 1930. There were also 25,000ers who committed various misdemeanors ranging from theft and drunkenness to moral transgression. The majority of these workers were recalled, dismissed, or run out of villages by angry peasants.

There was, however, another category of violation which was almost always a result of conflicts with officials and fell under the rubric of right deviation. From the limited evidence available, it appears that very few workers were labeled right deviationists and that very few who received this label actually merited the distinction. Right deviationism among the 25,000ers, and to a great extent, among rural cadres in general, meant some form of verbal opposition to or criticism of quotas or goals which appeared too high or unrealistic to local cadres in charge of their implementation; it could also mean nothing more than the customary inertia of rural officials or simply a label manipulated for use in power struggles.

A number of 25,000ers tried to resist demands of plenipotentiaries for what they considered unrealistic grain deliveries. Workers also sometimes attempted to intercede for collective farmers with higher authorities and were caught in the crossfire. Such actions, however, were generally not politically inspired.[71] The term *right deviation* was simply one of opprobrium, readily available for use when it was necessary to blitzkrieg the farms to obtain grain, increase sown acreage, or gather seed for sowing. For example, at a district course conference of 25,000ers, it was reported that there were "several individual manifestations" of the right deviation among 25,000ers. The 25,000er Kernozhitskii was reported to have said, "The control figures of collectivization, especially in Moscow Region, were unfulfillable and unrealistic." He was seconded by 25,000ers Likhov and Solozkov. The latter, who also commented on the absurdity of overly high industrialization targets and was also accused of right deviationism, protested against his newly acquired label, saying: "I don't even understand the issue [of right deviationism] . . . We students have the right to ask our teachers any questions and we can't be accused of right opportunism for this."[72] There were only three reported cases which seem likely to have merited the label: two Leningrad 25,000ers in the Lower Volga who wrote a declaration condemning the party line, and the worker Rakitskii who spoke in favor of the famous Mamaev article condemning the Central Committee for the excesses of the winter collectivization drive.[73] Even here, however, it should be noted that *Mamaevshchina* was not identical to, though identified with, the right, and that the real right of Bukharin and company stood by silently during the time the *Mamaevshchina* arose from the party ranks.

Workers who were accused of right deviationism were generally dismissed, purged, and sometimes even arrested. Many of these cases were simply the result of power struggles with rural officials. In other instances, these 25,000ers were simply disgusted with the outcome of collectivization, like the worker, who on returning to his factory, said, "There are too many injustices; it is not collectivism, it is pillage."[74]

Many other 25,000ers were caught up in the web of permanent purges and arrests of rural officials which was characteristic of the collectivization years and which decimated the ranks of collective farm and *sel' sovet* officials. Like other lower-level rural officials, the 25,000ers were continuously vulnerable to accusations of abuse of office. Most often these accusations came from the district organs and were linked to the failure to fulfill some unrealistic demand placed upon the collective farms. In other cases they derived from power struggles and were centered in the realm of the absurd. For example, the 25,000er Kondrat'ev was tried for discrediting the government. He saw some twine hanging from a telegraph pole, tried to remove the twine, and accidently damaged the pole. The 25,000er Antonov was tried in court for the death of sixty-three collective farm horses. However, Antonov claimed that he had nothing to do with that sector of the farm because he was in charge of cultural work; he was therefore charged, more appropriately, with insufficient cultural work among horses.[75] Such was the mentality of the times and such were the risks of rural office.

Material and cultural difficulties and the isolation of the 25,000ers also accounted for many of their departures. These causes for departure tended to be more prevalent in the later stages of the campaign, in late 1930 and in 1931, when the campaign entered into a state of siege. Most of the 25,000ers who survived the dizzying events of the first half of 1930 "dug in" and became hardened in their convictions; others were worn down by the experience, and about one half of the departures occurred at this time.

Most of these departures were a matter of simple demoralization, the type of demoralization which can easily grip soldiers living in a foreign land, fighting a seemingly losing battle, and living below their own standards of civilization. In their letters the 25,000ers described their response to life in the countryside after almost two years of work.

As demoralization set in, some 25,000ers deserted, but many managed to hold out until the end of the campaign and others sought official permission to leave. One 25,000er wrote, ''I will manage somehow until the end of the year and then I will return to production; let another work in my place . . . until the fall, until the fall and then demobilization.''[76] The 25,000er Baronov was gripped by a similar mood. He wrote:

> I consider that there is no purpose for me. I am simply an overhead expense for both the collective farm and the government. I am a worker from the bench, [I] worked in production for 13 years, [am] completely unfamiliar with collective farm construction, don't know the local language, and there are no translators. No one has helped me at all in my work.[77]

Baronov saw no purpose to his presence. This, too, was cause for demoralization and was also expressed by the 25,000er Sharov:

> Because of the presence of such a small amount of knowledge which I have, it is impossible to measure up to the work laid before me and to fulfill in time that great cause which the party entrusted me . . . I have entered such an impasse from which I cannot get out. I walk around like a fool and can think of nothing and I don't know what to do. I ask [you] to take measures to remove me from this post.[78]

Demoralization led many workers to attempt to obtain permission to return to the factories. One woman 25,000er, who was obviously desperate, tried to gain permission to leave by having her husband write the district party committee that she was pregnant. When this failed, her mother wrote the district committee that she was ill and must be released from work. The outcome of her attempts to depart with permission is not known, but she was criticized in the press.[79] Most often, however, workers who sought official permission to leave simply wrote straightforward letters expressing a desire to return to production.[80] And although asking permission to leave was formally not desertion, these workers were often labeled deserters for their inability to complete their tour of duty.

There was another form of desertion, which, like asking for permission to leave, was a kind of variation on an original theme. This was suicide, and as indicated earlier, there were seven reported cases of this, the most complete form of desertion. An interesting and well-documented case is contained in the Smolensk Archive. This was the case of A. K. Shevchenko, a Red army veteran and party member since 1926, a ''hereditary proletarian'' in his late twenties or early thirties who came from a plant in Ivanovo-Voznesensk. Different explanations were given for Shevchenko's suicide. The local authorities concluded that he was personally unstable and that he should never have been recruited, thus placing the blame on his factory's recruiting committee. The outside plenipotentiary sent to investigate the case blamed the local and district officials for failing to come to Shevchenko's aid and for Shevchenko's substandard material conditions. The witness Averbukh, a friend of the "deserter," blamed the suicide on Shevchenko's dissatisfaction with his family life. Probably these were all factors in the suicide, but Shevchenko, himself, should be consulted. He wrote two rather contradictory suicide notes to his factory. The fact that he would address his suicide notes to the factory is itself significant, and the contradictions in the tone of the two notes reveal both his identity as a worker, his feelings of isolation, and his hostility to the factory which no longer needed him. In the first suicide note Shevchenko wrote, "Comrades. Forgive me for this act but there is nothing more for me to do. There is no way out. I am not a coward and not a timid person. I have not stained the dignity of the worker . . . But when I came to the countryside, I saw that it is different from what they told us . . ." In his second letter Shevchenko's tone is somewhat altered, for it is less despairing and much more bitter. He wrote, "Comrades. Forgive me for this dirty affair but I ask that you send my body to Ivanovo-Voznesensk. I ask you not to refuse my request but if I don't deserve it then throw [it] to the dogs." Shevchenko addressed the third of his suicide notes to his wife, Shura. He wrote, "Forgive me for not saying goodbye to you but it doesn't really matter. Shura, you said to go to the collective farm. I don't advise [anyone?] to work here. There is such chaos. The peasants work day and night. There is no time to rest. All you do is work." Here, Shevchenko expressed his complete demoralization. There was nowhere to turn for help so Shevchenko "deserted" from the ranks.[81]

There was a less drastic and more common form of desertion which offered a way out of the countryside. This was simply to leave—to return to the factory or to escape onto the vast construction site which was the Soviet Union in those days and seek work elsewhere and anonymously. There were, however, penalties for desertion if caught. Party workers were subject to party discipline, including the possibility of expulsion, while nonparty workers could be expelled from the trade unions and possibly fired from their factory jobs.[82] It is more likely that most deserters simply returned to their factories and resumed their former positions. The factories needed skilled labor, and many even attempted to recall 25,000ers. Having resisted the original recruitment, the factories were not all that likely to punish or turn in their much-needed deserters. Nor were the district organs which were anxious to be rid of 25,000ers and, in any case, likely to be held responsible for desertions.[83] In fact, according to Kolkhoztsentr data from July 1931, there were only 788 cases of documented desertion, as compared to 1,015 justified departures and 6,079 workers who were simply unaccounted for.[84] Given the country's wide open spaces, the demand for skilled labor, and the chaos which facilitated flight, desertion—despite the penalties—was a fairly easy option for 25,000ers.

However, relatively few 25,000ers chose desertion as a way out. The majority (64 percent) did not forsake the campaign. These workers lived under the same conditions as those workers who chose, or were forced, to leave the countryside. Their response to their experience, however, was different. These 25,000ers viewed themselves as soldiers in the trenches, holding out against the enemy. The civil war mentality which had led many of them to volunteer in the recruitment campaign was reinforced by the material difficulties, the dangers, and the isolation from factory and class. The experience of the siege served to bolster their identity as workers, Communists, and 25,000ers.

This response is evident, first of all, in the 25,000ers' condemnation of the deserters. In their letters and statements, the workers compared the deserters to wartime deserters. The center, to be sure, made the same analogy and probably influenced the workers' choice of words. Nonetheless, the 25,000ers were no strangers to the language of struggle, militancy, and omnipresent enemies. Commenting on the desertion of a former comrade, a Leningrad 25,000er stated, "I am not boasting, but I say firmly—as a communist, as a Petersburg man, as a worker—that I took upon myself this cause that the VKP (b) entrusted me with and I will not retreat . . . let them kill me but I will not do such a deceitful thing."[85] In Belgorodskii *Okrug*, Central Black Earth Region, a group of 25,000ers condemned the deserters Kuznetsov, Loginov, and Seleznov at an *okrug* conference of 25,000ers:

> Don't believe Kuznetsov, Loginov, and Seleznov, those cowards and scoundrels who shamefully and treacherously left the front of collective farm construction and tried to justify their desertion with dirty slander.

> These scoundrels have no place in the ranks of the working class. We demand the most extreme measures—remove them from the ranks of the working class.[86]

The 25,000ers Kozyrev and Romanov proudly stated: "In other districts, over half the 25,000ers have returned, but we are monolithic . . ."[87] Needless to say, not all 25,000ers were "monolithic," yet because a politically significant proportion of them were, it is necessary to determine why the workers refused to "retreat."

Most often, the 25,000ers explained why they chose to remain in terms of defensive motivations—such as resisting the class enemy, terror, and so on—or in terms of class solidarity, party loyalty, or Soviet patriotism. Quite logically, the latter were often reinforced by the former. This is clear from the 25,000ers' letters on the difficulties which they faced and in their pledges to remain in the countryside to the end of the First Five-Year Plan.

The 25,000ers perceived themselves as worker-revolutionaries in the thick of battle, in the forefront of the class struggle, and as the soldiers who would complete the work of those—often including the 25,000ers, themselves—who had fought for socialism on the fronts of the civil war. The Moscow 25,000ers G. M. Kresnoshchekov (a Communist since 1918) and A. I. Gorbachev (a Communist since 1928) exemplified this mood in the following declaration:

> Work has turned out to be more difficult than we could have ever imagined. But neither slander, nor persecution, nor arson of our lodgings, nor shots in the windows from our class enemies will cause our enthusiasm to waver for one minute in the cause to fulfill our tasks to party and government . . . We will strike down the kulak in open battle on the economic and political front.[88]

The worker Markov wrote that the 25,000ers worked with the same enthusiasm as they did at the factory with the one essential difference that the issue of *kto-kogo* (roughly, "who will beat whom") was clearer in the countryside. This issue was indeed clear to the workers, for many lived in constant danger. In fact, workers at a conference of 25,000ers in the Northern Region in late 1930 condemned the regional procurators for their leniency in dealing with the kulak.[89]

The clarity of *kto-kogo* often served to enhance the workers' class and political solidarity in the countryside. When 25,000ers were murdered by "class enemies," there was a tendency for workers to pull closer together. When a Putilov 25,000er was murdered, ten Putilov workers, including the oldest worker at the plant, volunteered to take his place. In response to terror the 25,000er Shumar' stated, "Not in any case . . . should we shirk before the difficulties in the countryside." Shumar' urged his comrades at a 25,000ers' meeting not to let the terrorist acts of the "enemy" frighten them into retreat.[90] When the 25,000er Inzhevatkin was murdered, one of the speeches eulogizing him resembled very much a sermon for a dead soldier and called for greater class solidarity: "He fell, as a valiant soldier of the revolution, at his post of socialist construction . . . His glorious death will give our ranks still more firmness and unity."[91] Many 25,000ers viewed their campaign as—in the words of one group of workers—"our last and decisive battle."[92] Due to their isolation and siegelike existence, the 25,000ers, perhaps even more than their comrades still at the factories, continued to live in the world of class war, fronts, and a perpetual struggle with enemies. Resolutions passed at meetings of 25,000ers continued to lash out at the all-dangerous right deviation, left extremists, "right-left double dealers," kulaks, and pernicious "sabotage" of the "agents of the world bourgeoisie." This mentality was further reinforced by the infrequent letters sent to the 25,000ers from the center which, while failing to address individual needs or to insert a personal note, never failed to bring the workers the latest news on the machinations of the class enemy, the most recent trials of saboteurs, and reminders of the importance of vigilance.[93]

This mentality, in part, explains why so many 25,000ers managed to endure the hardships of life in the countryside. Not all 25,000ers, however, were so persistent in their militancy and dedication to struggle. Many 25,000ers simply viewed their assignments as a class or party duty for the good of the cause and the nation and got down to work, in the words of one district official, "in proletarian style."[94] Inzhevatkin, the "fallen soldier," had expressed this side of the 25,000ers' determination in a letter to his wife:

> I have told you and written lots of times explaining why I had to leave. No one is to blame—neither you nor I. I am here. The life here doesn't attract me personally and it isn't pleasant for me to be so far from my family, but on the other hand, it is for the good of the common cause. We must arouse the masses . . . in the backward national regions to the great work of construction. That is all we are living for and all we are concerned with. I have no personal interests here . . . [95]

Moreover, personal interests were to be subordinated to the cause, to the party, as revolutionary tradition dictated. Some deserters were even condemned for putting personal or material interests above the cause.[96] This, according to the 25,000er Mikhailov, was as it should be. Speaking in the language of bolshevism and the militant civil war tradition of the party, he said:

> We 25,000ers are not a little force. The reason we are Bol'sheviks is to overcome all sorts of "trifles." There are no conditions under which we will not be victorious, but for this we must struggle—must struggle, clench our teeth as we did on the front.[97]

The workers had an obligation to uphold before class and party, and if their revolutionary faith or belief in the class war was not sufficient to motivate them in their struggles, there was always the traditional appeal to party discipline. Party discipline, moreover, was expected to be second nature to a Bolshevik and a natural political trait of the proletariat. General Grigorenko, in his memoirs, captured the attitude of the party rank and file in his description of party discipline and obligations. He wrote, "I felt that my voluntary entry into the party had given the party the right to control my fate as it saw fit. For me, observance of party discipline and unconditional subordination to party decisions were absolutely natural."[98] Sacrifice and hard work, battle with the class enemy, and struggles on all sorts of revolutionary fronts came with the party card.

These were some of the forces which served to hold the 25,000ers' detachment together through the First Five-Year Plan and were also instrumental in leading to a campaign within the 25,000ers' movement to pledge to remain at rural work to the end of the First Five-Year Plan. This campaign, which had a most definite central impetus, was launched at the regional meetings of 25,000ers which took place on the eve of the First All-Union Rally. A group of Moscow 25,000ers submitted the following statement, which was a typical example of the pledges:

> In answer to sabotage within the country and preparations for imperialist intervention, we 25,000ers working in Orekhovo-Zuevskii district, Moscow Region, will stay until the end of the five-year plan and promise the party that [we] will struggle until the end with unflagging energy for the final rooting out of . . . capitalism in the countryside, for the full elimination of the kulak as a class on the basis of wholesale collectivization, for the quickest victory of socialism in our country.[99]

The civil war tradition remained alive in the ranks of the 25,000ers, and, significantly, its last major expression among the workers appeared in pledges which looked ahead to the end of the First Five-Year Plan, to the end of the revolution.

The campaign of the 25,000ers held together as long as the First Five-Year Plan revolution surged through the country. The campaign came to be based on the same elements which had impelled the original recruitment drive to success. The campaign had no other resource to fall back upon but those elements of revolutionary faith, militancy, party loyalty, and patriotism, which had been so important in recruitment and which served, in large part, as the sustaining forces of the revolution. However, like the nation as a whole, the campaign came increasingly under siege, and as conditions deteriorated and convictions hardened, the civil war mentality and the defensive motivations began to subsume much of the original idealism.

The campaign of the 25,000ers was concluded at the end of the First Five-Year Plan. Symbolically, this was its logical end point, for with the end of the First Five-Year Plan came the conclusion of the final chapter of the Russian Revolution as a force of dynamic transformation. With the revolution's end, the militant fervor, revolutionary ardor, and accentuated patriotism which held the 25,000ers' campaign together and which was required for Bolshevik fortress storming began gradually to drift away into the realm of consolidation and, in terms of the rural revolution, retreat. The siege mentality which had overcome the campaign gradually overtook the nation, setting the scene for the remainder of the 1930s.

Epilogue

The campaign of the 25,000ers was officially concluded in late 1931 with the publication of the December Central Committee decree. At this time many 25,000ers returned to the cities voluntarily or were recalled by their factories. According to the Soviet scholar Iu. S. Borisov, 30 percent (about 8,256) of the 25,000ers were still employed within the collective farm system in 1932; Borisov estimates further that approximately 40 percent (11,008) remained in the countryside in early 1933 according to all categories of rural employment. The number of 25,000ers had fallen from 18,000 in 1931 to approximately 11,008 in 1933, thereby indicating that about 7,000 workers left the countryside as a consequence of the December decree.[100]

Most of the 7,000 workers who left at this time, along with the majority of those who had left earlier, returned to work in the factories. Workers who had left their families behind in the cities were especially anxious to return. Some 25,000ers, like the worker Frederick Legran, who went on to work at Magnitogorsk, continued the work of socialist construction making themselves available for other campaign work. A number of 25,000ers returned to the countryside in the special mobilization of party workers to serve in the machine tractor stations' political sections created in 1933. Many returning 25,000ers were offered the opportunity to study or were promoted at their factories. The 25,000er F. Savin attended a technical institute in Moscow to become an engineer. I. Kozlov, another Moscow 25,000er, was sent to a trade union school, where he studied in the press department; he later worked as a journalist for the Soviet news agency TASS. The worker S. Basagin became the director of the factory apprenticeship school at Trekhgornaia Manufaktura upon return from the countryside; soon afterwards, he was mobilized for work as a deputy in the political section of the Omsk railroad. The metalist, A. E. On'kov, returned to his factory to become the secretary of the Komsomol cell; shortly after this, he enlisted in the army and was to die in the defense of Leningrad during the war. A. P. Iagnenkov went on to study aviation at a technical school and upon graduation became a foreman at an aviation plant; following this, he was sent to study in a Moscow party school, after which he did some sort of party work in connection with the construction of the Moscow metro. Iagnenkov was mobilized once again in 1938 to go to the countryside to assume the duties of director of a state farm; he returned to Moscow to study once more, and the last report on him indicated that he had assumed the duties of editor of a Kirgiz regional newspaper.[101]

The 25,000ers who remained in the countryside were also offered the opportunity to study at agricultural institutes and colleges or were promoted within the bureaucracy. The December 1931 decree had authorized 1,000 of the 25,000ers to be sent to school; another 2,362 had already been promoted within the Kolkhoztsentr bureaucracy on the basis of an earlier directive from Kolkhoztsentr. Many of the 25,000ers who chose to remain in the countryside after December 1931 moved away from work on the collective farms into "leading cadre work" on the state farms and in the machine tractor station, party, and soviet networks. After 1933, statistics were no longer collected on the 25,000ers, and it is therefore not possible to trace their fate as a group into the later 1930s and subsequent decades of Soviet history. It is possible, however, to follow the careers of individual 25,000ers who chose to remain in the countryside.

In the 1950s and 1960s the campaign of the 25,000ers was celebrated as a part of Khrushchev's attempts to improve collectivized agriculture and, in particular, the level of leadership in the countryside. Khrushchev ordered the mobilization of 35,000 cadres from the cities for work in the countryside and attempted to liken this mobilization to the campaign of the 25,000ers. It was time to inject new vigor into the collective farms, to create a new type of leader sadly absent from the countryside—so it was claimed—since the heyday of collectivization, when the worker-25,000ers had served as the pioneers of collective farming. Consequently, individual 25,000ers received a great deal of press attention at this time. This attention was directed to 25,000ers who had remained in the countryside into the Khrushchev years and whose careers, although on a lesser scale, paralleled those of the "Brezhnev generation" of former First Five-Year Plan affirmative-action recruits. These 25,000ers were not typical, however, of the original detachment, but were nonetheless an extremely interesting group, for they were typical of the 25,000ers who chose to remain in collective farm work. They represented the minority among the workers who had been born in the countryside and who had volunteered as 25,000ers in order to promote the cultural revolution in the villages of rural Soviet Russia.

Among this group was the former worker V. F. Liukshin, who remained a collective farm chairman into the late 1950s. Liukshin had been born in the village in which his collective farm now stood. In 1932, at the end of the campaign, he decided not to return to the factory. He later recalled:

> I received, I remember, a paper in 1932. It was from the administration of the Moscow-Kursk railroad. They wrote that the 25,000ers had fulfilled their tasks, the collective farm order was victorious. They suggested that I return to my former job. Actually, with a clear conscience, I could have returned to the city, to my former work, to my old comrades. Part of the 25,000ers returned to production at that time, especially those whose families had remained in the old place. But I decided to stay here: my family was with me, and the main thing, I wanted to see the fruits of my labor . . .

In an interview with a Soviet historian in the late 1950s, Liukshin said very little about agriculture, collective farm administration, or the ideas of socialism; instead he emphasized the cultural progress of the village, comparing it to the village of his childhood and pointing with pride to the television antennas and the new two-story collective farm clubhouse.[102]

The 25,000er I. A. Buianov also remained in the countryside into the Khrushchev period as a collective farm chairman. He, too, was born in the village where his collective farm was located. Buianov was the chairman of one of the most advanced collective farms in the Soviet Union from 1930 to 1963. In addition, he was twice a deputy to the Supreme Soviet of the USSR, attended the Twenty-First and Twenty-Second Congresses of the Communist party as a delegate, was twice hero of socialist labor, and was awarded the Order of Lenin.[103]

Buianov was rivaled in his accomplishments by another former 25,000er, G. P. Litovchenko. Litovchenko, although not born in the countryside, had worked as a farmhand in his youth before coming to the factory. He studied at an agricultural institute after the campaign ended. With the exception of the war years, he remained at work in the countryside. Litovchenko was twice a deputy to the Supreme Soviet of the USSR, a member of the revision commission of the Ukrainian Communist party, and a member of the Khersonskii and Genicheskii committees of the party.[104]

As of 1962, the 25,000er Tarasov was director of the large state farm Pervomaiskii in the Leningrad Region. Tarasov, a former Leningrad metalworker, was born in the countryside. After the 25,000ers' campaign, he attended the Kirov Higher Communist Agricultural School, where he studied agronomy. After graduation in 1935 he returned to work in agriculture and, with the exception of the war years, remained in the countryside into the 1960s.[105]

Other former workers also went on to become leaders of major state or collective farms, members of Communist party regional committees, and Supreme Soviet delegates.[106] It was not pure coincidence that most of these workers had been born in the countryside and motivated by "cultural" concerns. As noted earlier, adaptation to tradition and a sensitivity to peasant ways often brought the best results in the workers' attempts to bring the idea of socialism to the countryside. Workers who themselves were from the village or able to grasp the meaning of rural backwardness were those most likely to be sensitive to the traditions and ways of the countryside. Yet these workers still represented a small minority, at best, among the 25,000ers.

The majority of the 25,000ers were children of the First Five-year Plan revolution, and when the revolution was over, their work was finished. Although many later served on other important fronts, including those of

World War II,[107] the historical legacy of the 25,000ers rests on their First Five-Year Plan revolutionary credentials. They were the cadres of the Stalin revolution who, as advanced workers, served in the vanguard of the revolution. This is how they are remembered today in the Soviet Union. In a speech celebrating the October Revolution, Brezhnev hailed them as "worker-revolutionaries."[108] And, in fact, they were the last of a generation. After the First Five-Year Plan the Soviet working class was radically transformed. The old vanguard which had fought in the civil war, struggled through the NEP years, and served on the fronts of the First Five-Year Plan was gone—into administration, party leadership, school. It was replaced by a new working class, which would not share in the revolution's fruits to the same degree. The age of worker-revolutionaries was over, and the 25,000ers would be remembered as the "best sons of the fatherland" and as that "legendary detachment which left a memorable heritage in the history of the Soviet working class, in the history of our country."[109] The temper of the nation was transformed, as revolutionary idealism and militancy came to be replaced by a siege mentality bereft of the earlier dynamism and crusading spirit. The 25,000ers were to become a symbol of the old radicalism, of a lost idealism, and of the early pioneers in the creation of a new society. Their campaign was a microcosm of the revolution. As such, the campaign's history and fate were ultimately bound to the offensives, fronts, retreats, and entrenchment of the First Five-Year Plan revolution.

Conclusion

The campaign of the 25,000ers was an integral part of the First Five-Year Plan revolution and the collectivization of Soviet agriculture in the years 1929–31. The campaign reflected the development and fate of the revolution as it was transported to the countryside. The 25,000ers' campaign coincided with the heroic, crusading phase of collectivization which was characterized by an often unrestrained revolutionary militancy and by ubiquitous disorder and Moscow's inability to exert full control over rural officialdom and the implementation of policy. The task of the 25,000ers was to bring consciousness to the spontaneity of rural Soviet Russia. They were to represent the interests of Moscow in its efforts to exert control over the revolution. As they attempted to do this—in their positions as collective farm leaders, their attempts to introduce industrial methods on the farms, and their participation in the transformation of rural officialdom through purge and promotions— their campaign evolved from a crusade to a state of siege. The transformation of the campaign was a reflection and consequence of the transformation which the revolution as a whole underwent as it confronted the realities of the countryside. The legacy of the initial radical phase of collectivization was an incremental decline of ideology together with a cumulative expansion of a defensive, siege mentality, bolstered by the isolation of the proletarian dictatorship in the countryside and the increasing use of repression as the primary means of rural administration. This was the denouement of the final chapter of the Russian Revolution and the prelude to the 1930s.

The campaign of the 25,000ers had begun under very different circumstances, however. It was launched in the midst of the First Five-Year Plan revolution from above. In order to circumvent a bureaucracy which appeared to be unable or unwilling to implement the revolution, the leadership appealed to its party rank and file and the working class for active support in the revolution's implementation. According to the logic of the times, a revolution from above meant a revolution directed by the self-proclaimed conscious forces of Soviet society, a revolution carried out by a vanguard. The revolution could not have taken place without the aid of key sectors of Soviet (primarily urban) society. Constituting one detachment of the soldiers of the Stalin revolution, the 25,000ers were the most important cadres of the revolution to be sent to the countryside during the early years of collectivization.

The decision to recruit the 25,000ers was made at the November 1929 Central Committee plenum. The 25,000ers' campaign began in a massive recruitment drive calling to mind a wartime mobilization. The recruitment drive was an enormous success, hindered only by the opposition of the factories, which resisted the loss of their skilled workers. Factory workers proved highly responsive to the campaign; in all, over seventy thousand workers from the major industrial centers of the Soviet Union volunteered. The workers selected to become 25,000ers represented the so-called vanguard of the Soviet working class: the cadre workers, Communist party and Komsomol members, factory activists, skilled or highly skilled workers, and workers who had fought for Soviet power during the civil war. The 25,000ers were representative of a select group of Soviet workers forming a key part of the social base of the Stalin revolution. It was from this group that emerged the generation of leaders who would replace the cadres purged in the late 1930s and who would later come to be identified as the cohort of the Brezhnev generation. This stratum of the working class identified with the emphasis on the proletarian ethos— particularly after the uneventful NEP years, which many perceived as a time of retreat and unjustified compromise—and looked to the Stalin revolution for the final victory of socialism after years of war, hardship, and deprivation. Most important, the 25,000ers, along with many workers, were caught up in the civil war atmosphere engendered by the war scare and the grain-procurement crisis of the late 1920s. They saw the revolution as a solution to backwardness, seemingly endemic food shortages, and capitalist encirclement. Joining the ranks of the 25,000ers became an expression of Soviet patriotism, as workers volunteered to defend their country on the fronts of the First

Five-Year Plan and of collectivization, as they had during the revolutionary-heroic period of the civil war.

The 25,000ers entered the countryside in the midst of the frenzied drive to collectivize agriculture in the winter of 1929–30. Central policy on collectivization at this time assumed the nature of a series of ad hoc responses to the actions of the regional and district organs of the party and government as Moscow sought to gain control of the collectivization campaign. In the period between November 1929 and March 1930, the collectivization campaign demonstrated a dizzyingly wide gap between policy and policy implementation, between central intentions and local realities. The 25,000ers were unable to exert an influence on socialist construction as long as the center was unable to gain full control of its rural cadres. The center's attempts to gain control of the situation culminated in March 1930 when Stalin's famous article "Dizzyness from Success" and the March Central Committee decree were published. After this, the 25,000ers began gradually to enter into positions of authority in the collective farm system.

Following the March decisions the rural party rebelled against what it perceived to be either a retreat from the revolution or an effort to scapegoat rural cadres for the chaos of the campaign. The task of the center was to rein in the rural cadres and—in the aftermath of the collectivization campaign, massive peasant resistance, and the consequent discrediting of rural officials—to rebuild local authority. The 25,000ers' participation in these efforts was designed to serve as a breakthrough policy to enable the regime to implement the momentous transformation of agriculture and peasant life which took place at this time. The workers participated in the purge of rural officialdom in the spring of 1930 and promoted loyal supporters into positions of authority in the collective farms, the party cells, and the *sel'sovet*s. They engaged in power struggles with rural officials in order to establish their authority as collective farm leaders. By the summer of 1930 the workers represented a significant proportion of the first cadre of collective farm leaders, and 78.6 percent of them had entered office on the collective farm administrative boards. The workers were also responsible for roughly one half of the growth of the rural party in the first quarter of 1930 and frequently served as secretaries of collective farm party cells and as district party committee members. They were, as one worker boasted, "a force to be reckoned with."

Once in office, the 25,000ers served as the pioneers of the early collective farms. The workers attempted to bring the industrial revolution to the countryside by introducing factory methods of management and labor organization to the collective farms. Their work as collective farm administrators was influenced by their experience as factory workers and the instructions of the center, but ultimately was shaped by the necessity to respond and adjust to peasant tradition and demands. Those who sought to replicate the Putilov factory in the village faced insurmountable obstacles in their work with the collective farmers. The post-1932 retreat from the most extreme aims and uncompromising stance of the initial phase of collectivization was, in many cases, anticipated by the experience of 25,000er–collective farm leaders in this period who were forced to compromise with tradition and, indeed, reality in response to peasant demands, practicality, and the simple necessity of attempting to make the farms viable units of production. The primary obstacle in their efforts to transport the revolution to the countryside was the all-pervasive backwardness of rural Soviet Russia. The workers quickly found that the base for building socialism in peasant Russia was too weak to support the superstructure of collectivization.

The experience of the 25,000ers reflected the revolution's fate in the countryside. As the workers confronted obstacle upon obstacle in the form of material and cultural deprivation, the resistance of peasants and officals, and the inadequacy of the "base," their campaign gradually came to resemble a state of siege. They and the party which they represented lived and worked in isolation in the countryside. The majority of the workers remained loyal to the cause and stayed at their posts until the end of the First Five-Year Plan. At that time the Central Committee issued a decree announcing, in effect, the successful completion of the campaign of the 25,000ers. The 25,000ers had accomplished their mission: wholesale collectivization was victorious.

The Central Committee decree on the 25,000ers had been anticipated by decrees issued in October 1930 and March 1931 which ordered the cessation of working-class mobilizations for campaign work. Although the October and March decrees were not entirely effective, both these decrees and the decree on the 25,000ers marked the end of an era. The working class had played an instrumental role in the implementation of the revolution from above. The experience of the 25,000ers was shared by thousands of other workers who had participated in collectivization in patronage brigades and less-celebrated mobilizations. With the end of the revolution the working class lost its officially designated vanguard role. The composition of the labor force was radically transformed. The working class of 1932 was largely peasant in origin and new to the factory; the working class of 1929 had been transformed through the mass programs of training and promotion of the First Five-Year Plan period. The state would no longer appeal to a working-class vanguard for aid in policy implementation in order to circumvent a suspect bureaucracy; the state would now rely (albeit with major lapses into paranoia) on a transformed bureaucracy which had become, at least to the satisfaction of the state, a bastion of the working class or the new preserve of the old vanguard.

The 25,000ers had successfully completed their campaign, playing a pivotal role in a time of monumental transformations. Further working-class mobilizations were suspended as the temper of the times changed from revolutionary to pragmatic, and the protests of the industrial concerns were finally heeded. The state proclaimed victory in the countryside with well over one half of all peasant households collectivized in the country as a whole, over 80 percent of peasant households collectivized in the major grain-producing regions, and the elimination of the kulak as a class basically completed. Victory, however, was accompanied by retreat and compromise. Peasant leaders replaced working-class leaders. Collective farmers were granted permission to own a private plot of land and to trade on the market after fulfillment of the state grain order. The victory, moreover, would soon give way to crisis. The unsteady foundations of the collective farm system and the dizzying events of 1929–30 led to profound structural problems in agriculture which would result in an unprecedented famine in 1932–33 and the chronic weakness and inefficiency of collective farming which persists to the present.

The legacy of collectivization would be an enduring distrust of peasant spontaneity, a continued reliance on appointed officials and campaign methods of policy implementation, and the perpetuation of a siege mentality which colored the relations of the state and countryside throughout the 1930s. Although the state would no longer recruit workers en masse for rural work as it had in the case of the 25,000ers, it would continue to rely on appointed officials, who, like the 25,000ers before them, would remain isolated actors in a sea of peasant spontaneity under constant siege from above and below. The new vanguard would be recruited from the state's new social constituency in the countryside, the collective farmers. It would not replicate the ardent loyalty and revolutionary vigor of the 25,000ers, nor would it maintain its ranks as steadfastly. The new peasant cadres would lack the authority of the 25,000ers in attempting to resist the increasingly onerous and repressive encroachments of the central and provincial organs of the state. In addition, they would not have the support and defense of the central authorities and urban ombudsmen against the arbitrary repressive measures taken against them by the district organs as they found themselves caught in the crossfire between the demands of collective farmers and the state. This would result in a basic instability of rural cadres and endemic problems of control throughout the 1930s. The proletarian revolution would remain an isolated outpost in agrarian Soviet Russia.

The contribution of the 25,000ers in the First Five-Year Plan revolution, when viewed from the perspective of the end of the revolution, appears slight. Collectivization was a massive endeavor; building socialism in peasant Russia was an uphill struggle against the course of history and the reality of the countryside. However, the workers did play an important role in the construction of the collective farm system—an entirely new experiment in agriculture—if not in the construction of the less concrete socialist society for which they strove. They were the first cadre of collective farm leaders, and much of the credit for that "first spring" in which collectivized agriculture was celebrated and victory declared belongs to this first cadre of leaders. They helped to establish the basic structure of the collective farm system, which, after 1930, would remain fundamentally unchanged throughout the Stalin years. Finally, and not of least importance, the 25,000ers played an instrumental role in cleansing the rural party of the extremist deviations which the center perceived in its undisciplined and disorderly administration of the countryside in the 1920s. This did not solve the rural cadre problem, but it did clear the way for the construction of the collective farm system after the chaotic collectivization drive of the winter of 1929–30.

The importance of the campaign of the 25,000ers, however, lies less in any concrete contribution it made to the birth of the collective farm system than in the light it sheds upon the workings of the First Five-Year Plan revolution. The campaign has demonstrated how the state gained the active support and participation of important sectors of society in the implementation of the revolution in the countryside. It has shown that the most active supporters of the revolution from among the working class were drawn from that key sector of the industrial proletariat which made up the politically active cadre workers who helped to implement the Stalin revolution. Moreover, the revolution could not have been implemented without the support of these sectors of society. Collectivization was implemented in the face of overwhelming peasant resistance and the obstructions of rural officialdom, which were expressed either through opposition and inertia or a tendency to run far ahead of Moscow, defying any and all constraints. The revolution was not implemented through regular administrative channels; instead the state appealed directly to the party rank and file and key sectors of the working class in order to circumvent rural officialdom. The mass recruitments of workers and other urban cadres and the circumvention of the bureaucracy served as a breakthrough policy in order to lay the foundations of a new system. Collectivization was to be a revolution from above, directed and controlled by the conscious forces of the Communist party and the working class and carried out in accordance with the dictates of history.

The irony of revolution from above in the countryside, however, was that it owed its outcome less to the conscious leadership of the center and its cadres than to forces and actions which were beyond the center's control. Although centrally initiated and endorsed, collectivization became, to a great extent, a series of ad hoc policy responses to the unbridled initiatives of regional and district rural party and government organs. Collectivization and collective farming were shaped less by Stalin and the central authorities than by the undisciplined and irresponsible activity of rural officials, the experimentation of collective farm leaders left to fend for themselves, and the realities of a backward countryside and a traditional peasantry which defied Bolshevik fortress storming.

The center never managed to exert its control over the countryside as it had intended in the schema of revolution from above. The experience of the 25,000ers has demonstrated the gap between policy and central intentions, as viewed from the vantage point of the Kremlin, and policy as it was implemented in reality in the countryside during the early years of collectivization. During this period Moscow loomed large and ever-more threatening as it attempted to extend its control into all facets of the life of the nation. A network of strict repressive measures mushroomed, and the state appeared to rule by administrative fiat. Repression increased as did the arbitrary authority of plenipotentiaries, party instructors, and control agencies. Rule by administrative fiat and repression, however, did not represent effective control, but its opposite. The state ruled by circular, it ruled by decree, but it had neither the organizational infrastructure nor the manpower to enforce its voice or to ensure correct implementation of its policy in the administration of the countryside. As a consequence of its inability to exert its control, the state was to rely on rule by repression for the duration of the Stalin years. And repression should not be confused with all-embracing controls, for it was, in fact, a substitution for an orderly system of administrative control. The roots of the Stalin system in the countryside do not lie in the expansion of state controls but in the very absence of such controls and of an orderly system of administration, which, in turn, resulted in repression as the primary instrument of rule in the countryside. The legacy of collectivization—so vividly reflected in the campaign of the 25,000ers—was a continued reliance on appointments of leaders; frequent purges of cadres and the consequent endemic turnover of personnel; and periodic campaigns to enforce policy in a blitzkrieg style, alternating with periods of inertia and drift in rural policy.

To a certain extent this development shows great continuity with age-old patterns of state rule of the Russian countryside, which was always undergoverned and viewed as a source of extraction—of grain, revenue, labor, and cannon fodder. There were also, however, important discontinuities, which were reflected in the campaign of the 25,000ers. First, a new system of agricultural production was indeed established, and this, although not without its problems, did end the periodic crises which characterized earlier market relations between the cities and the countryside. Second, and most important, it must be stressed that collectivization was a revolution. It was intended to be more than simply a way to take grain from the peasantry. The campaign of the 25,000ers brings into focus the revolutionary and utopian dimensions of collectivization. It has shown how the early revolutionary impulse evolved from a crusade to a state of siege, thereby altering the shape of the revolution and helping to precondition the terrain for the repressive climate of the later 1930s. Rule by repression was based not only on the failures of control, but on the militaristic mentality engendered by the early revolutionary phase of collectivization.

The dissipation of the enthusiasm and dynamism of the first phase of the revolution left in place the pale reminders of revolutionary upheaval in the form of a defensive, warlike mentality. The cadres who participated in collectivization—and, indeed, the state which oversaw the operation—came away from the campaign with the bitter taste and formative experience of a brutal and brutalizing war. Sabotage, class aliens, fronts, and the elimination of enemies became part of a standard vocabulary and world view. The bureaucracy of the 1930s came to practice the same crude, heavy-handed style of administration and human discourse as had become the practice during collectivization and the frenzied days of the First Five-Year Plan. The experience and the language entered the vernacular of routine politics, administration, and everyday observations of the surrounding world as many of the urban cadres of collectivization were demobilized and entered work in the urban party, government, and industrial enterprises. And it must be stressed that many of these cadres, unlike the 25,000ers, more easily adopted this mentality than that of the enthusiasm of building a new society. The formation of the mentality which would ride roughshod over the 1930s was predicated upon the low cultural level of the cadres, the hardening experience of years of war and revolution, and, most of all, the siege mentality and practices of rural socialist construction. The temper of the times was drastically altered and a new type of cadre was called for: the old militant idealism and revolutionary fervor of cadres like the 25,000ers would be supplanted by a tough-minded pragmatism and a paranoid, martial posture. This was the denouement of the revolution in the countryside and of the 25,000ers' campaign. The campaign of the 25,000ers was held together by the enthusiasm, revolutionary ardor, and accentuated patriotism which surged through the country at the beginning of the First Five-Year Plan and which was required for Bolshevik fortress storming and socialist construction.

The campaign of the 25,000ers coincided with the final chapter of the Russian Revolution. The 25,000ers were among the last of the revolutionaries, the final working-class vanguard. They were the cadres of the Stalin revolution and, on a more general level, they were the "true believers" about whom Kopelev writes. They dreamt revolution and envisioned the final victory of socialism to lie just beyond the next plan, the next construction site, the next Vladimir Il'ich collective farm. They were part of an entire generation of workers and revolutionaries who believed Stalin when he said that there were no fortresses a Bolshevik could not storm. The Bolsheviks, however, remained an urban party of fortress-stormers who were ultimately unable to penetrate the fortress of agrarian Russia with the idea of socialism. By 1932, with the end of the First Five-Year Plan, the revolution had once again retreated from the countryside, leaving in its wake the isolated outposts of the proletarian dictatorship on the collective farms and in the rural party and soviets. The initial contradictions of the revolution of 1917 remained, and the age of "workers-revolutionaries" receded into the heroic past.

NOTES

Introduction

1. *Sel'skaia zhizn'*, 7 July 1963, p. 1.
2. Personal interview with Professor V. M. Selunskaia of the Department of History, Moscow State University, 1981.
3. *Sovetskii rabochii klass. Kratkii istoricheskii ocherk (1917–1973)* (Moscow: Politizdat, 1975), p. 224; N. Ia. Timoshina, "Bor'ba kommunisticheskoi partii za ukreplenie soiuza rabochego klassa i krest'ianstva v period industrializatsii strany (1926–1929 gg.)," *Uch. zap. Moskovskogo gos. universiteta*, vyp. 173 (1955), p. 192.
4. *Sel'skaia zhizn'*, 7 July 1963, p. 1; L. I. Brezhnev, *Leninskim kursom*, vol. 2 (Moscow: Politizdat, 1970), p. 87.
5. Cited in *Current Digest of the Soviet Press*, vol. 35, no. 4 (23 Feb. 1982), p. 10.
6. E. H. Carr, *What Is History?* (New York: Random House, Vintage Books, 1961), p. 27.
7. Lev Kopelev, *To Be Preserved Forever*, trans. Anthony Austin (New York: J. B. Lippincott, 1977), p. 11.

Chapter 1

1. V. P. Danilov, "Dinamika naseleniia SSSR za 1917–1929 gg.," *Arkheograficheskii ezhegodnik za 1968 god* (Moscow: Nauka, 1970), p. 245; A. G.

Rashin, "Dinamika promyshlennykh kadrov SSSR za 1917–1958 gg.," *Izmeneniia v chislennosti i sostave Sovetskogo rabochego klassa* (Moscow: AN SSSR, 1961), p. 9.

2. Danilov, "Dinamika," pp. 245–46.

3. Iu. K. Strizhkov, *Prodovol'stvennye otriady v gody grazhdanskoi voiny i inostrannoi interventsii, 1917–1921 gg.* (Moscow: Nauka, 1973), pp. 31–35; George Yaney, *The Urge to Mobilize: Agrarian Reform in Russia, 1861–1930* (Urbana, Ill.: Univ. of Illinois Press, 1982), pp. 401–62, 485–96.

4. Yaney, *The Urge to Mobilize*, p. 496.

5. V. I. Lenin, *Polnoe sobranie sochinenii*, 5th ed., vol. 36 (Moscow: Gospolitizdat, 1960), pp. 357–64 (hereafter cited as Lenin, *PSS*).

6. Lenin, *PSS*, vol. 36, pp. 357–64, 395–414, 424–25, 430–32, 521–22.

7. Lenin, *PSS*, vol. 35, pp. 146–48; vol. 36, pp. 521–22; Strizhkov, *Prodovol'stvennye otriady*, pp. 19–57.

8. Iu. S. Kulyshev and S. F. Tylik, *Bor'ba za khleb* (Leningrad: Lenizdat, 1972), pp. 24–54; V. M. Selunskaia, *Rabochii klass i Oktiabr' v derevne* (Moscow: Mysl', 1968), pp. 159, 166–76; Strizhkov, *Prodovol'stvennye otriady*, pp. 104–6, 114–15, 299.

9. Estimates of the number of Committees of Village Poor in the RSFSR in the early fall of 1918 range from 122,000 to 140,000. See A. Chernobaev, *Kombed* (Moscow: Moskovskii rabochii, 1978), p. 32.

10. Chernobaev, *Kombed*, pp. 14–16; B. M. Morozov, *Sozdanie i ukreplenie Sovetskogo gosudarstvennogo apparata* (Moscow: Gospolitizdat, 1957), pp. 166–67, 173; Olga A. Narkiewicz, *The Making of the Soviet State Apparatus* (Manchester, Eng.: Manchester Univ. Press, 1970), p. 64.

11. Selunskaia, *Oktiabr'*, pp. 203–5.

12. In the summer and fall of 1918 alone, 7,309 of the People's Commissariat of Food detachment cadres were wounded or murdered in the villages. Strizhkov, *Prodovol'stvennye otriady*, p. 142.

13. Selunskaia, *Oktiabr'*, pp. 155–58.

14. A. S. Bubnov, "Statisticheskie svedeniia o VKP (b)," *Bol'shaia Sovetskaia entsiklopediia*, 1st ed., vol. 11 (Moscow: Ogiz, 1930), p. 533.

15. F. V. Chebaevskii, "Stroitel'stvo mestnykh sovetov v kontse 1917 i pervoi polovine 1918 g.," *Istoricheskie zapiski*, vol. 61 (1957), p. 250; Morozov, *Sozdanie*, p. 150.

16. Morozov, *Sozdanie*, pp. 166–67, 184; Selunskaia, *Oktiabr'*, p. 230.

17. Selunskaia, *Oktiabr'*, p. 252; Strizhkov, *Prodovol'stvennye otriady*, pp. 124, 195.

18. See Bubnov, "Statisticheskie svedeniia," p. 533; and I. N. Iudin, *Sotsial'naia baza rosta KPSS* (Moscow: Politizdat, 1973), p. 144.

19. The party was purged of 30.3 percent of its membership in the 1921 party purge. Only 21 percent of the working-class membership was purged compared to the 44.7 percent of rural Communists purged. *Sotsial'nyi i natsional'nyi sostav VKP (b). Itogi vsesoiuznoi partiinoi perepisi 1927 goda* (Moscow and Leningrad: Gosizdat, 1928), p. 15.

20. Selunskaia, *Oktiabr'*, p. 246.

21. For further information on these developments, see Robert Service, *The Bolshevik Party in Revolution: A Study in Organizational Change, 1917–1923* (New York: Macmillan, 1979), chap. 8.

22. G. P. Andreiuk, "Vydvizhenchestvo i ego rol' v formirovanii intelligentsii (1921–1932 gg.)," *Iz istorii Sovetskoi intelligentsii* (Moscow: Mysl', 1966), pp. 9–16; V. Z. Drobizhev, "Rol' rabochego klassa SSSR v formirovanii komandnykh kadrov sotsialisticheskoi promyshlennosti (1917–1936 gg.)," *Istoriia SSSR*, no. 4 (1961), pp. 58–62; idem, "Statisticheskie dannye o roli rabochego klassa v formirovanii organov upravleniia promyshlennosti (1917–1922 gg.)," *Iz istorii rabochego klassa SSSR* (Leningrad: LGU, 1962), pp. 67–75.

23. *Bol'shevik*, nos. 3–4 (Feb. 1925), pp. 51–52. See E. G. Gimpel'son, *"Voennyi kommunizm": politika, praktika, ideologiia* (Moscow: Mysl', 1973), p. 80, for breakdowns of collectives according to degree of socialization.

24. *Bol'shevik*, ibid.; E. H. Carr, *The Bolshevik Revolution, 1917–1923*, vol. 2 (New York: Macmillan, 1952), pp. 154–57, 168; Gimpel'son, *"Voennyi kommunizm,"* pp. 68–80.

25. See Gimpel'son, *"Voennyi kommunizm,"* pp. 193–208, 243, 298–99.

26. Lenin, *PSS*, vol. 45, pp. 378–82.

27. Ibid., pp. 369–77, 389–406.

28. Ibid., pp. 404–5.

29. Ibid., pp. 363–68.

30. Ibid., p. 372.

31. Danilov, "Dinamika," p. 246.

32. V. P. Danilov, *Sozdanie material'no-tekhnicheskikh predposylok kollektivizatsii sel'skogo khoziaistva v SSSR* (Moscow: AN SSSR, 1957), p. 36.

33. M. Lewin, *Russian Peasants and Soviet Power: A Study of Collectivization*, trans. Irene Nove (New York: Norton, 1975), p. 85; Y. Taniuchi, *The Village Gathering in Russia in the mid-1920s*, Birmingham Univ. Soviet and East European Monographs, no. 1 (Birmingham, Eng.: Birmingham Univ., 1968), p. 23. The commune, which was given new life by the 1917 revolution when it became the vehicle through which the peasants seized land, was strongest in the major grain-producing regions.

34. However, even the rudiments of primitive technology were not to be had in many peasant households. In 1927 31.6 percent of peasant farms did not have their own farming equipment; in that same year 28.3 percent of households had no draft animal. See Danilov, *Sozdanie*, p. 293; and idem, "Sotsial'no-ekonomicheskie otnosheniia v Sovetskoi derevne nakanune kollektivizatsii," *Istoricheskie zapiski*, vol. 55 (1956), pp. 96–97.

35. Danilov, *Sozdanie*, pp. 99–100.

36. Stalin, along with Molotov and Andreev, quickly disassociated himself from this statement. See I. V. Stalin, "Vsem chlenam redaktsii 'Komsomol'skoi pravdy,' " *Sochineniia*, vol. 7 (Moscow: Gospolitizdat, 1952), p. 153.

37. See chap. 1, n. 19.

38. T. H. Rigby, *Communist Party Membership in the USSR, 1917–1967* (Princeton, N.J.: Princeton Univ. Press, 1968), pp. 101–2, 134, 139, 144–53.

39. L. I. Zharov and A. V. Ovcharova, "Mobilizatsiia 3000 kommunistov na rabotu v derevniu (1924 g.)," *Istoricheskii arkhiv*, no. 1 (1959), pp. 61–85.

40. See Bubnov, "Statisticheskie svedeniia," p. 533, and Iudin, *Sotsial'naia baza*, p. 164.

41. *Sotsial'nyi i natsional'nyi sostav*, pp. 18, 36.

42. Ibid., p. 87; and Rigby, *Communist Party*, p. 134.

43. *Sotsial'nyi i natsional'nyi sostav*, p. 41.

44. Ibid., pp. 33, 85.

45. *Derevenskii kommunist*, nos. 11–12 (21 June 1930), pp. 44–49. In the party purge of 1929–30, 16.9 percent of rural Communists were purged, 14.6 percent were reprimanded, and 10.2 percent were removed from responsible positions. These Communists were purged on the following basis: 12.7 percent as alien elements, 15.1 percent for drunkenness, 13.6 percent for passivity, 4.6 percent for embezzlement, 6.4 percent for ties to alien elements, 4.6 percent for religious activity, 4.7 percent for refusal to enter a collective farm, and 2.5 percent for hidden grain reserves. In addition, according to an article in *Bol'shevik*, nos. 9–10 (31 May 1929), pp. 76, 81, rural party members tended to be drawn from the wealthier strata of the rural population. They hired labor more often than nonparty peasants and were wealthier in terms of the values of the means of production (e.g., draft animals, inventory) on their farms.

46. Some rural Communists objected to the reigning spirit of NEP and to the concept of class peace throughout the 1920s. Many of these Communists had actively resisted the introduction of NEP. See V. M. Shein, "Deiatel'nost' partiinykh organizatsii Zapadnoi Sibiri po raz"iasneniiu novoi ekonomicheskoi politiki sredi kommunistov," *Nauchnye trudy*, vyp. 46 (Novosibirsk: Novosibirskii gos. pedinstitut, 1970), pp. 75–86.

47. *Sovetskoe stroitel'stvo*, no. 12 (Dec. 1929), pp. 7, 11; no. 2 (Feb. 1930), pp. 38–40; and A. I. Lepeshkin, *Mestnye organy vlasti Sovetskogo gosudarstva* (Moscow: Gosiurizdat, 1959), pp. 59, 60, 237.

48. Taniuchi, *The Village Gathering*, p. 28.

49. By 1929, 31 percent of all strong peasants (*zazhitochnye*) and 43.6 percent of all kulaks belonged to a cooperative; only 20.6 percent and 30.3 percent of poor peasants and middle peasants, respectively, were members of a cooperative. Danilov, *Sozdanie*, p. 139; *Sovetskoe stroitel'stvo*, no. 1 (Jan. 1929), p. 41.

50. George L. Yaney, "Agricultural Administration in Russia from the Stolypin Land Reform to Forced Collectivization: An Interpretive Study," in *The Soviet Rural Community*, ed. James Millar (Urbana, Ill.: Univ. of Illinois Press, 1971), p. 6.

51. Danilov, "Sotsial'no-ekonomicheskie otnosheniia," p. 118.

52. *Voprosy shefstva*, no. 1 (Jan. 1926), pp. 3–4; no. 5 (May 1926), p. 35.

53. Ibid., no. 1 (July 1925), p. 3; no. 1 (Jan. 1926), pp. 3–4, 30; no. 2 (Feb. 1926), p. 12; no. 4 (Apr. 1926), p. 3; no. 6 (June 1926), pp. 3–5.

54. Ibid., no. 1 (July 1925), p. 17.

55. Ibid., no. 4 (Oct. 1925), p. 33; no. 4 (Apr. 1926), p. 19.

56. Ibid., no. 3 (Mar. 1926), p. 22.

57. L. S. Rogachevskaia, *Likvidatsiia bezrabotitsy v SSSR, 1917–1930* (Moscow: Nauka, 1973), pp. 75–76, 142, 249.

58. William J. Chase, "Moscow and Its Working Class, 1918–1928: A Social Analysis," Diss. Boston College, 1979, pp. 251–57.

59. E. H. Carr and R. W. Davies, *Foundations of a Planned Economy*, vol. 1, pt. 2 (New York: Macmillan, 1969), p. 603.

60. M. Fischer, *My Lives in Russia* (New York: Harper and Brothers, 1944), pp. 10–11. For examples of literature from the 1920s portraying NEP society in all of its decadence and corruption, see Lev Goomilevsky, *Dog Lane*; Valentine Kataev, *The Embezzlers*, V. Kirshon and A. Uspenskii, *Red Rust*; Leonid Leonov, *The Thief*; P. Romanof, *Three Pairs of Silk Stockings*; idem, *Without Cherry Blossom*, to name a few.

61. Chase, "Moscow and Its Working Class," pp. 243–44, 342–43; L. F. Morozov, *Reshaiushchii etap bor'by s nepmanskoi burzhuaziei* (Moscow: Akad. obshchest. nauk pri TsK KPSS, 1960), pp. 48–49.

62. Roger Pethybridge, *The Social Prelude to Stalinism* (New York: St. Martin's Press, 1974), pp. 200, 235–36.

63. See chap. 1, n. 61.

64. This was, for example, the most frequent issue raised at factory meetings during the soviet election campaign of 1929. See TsGAOR, f. 5469, op. 13, d. 126, ll. 12, 53, 57–58, 63.

65. Narkiewicz, *The Making of the Soviet State Apparatus*, pp. 110–11, 114, 181–82, 183. See also V. Molotov, *Stroitel'stvo sotsializma i protivorechiia rosta. Doklad o rabote TsK VKP (b) na I Moskovskoi oblastnoi partiinoi konferentsii. 14 sentiabria 1929 goda* (Moscow: Moskovskii rabochii, n.d.), pp. 47–49; and speeches by Stalin in *Sochineniia*, vol. 10, p. 259; vol. 11, pp. 1, 172–73.

66. Narkiewicz, *The Making of the Soviet State Apparatus*, pp. 110–11, 114, 181–82, 183; Pethybridge, *The Social Prelude to Stalinism*, pp. 200, 235–36.

67. Stalin, *Sochineniia*, vol. 11, pp. 1–19, 81–97, 139–46, 222–38; vol. 12, pp. 1–107.

68. Ibid., vol. 11, pp. 176–77.

69. Ibid., vol. 12, pp. 47–59.

70. Ibid.

71. R. W. Davies, *The Socialist Offensive: The Collectivization of Soviet Agriculture, 1929–1930* (Cambridge, Mass.: Harvard Univ. Press, 1980), pp. 116–37, 442.

72. Ibid., p. 133.

73. Ibid., p. 170.

74. Part 2 of *KPSS v rezoliutsiiakh i resheniiakh s"ezdov, konferentsii i plenumov TsK*, 7th ed. (Moscow: Gospolitizdat, 1953), pp. 544–47. Also see I. Stalin, "Otvet tovarishcham kolkhoznikam," *Sochineniia*, vol. 12, p. 208, where he claims that the Politburo planned a 1933 deadline for collectivization in regions not mentioned in the original decree. It should be noted that great controversy surrounds the December Politburo commission's work. Soviet secondary sources claim (on the basis of archival sources) that there was disagreement among the commission's members on such key issues as collectivization tempos and kulak policy. They claim further that the

commission proposed a "realistic" plan of collectivization which was then radically revised by Stalin, Molotov, and Kaganovich. The intent of this line of analysis is to ascribe blame for the excesses of the winter of 1930 collectivization drive. The main problem with this viewpoint is that the commission's supposedly moderate and realistic plan on collectivization tempos was only slightly less radical than the revised plans, setting timetables for the completion of collectivization in the three different zones, at best, only a half year later than the revised plans (i.e., the legislation in the 5 January decree). The Soviet scholar Ivnitskii presents by far the most convincing description of the commission's activities and problems. He indicates that Stalin did not actually personally revise the commission's plans but simply aligned himself with radicals on the commission such as Ryskulov, the deputy commissar of the RSFSR Council of People's Commissars. For further information on the commission, see B. A. Abramov, "O rabote komissii Politbiuro TsK VKP (b) po voprosam sploshnoi kollektivizatsii," *Voprosy istorii KPSS*, no. 1 (1964), pp. 33–35; M. L. Bogdenko, "K istorii nachal'nogo etapa sploshnoi kollektivizatsii sel'skogo khoziaistva SSSR," *Voprosy istorii*, no. 5 (1963), p. 27; N. A. Ivnitskii, "Istoriia podgotovki postanovleniia TsK VKP (b) o tempakh kollektivizatsii sel'skogo khoziaistva ot 5 ianvaria 1930 g.," *Istochnikovedenie istorii Sovetskogo obshchestva*, vyp. 1 (Moscow: Nauka, 1964), pp. 279–84; and M. A. Vyltsan, N. A. Ivnitskii, and Ia. A. Poliakov, "Nekotorye problemy istorii kollektivizatsii v SSSR," *Voprosy istorii*, no. 3 (1965), pp. 4–6.

75. Davies, *Socialist Offensive*, pp. 177–180, 237. Also see my discussion of collectivization in chap. 4.

76. *Partiinoe stroitel'stvo*, no. 9 (May 1932), p. 48.

77. See chap. 1, n.45.

78. The *sel'sovet*s had a very weak cadre of party members. In 1929 only 10 percent of all *sel'sovet* members were party members while 32.2 percent of *sel'sovet* chairmen were party members. The percentage of *sel'sovet*s which had neither party nor Komsomol members was 25.7. See *Sovetskoe stroitel'stvo*, no. 12 (Dec. 1929), pp. 12–14.

79. See chap. 3 for further details.

80. It should be noted, however, that a wide range of reforms were in the planning stages (e.g., the establishment of independent budgets for the *sel'sovet*s, training programs for cadres, the elimination of the subdivision of the *okrug*, the transfer of party cells from a territorial to a production basis, etc.).

81. I. Stalin, "God velikogo pereloma. K XII godovshchine Oktiabria," *Sochineniia*, vol. 12, pp. 128–32.

82. I. Stalin, "K voprosam agrarnoi politiki v SSSR. Rech' na konferentsii agrarnikov-marksistov. 27 dekabria 1929 gg.," *Sochineniia*, vol. 12, p. 149.

83. Molotov, *Stroitel'stvo sotsializma i protivorechiia rosta*, pp. 44–45, 68–69, 96.

84. This climaxed in the case of the false collective farm Krasnyi Meliorator. See *Pravda*, 17 Sept. 1929, p. 5; and F. Frolov and V. Barchuk, *Kolkhoz "Krasnyi meliorator" (Kak kulak "vrastaet v sotsializm")* (Moscow: Knigosoiuz, 1930).

85. *Sovetskoe stroitel'stvo*, no. 4 (Apr. 1929), p. 73.

86. *XVI s''ezd VKP (b). Sten. otchet* (Moscow and Leningrad: Gosizdat, 1930), p. 66.

87. Decree of 25 Mar. 1931 in *Direktivy VKP (b) po khoziaistvennym voprosam*, ed. M. Savel'ev and A. Poskrebyshev (Moscow and Leningrad: Gos. sots.-ekon. izd-vo, 1931), p. 844. See also Central Committee decree of 20 October 1930 temporarily limiting recruitment of workers into administration in *Ezhegodnik Sovetskogo stroitel'stva i prava na 1931 god (za 1929/30 god)* (Moscow and Leningrad: Gos. sots.-ekon. izd-vo, 1931), p. 12.

Chapter 2

1. *KPSS v rezoliutsiiakh*, p. 528.

2. V. M. Selunskaia, *Rabochie-dvadtsatipiatitysiachniki* (Moscow: MGU, 1964), p. 43.

3. *Pravda*, 3 Dec. 1929, p. 3.

4. *Pravda*, 3 Dec. 1929, p. 3; TsGAOR, f. 5469, op. 13, d. 124, ll. 8–12; *Informatsionnaia svodka tsentral'nogo komiteta vsesoiuznogo soiuza rabochikh metallistov* [TsK VSRM], no. 2/150 (20 Mar. 1930), p. 2.

5. A. N. Timofeev, ''Dvadtsatipiatitysiachniki-provodniki politiki partii v kolkhoznom stroitel'stve na Ukraine (1929–1930 gg.),'' *Iz istorii bor'by kommunisticheskoi partii Ukrainy za sotsialisticheskoe pereustroistvo sel'skogo khoziaistva* (Kiev: Kievskii gos. universitet, 1961), pp. 80–81.

6. See circular letter of 24 December 1929 issued by Kolkhoztsentr in TsGANKh, f. 7446, op. 12, d. 3, ll. 2–3.

7. *Informatsionnaia svodka TsK VSRM*, no. 7/148 (10 Dec. 1929), p. 10; N. A. Ivnitskii and D. M. Ezerskii, eds., ''Dvadtsatipiatitysiachniki i ikh rol' v kollektivizatsii sel'skogo khoziaistva v 1930 g.,'' *Materialy po istorii SSSR. Dokumenty po istorii Sovetskogo obshchestva*, vyp. 1 (Moscow: AN SSSR, 1955), pp. 431–32; *Pravda*, 3 Dec. 1929, p. 3; Ia. A. Rozenfel'd, *Dvadtsatipiatitysiachniki* (Moscow: Sel'khozgiz, 1957), pp. 13, 23; Selunskaia, *Rabochie-dvadtsatipiatitysiachniki*, p. 43; TsGAOR, f. 5452, op. 11, d. 38, l. 26; f. 5469, op. 13, d. 124, ll. 8–10.

8. N. V. Efremenkov and V. I. Mukhachev, ''Dvadtsatipiatitysiachniki-Ural'tsy na kolkhoznoi rabote v 1930 godu,'' *Trudy Ural'skogo politekhnicheskogo instituta (raboty kafedry Marksizma-Leninizma)*, sb. 86 (1957), p. 124; I. A. Ivanov, ''Uchastie rabochikh Leningrada v kollektivizatsii sel'skogo khoziaistva SSSR (1929–1932 gg.),'' *Istoriia rabochego klassa Leningrada*, vyp. 1 (Leningrad: LGU, 1962), p. 81; Ivnitskii and Ezerskii, ''Dvadtsatipiatitysiachniki,'' p. 425; Rozenfel'd, *Dvadtsatipiatitysiachniki*, pp. 13–15; Selunskaia, *Rabochie-dvadtsatipiatitysiachniki*, p. 58.

9. Ivnitskii, ''Istoriia podgotovki postanovleniia TsK VKP (b),'' p. 277.

10. *Na fronte kollektivizatsii*, no. 1 (15 Nov. 1929), p. 31; Selunskaia, *Rabochie-dvadtsatipiatitysiachniki*, p. 79.

11. V. Molotov, ''O kolkhoznom dvizhenii,'' *Bol'shevik*, no. 22 (30 Nov. 1929), p. 21.

12. Selunskaia, *Rabochie-dvadtsatipiatitysiachniki*, p. 75.

13. For further information, see Lynne Viola, "The Campaign of the 25,000ers: A Study of the Collectivization of Soviet Agriculture, 1929–1931," Diss. Princeton University, 1984, chap. 3.

14. *Pravda*, 3 Dec. 1929, p. 3; Rozenfel'd, *Dvadtsatipiatitysiachniki* p. 23; Selunskaia, *Rabochie-dvadtsatipiatitysiachniki*, p. 62; TsGANKh, f. 7446, op. 12, d. 5, l. 16. In addition, a select group of 150 workers was to be sent to study in a special course for machine tractor station directors.

15. *Trud*, 19 Jan. 1930, p. 4.

16. *Pravda*, 3 Dec. 1929, p. 3; 10 Dec. 1929, p. 1; 16 Dec. 1929, p. 2.

17. These rumors were based on plans submitted by Kolkhoztsentr. See *Izvestiia*, 21 Dec. 1929, p. 7; *Leningradskaia pravda*, 7 Dec. 1929, p. 3; *Moskovskaia derevnia*, 20 Dec. 1929, p. 1; *Rabochaia Moskva*, 27 Dec. 1929, p. 4; *Sel'skokhoziaistvennaia gazeta*, 6 Dec. 1929, p. 2; 20 Dec. 1929, p. 4; and Kolkhoztsentr decision in TsGANKh, f. 7446, op. 12, d. 1, ll. 1, 6.

18. *Rabochaia gazeta*, 6 Dec. 1929, p. 5; *Trud*, 8 Dec. 1929, p. 2.

19. See the Peoples' Council of Commissars' decree on salary and rights in *Sobranie zakonov i rasporiazhenii raboche-krest'ianskogo pravitel'stva SSSR*, no. 1 (1 Jan. 1930), pp. 12–14.

20. Timofeev, "Dvadtsatipiatitysiachniki," pp. 80–81.

21. N. Ezhov of later notoriety was good enough to provide us with a definition of the Soviet usage of the term *mobilization*. He said that the term was "usually used in the sense of a certain compulsion." See *Sputnik agitatora (dlia derevni)*, no. 8 (Mar. 1930), p. 7.

22. *Rabochaia gazeta*, 24 Dec. 1929, p. 3; *Sel'skokhoziaistvennaia gazeta*, 22 Nov. 1929, p. 1; *Ural'skii rabochii*, 14 Dec. 1929, p. 2 (Ural regional party committee decree on campaign); and TsGAOR, f. 5469, op. 13, d. 124, ll. 8–10 (VSRM directives).

23. *Leningradskaia pravda*, 3 Dec. 1929, p. 1.

24. *Politicheskii i trudovoi pod"em rabochego klassa SSSR (1928–1929 gg.). Sbornik dokumentov* (Moscow: Gospolitizdat, 1956), p. 529.

25. *Pravda*, 13 Dec. 1929, p. 5.

26. Ivnitskii and Ezerskii, "Dvadtsatipiatitysiachniki," pp. 462, 489.

27. Selunskaia, *Rabochie-dvadtsatipiatitysiachniki*, p. 54.

28. *Krest'ianskaia pravda*, 27 Dec. 1929, p. 1; S. Kostiuchenko, I. Khrenov, and Iu. Fedorov, *Istoriia Kirovskogo zavoda, 1917–1945* (Moscow: Mysl', 1966), p. 327.

29. Even among oil refinery workers and Leningrad metalworkers, two groups of workers with high party "saturation," percentages of party members were still only 31.1 and 24.6, respectively. See data in *Trud v SSSR. Spravochnik 1926–1930 gg.* (Moscow: Plankhozgiz, 1930), pp. 25, 34. For party composition of shock workers, see *Partiinoe stroitel'stvo*, no. 2 (Feb. 1930), pp. 46–47, 69–70.

30. According to data on workers from Leningrad, Ivanovo-Voznesensk, and the Western Region, approximately one half of the 25,000ers who were Communists had entered the party between 1924 and 1927. Only about 10 percent had entered the party prior to 1924. Information from E. Iakubovskii, *Profsoiuzy v bor'be za kollektivizatsii*

derevni (Moscow and Leningrad: VTsSPS, 1930), p. 16; *Kollektivizatsiia sel'skogo khoziaistva v Zapadnom raione RSFSR (1927–1937 gg.)* (Smolensk: Arkhivnye otdely, gos. i partiinye arkhivy Smolenskoi i Brianskoi oblastei, 1968), document no. 53; and *Na Leninskom puti*, no. 2 (Feb. 1930), pp. 8–10.

31. V. Denisov, *Odin iz dvadtsatipiatitysiach* (Krasnoiarsk: Krasnoiarskoe knizhnoe izd-vo, 1967), pp. 4–6; A. Isbakh, *1 iz 25 tysiach. (Povest' v tridtsati chetyrekh dokumentov)* (Moscow and Leningrad, 1931), p. 10; V. P. Tiushev, "Dvadtsatipiatitysiachniki v Buriat-Mongol'skoi ASSR," *Zapiski Buriat-Mongol'skogo nauchno-issledovatel'skogo instituta kul'tury*, vol. 15 (1952), pp. 6–7.

32. Z. Amangaliev, "Rol' rabochikh brigad i dvadtsatipiatitysiachnikov v ukreplenii soiuza rabochego klassa i trudiashchegosia krest'ianstva (1929–1930 gg.) po materialam Kazakhstana," *Uch. zap. Alma-Atinskogo gos. zhen. pedinstituta*, vyp. 1 (1958), p. 56; V. F. Romanov, "Tverskie 25-tysiachniki-aktivnye boitsy za pobedu kolkhoznogo stroia v SSSR," *Uch. zap. Moskovskogo pedinstituta*, no. 250 (1967), p. 179; A. S. Rusakov, "Poslantsy russkogo rabochego klassa v Tadzhikistan," *Voprosy istorii*, no. 7 (1972), p. 118.

33. TsGAOR, f. 5469, op. 13, d. 124, ll. 37–54.

34. The average 25,000er tended to earn a good deal more than the average factory worker, who in the second quarter of 1929–30 earned 76.65 rubles per month, or even the average adult metalworker, who received in 1929 (March) a comparatively high salary of 94.74 rubles per month. According to data based on 6,767 Moscow and Leningrad 25,000ers, 9 percent received less than 75 rubles per month, 18 percent received 75–100 rubles per month, 26 percent received 100–125 rubles per month, 21 percent received 125–150 rubles per month, and 25 percent received over 150 rubles per month. Moscow and Leningrad workers, in general, received higher wages than workers in most other regions, but even in the Western Region, where wages were relatively low, 63 percent of the 25,000ers earned more than 80 rubles per month and 36 percent earned over 100 rubles per month. Information from Iakubovskii, *Profsoiuzy*, p. 16; *Kollektivizatsiia sel'skogo khoziaistva v Zapadnom raione*, document no. 53; and *Trud v SSSR*, pp. 38, 46. According to data based on Leningrad 25,000ers working in Siberia, 81.6 percent had an elementary education, 10.9 percent had completed secondary school, and 7.5 percent had an incomplete secondary education. In the Western Region, 90 percent of the 25,000ers had an elementary education, while the remaining 10 percent claimed to have passed through some form of schooling. See *Kollektivizatsiia sel'skogo khoziaistva v Zapadnom raione*, document no. 53; and *Kollektivizatsiia sel'skogo khoziaistva Zapadnoi Sibiri (1927–1937 gg.)* (Tomsk: Zapadno-Sibirskoe knizhnoe izd-vo, 1972), pp. 129–30.

35. *Kollektivizatsiia sel'skogo khoziaistva v Severo-Zapadnom raione (1927–1937 gg.)* (Leningrad: LGAOR SS, LGU, Gos. i partiinye arkhivy Leningradskoi, Murmanskoi, Novgorodskoi, Pskovskoi oblastei, Karel'skoi ASSR, 1970), p. 159; *Politicheskii i trudovoi pod''em rabochego klassa SSSR*, p. 530; Selunskaia, *Rabochie-dvadtsatipiatitysiachniki*, p. 23; and TsGAOR, f. 5469, op. 13, d. 124, ll. 37–54.

36. For examples, see *Krest'ianskaia pravda*, 27 Dec. 1929, p. 1; *Molot*, 7 Jan. 1930, p. 3; *Rabochaia Moskva*, 10 Dec. 1929, pp. 2–3; and *Po zovu partii. Sbornik*

vospominanii i statei Leningradtsev-dvadtsatipiatitysiachnikov (Leningrad: Lenizdat, 1961), pp. 95, 307–8.

37. V. A. Smyshliaev and P. V. Solov'ev, "Na perednem krae bor'by za sotsialisticheskoe preobrazovanie derevni," *Leningradskie rabochie v bor'be za sotsializm, 1926–1937* (Leningrad: Lenizdat, 1965), p. 245.

38. There are no overall statistics for percentages of civil war veterans among the 25,000ers, but contemporary reports emphasized that large numbers of volunteers were veterans. See, for examples, *Krest'ianskaia pravda*, 27 Dec. 1929, p. 1; *Molot*, 7 Jan. 1930, p. 3; *Za urozhai*, nos. 1–2 (Jan. 1930), pp. 4–5.

39. For biographical data on women, see I. Kats-Kagan, *25,000 proletariev u rulia kolkhozov* (Moscow: VTsSPS, 1930), p. 8; *Leningradskaia pravda*, 4 Dec. 1929, p. 2; *Po zovu partii*, p. 307; V. P. Tiushev, "Novye dannye o rabote dvadtsatipiatitysiachnikov v Vostochnoi Sibiri (po materialam Krasnoiarskikh arkhivov)," *Uch. zap. Irkutskogo pedinstituta (Seriia istoricheskaia)* under separate title *Voprosy istorii Sibiri*, vyp. 28 (1967), p. 81; E. Zombe, "Dvadtsatipiatitysiachniki," *Voprosy istorii*, no. 5 (1947), p. 9.

40. *Leningradskaia pravda*, 7 Dec. 1929, p. 3; 10 Dec. 1929, p. 2; for praise of the Leningrad campaign, see *Pravda*, 5 Dec. 1929, p. 5; 8 Dec. 1929, p. 5; 11 Dec. 1929, p. 5; 19 Dec. 1929, p. 2; 3 Jan. 1930, p. 2.

41. *Pravda*, 3 Jan. 1930, p. 2; Ivnitskii and Ezerskii, "Dvadtsatipiatitysiachniki," pp. 410, 434–35; *Rabochaia Moskva*, 29 Dec. 1929, p. 3; and for chemical industry, see V. S. Lel'chuk, "O nekotorykh sdivakh v riadakh rabochikh khimicheskoi promyshlennosti SSSR, 1917–1937," *Formirovanie i razvitie Sovetskogo rabochego klassa (1917–1961 gg.)* (Moscow: Nauka, 1964), pp. 219–24.

42. *Bednota*, 15 Dec. 1929, p. 4; *Izvestiia*, 21 Dec. 1929, p. 7; *Leningradskaia pravda*, 4 Dec. 1929, p. 2; *Pravda*, 16 Dec. 1929, p. 2; 18 Dec. 1929, p. 1; *Sel'skokhoziaistvennaia gazeta*, 5 Dec. 1929, p. 1; *Trud*, 11 Dec. 1929, p. 2; 19 Dec. 1929, p. 4; TsGAOR, f. 5469, op. 13, d. 124, ll. 37–38, 40.

43. *Rabochaia Moskva*, 24 Dec. 1929, p. 3; *Sel'skokhoziaistvennaia gazeta*, 6 Dec. 1929, p. 2; TsGAOR, f. 5469, op. 13. d. 124, ll. 36, 40; f. 5452, op. 11, d. 38, l. 6; f. 5470, op. 14, d. 204, l. 47.

44. *Pravda*, 3 Jan. 1930, p. 2.

45. TsGAOR, f. 5469, op. 13, d. 124, ll. 37–38; also cited in part in *Trud*, 14 Jan. 1930, p. 2.

46. *Vecherniaia Moskva*, 10 Jan. 1930, p. 2.

47. TsGAOR, f. 5469, op. 13, d. 124, ll. 37–38, 46–54; *Trud*, 14 Jan. 1930, p. 2.

48. TsGAOR, f. 5469, op. 13, d. 124, ll. 46–54.

49. TsGAOR, f. 5469, op. 13, d. 124, ll. 37–38; *Trud*, 19 Dec. 1929, p. 4.

50. TsGAOR, f. 5469, op. 13, d. 124, ll. 55–56.

51. *Rabochaia Moskva*, 8 Dec. 1929, p. 1; 11 Jan. 1930, p. 3.

52. See the account of these efforts given in Paddy Dale, "The Instability of the Infant Vanguard: Worker Party Members, 1928–1932," *Soviet Studies*, vol. 35, no. 4 (Oct. 1983), pp. 504–24.

53. TsGAOR, f. 5469, op. 13, d. 124, ll. 37–38, 46–54.

54. *Litsom k derevne*, no. 24 (Dec. 1929), p. 22; *Trud*, 4 Dec. 1929, p. 1.

55. Ivnitskii and Ezerskii, "Dvadtsatipiatitysiachniki," p. 412.

56. Kats-Kagan, *25,000 proletariev*, p. 14.

57. *Litsom k derevne*, no. 24 (Dec. 1929), p. 22; *Rabochaia gazeta*, 8 Jan. 1930, p. 2; TsGAOR, f. 5469, op. 13, d. 124, l. 40.

58. In fact, at this point, it was still not certain who would pay the workers' salaries if they were maintained at their former level. *Leningradskaia pravda*, 13 Jan. 1930, p. 3; *Rabochaia gazeta*, 24 Jan. 1930, p. 2.

59. *Bednota*, 26 Jan. 1930, p. 1; *Pravda*, 24 Jan. 1930, p. 5.

60. *Biulleten' Ural'skogo oblastnogo komiteta VKP (b)*, no. 15 (26 Dec. 1929), p. 7; *Izvestiia Nizhegorodskogo kraevogo komiteta VKP (b)*, nos. 11–12 (31 Dec. 1929), p. 24.

61. *Rabochaia Moskva*, 11 Jan. 1930, p. 3.

62. *Komsomolskaia pravda*, 27 Nov. 1929, p. 4; *Trud*, 27 Nov. 1929, p. 2. See the especially strident attacks on Dogadov, who was accused of adhering to the right opposition's platform, at the Sixteenth Party Congress, in *XVI s"ezd VKP (b)*. *Sten. otchet* (Moscow and Leningrad: Gosizdat, 1930), pp. 276–77. Also see Shvernik's speech at the congress, in which he accuses the right opposition and the former trade union leadership of opposition to the use of workers in the countryside, p. 646.

63. *Izvestiia*, 10 Jan. 1930, p. 1; *Trud*, 22 Nov. 1929, p. 1; 13 Dec. 1929, p. 1.

64. *Pravda*, 20 Dec. 1929, p. 2; 1 Jan. 1930, p. 2; *Trud*, 19 Dec. 1929, p. 4; *Vecherniaia Moskva*, 31 Dec. 1929, p. 1; 3 Feb. 1930, p. 1.

65. See the case of Moscow's refusal to recant after Stalin published "Dizzyness from Success" in chap. 5 and also see the case of the Moscow Regional Council of Trade Unions exerting its authority in the mobilization of the "thousanders" for higher education in Sheila Fitzpatrick, *Education and Social Mobility in the Soviet Union, 1924–1934* (Cambridge: Cambridge Univ. Press, 1979), p. 185.

66. *Moskovskaia derevnia*, 8 Jan. 1930, p. 1; *Rabochaia gazeta*, 27 Dec. 1929, p. 4.

67. See *Kollektivizatsiia sel'skogo khoziaistva v Zapadnom raione RSFSR*, pp. 220–21.

68. *Za industrializatsiiu*, 22 Jan. 1930, p. 3.

69. For example, Rozenfel'd, *Dvadtsatipiatitysiachniki*, pp. 17–18, 28; Selunskaia, *Rabochie-dvadtsatipiatitysiachniki*, pp. 33–34.

70. For example, Charles P. Cell, *Revolution at Work* (New York: Academic Press, 1977), p. 10; Robert C. Tucker, "Stalinism as Revolution from Above," in *Stalinism: Essays in Historical Interpretation*, ed. Robert C. Tucker (New York: Norton, 1977), p. 101.

71. Ivnitskii and Ezerskii, "Dvadtsatipiatitysiachniki," pp. 434–35; *Pravda*, 18 Jan. 1930, p. 3; N. Nemakov and T. Isakov, "Dvadtsatipiatitysiachniki v kollektivizatsii sel'skogo khoziaistva," *Iz istorii kommunisticheskoi partii Kirgizii*, vyp. 2 (Frunze: Mektep, 1965), p. 31.

72. Kats-Kagan, *25,000 proletariev*, pp. 6–7; *Pravda*, 18 Jan. 1930, p. 3.

73. TsGAOR, f. 5469, op. 13, d. 124, ll. 8–10 (VSRM directive); *Ural'skii rabochii*, 14 Dec. 1929, p. 2 (Urals regional party committee directive).

Notes

. *Rabochaia Moskva*, 8 Dec. 1929, p. 1.

75. See the case of Cherednichenko in Lev Kopelev, *I sotvoril sebe kumira* (Ann Arbor: Ardis, 1978), pp. 209–10.

76. Nemakov and Isakov, "Dvadtsatipiatitysiachniki," pp. 28–29.

77. Efremenkov and Mukhachev, "Dvadtsatipiatitysiachniki," p. 124.

78. *Leningradskaia pravda*, 10 Jan. 1930, p. 3.

79. TsGAOR, f. 5469, op. 13, d. 124, ll. 46–54.

80. The questionnaires (*ankety*) were available from a total of seventy-six 25,000ers. Each questionnaire included a question on the "form" of recruitment—that is, "voluntary" or "mobilized." See TsGAOR, f. 5469, op. 13, d. 125; continued in f. 7676, op. 6, d. 180.

81. This is actually more than probable, given the statistical profile of the workers in terms of skill and party membership.

82. *Sobranie zakonov*, no. 1 (1 Jan. 1930), pp. 12–14.

83. Anton Ciliga, *The Russian Enigma* (London: George Routledge and Sons, 1940), p. 111; *Leningradskaia pravda*, 15 Dec. 1929, p. 3.

84. *Rabochaia gazeta*, 13 Feb. 1930, p. 8.

85. Although this was never "official" policy, some families did, in fact, receive the difference payment while the worker was in the countryside. *Rabochaia gazeta*, 8 Dec. 1929, p. 2; *Rabochaia Moskva*, 6 Dec. 1929, p. 3, for information about rumors.

86. A. I. Iulina, "Kuzbasskie dvadtsatipiatitysiachniki na kolkhoznoi stroike Zapadnoi Sibiri (1929–1930 gg.)," *Iz istorii rabochego klassa Sibiri*, vyp. 3 (Kemerovo: Kuzbas. politekhn. insitut, kafedr istorii KPSS, 1970), p. 70. For an indication of salaries of chairmen and secretaries of district soviet executive committees and *sel' sovet*s, see *Ezhegodnik Sovetskogo stroitel' stva i prava na 1931 god (za 1929/30 god)*, pp. 123, 163.

87. For examples, see *Rabochaia Moskva*, 24 Dec. 1929, p. 3; *Sel' skokhoziaistvennaia gazeta*, 6 Dec. 1929, p. 2; TsGAOR, f. 5452, op. 11, d. 38, l. 6; f. 5469, op. 13, d. 124, ll. 36, 37–38, 40, 47; f. 5470, op. 14, d. 204, l. 47.

88. Ciliga, *Russian Enigma*, p. 111; *Kollektivizatsiia sel'skogo khoziaistva na Severnom Kavkaze, 1927–1937* (Krasnodar: Knizhnoe izd-vo, 1972), pp. 356–57.

89. *Spravochnik partiinogo rabotnika*, vol. 8 (Moscow: Partizdat, 1934), p. 315.

90. See chap. 7.

91. For biographical information on these men, see *Bol'shaia Sovetskaia entsiklopediia*, vol. 4, 3d ed. (Moscow: Sovetskaia entsiklopediia, 1971), p. 177; *Pravda*, 15 Apr. 1955, p. 2; 7 July 1963, p. 1; Selunskaia, *Rabochie-dvadtsatipiatitysiachniki*, pp. 213, 216.

92. *Izvestiia*, 25 Jan. 1930, p. 1; *Leningradskaia pravda*, 11 Jan. 1930, p. 2; *Pravda*, 18 Jan. 1930, p. 3; Rozenfel'd, *Dvadtsatipiatitysiachniki*, pp. 97–98; Rusakov, "Poslantsy," p. 119.

93. For further information on attitudes among workers at the end of NEP, see Chase, "Moscow and Its Working Class," pp. 84, 218, 243–44, 251–57, 288, 365–66; Sheila Fitzpatrick, "Cultural Revolution as Class War," in *Cultural Revolution in Russia, 1928–1931*, ed. Sheila Fitzpatrick (Bloomington, Ind.: Indiana Univ. Press, 1978), p. 19; Maurice Hindus, *Red Bread* (New York: Jonathan Cape and

Harrison Smith, 1931), pp. 114, 118–22, especially on urban-rural relations; and William G. Rosenberg, "Smolensk in the 1920s: Party-Worker Relations and the 'Vanguard' Problem," *Russian Review*, vol. 36, no. 2 (Apr. 1977), pp. 132–40.

94. For a discussion of the heterogeneity of the Soviet working class in the late 1920s and the relation of the party to different strata of workers, see Hiroaki Kuromiya, "The Crisis of Proletarian Identity in the Soviet Factory, 1928–1929," *Slavic Review*, vol. 44, no. 2 (Summer 1985).

95. Data from A. G. Rashin, "Dinamika promyshlennykh kadrov SSSR za 1917–1958 gg.," *Izmeneniia v chislennosti i sostave Sovetskogo rabochego klassa* (Moscow: AN SSSR, 1961), pp. 13–15, 38, 44, 50, 57; idem, *Sostav fabrichno-zavodskogo proletariata SSSR. Predvaritel'nye itogi perepisi metallistov, gornorabochikh i tekstil'shchikov v 1929 g.* (Moscow: VTsSPS, 1930), pp. ix, 12–13, 15–17, 21, 24–25; and *Trud v SSSR*, pp. 26, 34.

96. *Politicheskii i trudovoi pod''em*, pp. 541–43; Smolensk Archive, T 87/31, WKP 261, pp. 62–63; TsGAOR, f. 5453, op. 14, d. 58, l. 74; f. 5453, op. 14, d. 150, l. 48; f. 5469, op. 13, d. 124, l. 90; f. 5470, op. 14, d. 204, l. 47.

97. *Molot*, 18 Jan. 1930, p. 2 (speech of 13 Jan.).

98. *Izvestiia*, 27 Jan. 1930, p. 2.

99. *Trud*, 2 Feb. 1930, p. 3; P. M. Diuvbanov, *Vedushchaia rol' rabochego klassa v sotsialisticheskom pereustroistve sel'skogo khoziaistva (na materialakh avtonomykh respublik Srednego Povolzh'ia)* (Kazan: Kazanskii universitet, 1975), p. 68.

100. *Kollektivizatsiia sel'skogo khoziaistva na Severnom Kavkaze*, p. 200.

101. *Za urozhai*, nos. 1–2 (Jan. 1930), pp. 4–5.

102. *Litsom k derevne*, no. 1 (Jan. 1930), p. 15; also see Rozenfel'd, *Dvadtsatipiatitysiachniki*, p. 41.

103. TsGAOR, f. 5469, op. 13, d. 124, ll. 99–100.

104. TsGAOR, f. 5470, op. 14, d. 204, l. 47.

105. *Molot*, 28 Jan. 1930, p. 1.

106. Ivnitskii and Ezerskii, "Dvadtsatipiatitysiachniki," p. 455.

107. TsGAOR, f. 5469, op. 13, d. 124, ll. 99–100.

108. I. I. Alekseenko, "Rabochie-dvadtsatipiatitysiachniki—provodniki politiki kommunisticheskoi partii v kolkhoznom stroitel'stve," *K sorokaletiiu velikoi Oktiabr'skoi sotsialisticheskoi revoliutsii* (Krasnoiarsk: Knizhnoe izd-vo, 1957), p. 419.

109. *Litsom k derevne*, no. 4 (Feb. 1930), p. 6.

110. Ibid., no. 24 (Dec. 1929), p. 26; Timofeev, "Dvadtsatipiatitysiachniki," p. 80.

111. *Litsom k derevne*, no. 4 (Feb. 1930), p. 5.

112. *Rabochaia gazeta*, 28 Jan. 1930, p. 3.

113. *Politicheskii i trudovoi pod''em*, p. 543.

114. Zombe, "Dvadtsatipiatitysiachniki," p. 10.

115. See cases in V. Eroshkin, *Na ikh doliu vypalo schast'e* (Ioshkar-Ola: Mariisk. knizhnoe izd-vo, 1976), pp. 13–15, 31–34, 48–49; and Rusakov, "Poslantsy," pp. 118–21.

116. N. Ia. Gushchin, *Rabochii klass Sibiri v bor'be za sozdanie kolkhoznogo*

stroia (Novosibirsk: Nauka, Sibirskoe otdelenie, 1965), p. 73; Kats-Kagan, *25,000 proletariev*, p. 8.

117. Lev Kopelev, *I sotvoril sebe kumira*, pp. 209–10.

118. *Litsom k derevne*, no. 24 (Dec. 1929), p. 4. For interesting data on the intensity of rural violence in reference to the 1926 wave of *sel'kory* (rural newspaper correspondent) murders, see William Reswick, *I Dreamt Revolution* (Chicago: Henry Regnery, 1952), pp. 153–55, 162–64.

119. Ciliga, *Russian Enigma*, pp. 111–12; I. A. Ivanov, "Pomoshch' Leningradskikh rabochikh v kollektivizatsii sel'skogo khoziaistva podshefnykh raionov," *Rabochie Leningrada v bor'be za pobedu sotsializma* (Moscow and Leningrad: AN SSSR, 1963), pp. 203–4.

120. See chap. 7.

121. Mikhail Sholokhov, *Virgin Soil Upturned*, trans. Robert Daglish, vol. 1 (Moscow: Progress Publishers, 1980), pp. 282–83.

122. *Litsom k derevne*, no. 1 (Jan. 1930), p. 15.

123. Ibid.; *Politicheskii i trudovoi pod"em*, p. 543.

124. *Po zovu partii*, pp. 52, 125–26, 306–8; Rozenfel'd, *Dvadtsatipiatitysiachniki*, pp. 18–19.

125. *Bastiony revoliutsii. Stranitsy istorii Leningradskikh zavodov*, vyp. 3 (Leningrad: Lenizdat, 1960), pp. 48, 238–39; *Rabochaia gazeta*, 30 Nov. 1929, p. 3.

126. *Moskovskaia derevnia*, 26 Jan. 1930, p. 3; *Rabochaia gazeta*, 22 Mar. 1930, p. 3 (for slightly later period); TsGAOR, f. 5469, op. 13, d. 123, ll. 72–76.

127. *Moskovskaia derevnia*, 22 Jan. 1930, p. 3; TsGAOR, f. 5469, op. 13, d. 122, ll. 2–7, 14, 152–54, 162–169.

128. TsGAOR, f. 5469, op. 13, d. 123, ll. 78–91.

129. For example, see discussion of this in A. Mel'kumov, *Proletariat i sotsialisticheskoe pereustroistvo derevni* (Moscow: Moskovskii rabochii, 1930), pp. 53, 55, 61. Mel'kumov claims that up to 50 percent of households in some Moscow Region *okrug*s self-liquidated their farms and permanently moved to the cities at this time.

130. See trade union efforts to "reeducate" these workers via circles, lectures, newspaper readings, etc., in TsGAOR, f. 5469, op. 13, d. 123, ll. 72–76, 78–91.

131. *Rabochaia gazeta*, 24 Jan. 1930, p. 2; *Rabochaia Moskva*, 15 Feb. 1930, p. 3; 20 Feb. 1930, p. 3; TsGAOR, f. 5469, op. 13, d. 124, l. 90.

132. K. K. German, *Dvadtsatipiatitysiachniki Belorussii* (Minsk: BGU, 1971), pp. 23–24; Selunskaia, *Rabochie-dvadtsatipiatitysiachniki*, p. 57.

133. Kopelev, *I sotvoril sebe kumira*, pp. 209–10.

134. *Ural'skii rabochii*, 26 Dec. 1929, p. 3.

135. *Rabochaia gazeta*, 10 Jan. 1930, p. 5.

136. TsGAOR, f. 5452, op. 11, d. 38, l. 6.

137. According to data on the selection of workers among Leningrad volunteers, approximately 40 percent of volunteers were cut at the level of the factory selection committee, 15 to 20 percent were cut by the individual regional trade unions representing the worker's profession, and 10 percent were cut by the regional trade union council committees. Selunskaia, *Rabochie-dvadtsatipiatitysiachniki*, p. 58.

138. *Informatsionnaia svodka tsentral'nogo komiteta VSRM*, no. 1/149 (15 Jan. 1930), p. 12; *Litsom k derevne*, no. 1 (Jan. 1930), pp. 17, 20–21; Ivnitskii and Ezerskii, "Dvadtsatipiatitysiachniki," pp. 415–16; *Politicheskii i trudovoi pod''em*, pp. 529–30; Rozenfel'd, *Dvadtsatipiatitysiachniki*, pp. 14–15; TsGAOR, f. 5452, op. 11, d. 38, l. 7; f. 5470, op. 14, d. 204, l. 47; Zombe, "Dvadtsatipiatitysiachniki," p. 8.

139. Rozenfel'd, *Dvadtsatipiatitysiachniki*, p. 15; Selunskaia, *Rabochie-dvadtsatipiatitysiachniki*, p. 57; TsGAOR, f. 5469, op. 13, d. 124, l. 90.

140. Rashin, "Dinamika," p. 61; idem, *Sostav*, pp. v, xii, 16, 30, 38, 39, 64, 128; *Trud v SSSR*, pp. 26–27, 34.

Chapter 3

1. N. A. Ivnitskii, ed., "Dvadtsatipiatitysiachniki-Moskvichi na kolkhoznoi rabote," *Istoricheskii arkhiv*, no. 1 (1956), p. 106; Ivnitskii and Ezerskii, "Dvadtsatipiatitysiachniki," pp. 423–25, 440; TsGANKh, f. 7446, op. 12, d. 5, ll. 2–4.

2. *Bednota*, 15 Aug. 1930, p. 2.

3. *Kollektivizatsiia sel'skogo khoziaistva. Vazhneishie postanovleniia kommunisticheskoi partii i sovetskogo pravitel'stva, 1927–35* (Moscow: AN SSSR, 1957), p. 253; *Pravda*, 3 Dec. 1929, p. 3.

4. *Bednota*, 2 Feb. 1930, p. 1; *Izvestiia*, 9 Feb. 1930, p. 4.

5. *Izvestiiu*, 27 Jan. 1930, p. 2; *Pravda*, 27 Jan. 1930, p. 4.

6. *Vecherniaia Moskva*, 10 Feb. 1930, p. 2; G. Kolesnikova and N. Kovanov, *Udarniki sotsialisticheskoi stroiki (dvadtsatipiatitysiachniki)* (Moscow: Krasnaia gazeta, 1931), pp. 3–6.

7. *Bednota*, 29 Jan. 1930, p. 4; Ivnitskii and Ezerskii, "Dvadtsatipiatitysiachniki," pp. 433, 479.

8. *Bednota*, 6 Feb. 1930, p. 4; *Pravda*, 5 Feb. 1930, pp. 2, 5; *Trud*, 27 Jan. 1930, p. 1; 31 Jan. 1930, p. 3.

9. *Pravda*, 5 Feb. 1930, p. 2.

10. *Zapadnyi oblastnoi komitet VKP (b). Vtoraia oblastnaia partkonferentsiia (5–12 iiunia 1930 g.). Sten. otchet* (Moscow and Smolensk: Zapadnoe oblastnoe otdelenie Ogiza, 1931), p. 269.

11. *Derevenskii kommunist*, nos. 11–12 (21 June 1930), p. 46. A total of 15 percent of rural Communists were purged according to the final data. See Rigby, *Communist Party*, p. 187.

12. Ibid., nos. 23–24 (25 Dec. 1929), p. 51; *Put' sovetov* (North Caucasus), no. 14 (31 July 1930), pp. 23–24; *Sovetskoe stroitel'stvo*, no. 2 (Feb. 1930), p. 58.

13. Central Executive Committee of the Soviets of the USSR decree of 25 January 1930; see *Izvestiia*, 26 Jan. 1930, p. 1.

14. *Put' sovetov* (M. Volga), no. 10 (May 1930), p. 1; B. Levin and I. Suvorov, "Sovety i stroitel'stvo sotsializma," in *15 let Sovetskogo stroitel'stva*, ed. E. Pashukanis (Moscow: Gosizdat, 1932), pp. 465–66.

15. *Derevenskii kommunist*, no. 2 (25 Jan. 1930), p. 21.

16. *Sovetskoe stroitel'stvo*, no. 11 (Nov. 1929), pp. 80–86.

17. *Izvestiia*, 11 Sept. 1929, p. 3; 20 Jan. 1930, p. 1; 22 Jan. 1930, p. 1; *Rabochaia Moskva*, 19 Sept. 1929, p. 3; *Sovetskoe stroitel'stvo*, no. 9 (Sept. 1929), pp. 32–41; no. 12 (Dec. 1929), pp. 75–84; no. 1 (Jan. 1930), pp. 64–79; no. 2 (Feb. 1930), pp. 2–4.

18. Selunskaia, *Rabochie-dvadtsatipiatitysiachniki*, pp. 71–72.

19. Letters of 18 December, 24 December, and 6 January in TsGANKh, f. 7446, op. 12, d. 3, ll. 2–3, 9; d. 22a, ll. 1–2.

20. *Pravda*, 25 Jan. 1930, p. 3; *Rabochaia gazeta*, 19 Jan. 1930, p. 3.

21. *Pravda*, 25 Jan. 1930, p. 3.

22. *Bednota*, 30 Jan. 1930, p. 1.

23. TsGANKh, f. 7446, op. 12, d. 21a, ll. 3–4.

24. *Izvestiia*, 28 Jan. 1930, p. 4.

25. TsGANKh, f. 7446, op. 12, d. 21a, ll. 3–4.

26. The first official statistics on the 25,000ers were dated 21 February 1930. These statistics were based on information available for 15,898 25,000ers. According to this data, 10,685 were employed on the collective farms, 2,457 on the group collective farms, 1,720 in the district offices of Kolkhoztsentr, 960 in machine tractor stations, 63 in Kolkhoztsentr *okrug* offices, and 13 in regional-level Kolkhoztsentr offices. Within two weeks of this initial compilation, 594 additional 25,000ers surfaced. According to this data, 10,729 25,000ers were employed on collective farms; 1,624 on group collective farms; 495 in machine tractor stations; 2,338 in Kolkhoztsentr district offices; 97 in Kolkhoztsentr *okrug* offices; 106 in soviet, party, and cooperative work; 4 in Kolkhoztsentr, and 1,099 in an unclear capacity. A comparison of these two sets of data indicates high turnover in offices and continued fluidity of the 25,000ers' situation. Data from Ivnitskii and Ezerskii, "Dvadtsatipiatitysiachniki," pp. 456, 476–77.

27. Ivnitskii and Ezerskii, "Dvadtsatipiatitysiachniki," p. 462. Several Soviet scholars have argued convincingly that there were actually some thirty-five thousand 25,000ers. For example, see Iu. S. Borisov, *Podgotovka proizvodstvennykh kadrov sel'skogo khoziaistva SSSR v rekonstruktivnyi period* (Moscow: AN SSSR, 1960), pp. 81–83; V. P. Danilov, M. P. Kim, and N. V. Tropkin, eds., *Sovetskoe krest'ianstvo: kratkii ocherk istorii (1917–1970)* (Moscow: Politizdat, 1973), p. 255. Part of the reason for this disparity lay in the fact that a secondary wave of workers, not selected as 25,000ers, but placed in a "25,000er reserve," called for by the Central Committee on 15 January 1930, were often counted as 25,000ers. See *Pravda*, 24 Jan. 1930, p. 5, for information on the reserve. Whatever the case, all further data on the 25,000ers were based on a figure more closely approximate to the official figure of 27,519; therefore this figure will be used as the base number for further calculations in this study.

28. Nemakov and Isakov, "Dvadtsatipiatitysiachniki," p. 40; V. P. Tiushev, "Deiatel'nost' rabochikh-dvadtsatipiatitysiachnikov v kolkhozakh Irkutskoi oblasti," *Oktiabr' i Vostochnaia Sibir'* (Irkutsk: Irkutskii gos. pedinstitut, 1968), p. 73.

29. *Bednota*, 17 Apr. 1930, p. 2; *Vlast' sovetov*, nos. 13–14 (1931), pp. 42–43.

30. *Bednota*, 15 Aug. 1930, p. 2.

31. TsGANKh, f. 7446, op. 13, d. 55, ll. 76–84.
32. TsGANKh, f. 7446, op. 12, d. 21a, ll. 3–4, 21.
33. See, for example, the case in *Izvestiia Donskogo okruzhnogo komiteta VKP (b)*, nos. 3–4 (Mar.–Apr. 1930), pp. 8–9.
34. *Pravda*, 9 Feb. 1930, p. 4. The 25,000ers had been requested (*Pravda*, 26 Jan. 1930, p. 3) to send their names, addresses, and other pertinent information to this party department.
35. *Izvestiia*, 6 Mar. 1930, p. 4; TsGANKh, f. 7446, op. 13, d. 55, ll. 76–84.
36. *Izvestiia*, 6 Mar. 1930, p. 4.
37. Ivnitskii and Ezerskii, "Dvadtsatipiatitysiachniki," p. 441.
38. *Litsom k derevne*, no. 8 (Apr. 1930), p. 15.
39. Ibid., p. 3.
40. Kats-Kagan, *25,000 proletariev*, p. 13.
41. German, *Dvadtsatipiatitysiachniki Belorussii*, p. 31.
42. Ivnitskii and Ezerskii, "Dvadtsatipiatitysiachniki," p. 482.
43. TsGAOR, f. 5470, op. 14, d. 204, l. 54.
44. *Rabochaia gazeta*, 1 Mar. 1930, p. 4.
45. *Trud*, 12 June 1930, p. 4.
46. On staff shortages in Kolkhoztsentr's provincial network, see R. W. Davies, *The Soviet Collective Farm, 1929–1930* (Cambridge, Mass.: Harvard Univ. Press, 1980), p. 7.
47. *Bednota*, 2 Feb. 1930, p. 1; TsGANKh, f. 7446, op. 11, d. 44, ll. 93–109.
48. *Rabochaia Moskva*, 5 Mar. 1930, p. 2; *Vecherniaia Moskva*, 24 Feb. 1930, p. 1.
49. The Central Committee and Kolkhoztsentr had issued orders that not one 25,000er was to be retained in the offices of the Kolkhoztsentr network, with possible exceptions for 25,000ers in district-level offices in districts of wholesale collectivization. *Pravda*, 18 Jan. 1930, p. 3; 25 Jan. 1930, p. 3; TsGANKh, f. 7446, op. 12, d. 3, ll. 1–2; d. 21a. ll. 3–4.
50. *Nizhnevolzhskii kolkhoznik*, no. 1 (July 1930), p. 41.
51. *Bednota*, 15 Feb. 1930, p. 1.
52. Rozenfel'd, *Dvadtsatipiatitysiachniki*, p. 58.
53. Ivnitskii and Ezerskii, "Dvadtsatipiatitysiachniki," p. 456. This percentage was based on data available for only 15,898 25,000ers and, consequently, should be read as an extreme underestimation.
54. *Bednota*, 11 Feb. 1930, p. 4; 8 Mar. 1930, p. 4; *Izvestiia*, 10 Feb. 1930, p. 1; 21 Feb. 1930, p. 4; *Vecherniaia Moskva*, 24 Feb. 1930, p. 1; Ivnitskii and Ezerskii, "Dvadtsatipiatitysiachniki," p. 456; Kats-Kagan, *25,000 proletariev*, p. 28; M. Kureiko, *25-tysiachniki na kolkhoznoi stroike* (Moscow and Leningrad: Sel'kolkhozgiz, 1931), pp. 18–19.
55. *Izvestiia Donskogo okruzhnogo komiteta VKP (b)*, nos. 3–4 (Mar.–Apr. 1930), pp. 8–9; *Pravda*, 9 Feb. 1930, p. 4; *Rabochaia gazeta*, 1 Mar. 1930, p. 4; TsGANKh, f. 7446, op. 12, d. 21a, l. 23.
56. TsGANKh, f. 7446, op. 12, d. 21a, l. 23.
57. Ibid., f. 7446, op. 12, d. 21a, ll. 32–33.

58. See my dissertation (p. 195) for a list of these organizations. Cited in chap. 2, n. 13.

Chapter 4

1. See discussion of "teleological planning" in Carr and Davies, *Foundations of a Planned Economy*, vol. 1, pt. 2, pp. 790–94.

2. *Krest'ianskaia gazeta*, 14 Jan. 1930, p. 1.

3. *Pravda*, 10 June 1930, p. 3.

4. *KPSS v rezoliutsiiakh*, pp. 544–47.

5. See chap. 1 on regional rates of collectivization.

6. *KPSS v rezoliutsiiakh*, p. 547.

7. Davies, *Socialist Offensive*, pp. 177–80.

8. This was most dramatically demonstrated in Siberia, which had percentages of 4.8 collectivized households on 1 October 1929, 20.1 on 1 February 1930, 32 on 10 February 1930, 39.5 on 20 February 1930, and 47.7 on 1 March 1930. TsGANKh, f. 4108, op. 16, d. 48, l. 83.

9. *XVI s"ezd VKP (b). Sten. otchet.*, pp. 114, 214–16, 226, 230, 352, 360.

10. Davies, *Socialist Offensive*, pp. 177–80.

11. P. N. Sharova, *Kollektivizatsiia sel'skogo khoziaistva v TsChO, 1928–32 gg.* (Moscow: AN SSSR, 1963), pp. 153–54.

12. I. I. Iakovlev, "Iz istorii dvadtsatipiatitysiachnikov na Altae v pervoi polovine 1930 goda," *Nekotorye voprosy istorii KPSS* (Barnaul: Barnaulskii gos. pedinstitut, 1973), p. 70.

13. Davies, *Socialist Offensive*, pp. 177–79; M. L. Bogdenko, "Kolkhoznoe stroitel'stvo vesnoi i letom 1930 g.," *Istoricheskie zapiski*, vol. 76 (1965), p. 20; L. Kozlova, *K pobede kolkhoznogo stroia. Bor'ba Moskovskoi partiinoi organizatsii za podgotovku i provedenie kollektivizatsii* (Moscow: Moskovskii rabochii, 1971), pp. 193–96; *Za kollektivizatsiiu*, 1 June 1930, p. 1.

14. K. F. Shalina, "Rol' 25-tysiachnikov v sotsialisticheskom pereustroistve sel'skogo khoziaistva," *Izvestiia Krymskogo pedinstituta*, vol. 36 (1961), p. 10.

15. *XVI s"ezd VKP (b). Sten. otchet*, p. 82.

16. *Zapadnyi oblastnoi komitet VKP (b). Vtoraia oblastnaia partkonferentsiia. Sten. otchet*, pp. 169, 223, 254.

17. Stalin, "Golovokruzhenie ot uspekhov. K voprosam kolkhoznogo dvizheniia," *Sochineniia*, vol. 12, pp. 191–99; *KPSS v rezoliutsiiakh*, pp. 548–51.

18. Stalin, "K voprosam agrarnoi politiki v SSSR. (Rech' na konferentsii agrarnikov-marksistov 27 dekabria 1929 g.)," *Sochineniia*, vol. 12, pp. 169–70.

19. *KPSS v rezoliutsiiakh*, p. 545.

20. For information on the Bauman commission, see N. A. Ivnitskii, *Klassovaia bor'ba v derevne i likvidatsiia kulachestva kak klassa* (Moscow: Nauka, 1972), pp. 169–78.

21. Ibid., pp. 177–78; B. A. Abramov, F. M. Vagonov, and V. A. Golikov, "O nekotorykh voprosakh istorii pervogo etapa sploshnoi kollektivizatsii sel'skogo khoziaistva," *Voprosy istorii KPSS*, no. 4 (1972), pp. 27–28.

22. There were three documents on dekulakization. The first, a Central Committee decree of 30 January 1930, was never published but a regional variant of it can be found in the decree of the Western Region party committee in *Kollektivizatsiia sel'skogo khoziaistva v Zapadnom raione RSFSR*, pp. 246–50. The second, a Central Executive Committee and Council of People's Commissars USSR decree of 1 February 1930 was published in *Sobranie zakonov*, no. 9 (24 Feb. 1930), pp. 187–88. The third, instructions issued by the Central Executive Committee and the Council of People's Commissars on 4 February 1930, was not published but reflected in regional decrees issued by the North Caucasus, the Middle Volga, and Siberia in *Kollektivizatsiia sel'skogo khoziaistva na Severnom Kavkaze*, pp. 248–52; *Kollektivizatsiia sel'skogo khoziaistva v Srednem Povolzh'e* (Kuibyshev: Kuibyshevskoe knizhnoe izd-vo, 1970), pp. 156–58; and *Kollektivizatsiia sel'skogo khoziaistva Zapadnoi Sibiri*, pp. 135–38.

23. For further information on dekulakization, see Davies, *Socialist Offensive*, pp. 232–37.

24. Abramov, Vaganov, and Golikov, "O nekotorykh voprosakh," pp. 27–28; Danilov, Kim, and Tropkin, *Sovetskoe krest'ianstvo*, p. 228.

25. Ivnitskii, *Klassovaia bor'ba*, p. 180.

26. Ibid., p. 213.

27. See Lewin, *Russian Peasants and Soviet Power*, pt. 2; and V. P. Danilov, "K kharakteristike obshchestvenno-politicheskoi obstanovki v Sovetskoi derevne nakanune kollektivizatsii," *Istoricheskie zapiski*, vol. 79 (1967), pp. 30–34, 40, 44.

28. P. V. Semernin, "O likvidatsii kulachestva kak klassa," *Voprosy istorii KPSS*, no. 4 (1958), pp. 75–78; V. A. Sidorov, "Likvidatsiia v SSSR kulachestva kak klassa," *Voprosy istorii*, no. 7 (1968), p. 27; also see *Derevenskii kommunist*, nos. 15–16 (21 Aug. 1929), p. 17, and no. 19 (14 Oct. 1929), pp. 13–14, for local decisions to not admit kulaks to collective farms.

29. N. Ia. Gushchin, "Likvidatsiia kulachestva kak klassa v Sibirskoi derevne," *Sotsial'naia struktura naseleniia Sibiri* (Novosibirsk: Nauka, Sibirskoe otdelenie, 1970), pp. 125–26; Iu. A. Moshkov, *Zernovaia problema v gody sploshnoi kollektivizatsii sel'skogo khoziaistva SSSR (1929–32 gg.)* (Moscow: MGU, 1966), pp. 63–65.

30. Gushchin, "Likvidatsiia," pp. 125–26.

31. *Sobranie zakonov*, no. 6 (13 Feb. 1930), pp. 137–38.

32. V. M. Selunskaia et al., eds., *Izmeneniia sotsial'noi struktury Sovetskogo obshchestva 1921-seredine 30-kh godov* (Moscow: Mysl', 1979), p. 247.

33. V. K. Medvedev, "Likvidatsiia kulachestva v Nizhne-Volzhskom krae," *Istoriia SSSR*, no. 6 (1958), p. 18.

34. Gushchin, "Likvidatsiia," p. 127; idem, *Sibirskaia derevnia na puti k sotsializmu* (Novosibirsk: Nauka, Sibirskoe otdelenie, 1973), p. 418.

35. Cited in Bogdenko, "Kolkhoznoe stroitel'stvo," p. 21.

36. For example, see *Izvestiia*, 1 Feb. 1930, p. 1; 2 Feb. 1930, p. 1; *Krest'ianskaia pravda*, 5 Feb. 1930, pp. 1, 3; *Molot*, 2 Feb. 1930, p. 1; 4 Feb. 1930, p. 1; 6 Feb. 1930, p. 1; 7 Feb. 1930, p. 1; *Moskovskaia derevnia*, 2 Feb. 1930, p. 1; *Na fronte kollektivizatsii*, nos. 4–5 (1–15 Jan. 1930), pp. 12–13; *Partiinoe*

238 *Notes*

stroitel'stvo, nos. 3–4 (Feb. 1930), pp. 16–17; *Pravda*, 1 Feb. 1930, p. 4; 2 Feb. 1930, p. 3; *Rabochaia gazeta*, 2 Feb. 1930, p. 3; 4 Feb. 1930, p. 1; *Rabochaia Moskva*, 4 Feb. 1930, p. 2; *Sel'skokhoziaistvennaia zhizn'*, no. 4 (10 Feb. 1930), pp. 1–2; *Ural'skii rabochii*, 8 Feb. 1930, p. 3; *Vecherniaia Moskva*, 8 Feb. 1930, p. 2.

37. Stalin, "Otvet tovarishcham Sverdlovtsam," *Sochineniia*, vol. 12, pp. 187–88.

38. *Krest'ianskaia pravda*, 15 Feb. 1930, p. 1.

39. The first articles to criticize excesses appeared in *Molot*, 7 Jan. 1930, p. 5; 14 Jan. 1930, p. 2; 16 Jan. 1930, p. 1; 18 Jan. 1930, p. 2. *Izvestiia* also published several early critical articles (25 Jan. 1930, p. 3; 29 Jan. 1930, p. 3). For critical articles in first half of February, see *Krest'ianskaia pravda*, 5 Feb. 1930, pp. 1, 3; 15 Feb. 1930, p. 1; *Molot*, 2 Feb. 1930, p. 1; 4 Feb. 1930, p. 1; 6 Feb. 1930, p. 1; 7 Feb. 1930, p. 1; 11 Feb. 1930, p. 3; *Moskovskaia derevnia*, 2 Feb. 1930, p. 1; 7 Feb. 1930, p. 2; *Pravda*, 1 Feb. 1930, p. 4; 3 Feb. 1930, p. 1; *Rabochaia gazeta*, 7 Feb. 1930, p. 3 (Syrtsov speech); *Rabochaia Moskva*, 4 Feb. 1930, p. 2; *Sel'skokhoziaistvennaia zhizn'*, no. 4 (10 Feb. 1930), pp. 1–2; *Sotsialisticheskoe zemledelie*, 4 Feb. 1930, p. 2; 6 Feb. 1930, p. 2; *Ural'skii rabochii*, 12 Feb. 1930, p. 2 (Syrtsov speech); *Vecherniaia Moskva*, 8 Feb. 1930, p. 2; *Za kollektivizatsiiu*, 12 Feb. 1930, p. 2.

40. Anna Louise Strong, *I Change Worlds* (New York: Garden City Publishing Co., 1937), p. 292.

41. Abramov, Vaganov, and Golikov, "O nekotorykh voprosakh," pp. 34–35.

42. Ibid., p. 35; Ivnitskii, *Klassovaia bor'ba*, p. 214; F. A. Karevskii, "Likvidatsiia kulachestva kak klassa v Srednem povolzh'e," *Istoricheskie zapiski*, vol. 80 (1967), p. 94; also see article in *Izvestiia*, 2 Feb. 1930, p. 3, criticizing excesses in the Middle Volga.

43. Abramov, Vaganov, and Golikov, "O nekotorykh voprosakh," p. 35; see also article in *Sotsialisticheskoe zemledelie*, 4 Feb. 1930, p. 2, criticizing Moscow's activities.

44. B. A. Abramov, F. M. Vaganov, and V. I. Kulikov, "N. I. Nemakov. Kommunisticheskaia partiia—organizator massovogo kolkhoznogo dvizheniia (1929–32 gg.)," [book review] *Voprosy istorii KPSS*, no. 6 (1968), p. 116.

45. Medvedev, "Likvidatsiia," p. 26.

46. *Kollektivizatsiia sel'skogo khoziaistva v Srednem Povolzh'e*, p. 156; *Kollektivizatsiia sel'skogo khoziaistva Zapadnoi Sibiri*, p. 137.

47. *Kollektivizatsiia sel'skogo khoziaistva na Severnom Kavkaze*, p. 251; and *Molot*, 11 Feb. 1930, p. 2.

48. *XVI s"ezd VKP (b). Sten. otchet*, p. 360.

49. Kozlova, *K pobede*, p. 206.

50. Ivnitskii, *Klassovaia bor'ba*, p. 220; Sharova, *Kollektivizatsiia*, p. 153.

51. I. Vareikis, *O sploshnoi kollektivizatsii i likvidatsii kulachestva kak klassa* (Voronezh: Kommuna, 1930), p. 32.

52. V. N. Burkov, "Derevenskie partiinye organizatsii Zapadnoi Sibiri v bor'be za razvertyvanie sploshnoi kollektivizatsii i likvidatsiiu kulachestva kak klassa (konets 1929-vesna 1930 g.)," *Uch. zap. Tomskogo gos. universiteta (Sb. rabot aspirantov kafadry istorii KPSS)*, no. 56 (1965), p. 52.

53. Karevskii, "Likvidatsiia," p. 98.

54. Medvedev, "Likvidatsiia," p. 26.

55. The policy moves of the second half of February are treated in detail in Davies, *Socialist Offensive*, pp. 261–68.

56. Bogdenko, "Kolkhoznoe stroitel'stvo," pp. 23, 25–26; Abramov, Vaganov, and Golikov, "O nekotorykh voprosakh," p. 30.

57. *Sotsialisticheskoe zemledelie*, 28 Feb. 1930, p. 1; *Za kollektivizatsiiu*, 2 Mar. 1930, p. 1.

58. Roy A. Medvedev, *Let History Judge: The Origins and Consequences of Stalinism*, trans. Colleen Taylor, eds. David Joravsky and Georges Haupt (New York: Vintage, 1973), p. 87; N. I. Nemakov, *Kommunisticheskaia partiia—organizator massovogo kolkhoznogo dvizheniia* (Moscow: MGU, 1966), p. 191.

59. *KPSS v rezoliutsiiakh*, pp. 548–51. For a more complete review of the events leading up to the retreat, see, Lynne Viola, "The Campaign to Eliminate the Kulak as a Class, Winter 1930: A Note on the Legislation," *Slavic Review* (forthcoming).

60. For detailed information on the implementation of the campaign, see Davies, *Socialist Offensive*, 243–51; and Merle Fainsod, *Smolensk Under Soviet Rule* (Cambridge, Mass.: Harvard Univ. Press, 1958), chap. 12.

61. For information on plenipotentiaries, see my dissertation, pp. 217–18. Cited in chap. 2, n. 13.

62. E. N. Gurovich, *Proletariat na kolkhoznoi stroike* (Moscow: Moskovskii rabochii, 1931), p. 5; Sharova, *Kollektivizatsiia*, p. 144; *Izvestiia oblastnogo komiteta VKP (b) TsChO*, no. 6 (30 Mar. 1930), p. 15.

63. *Pravda*, 26 Jan. 1930, p. 3; V. M. Selunskaia, "Rabochie-dvadtsatipiatitysiachniki—provodniki politiki partii v kolkhoznom stroitel'stve (1929–30 gg.)," *Voprosy istorii*, no. 3 (1954), p. 24; *Pamiatka rabochemu dvadtsatipiatitysiachniku* (Moscow: Kolkhoztsentr, 1930), pp. 3–5; *XVI s"ezd VKP (b). Sten. otchet*, p. 95; TsGAOR, f. 5453, op. 14, d. 57, ll. 33, 51, 53; d. 150, l. 13; f. 7676, op. 1, d. 160, ll. 40, 59.

64. *Zapadnyi oblastnoi komitet VKP (b). Vtoraia oblastnaia partkonferentsiia. Sten. otchet*, pp. 238–39.

65. Iakovlev, "Iz istorii dvadtsatipiatitysiachnikov," p. 71.

66. Ivnitskii and Ezerskii, "Dvadtsatipiatitysiachniki," pp. 497–98; Shalina, "Rol' 25–tysiachnikov," pp. 12–13.

67. F. I. Anastasenko and A. O. Krichevskii, *25-tysiachniki Krasnoputilovtsy na kolkhoznoi stroike* (Leningrad: Sel'khozgiz, 1931), p. 14.

68. K. Onipko, *Pervye shagi. Zapiski dvadtsatipiatitysiachnika* (Moscow: Krest'ianskaia pravda, 1931), pp. 12–16. This problem and form of "socialization" was fairly common. See *Sel'skokhoziaistvennaia zhizn'*, no. 3 (30 Jan. 1930), pp. 26–27 for report of Kolkhoztsentr meeting at which this was discussed.

69. Anastasenko and Krichevskii, *25-tysiachniki*, p. 14.

70. *Litsom k derevne*, no. 7 (Apr. 1930), p. 24.

71. Anastasenko and Krichevskii, *25-tysiachniki*, p. 14; Nemakov, *Kommunisticheskaia partiia*, p. 179; Nemakov and Isakov, "Dvadtsatipiatitysiachniki," pp. 43–44.

72. *Trud*, 3 Jan. 1931, p. 4.
73. TsGAOR, f. 5453, op. 14, d. 57, l. 93.
74. Ibid., ll. 22–27.
75. S. Zamiatin, *Burnyi god. Opyt raboty piatitysiachnika v Rudnianskom raione na Nizhnei Volge* (Moscow: Krest'ianskaia gazeta, 1931), pp. 9–16.
76. L. Berson, *Vesna 1930 goda. Zapiski dvadtsatipiatitysiachnika* (Moscow: Ogiz, 1931), pp. 18–19.
77. TsGANKh, f. 4108, op. 16, d. 48, l. 86.
78. Petro Grigorenko, *V podpol'e mozhno vstretit' tol'ko krys* (New York: Detinits, 1981), p. 114.
79. M. N. Chernomorskii, ed., "Rol' rabochikh brigad v bor'be za sploshnuiu kollektivizatsiiu v Tambovskoi derevne," *Materialy po istorii SSSR. Dokumenty po istorii Sovetskogo obshchestva*, vyp. 1, p. 378.
80. Denisov, *Odin iz*, p. 22.
81. Hindus, *Red Bread*, pp. 169–70.
82. See Lynne Viola, "Bab'i Bunty and Peasant Women's Protest During Collectivization," *Russian Review*, vol. 45, no. 1 (Jan. 1986), for further information.
83. *Rabochaia gazeta*, 22 Mar. 1930, p. 6.
84. Kopelev, *I sotvoril sebe kumira*, p. 210; Rozenfel'd, *Dvadtsatipiatitysiachniki*, pp. 77, 81–82; Zombe, "Dvadtsatipiatitysiachniki," p. 13.
85. See reports of *sel'sovets* resisting collectivization in Chernomorskii, "Rol' rabochhikh," pp. 352–53, 360–61.
86. Sharova, *Kollektivizatsiia*, p. 145.
87. *Izvestiia*, 29 May 1930, p. 3; *Sotsialisticheskoe zemledelie*, 25 June 1930, p. 3.
88. Berson, *Vesna 1930 goda*, pp. 12–13.
89. This will be discussed in the next chapter.
90. N. Ia. Gushchin, "Rabochie Leningrada i Moskvy v bor'be za kollektivizatsiiu sel'skogo khoziaistva Sibiri," *Istoriia SSSR*, no. 6 (1965), p. 105; S. M. Zakharov, "Rabochie-dvadtsatipiatitysiachniki—aktivnye uchastniki sotsialisticheskoi perestroiki sel'skogo khoziaistva Uzbekistana," *Uch. zapiski Karshinskogo pedinstituta*, vyp. 4, ch. 1 (1960), pp. 18–19.
91. Rozenfel'd, *Dvadtsatipiatitysiachniki*, pp. 45–47.
92. TsGAOR, f. 5470, op. 14, d. 204, l. 52.
93. *Po zovu partii*, pp. 130–33.
94. This point will be discussed in the next chapter.
95. Smolensk Archive, T 87/31, WKP 261, pp. 75–76.
96. TsGAOR, f. 5453, op. 14, d. 58, ll. 38–57.
97. *Trud*, 28 Mar. 1930, p. 3.
98. Ivnitskii, "Dvadtsatipiatitysiachniki-Moskvichi," p. 118.
99. Gushchin, *Rabochii klass Sibiri*, p. 73.
100. G. Furman, *Kak pomogali kolkhozam 25-tysiachniki* (Moscow: Knigosoiuz, 1930), p. 36.
101. Smolensk Archive, T 87/31, WKP 151, p. 537.
102. Furman, *Kak pomogali*, p. 39.

103. TsGAOR, f. 5453, op. 14, d. 58, ll. 35–36.

104. Furman, *Kak pomogali*, p. 39; TsGAOR, f. 5453, op. 14, d. 58, l. 48; *Nizhnevolzhskii kolkhoznik*, no. 1 (July 1930), p. 41.

105. *XVI s"ezd VKP (b). Sten. otchet*, p. 633.

106. Stalin, "Otvet tovarishcham kolkhoznikam," and "Otvet t. M. Rafailu," *Sochineniia*, vol. 12, pp. 214–15, 231–32.

107. Stalin, "Otvet tovarishcham kolkhoznikam," *Sochineniia*, vol. 12, p. 212.

108. *KPSS v rezoliutsiiakh*, p. 551.

109. *Kollektivizatsiia sel'skogo khoziaistva na Severnom Kavkaze*, pp. 259–66.

110. *Sel'skokhoziaistvennyi informatsionnyi biulleten'*, nos. 32–33 (30 Sept. 1930), pp. 25–26; TsGANKh, f. 7446, op. 12, d. 27, ll. 3–13; TsGAOR, f. 5453, op. 14, d. 57, l. 2; and Iu. S. Borisov, *25-tysiachniki* (Moscow: Gospolitizdat, 1959), p. 73.

111. According to 1931 statistics, the overwhelming majority of 25,000ers were employed on collective farms organized before or by the spring of 1930. *Kolkhozy vesnoi 1931 goda* (Moscow and Leningrad: TsUNKhU, 1932), pp. 137–41.

112. Borisov, *Podgotovka*, p. 85; Ivnitskii and Ezerskii, "Dvadtsatipiatitysiachniki," pp. 460, 476–77; *Kolkhozy v 1930 g. Itogi raportov kolkhozov XVI s"ezdu VKP (b)* (Moscow and Leningrad: Ogiz, 1931), p. 224.

113. TsGANKh, f. 7446, op. 11, d. 44, ll. 93–109.

114. Ciliga, *Russian Enigma*, p. 108; *Rabochaia gazeta*, 14 Mar. 1930, p. 2.

Chapter 5

1. Stalin, "Otvet tovarishcham kolkhoznikam," *Sochineniia*, vol. 12, pp. 218–19.

2. *KPSS v rezoliutsiiakh*, p. 551.

3. *Izvestiia*, 29 Mar. 1930, p. 2; *Pravda*, 31 Mar. 1930, p. 3.

4. *XVI s"ezd VKP (b). Sten. otchet*, pp. 38–39.

5. Bogdenko, "Kolkhoznoe stroitel'stvo," p. 31; Davies, *Socialist Offensive*, pp. 442–43.

6. Burkov, "Derevenskie partiinye," p. 54.

7. Bogdenko, "Kolkhoznoe stroitel'stvo," p. 31.

8. Grigorenko, *V podpol'e mozhno vstretit' tol'ko krys*, p. 114; Khrushchev Memoirs Transcript, Lenta no. 1 (New York: Holdings of the Harriman Institute, Columbia University), pp. 10–11.

9. Berson, *Vesna 1930 goda*, pp. 72–73; Anna Louise Strong, *The Soviets Conquer Wheat* (New York: Henry Holt and Co., 1931), pp. 92–93.

10. *Izvestiia Nizhegorodskogo kraevogo komiteta VKP (b)*, nos. 7–8 (15 Apr. 1930), p. 6; *Pravda*, 2 Apr. 1930, p. 2; *Za kollektivizatsiiu*, 4 May 1930, p. 2; R. Belbei, *Za ili protiv (Kak rabochii ispravliaet peregiby v derevne)* (Moscow: VTsSPS, 1930), p. 28; Kostiuchenko, Khrenov, and Fedorov, *Istoriia Kirovskogo zavoda*, p. 331.

11. Belbei, *Za ili protiv*, p. 28.

12. The participation of Red army troops in repressing revolts is poorly documented for the RSFSR. For a frank and exceptional mention of this, see Danilov, Kim,

and Tropkin, *Sovetskoe krest'ianstvo*, pp. 280–82; and the description of a major revolt in P.G. Chernopitskii, *Na velikom perelome*. *Sel'skie sovety Dona v period podgotovki i provedeniia massovoi kollektivizatsii (1928–31 gg.)* (Rostov: Rostovskii universitet, 1965), pp. 101–2; also see Fainsod, *Smolensk Under Soviet Rule*, pp. 246–47, which discusses a 20 February 1930 letter from Western Region first party secretary Rumiantsev, condemning the use of Red army units in dekulakization, something which he described as a deviation from policy.

13. *Bastiony revoliutsii*, p. 239.

14. Burkov, "Derevenskie partiinye," p. 50; and Iakovlev, "Iz istorii dvadtsatipiatitysiachnikov," pp. 71–72.

15. G. I. Arsenov, *Lebedevka, selo kolkhoznoe* (Kursk: Knizhnoe izd-vo, 1964), pp. 43–44.

16. Davies, *Socialist Offensive*, chap. 7.

17. See article by Mamaev in *Pravda*, 9 June 1930, p. 3, and discussion which followed in *Pravda*, 10 June 1930, p. 3; 12 June 1930, p. 3; 16 June 1930, p. 3; 18 June 1930, p. 3; 28 June 1930, p. 3. See Davies, *Socialist Offensive*, pp. 324–26 for discussion of the Mamaev article.

18. Mamaev uses this formula, *Pravda*, 9 June 1930, p. 3; also see discussion of this issue in *Zapadnyi oblastnoi komitet VKP (b). Vtoraia oblastnaia part-konferentsiia. Sten. otchet*, pp. 258–59.

19. Ibid., p. 61; also see report of Ukhanov at the 27 April plenum of the Moscow committee of the Komsomol who stated that it was necessary to stop these "individual" comrades who spoke as if the excesses were the result of the Central Committee's leadership, in *Rabochaia Moskva*, 30 April 1930, p. 2.

20. V. P. Danilov and N. A. Ivnitskii, "Leninskii kooperativnyi plan i ego osushchestvlenie v SSSR," in *Ocherki istorii kollektivizatsii sel'skogo khoziaistva v soiuznykh respublikakh*, ed. V. P. Danilov (Moscow: Gospolitizdat, 1963), pp. 46–47.

21. *Litsom k derevne*, no. 7 (Apr. 1930), p. 2.

22. Berson, *Vesna 1930 goda*, pp. 74–75.

23. Belbei, *Za ili protiv*, p. 39.

24. *XVI s''ezd VKP (b). Sten. otchet*, p. 52.

25. Stalin, "Otvet tovarishcham kolkhoznikam," *Sochineniia*, vol. 12, p. 213.

26. Ibid., pp. 214–15; idem, "Otvet t. M. Rafailu," *Sochineniia*, vol. 12, pp. 231–32.

27. Stalin, "Otvet tovarishcham kolkhoznikam," *Sochineniia*, vol. 12, p. 217.

28. *KPSS v rezoliutsiiakh*, p. 551.

29. Characteristically, the North Caucasus's decree was published before the Central Committee's, on 3 Mar. 1930. See *Kollektivizatsiia sel'skogo khoziaistva na Severnom Kavkaze*, p. 277; for other regional decrees, see *Kollektivizatsiia sel'skogo khoziaistva v Srednom povolzh'e*, p. 178; and *Kollektivizatsiia sel'skogo khoziaistva v Zapadnom raione*, pp. 271–72.

30. Bogdenko, "Kolkhoznoe stroitel'stvo," p. 33.

31. Davies, *Socialist Offensive*, p. 280; Strong, *The Soviets Conquer Wheat*, p. 102.

32. Gushchin, *Sibirskaia derevnia*, p. 298; Nemakov, *Kommunisticheskaia partiia*, p. 196.

33. Martha Brill Olcott, "The Collectivization Drive in Kazakhstan," *Russian Review*, vol. 40, no. 2 (Apr. 1981), p. 131.

34. *Pravda*, 26 Mar. 1930, p. 3; *Stroitel'stvo sotsializma v SSSR i krakh opportunizma* (Moscow: Politizdat, 1982), p. 229.

35. Medvedev, *Let History Judge*, p. 89.

36. Kozlova, *K pobede*, pp. 188–96.

37. See table 4 and *Za kollektivizatsiiu*, 20 June 1930, p. 3.

38. Abramov, Vagonov, and Golikov, "O nekotorykh voprosakh," p. 35; Stalin, "Otvet tovarishcham Sverdlovtsam," *Sochineniia*, vol. 12, p. 186.

39. *Rabochaia Moskva*, 2 Apr. 1930, p. 2; 22 Apr. 1930, p. 2; *Za kollektivizatsiiu*, 13 Apr. 1930, p. 3; 4 May 1930, p. 2.

40. Kozlova, *K pobede*, pp. 212–13. For information on the Moscow organization's "theory" of the inevitability of exodus and the nature of the middle peasant, see speeches by Moscow regional party committee secretary F. Leonov in *Za kollektivizatsiiu*, 14 May 1930, p. 1; *Rabochaia Moskva*, 22 Apr. 1930, p. 2; and *XVI s"ezd VKP (b). Sten. otchet*, p. 114, as well as Bauman's speech at the congress, pp. 214–16.

41. Stalin, "Otvet tovarishcham kolkhoznikam," *Sochineniia*, vol. 12, pp. 208–9.

42. Kozlova, *K pobede*, pp. 213–215. The mistakes of the Moscow organization were discussed at the Fourth Plenum of the Moscow party city and regional committees in early April. This plenum followed very quickly on the heels of the late March Third Plenum, at which the Moscow organization had refused to recant.

43. *XVI s"ezd VKP (b). Sten. otchet*, pp. 214–16, 230, 351.

44. See Davies, *Socialist Offensive*, 312–14.

45. V. A. Sidorov, "Meropriiatiia po trudovomu perevospitaniiu byvshikh kulakov," *Voprosy istorii*, no. 11 (1964), p. 58. Sidorov cites an unpublished Politburo decree of 30 March 1930. Further exiles could only be of individuals and of small groups. Similar rulings were issued by *okrug* party committees in Tomsk and in Viazemskii *Okrug*. See *Kollektivizatsiia sel'skogo khoziaistva Zapadnoi Sibiri*, pp. 143–44; and *Kollektivizatsiia sel'skogo khoziaistva v Zapadnom raione*, p.315, which refers to a Central Committee telegram.

46. See Davies, *Socialist Offensive*, pp. 269, 281.

47. Sidorov, "Meropriiatiia," p. 58. By 25 May 1930 in the Central Black Earth Region 32,583 dekulakized households had been rehabilitated. This region was dubbed "region of excesses" at the Sixteenth Party Congress. See Sharova, *Kollektivizatsiia*, pp. 165–66.

48. *Izvestiia*, 29 Mar. 1930, p. 2; *Pravda*, 31 Mar. 1930, p. 3; *Rabochaia gazeta*, 11 Apr. 1930, p. 3.

49. *Rabochaia gazeta*, 11 Apr. 1930, p. 3; also see letters from the central committees of the trade unions asking 25,000ers to send detailed information on a large variety of issues in TsGAOR, f. 5453, op. 14, d. 57, ll. 33, 51, 53; d. 150, l. 13; f. 7676, op. 1, d. 160, ll. 40, 59.

50. For example, *Izvestiia*, 29 Mar. 1930, p. 2; *Kollektivist*, no. 18 (30 Sept.

1930), pp. 54–55; *Krest'ianskaia pravda*, 28 May 1930, p. 2; *Pravda*, 16 Dec. 1930, p. 4.

51. *Bednota*, 17 Apr. 1930, p. 2; *Kollektivist*, no. 18 (30 Sept. 1930), pp. 55–57; *Litsom k derevne*, no. 7 (Apr. 1930), p. 2; no. 9 (May 1930), p. 3; *Pravda*, 31 Mar. 1930, p. 3; *Rabochaia gazeta*, 17 Apr. 1930, p. 3; 14 May 1930, p. 1; *Trud*, 25 July 1930, p. 3.

52. *Sel'skokhoziaistvennyi informatsionnyi biulleten'*, no. 5 (10 May 1930), p. 14; nos. 8–9 (25–30 May 1930), p. 24; *Spravochnik partiinogo rabotnika*, vol. 8, p. 602; *Trud*, 12 May 1930, p. 1; 29 May 1930, p. 3; TsGANKh, f. 7446, op. 12, d. 21a, ll. 32–33.

53. E. A. Sultanova, "Leningradskie kommunisty v bor'be za sotsialisticheskoe pereustroistvo sel'skogo khoziaistva v 1925–30 gg. (Obzor fondov Leningradskogo partiinogo arkhiva)," *Voprosy istorii KPSS*, no. 5 (1964), p. 106.

54. Ibid.

55. *XVI s''ezd VKP (b). Sten. otchet*, p. 69.

56. TsGAOR, f. 5475, op. 13, d. 66, l. 120.

57. Kopelev, *I sotvoril sebe kumira*, pp. 212–13.

58. Decree of the Central Council of Trade Unions. See TsGANKh, f. 7446, op. 12, d. 21a, ll. 32–33; and Ivnitskii and Ezerskii, "Dvadtsatipiatitysiachniki," p. 487. In May 25,000ers deemed "unsuitable" for collective farm work were permitted to be sent back to the factories in individual cases or sent on to courses for further study. See Central Committee decree of 21 May 1930 in *Spravochnik partiinogo rabotnika*, vol. 8, p. 602.

59. *Rabochaia gazeta*, 1 Mar. 1930, p. 4; E. I. Bakst, "Uchastie Moskovskikh rabochikh brigad v kollektivizatsii sel'skogo khoziaistva osnovnykh zernovykh raionov strany (1929–31 gg.)," *Ot oktiabria k stroitel'stvu kommunizma* (Moscow: Nauka, 1967), p. 344; N. A. Ivnitskii, "Fond Kolkhoztsentra SSSR i RSFSR i ego znachenie dlia izucheniia istorii kolkhoznogo dvizheniia v SSSR (1927–32 gg.)," *Problemy istochnikovedeniia*, vyp. 4 (Moscow: AN SSSR, 1955), p. 92.

60. Ivnitskii and Ezerskii, "Dvadtsatipiatitysiachniki," pp. 472–73.

61. Belbei, *Za ili protiv*, pp. 32–35; Berson, *Vesna 1930 goda*, pp. 74–76.

62. See the collection of his letters in Isbakh, *1 iz 25 tysiach*.

63. N. Ia. Gushchin, Iu. V. Zhurov, and A. I. Bozhenko, *Soiuz rabochego klassa i krest'ianstva Sibiri v period postroeniia sotsializma (1917–37 gg.)* (Novosibirsk: Nauka, Sibirskoe otdelenie, 1978), p. 307.

64. V. A. Smyshliaev, *Po Leninskim zavetam* (Leningrad: LGU, 1969), p. 104.

65. *Bednota*, 15 Aug. 1930, p. 3. See also the case in *Bastiony revoliutsii*, pp. 238–39, of the 25,000er Trofimov, who went to work in a village where his enterprise recruited seasonal workers.

66. Ia. A. Iakovlev, *V pokhod za organizatsiiu kollektivnogo proizvodstva. Doklad Moskovskim rabochim uezzhaiushchim na rabotu v kolkhozy* (Moscow and Leningrad: Gosizdat, 1930), pp. 22–24; *Uchebnyi plan i programmy kursov po podgotovke rukovodiashchikh kadrov v kolkhozakh (v sviazi s napravleniem 25,000 rabochikh v kolkhozy)* (Moscow: VTsSPS, 1930), p. 29.

67. Ivnitskii and Ezerskii, "Dvadtsatipiatitysiachniki," p. 516; Rozenfel'd, *Dvadtsatipiatitysiachniki*, pp. 44–45.

68. TsGAOR, f. 5453, op. 14, d. 57, l. 9; f. 5475, op. 13, d. 66, l. 20.

69. *Sputnik agitatora (dlia derevni)*, nos. 15–16 (May–June 1930), pp. 42–43.

70. Smolensk Archive, T87/31, WKP 261, p. 59.

71. *Izvestiia*, 17 Apr. 1930, p. 3; Kats-Kagan, *25,000 proletariev*, p. 14; Rusakov, "Poslantsy," p. 120.

72. *Litsom k derevne*, no. 9 (May 1930), p. 15; *Metallist*, no. 39 (30 Dec. 1930), pp. 28–29; *Nizhnevolzhskii kolkhoznik*, no. 1 (July 1930), p. 41.

73. *Sputnik agitatora (dlia derevni)*, nos. 15–16 (May–June 1930), p. 43.

74. *Trud*, 29 Mar. 1930, p. 3.

75. Ivnitskii and Ezerskii, "Dvadtsatipiatitysiachniki," pp. 436–38, 457.

76. TsGAOR, f. 5470, op. 14, d. 204, l. 111.

77. Gushchin, *Rabochii klass Sibiri*, p. 72; Kats-Kagan, *25,000 proletariev*, p. 13.

78. Kats-Kagan, *25,000 proletariev*, p. 29.

79. Ibid., p. 13.

80. *Litsom k derevne*, no. 10 (May 1930), p. 22.

81. *Metallist*, no. 39 (30 Dec. 1930), pp. 27–28; Alekseenko, "Rabochie-dvadtsatipiatitysiachniki—provodniki politiki kommunisticheskoi partii," p. 428.

82. Ivnitskii and Ezerskii, "Dvadtsatipiatitysiachniki," p. 493; Kureiko, *25-tysiachniki*, p. 20; *Rabochaia gazeta*, 5 June 1930, p. 6; *Sotsialisticheskoe zemledelie*, 25 June 1930, p. 3.

83. Nemakov, *Kommunisticheskaia partiia*, pp. 179–80.

84. *Bednota*, 24 Nov. 1930, p. 2.

85. Nemakov, *Kommunisticheskaia partiia*, p. 179.

86. Shalina, "Rol' 25-tysiachnikov," p. 8.

87. *Izvestiia*, 29 Jan. 1930, p. 3; TsGANKh, f. 7446, op. 13, d. 55, ll. 76–84; German, *Dvadtsatipiatitysiachniki Belorussi*, p. 30.

88. Anastasenko and Krichevskii, *25-tysiachniki*, p. 12; Shalina, "Rol' 25-tysiachnikov," p. 9; *Sovetskoe stroitel'stvo*, no. 8 (Aug. 1930), p. 135.

89. *Bednota*, 15 Aug. 1930, p. 3; *Litsom k derevne*, no. 8 (Apr. 1930), p. 45; *Rabochaia gazeta*, 11 Apr. 1930, p. 3; *Sotsialisticheskoe zemledelie*, 17 July 1930, p. 3.

90. Shalina, "Rol' 25-tysiachnikov," p. 9; *Litsom k derevne*, no. 12 (June 1930), p. 25.

91. K. A. Bitaev, "Rol' 25-tysiachniki v provedenii kollektivizatsii sel'skogo khoziaistva Severnoi Osetii," *Uch. zap. Severo-Osetinskogo gos. pedinstituta*, vol. 23, vyp. 3 (1958), p. 175.

92. For example, see the case against a Leningrad 25,000er in G. V. Efimov and I. B. Marmorshtein, *O 25-ti tysiachniki* (Leningrad: Leningradskoe oblastnoe izd-vo, 1931), p. 38.

93. *Bednota*, 26 July 1930, p. 4; 15 Aug. 1930, p. 2; Smolensk Archive, T87/19, WKP 151, pp. 76–85; *Sotsialisticheskoe zemledelie*, 24 July 1930, p. 2; 6 Sept. 1930,

p. 3; *Sovetskoe stroitel'stvo*, no. 8 (Aug. 1930), p. 133; TsGANKh, f. 7446, op. 13, d. 55, l. 82; *Za kollektivizatsiiu*, 5 Oct. 1930, p. 3.

94. *Bednota*, 26 July 1930, p. 4; *Sotsialisticheskoe zemledelie*, 24 July 1930, p. 2.

95. Before May the only serious warning was issued by the Central Council of Trade Unions, which called attention to abuses in Tadzhikistan and Central Asia. Other pre-May warnings about problems in the field were issued by Kolkhoztsentr, the Don *okrug* party committee, and the Central Black Earth Region's party committee, but they lacked the force of the May decrees. See my dissertation, pp. 322, 355, n. 122 (cited in chap. 2, n. 13).

96. *Trud*, 12 May 1930, p. 1; 29 May 1930, p. 3; *Sel'skokhoziaistvennyi informatsionnyi biulleten'*, nos. 8–9 (25–30 May 1930), p. 24; no. 14 (25 June 1930), pp. 17–19; no. 26 (25 Aug. 1930), p. 23; *Izvestiia*, 14 June 1930, p. 4; *Spravochnik partiinogo rabotnika*, vol. 8, pp. 602–3; Gurovich, *Proletariat*, pp. 43–44; 50–51.

97. Ibid.

98. Ivnitskii and Ezerskii, "Dvadtsatipiatitysiachniki," pp. 107–10; Romanov, "Tverskie 25-tysiachniki," p. 196; Timofeev, "Dvadtsatipiatitysiachniki," pp. 91–92.

99. *Kontrol' mass. Biulleten' oblastnoi kontrol'noi komissii VKP (b) i RKI TsChO*, nos. 5–6 (May–June 1931), p. 35.

100. *Sovetskaia iustitsiia*, nos. 17–18 (30 June 1932), pp. 65–66; *Sudebnaia praktika*, no. 13 (30 Sept. 1931), pp. 11–12. On 22 March 1931 the People's Commissariat of Justice issued a circular calling on all regional courts to review cases against 25,000ers. See *Sovetskaia iustitsiia*, no. 10 (10 Apr. 1931), p. 30.

101. TsGAOR, f. 5470, op. 14, d. 204, ll. 9–11, 14.

102. TsGAOR, f. 5453, op. 14, d. 57, l. 31; d. 150, ll. 30–31.

103. TsGAOR, f. 7676, op. 1, d. 160, l. 48.

104. *Bednota*, 24 Nov. 1930, p. 2.

105. For example, see report in *Kollektivizatsiia sel'skogo khoziaistva v Severo-Zapadnom raione (1927–37 gg.)* (Leningrad: LGU, LGAOR SS, Gos. i partiinye arkhivy Leningradskoi, Murmanskoi, Novgorodskoi, Pskovskoi oblastei i Karel'skoi ASSR, 1970), p. 180.

106. Kolesnikova and Kovanov, *Udarniki*, pp. 16–19.

107. Ibid.; A. Maksimov, *Dvadtsatipiatitysiachniki v kolkhozakh* (Leningrad, 1931), p. 27.

108. TsGANKh, f. 7446, op. 11, d. 28, ll. 73–74; *Sel'skokhoziaistvennaia zhizn'*, no. 20 (18 May 1929), pp. 1–2; nos. 40–41 (14 Oct. 1929), p. 4; *Sotsialisticheskaia rekonstruktsiia sel'skogo khoziaistva*, nos. 9–10 (Sept.–Oct. 1930), pp. vi–vii, 1–9; no. 12 (Dec. 1930), p. 11; *Sovetskoe stroitel'stvo*, no. 3 (Mar. 1930), pp. 9–24; no. 7 (July 1930), pp. 19–24. For purge and new recruitments in Kolkhoztsentr, see Iu. S. Borisov, ed., "Iz istorii sozdaniia kolkhoznykh kadrov v pervyi god sotsialisticheskoi reorganizatsii sel'skogo khoziaistva (1930 g.)," *Istoricheskii arkhiv*, no. 2 (1956), pp. 67–90; and idem, *Podgotovka*, pp. 110–60.

109. Data in *Partiinoe stroitel'stvo*, nos. 11–12 (June 1930), p. 44.

110. I. I. Alekseenko, "Rabochie dvadtsatipiatitysiachniki v kolkhoznom

stroitel'stve Khakassi,'' *250 let vmeste s velikim russkim narodom* (Abakan: Khakknigizdat, 1959), p. 160; Rozenfel'd, *Dvadtsatipiatitysiachniki*, pp. 75, 97; V. P. Tiushev, ''Kommunisticheskaia partiia-organizator deiatel'nosti dvadtsati- piatitysiachnikov (Po materialam Vostochnoi Sibiri),'' *Velikii Oktiabr' i Vostochnaia Sibir'* (Irkutsk: Irkutskii gos. universitet, 1968), p. 294; Zombe, ''Dvadtsati- piatitysiachniki,'' p. 17.

111. Borisov, ''Iz istorii sozdaniia kolkhoznykh kadrov,'' p. 67.

112. Iu. S. Kukushkin, *Sel'skie sovety i klassovaia bor'ba v derevne* (Moscow: MGU, 1968), pp. 237, 246, 253; Levin and Suvorov, ''Sovety,'' p. 467.

113. *Pravda*, 13 Dec. 1929, p. 1; 15 Jan. 1930, p. 1; 18 Feb. 1930, p. 1.

114. *XVI s''ezd VKP (b). Sten. otchet*, pp. 69, 734; TsGANKh, f. 7446, op. 12, d. 27, ll. 3–13.

115. *Pravda*, 24 Jan. 1930, p. 5.

116. *KPSS v rezoliutsiiakh*, p. 542; *Partiinoe stroitel'stvo*, nos. 3–4 (Feb. 1930), pp. 10–18, 35–38.

117. For examples, cases in Ia. L. Gel'berg, ''K voprosu regulirovanii sostava partii v derevne v gody sploshnoi kollektivizatsii,'' *Uch. zap. Vitebskogo veterinarnogo instituta*, vol. 16, vyp. 2 (1958), pp. 33–34; *Kollektivizatsiia sel'skogo khoziaistva na Severnom Kavkaze*, pp. 356–57; Ivnitskii and Ezerskii, ''Dvadtsatipiatitysiachniki,'' p. 491.

118. *Kolkhozy v 1930 g.*, p. 224.

119. E. I. Lar'kina, *Podgotovka kolkhoznykh kadrov v period massovoi kollektivizatsii* (Moscow: Sotsekgiz, 1960), pp. 32–40; Selunskaia, *Rabochie- dvadtsatipiatitysiachniki*, pp. 187–89.

120. See Borisov, *Podgotovka*; and Iu. V. Arutiunian, *Mekhanizatory sel'skogo khoziaistva SSSR v 1929–57 gg.* (Moscow: AN SSSR, 1960).

121. T. Levichev, *Pomoshch' goroda derevne. Rabochie brigady v derevne* (Moscow: Vlast' sovetov, 1930), pp. 37–39.

122. *Izvestiia*, 25 June 1930, p. 2.

123. *Sel'skokhoziaistvennyi informatsionnyi biulleten'*, nos. 49–50 (25 Dec. 1930), pp. 28–29.

124. Kukushkin, *Sel'skie sovety*, pp. 253–54, 258.

125. See Fitzpatrick, *Education and Social Mobility*, pt. 2.

126. For problems with rural cadres, see Borisov and Arutiunian cited in chap. 5, n. 120.

Chapter 6

1. Anastasenko and Krichevskii, *25-tysiachniki* p. 9; Bitaev, ''Rol' 25- tysiachnikov,'' p. 175; Iakovlev, ''Iz istorii dvadtsatipiatitysiachnikov,'' p. 68; Ivnitskii and Ezerskii, ''Dvadtsatipiatitysiachniki,'' pp. 425–26.

2. Amangaliev, ''Rol' rabochikh,'' p. 57; Bitaev, ''Rol' 25-tysiachnikov,'' p. 175; G. V. Machin, ''Priezd rabochikh-dvadtsatipiatitysiachnikov v Uzbekistan,'' *Sbornik nauch. trudov Tashkentskogo gos. universiteta (Materialy po istorii, istori- ografii i arkheologii)*, no. 556 (1978), p. 95.

3. Ivnitskii and Ezerskii, "Dvadtsatipiatitysiachniki," p. 422.

4. *Kollektivist*, nos. 1–2 (Jan. 1931), p. 83.

5. Anastasenko and Krichevskii, *25-tysiachniki*, p. 9; *Metallist*, no. 39 (30 Dec. 1930), p. 27.

6. Kostiuchenko, Khrenov, and Fedorov, *Istoriia Kirovskogo zavoda*, p. 329.

7. *Bednota*, 27 Feb. 1930, p. 2.

8. Rozenfel'd, *Dvadtsatipiatitysiachniki*, p. 32.

9. *Po zovu partii*, p. 43.

10. K. A. Bogomolova, "Dvadtsatipiatitysiachniki v Tadzhikistane," *Doklady AN Tadzh. SSR*, vyp. 9 (1953), p. 15; Efimov and Marmorshtein, *O 25-ti tysiachnikakh*, p. 32; Kolesnikova and Kovanov, *Udarniki*, pp. 20–23; Kostiuchenko, Khrenov, and Fedorov, *Istoriia Kirovskogo zavoda*, p. 332; A. Nuritov and A. Iunuskhodzhaev, "O roli 25-tysiachnikov v kollektivizatsii sel'skogo khoziaistva v Uzbekistane," *Nauchnye trudy Tashkentskogo gos. universiteta*, vyp. 373 (1970), p. 53.

11. *Izvestiia Severno-Kavkazskogo kraevogo komiteta VKP (b)*, no. 24 (1 Jan. 1930), pp. 23–25; *Kollektivizatsiia sel'skogo khoziaistva v Severo-Zapadnom raione*, p. 180; V. M. Selunskaia et al., eds., *Soiuz sozidatelei novogo obshchestva* (Moscow: Politizdat, 1979), p. 148; TsGANKh, f. 7446, op. 12, d. 21a, ll. 3–4.

12. Sholokhov, *Virgin Soil Upturned*, vol. 1, p. 384.

13. TsGAOR, f. 5453, op. 14, d. 58, ll. 35–36.

14. Maksimov, *Dvadtsatipiatitysiachniki*, p. 37.

15. Belbei, *Za ili protiv*, pp. 5–6, 14–16.

16. *Bastiony revoliutsii*, pp. 238–39; *Kollektivist*, no. 8 (30 Apr. 1931), p. 57; Tiushev, "Novye dannye," p. 86.

17. TsGAOR, f. 7676, op. 1, d. 160, l. 9; *Metallist*, no. 18 (30 May 1930), p. 51; Ivnitskii, "Dvadtsatipiatitysiachniki-Moskvichi," pp. 119–20, 128–31; Anastasenko and Krichevskii, *25-tysiachniki*, pp. 20–21; *Bastiony revoliutsii*, pp. 82–83; Gurovich, *Proletariat*, p. 10; Frederick Legran, *16 let v SSSR* (Moscow: Profizdat, 1933), p. 20.

18. Fainsod, *Smolensk Under Soviet Rule*, chap. 13.

19. *Kollektivist*, no. 7 (15 Apr. 1931), pp. 55–56; TsGAOR, f. 5453, op. 14, d. 57, ll. 35–36; *Zapadnyi oblastnoi komitet VKP (b). Vtoraia oblastnaia partkonferentsiia. Sten. otchet*, pp. 238–39.

20. *Sovetskaia iustitsiia*, no. 19 (10 July 1931), pp. 3–4. Krasavin's case was overturned; it is not clear what happened to Iarochik.

21. Furman, *Kak pomogali*, p. 22.

22. TsGAOR, f. 7676, op. 1, d. 160, l. 86; Ivnitskii and Ezerskii, "Dvadtsatipiatitysiachniki," p. 491; *Kollektivist*, nos. 23–24 (Dec. 1930), p. 72; *Rabochaia gazeta*, 14 May 1930, p. 3.

23. Kostiuchenko, Khrenov, and Fedorov, *Istoriia Kirovskogo zavoda*, p. 331.

24. *Izvestiia*, 27 Jan. 1930, p. 2.

25. Sholokhov, *Virgin Soil Upturned*, vol. 2, p. 195.

26. Sholokhov, *Virgin Soil Upturned*, vol. 1, p. 321.

27. *Sotsialisticheskoe zemledelie*, 14 May 1930, p. 3.

28. *Litsom k derevne*, no. 9 (Apr. 1930), p. 15.

29. Efimov and Marmorshtein, *O 25-ti tysiachnikakh*, p. 24; Maksimov, *Dvadtsatipiatitysiachniki*, pp. 12–13.

30. For a good example, see letter of the 25,000er Leonov in *Rabochaia Moskva*, 6 Apr. 1930, p. 2.

31. Selunskaia, *Rabochie-dvadtsatipiatitysiachniki*, p. 145.

32. Efimov and Marmorshtein, *O 25-ti tysiachnikakh*, pp. 11–12; V. A. Eroshkin, "Rabochie-dvadtsatipiatitysiachniki v Mariiskoi ASSR," *Voprosy istorii rabochego klassa Mariiskoi ASSR* (Ioshkar-Ola: Kirovskii gos. pedinstitut im. V. I. Lenina, 1969), p. 81; *Litsom k derevne*, nos. 23–24 (Dec. 1930), pp. 34–35.

33. *Litsom k derevne*, no. 6 (Mar. 1930), pp. 16–17.

34. TsGANKh, f. 7446, op. 13, d. 55, ll. 76–77; *Izvestiia*, 22 June 1930, p. 3; *Sotsialisticheskoe zemledelie*, 17 July 1930, p. 3; Alekseenko, "Rabochie dvadtsatipiatitysiachniki v kolkhoznom stroitel'stve Khakassi," p. 156; Ivanov, "Uchastie rabochikh Leningrada v kollektivizatsii," p. 89; I. L. Portnoi, "Dvadtsatipiatitysiachniki i soiuz sel'khozrabochikh KazSSR v bor'be za kollektivizatsiiu sel'skogo khoziaistva respubliki (1930–32 gg.)," *Izvestiia AN Kazakhskoi SSR (Seriia obshch. nauka)*, no. 5 (1975), pp. 64–65.

35. *Rabochaia gazeta*, 5 Jan. 1930, p. 3; *Litsom k derevne*, no. 3 (Feb. 1930), p. 16; *XVI s''ezd VKP (b). Sten. otchet*, p. 216.

36. *Bol'shevik*, no. 22 (30 Nov. 1929), pp. 14, 18; *Izvestiia*, 1 Jan. 1930, p. 2; *Leningradskaia pravda*, 10 Jan. 1930, p. 1; *Pravda*, 3 Mar. 1930, p. 3; *Trud*, 23 Nov. 1929, p. 2.

37. See my dissertation, pp. 423–24, n. 48. Cited in chap. 2, n. 13.

38. *Kolkhozy v 1930 g.*, pp. 247 58.

39. Furman, *Kak pomogali*, p. 8.

40. *Pravda*, 27 Jan. 1930, p. 4.

41. Sholokhov, *Virgin Soil Upturned*, vol. 1, p. 185.

42. Furman, *Kak pomogali*, p. 23.

43. Sholokhov, *Virgin Soil Upturned*, vol. 1, p. 188.

44. *Bednota*, 8 June 1930, p. 2.

45. Sholokhov, *Virgin Soil Upturned*, vol. 1, pp. 89–90.

46. Efimov and Marmorshtein, *O 25-ti tysiachnikakh*, p. 19; Kats-Kagan, *25,000 proletariev*, pp. 20–21.

47. Hindus, *Red Bread*, pp. 175–76.

48. Kolesnikova and Kovanov, *Udarniki*, pp. 29–31.

49. N. V. Simonov, *Kak my organizovali trud v kolkhoze (Opyt kolkhoza im. Kalinina v vesnu 1930 g.)* (Moscow: Krest'ianskaia gazeta, 1930), pp. 40–41.

50. Anastasenko and Krichevskii, *25-tysiachniki*, p. 16; Efimov and Marmorshtein, *O 25-ti tysiachnikakh*, p. 19.

51. Hindus, *Red Bread*, p. 25.

52. Sholokhov, *Virgin Soil Upturned*, vol. 2, p. 90.

53. Davies, *The Soviet Collective Farm*, p. 140.

54. *S''ezdy sovetov soiuza sovetskikh sotsialisticheskikh respublik. Sbornik dokumentov*, vol. 3 (Moscow: Gosiurizdat, 1960), p. 189.

55. *Uchebnyi plan i programmy kursov*, pp. 35–37.

---

56. *Izvestiia*, 24 Jan. 1930, p. 2; *Pravda*, 6 Feb. 1930, p. 5; 6 Mar. 1930, p. 4.

57. *Pravda*, 6 Mar. 1930, p. 4; Davies, *The Soviet Collective Farm*, p. 136.

58. *Pravda*, 18 Apr. 1930, p. 1.

59. *XVI s"ezd VKP (b). Sten. otchet*, pp. 643–44.

60. Davies, *The Soviet Collective Farm*, pp. 140–41.

61. G. Shustov, *Kak organizovat' sdel'nye raboty v kolkhozakh* (Moscow: Sel'kolkhozgiz, 1931), p. 4.

62. *Sotsialisticheskoe zemledelie*, 12 Dec. 1930, p. 4.

63. Ibid.; Shustov, *Kak organizovat'*, pp. 3–5; Simonov, *Kak my organizovali*, p. 21.

64. Davies, *The Soviet Collective Farm*, p. 151.

65. *XVI s"ezd VKP (b). Sten. otchet*, pp. 574–75; M. L. Bogdenko, "Materialy sploshnogo ucheta kolkhozov 1930 g.," *Istochnikovedenie istorii Sovetskogo obshchestva*, vyp. 2 (Moscow: Nauka, 1968), p. 316.

66. Rozenfel'd, *Dvadtsatipiatitysiachniki*, pp. 71, 76; Shustov, *Kak organizovat'*, pp. 14–19.

67. *Kolkhozy v 1930 g.*, pp. 247–58.

68. Anastasenko and Krichevskii, *25-tysiachniki*, pp. 19–20; *Bastiony revoliutsii*, p. 109; Ivnitskii and Ezerskii, "Dvadtsatipiatitysiachniki," pp. 505–6; *Metallist*, no. 39 (30 Dec. 1930), p. 27; *Vasileostrovtsy v bor'be za sotsialisticheskuiu derevniu, 1923–33* (Leningrad: Raisovet, 1933), p. 38; Ivanov, "Pomoshch' Leningradskikh rabochikh," pp. 213–14; Romanov, "Tverskie 25-tysiachniki," pp. 190–91.

69. *Bastiony revoliutsii*, p. 108; Rozenfel'd, *Dvadtsatipiatitysiachniki*, pp. 31, 158–59.

70. Anastasenko and Krichevskii, *25-tysiachniki*, pp. 15–18.

71. Rozenfel'd, *Dvadtsatipiatitysiachniki*, p. 84.

72. *Po zovu partii*, p. 92.

73. *XVI s"ezd VKP (b). Sten. otchet*, pp. 69–70.

74. Anastasenko and Krichevskii, *25-tysiachniki*, p. 15; Ivanov, "Pomoshch' Leningradskikh rabochikh," p. 213.

75. Ibid.

76. Anastasenko and Krichevskii, *25-tysiachniki*, p. 1; *Izvestiia Severno-Kavkazskogo kraevogo komiteta VKP (b)*, no. 3 (15 Feb. 1930), p. 6.

77. Kolesnikova and Kovanov, *Udarniki*, p. 14.

78. Eroshkin, *Na ikh doliu vypalo schast'e*, p. 22.

79. Efimov and Marmorshtein, *O 25-ti tysiachnikakh*, p. 43; Ivnitskii, "Dvadtsatipiatitysiachniki-Moskvichi," p. 119.

80. Anastasenko and Krichevskii, *25-tysiachniki*, pp. 15–18, 30; Rozenfel'd, *Dvadtsatipiatitysiachniki*, pp. 55, 59–60, 61–62.

81. Ivnitskii and Ezerskii, "Dvadtsatipiatitysiachniki," pp. 491, 505–6; Rozenfel'd, *Dvadtsatipiatitysiachniki*, pp. 31–33, 71.

82. TsGAOR, f. 5475, op. 13, d. 66, l. 18; *Kollektivist*, no. 8 (30 Apr. 1931), pp. 57–58; *Sotsialisticheskoe zemledelie*, 25 June 1930, p. 3; *Zapadnyi oblastnoi komitet VKP (b). Vtoraia oblastnaia partkonferentsiia. Sten. otchet*, pp. 220–21.

83. TsGAOR, f. 5453, op. 14, d. 57, ll. 16, 47–49; d. 58, l. 43; TsGANKh, f. 7446, op. 11, d. 44, ll. 93–109; *Litsom k derevne*, no. 9 (May 1930), p. 15.

84. *Zapadnyi oblastnoi komitet VKP (b). Vtoraia oblastnaia partkonferentsiia. Sten. otchet*, pp. 65, 67; *XVI s''ezd VKP (b). Sten. otchet*, p. 622; Ivnitskii, "Dvadtsatipiatitysiachniki-Moskvichi," pp. 119–20.

85. TsGAOR, f. 5453, op. 14, d. 57, ll. 54–55; f. 5470, op. 14, d. 204, l. 94; Ivnitskii, "Dvadtsatipiatitysiachniki-Moskvichi," pp. 120–22; *Metallist*, no. 18 (30 May 1930), p. 51; *Rabochaia Moskva*, 28 Mar. 1930, p. 3.

86. TsGAOR, f. 5453, op. 14, d. 57, ll. 10, 16, 50; f. 5475, op. 13, d. 66, l. 18; *Izvestiia*, 25 June 1930, p. 2; *Kollektivist*, no. 8 (30 Apr. 1931), p. 58; *Litsom k derevne*, no. 14 (July 1930), p. 30; *Rabochaia Moskva*, 28 Mar. 1930, p. 3; *Sotsialisticheskoe zemledelie*, 25 June 1930, p. 3.

87. *XVI s''ezd VKP (b). Sten. otchet*, p. 734.

88. Lar'kina, *Podgotovka*, p. 39; Onipko, *Pervye shagi*, p. 32; Rozenfel'd, *Dvadtsatipiatitysiachniki*, pp. 61–62, 86; Selunskaia, *Rabochie-dvadtsatipiatitysiachniki*, p. 189.

89. *Kollektivizatsiia sel'skogo khoziaistva na Severnom Kavkaze*, pp. 354–56; *Po zovu partii*, p. 67; Rozenfel'd, *Dvadtsatipiatitysiachniki*, pp. 71, 77–78, 86.

90. Stalin, "Otvet tovarishcham kolkhoznikam," *Sochineniia*, vol. 12, pp. 226–27.

91. Roberta Thompson Manning, *The Crisis of the Old Order in Russia: Gentry and Government* (Princeton N.J.: Princeton Univ. Press, 1982), p. 367.

92. *Bastiony revoliutsii*, pp. 228–29; Ivnitskii and Ezerskii, "Dvadtsatipiatitysiachniki," p. 491; Rozenfel'd, *Dvadtsatipiatitysiachniki*, pp. 58–59.

93. TsGAOR, f. 5453, op. 14, d. 58, l. 44; Ivnitskii, "Dvadtsatipiatitysiachniki-Moskvichi," pp. 114–15; *Po zovu partii*, pp. 17–18; Romanov, "Tverskie 25-tysiachniki," p. 192.

94. TsGAOR, f. 5453, op. 14, d. 57, ll. 54–55.

95. Maksimov, *Dvadtsatipiatitysiachniki*, p. 33.

96. *Izvestiia*, 25 June 1930, p. 2.

97. TsGAOR, f. 5453, op. 14, d. 57, ll. 32–33.

98. *Bednota*, 24 Nov. 1930, p. 2.

99. *Zapadnyi oblastnoi komitet VKP (b). Vtoraia oblastnaia partkonferentsiia. Sten. otchet*, pp. 104–05, 188, 193.

100. *Kollektivist*, nos. 1–2 (Jan. 1931), p. 74.

101. *Bednota*, 24 Nov. 1930, p. 2; *Sotsialisticheskoe zemledelie*, 2 Nov. 1930, p. 3.

102. *Rabochaia gazeta*, 25 June 1930, p. 8.

103. *Sotsialisticheskoe zemledelie*, 2 Nov. 1930, p. 3.

104. Furman, *Kak pomogali*, pp. 37–38.

105. *Zapadnyi oblastnoi komitet VKP (b). Vtoraia oblastnaia partkonferentsiia. Sten. otchet*, pp. 210–11.

106. *Za kollektivizatsiiu*, 5 Oct. 1930, p. 3. Khaliuzov wrote an official self-condemnatory statement to *Za kollektivizatsiiu*:

I request the editor to publish my letter so that I can condemn my suicide attempt before all society.

For eight months, I worked as a 25,000er on a collective farm . . . The farm was almost in ruins, there was no discipline among the collective farmers. During the harvest . . . the situation deteriorated further.

I saw that I had not lived up to the tasks set for me as a 25,000er. No one helped me and I tried to desert from the detachment—I shot myself. Now I am conscious that I did not pass the class exam.

Chapter 7

1. *Trud*, 30 Jan. 1931, p. 1; 9 Feb. 1931, p. 3; TsGANKh, f. 7446, op. 13, d. 55, l. 88; *Za kollektivizatsiiu*, 3 Feb. 1931, p. 3.

2. *Spravochnik partiinogo rabotnika*, vol. 8, p. 315.

3. Iu. V. Arutiunian, "Kollektivizatsiia sel'skogo khoziaistva i vysvobozhdenie rabochei sily dlia promyshlennosti," *Formirovanie i razvitie Sovetskogo rabochego klassa (1917–61 gg.)* (Moscow: Nauka, 1964), p. 111; A. G. Rashin, "Rost gorodskogo naseleniia v SSSR," *Istoricheskie zapiski*, vol. 66 (1960), p. 270; for information on turnover and travel to the city by newly trained cadres, see Arutiunian, *Mekhanizatory*, pp. 27–31; Borisov, *Podgotovka*, pp. 158, 277–78; Lar'kina, *Podgotovka*, 106–8.

4. *Sobranie zakonov*, no. 1 (1 Jan. 1930), pp. 12–14; ibid., no. 47 (29 Sept. 1930), pp. 911–12; *Spravochnik partiinogo rabotnika*, vol. 8, p. 315.

5. *Izvestiia*, 17 June 1930, p. 2; *Kollektivist*, nos. 11–12 (June 1930), p. 76; *Rabochaia gazeta*, 22 Mar. 1930, p. 6; 2 Feb. 1931, p. 3; *Trud*, 28 Feb. 1930, p. 3; 1 June 1930, p. 3.

6. *Izvestiia*, 17 June 1930, p. 2.

7. *Izvestiia*, 24 Feb. 1930, p. 4; Gurovich, *Proletariat*, pp. 50–51; *Sel'skokhoziaistvennyi informatsionnyi biulleten'*, no. 11 (25 Mar. 1931), pp. 36–37; no. 19 (20 June 1931), p. 3; *Spravochnik partiinogo rabotnika*, vol. 8, pp. 315, 602–3; *Trud*, 12 May 1930, p. 1; 24 May 1930, p. 4.

8. TsGANKh, f. 7446, op. 12, d. 21a, ll. 3–4.

9. *Kollektivist*, nos. 11–12 (June 1930), p. 75; *Sel'skokhoziaistvennyi informatsionnyi biulleten'*, no. 5 (10 May 1930), p. 14; *Sovetskoe stroitel'stvo*, no. 8 (Aug. 1930), p. 135; TsGAOR, f. 5453, op. 14, d. 58, l. 29.

10. *Sovetskoe stroitel'stvo*, no. 8 (Aug. 1930), p. 135; *Trud*, 1 June 1930, p. 3; TsGAOR, f. 5453, op. 14, d. 57, ll. 9, 32.

11. *Bednota*, 15 Aug. 1930, p. 2; Ivnitskii and Ezerskii, "Dvadtsatipiatitysiachniki," p. 458; *Trud*, 3 Jan. 1931, pp. 3–4.

12. Smolensk Archive, T87/31, WKP 151, p. 545; TsGANKh, f. 7446, op. 13, d. 55, ll. 76–84; TsGAOR, f. 5453, op. 14, d. 150, ll. 38–39; f. 7676, op. 1, d. 160, ll. 54–58.

13. See decrees to this effect in Gurovich, *Proletariat*, pp. 45, 50–51; *Sel'skokhoziaistvennyi informatsionnyi biulleten'*, no. 14 (25 June 1930), pp. 17–19; nos. 32–33 (30 Sept. 1930), pp. 26–27; *Spravochnik partiinogo rabotnika*, vol. 8, p. 603.

14. *Trud*, 3 Jan. 1931, p. 3.

15. Gurovich, *Proletariat*, p. 63; *Sel'skokhoziaistvennyi informatsionnyi biulleten'*, no. 11 (25 Mar. 1931), pp. 36–37; no. 19 (20 June 1931), p. 3; no. 26 (30 Aug. 1931), pp. 28–29; *Spravochnik partiinogo rabotnika*, vol. 8, p. 315.

16. Smolensk Archive, T87/31, WKP 151, p. 545; TsGANKh, f. 7466, op. 13, d. 55, ll. 76–84; TsGAOR, f. 5453, op. 14, d. 57, ll. 35–36.

17. *Bednota*, 15 Aug. 1930, p. 3; Ivnitskii and Ezerskii, "Dvadtsatipiatitysiachniki," p. 474; *Sotsialisticheskoe zemledelie*, 12 June 1930, p. 5; TsGANKh, f. 7446, op. 13, d. 55, ll. 76–84.

18. *Litsom k derevne*, nos. 19–20 (Oct. 1930), p. 35; *Rabochaia gazeta*, 15 Aug. 1930, p. 3; TsGANKh, f. 7446, op. 13, d. 55, l. 79; TsGAOR, f. 5453, op. 14, d. 57, ll. 35–36.

19. Smolensk Archive, T87/31, WKP 261, pp. 62–63; TsGAOR, f. 7676, op. 1, d. 160, ll. 54–58.

20. *Bednota*, 15 Aug. 1930, p. 2.

21. TsGAOR, f. 5453, op. 14, d. 57, ll. 35–36; f. 7676, op. 1, d. 160, l. 72.

22. TsGAOR, f. 5453, op. 14, d. 57, l. 9; f. 5470, op. 14, d. 204, ll. 113–14.

23. Ivnitskii and Ezerskii, "Dvadtsatipiatitysiachniki," p. 474.

24. *Pravda*, 10 Dec. 1929, p. 1.

25. *Metallist*, no. 22 (10 July 1930), p. 34; *Rabochaia gazeta*, 14 May 1930, p.3.

26. *Rabochaia gazeta*, 18 Mar. 1930, p. 6; *Sel'skokhoziaistvennyi informatsionnyi biulletin'*, no. 14 (25 June 1930), pp. 17–19; TsGANKh, f. 7446, op. 12, d. 21a, ll. 3–4.

27. *Trud*, 16 Mar. 1930, p. 1.

28. *Trud*, 12 May 1930, p. 1; 29 May 1930, p. 3; *Spravochnik partiinogo rabotnika*, vol. 8, p. 602.

29. *Trud*, 19 Mar. 1930, p. 1; 17 May 1930, p. 2; 30 May 1930, p. 1; 1 June 1930, p. 3; 12 June 1930, p. 4.

30. *Bednota*, 15 Aug. 1930, p. 2; *Trud*, 1 June 1930, p. 3; 14 Jan. 1931, p. 4; for initial condemnation of Babaev plant, see *Trud*, 12 May 1930, p. 1, and 25 June 1930, p. 8.

31. Kats-Kagan, *25,000 proletariev*, p. 32; *Metallist*, no. 18 (30 May 1930), p. 50; *Trud*, 6 May 1930, p. 4; 1 June 1930, p. 3; 14 Jan. 1931, p. 4. (It was reported that Moscow factories had lost 148 of their 25,000ers and that Urals factories had lost *all* of their 25,000ers.)

32. *Kollektivist*, nos. 11–12 (June 1930), p. 76; *Metallist*, no. 22 (10 July 1930), p. 35; *Sotsialisticheskoe zemledelie*, 12 June 1930, p. 5.

33. *Sovetskoe stroitel'stvo*, no. 8 (Aug. 1930), p. 131.

34. Ibid.; *Rabochaia gazeta*, 14 May 1930, p. 3; *Sotsialisticheskoe zemledelie*, 17 July 1930, p. 3; *Trud*, 25 July 1930, p. 3; TsGAOR, f. 5453, op. 14, d. 57, l. 82; d. 150, l. 33.

35. *Trud*, 12 June 1930, p. 4.

36. Ibid., 25 July 1930, p. 3.

37. *Rabochaia gazeta*, 5 Mar. 1930, p. 4; *Spravochnik partiinogo rabotnika*, vol. 8, p. 603.

38. *Trud*, 1 June 1930, p. 3; 29 Oct. 1930, p. 5.

39. *Izvestiia*, 29 May 1930, p. 3.

40. *Metallist*, no. 22 (10 July 1930), p. 35.

41. *Trud*, 9 Jan. 1931, p. 3.

42. *Metallist*, no. 22 (10 July 1930), p. 34.

43. TsGAOR, f. 5453, op. 14, d. 57, ll. 54–55 (letter dated 19 July 1930); *Rabochaia gazeta*, 14 Mar. 1930, p. 2.

44. *Bastiony revoliutsii*, p. 278.

45. *Sputnik agitatora (dlia derevni)*, nos. 15–16 (May–June 1930), p. 43.

46. *Litsom k derevne*, no. 10 (May 1930), p. 22.

47. K. K. German, *Vedushchaia rol' rabochego klassa v sozdanie kolkhoznogo stroia v Belorussii* (Minsk: BGU, 1968), p. 106.

48. *Rabochaia gazeta*, 25 June 1930, p. 8.

49. *Trud*, 22 Oct. 1930, p. 3; 9 Feb. 1931, p. 3.

50. *Spravochnik partiinogo rabotnika*, vol. 8, pp. 315, 602–3.

51. See my dissertation, p. 524, n. 106, for a detailed listing of these decrees and directives. Cited in chap. 2, n. 13.

52. *Spravochnik partiinogo rabotnika*, vol. 8, pp. 602–3; see results of one inspection in *K dvukhnedel'niku po massovoi proverke uslovii raboty 25-ti tysiachnikov i uluchsheniia sviazi s nimi* (Baku: Azerbaidzh. SPS, 1930).

53. *Bednota*, 13 June 1930, p. 4; *Rabochaia gazeta*, 25 June 1930, p. 8.

54. For example, see *Rezoliutsii priniatye pervoi Ostrogozhskoi okruzhnoi konferentsii "25000". 28–30 iiulia 1930 g.* (Ostrogozhsk: Ostrogozhsk. tip. poligraftresta TsChO, 1930).

55. *Pravda*, 4 Dec. 1929, p. 6; Rozenfel'd, *Dvadtsatipiatitysiachniki*, p. 92; Lar'kina, *Podgotovka*, p. 45; TsGANKh, f. 7446, op. 11, d. 110; d. 153; l. 156; op. 12, d. 27; op. 13, d. 55, l. 53; *Vlast' sovetov*, nos. 13–14 (1931), pp. 42–43.

56. Portnoi, "Dvadtsatipiatitysiachniki," pp. 64–65; *Izvestiia*, 22 June 1930, p. 2; Ivanov, "Uchastie rabochikh Leningrada," p. 89; Zombe, "Dvadtsatipiati-tysiachniki," p. 19.

57. *Spravochnik partiinogo rabotnika*, vol. 8, p. 603.

58. *Sel'skokhoziaistvennyi informatsionnyi biulleten'*, no. 37 (20 Oct. 1930), p. 12.

59. *Spravochnik partiinogo rabotnika*, vol. 8, p. 315.

60. Six 25,000ers were elected to membership in the regional committee of the Western regional party. See *Zapadnyi oblastnoi komitet VKP (b). Vtoraia oblastnaia partkonferentsiia. Sten. otchet*, p. 390; also see Rozenfel'd, *Dvadtsatipiatitysiachniki*, p. 97, for information on 25,000ers on party district committees.

61. Iu. S. Borisov, *25-tysiachniki* (Moscow: Gospolitizdat, 1959), p. 60; his name appears in the list of delegates at the end of *XVI s''ezd VKP (b). Sten. otchet* (Moscow: Partizdat, 1935), p. 1336.

62. *Kollektivist*, nos. 15–16 (Aug. 1930), pp. 31–32; Smolensk Archive, T87/31, WKP 152, p. 269.

63. Selunskaia, *Rabochie-dvadtsatipiatitysiachniki*, p. 116.

64. *Sel'skokhoziaistvennyi informatsionnyi biulleten'*, no. 6 (5 Feb. 1931), pp. 19–20.

65. Ivnitskii and Ezerskii, "Dvadtsatipiatitysiachniki," pp. 460, 462–463; *Kolkhozy vesnoi 1931 goda*, p. 137; TsGANKh, f. 7446, op. 13, d. 55, l. 89.

66. Borisov, *25-tysiachniki*, p. 83; Lar'kina, *Podgotovka*, p. 46.

67. For information on labor turnover, see Solomon M. Schwarz, *Labor in the Soviet Union* (London: Cresset Press, 1953), p. 87; and A. I. Vdovin and V.I. Drobizhev, *Rost rabochego klassa, 1917–40 gg.* (Moscow: Mysl', 1976), pp. 189–92.

68. Rozenfel'd, *Dvadtsatipiatitysiachniki*, pp. 97–98; Selunskaia, *Rabochie-dvadtsatipiatitysiachniki*, p. 213.

69. *Izvestiia oblastnogo komiteta VKP (b) TsChO*, no. 20 (30 Oct. 1930), p. 19.

70. TsGANKh, f. 7446, op. 11, d. 153, l. 42.

71. Nemakov, *Kommunisticheskaia partiia*, p. 180; Nemakov and Isakov, "Dvadtsatipiatitysiachniki," pp. 43–44.

72. *Za kollektivizatsiiu*, 26 Dec. 1930, p. 2.

73. Efimov and Marmorshtein, *O 25-ti tysiachnikakh*, p. 18; *Izvestiia Nizhegorodskogo kraevogo komiteta VKP (b)*, nos. 14–15 (18 Sept. 1930), pp. 22–23.

74. Ciliga, *Russian Enigma*, pp. 108–9.

75. *Sovetskaia iustitsiia*, no. 19 (10 July 1931), pp. 3, 5.

76. Gurovich, *Proletariat*, p. 11.

77. Romanov, "Tverskie 25-tysiachniki," p. 194.

78. Maksimov, *Dvadtsatipiatitysiachniki*, p. 32.

79. *Litsom k derevne*, no. 10 (May 1930), p. 13.

80. For example, see letter in *Komsomolskaia pravda*, 7 May 1930, p. 2.

81. Smolensk Archive, T87/19, WKP 151, pp. 76–84. (The documents contain many grammatical errors and are paraphrased, in part.)

82. The penalties for desertion were not specified, but according to information issued by the Shuiskii *okrug* party committee, Western Region, if a 25,000er–party member deserted, the issue of party expulsion was to be examined. If a nonparty-25,000er deserted, he was to be sent back to his former factory. Smolensk Archive, T87/31, WKP 261, pp. 62–63. The Central Council of Trade Unions, however, issued a decree calling for the expulsion of deserters from the trade unions. *Izvestiia*, 16 Mar. 1930, p. 4, and 29 May 1930, p. 3.

83. For articles on the deserter Sudakov, whose factory was pressured into firing him after he resumed his old job, see *Trud*, 26 Feb. 1930, p. 3; 9 Mar. 1930, p. 3; 29 Mar. 1930, p. 3. Also see article in *Pravda*, 11 Apr. 1930, p. 6, ordering all factories to report deserters. The chairmen of the district Kolkhoztsentr offices were to be held responsible for desertions caused by bad conditions according to instructions of Kolkhoztsentr. See TsGANKh, f. 7446, op. 12, d. 21a, ll. 3–4, 23. The press, while condemning deserters, softened the issue by placing the real blame on rural officialdom and the factories for lack of support. See, for example, *Pravda*, 31 Mar. 1930, p. 3; *Rabochaia gazeta*, 14 May 1930, p. 3; *Sovetskoe stroitel'stvo*, no. 8 (Aug. 1930), p. 136. Finally, it should be noted that in the Urals in 1930, of two hundred deserters, only eleven were expelled from the party, according to Efremenkov and Mukhachev, "Dvadtsatipiatitysiachniki-Ural' tsy," p. 141.

84. TsGANKh, f. 7446, op. 13, d. 55, l. 86.

256   *Notes*

85. Cited from party archives in Sultanova, "Leningradskie kommunisty," p. 106.

86. Ivnitskii, "Dvadtsatipiatitysiachniki-Moskvichi," p. 113.

87. Kolesnikova and Kovanov, *Udarniki*, p. 37.

88. Shalina, "Rol' 25-tysiachnikov," p. 10.

89. *Trud*, 5 Aug. 1930, p. 3; TsGANKh, f. 7446, op. 12, d. 40, ll. 2–5.

90. Ciliga, *Russian Enigma*, p. 112; Rozenfel'd, *Dvadtsatipiatitysiachniki*, p. 40.

91. Isbakh, *1 iz 25 tysiach*, pp. 53–54.

92. Kolesnikova and Kovanov, *Udarniki*, p. 5.

93. TsGANKh, f. 7446, op. 12, d. 40, ll. 9–12; TsGAOR, f. 5453, op. 14, d. 57, l. 8; *Resoliutsii priniatye pervoi Ostrogozhskoi okruzhnoi konferentsii "25000"*, p. 10.

94. *"Po-rabochumu." Kollektivizatsiia sel'skogo khoziaistva v Srednem Povolzh'e*, pp. 194–95.

95. A. Isbach, *One of the 25,000* (Moscow: Cooperative Publishing Society of Foreign Workers in the USSR, 1931), pp. 36–37.

96. Ivnitskii and Ezerskii, "Dvadtsatipiatitysiachniki," p. 470.

97. *Sotsialisticheskoe zemledelie*, 31 Dec. 1930, p. 3.

98. Petro G. Grigorenko, *Memoirs*, trans. Thomas P. Whitney (New York: Norton, 1982), p. 33.

99. *Kollektivist*, nos. 23–24 (Dec. 1930), p. 74. Also see pledges in Ivnitskii and Ezerskii, "Dvadtsatipiatitysiachniki," p. 499; *Pravda*, 16 Dec. 1930, p. 4; *Sotsialisticheskoe zemledelie*, 31 Dec. 1930, p. 3; and *Za kollektivizatsiiu*, 7 Jan. 1931, p. 3.

100. Borisov, *25-tysiachniki*, p. 83.

101. Bogomolova, "Dvadtsatipiatitysiachniki," p. 19; Eroshkin, *Na ikh doliu vypalo schast'e*, pp. 31–76; V. A. Smyshliaev, *Po Leninskim zavetam* (Leningrad: LGU, 1969), p. 137; Rusakov, "Poslantsy," p. 121; Legran, *16 let v SSSR*, p. 23.

102. Borisov, *25-tysiachniki*, pp. 6–7; Selunskaia, *Rabochie-dvadtsatipiatitysiachniki*, pp. 213–14; *Sovetskii rabochii klass*, p. 228.

103. *Bol'shaia Sovetskaia entsiklopediia*, vol. 4, 3d ed. (Moscow: Sovetskaia entsiklopediia, 1971), p. 177; Selunskaia, *Rabochie-dvadtsatipiatitysiachniki*, pp. 213–14.

104. *Pravda*, 15 Apr. 1955, p. 2.

105. *Po zovu partii*, pp. 163, 308; Selunskaia, *Rabochie-dvadtsatipiatitysiachniki*, p. 217.

106. For example, see cases in Bogomolova, "Dvadtsatipiatitysiachniki," p. 19; German, *Dvadtsatipiatitysiachniki Belorussi*, p. 81; and I. G. Pichugin, "Rol' 25-tysiachnikov v kollektivizatsii sel'skogo khoziaistva Kazakhstana," *Uch. zap. Kazakhskogo universiteta*, vol. 31, vyp. 3 (1957), p. 31; Rusakov, "Poslantsy," p. 127.

107. For example, see Eroshkin, *Na ikh doliu vypalo schast'e*, pp. 13–15, 31–34, 48–49, 58, 77–78.

108. L. I. Brezhnev, *Leninskim kursom*, vol. 2 (Moscow: Politizdat, 1970), p. 87.

109. *Sovetskii rabochii klass*, p. 224; N. Ia. Timoshina, "Bor'ba kommunisticheskoi partii za ukreplenie soiuza rabochego klassa i krest'ianstva v period industrializatsii strany (1926–29 gg.)," *Uch. zap. Moskovskogo gos. universiteta*, vyp. 173 (1955), p. 192.

GLOSSARY

artel
: type of collective farm midway between *kommuna* and *toz* in degree of socialization; since March 1930 the officially accepted form of collective

basmachi
: members of anti-Soviet nationalist movement in Central Asia

Central Committee
: unless otherwise indicated, the Central Committee of the Communist party

control commission
: internal party inspection agency

district
: *raion*; administrative-territorial unit above the village level

grubost'
: crudeness

Kolkhoztsentr
: All Russian (later All Union) Union of Agricultural Collectives; the primary agency in charge of the collective farm system and nominally under the jurisdiction of the People's Commissariat of Agriculture

kommuna
: most advanced type of collective farm, in which all property is socialized and production is collectively organized

Komsomol
: Communist Youth League

kulak
: literally a "fist"; a wealthy peasant who exploits the labor of others; most often used as a term of political opprobrium against opponents of the collective farm and/or other policies; used in this text (unless otherwise noted) in the political, rather than the socioeconomic, sense

MTS
: machine tractor station

mullah
: Islamic religious leader in Central Asia

muzhik
: peasant man (slightly pejorative)

258   *Glossary*

OGPU
Ob''edinennoe Gosudarstvennoe Politicheskoe Upravlenie; Unified State Political Administration, or internal security police

okrug
administrative-territorial unit between the district and regional levels; abolished in the summer of 1930

peregibshchik
one who commits excesses (*peregiby*—term used for violations in the collectivization campaign)

pod''em
upsurge or upward thrust; used to designate a revolutionary or radical mood among workers

podkulachnik
kulak agent

region
oblast', *krai*, or republic; administrative-territorial units below the central level

RSFSR
Russian Soviet Federative Socialist Republic

sel'sovet
lowest level of rural government

stazh
term of tenure or service at the factory bench, in the Communist party, or in the trade union

toz
least advanced type of collective farm, where only the land and part of the inventory are socialized

A NOTE ON SOURCES

Western specialists working on the Soviet period and, in particular, the Stalin years face major difficulties in their access to and use of sources. Western scholars are not admitted to Communist party archives, and only with difficulty can they obtain access to government archives. Central newspapers and journals are available but regional and district press publications are more difficult to obtain. Problems of access are compounded by the problem of extreme source-bias, which has resulted from state ownership and control of publishing in the USSR. These problems have served as a major factor in determining the relatively narrow source base upon which much of the Western literature on the Stalin years is founded.

Despite serious problems of access and bias, there is a massive amount of available source material which either has not been used or has been underutilized by Western scholars. This raises a third problem—the problem of the researcher's own bias in approaching and selecting sources. Western scholars have relied predominantly on a restricted range of sources reflecting either political history and political science approaches or political biases: official statements, laws, theoretical tracts of leaders and members of the opposition, and, in the main, émigré and dissident memoirs. Other types of sources (e.g., newspapers, journals, document collections, popular pamphlets, workers' memoirs, etc.) have been neglected. This has led to two consequences. First, the initial bias which influenced source selection is often mirrored in these traditional sources and, therefore, serves to reaffirm traditional views and preconceptions. Second, reliance on certain types of sources has become a standard, if not orthodox, procedure. These are both serious consequences because they have served to increase the already fixed rigidity of outlook and approach in the field.

This situation has begun to change over the last decade with the advent of the study of Soviet social history. Social historians have contributed to the field of Soviet studies by broadening the available data base of the early 1930s through the introduction of new sources and evidence, which, in turn, has led to new interpretations of the period. This book is intended to contribute further to the data base by introducing Western scholars to new sources and evidence on the early years of collectivization—most notably, materials from Soviet government archives. Problems of bias in the sources and of access have not been completely overcome, needless to say. A broad range of sources, compared and contrasted, has served in part to minimize the bias; in other cases, the bias has been retained and put to use in order to illuminate the mentality of the leading actors in the study. Although access to and selection from sources has been broad, certain problems have proved insurmountable. For example, Communist party and regional archives were closed to the author, despite permission to work in central government archives. In addition, data on the 25,000ers after 1932 is scant and some of the statistical sources on the 25,000ers are problematic. (While trade union statistics are, in general, good, statistics from Kolkhoztsentr and its regional affiliates are often marred by omissions and arithmetical errors.) These problems have been offset, for the most part, by a broad variety of sources, ranging from secondary material to popular pamphlets and workers' memoirs and from the periodical press to archival documents.

Soviet secondary sources constitute the first category of source used in this study. Although their interpretations are often unacceptable to Western researchers, these sources provide Western scholars with useful raw material, excerpted from unpublished statistical data, central and regional laws, Communist party plenums, regional party conferences, and personal correspondence. This material is derived from central and regional Communist party and government archives, regional and district periodicals, and factory newspapers, all of which are generally not accessible to Western scholars. This source's value is governed by such factors as author, date of publication, and, in particular, region of publication. The interpretations offered by most Soviet authors are heavily oriented to the politics of the current leadership, although since the 1960s there has been a greater detachment in Soviet works on collectivization. Publisher and place of publication are often decisive in determining the value of a given work. This study has drawn heavily on regional publications, which have often proved to be an invaluable source of information on regional developments, sometimes neglected in central publications. In some cases they also provide sensitive data which may not have escaped the censors in Moscow and Leningrad.

Contemporary political pamphlets are another important source of information used in this study. Political pamphlets often contain sensitive material (such as descriptions of peasant riots) when their purpose is to popularize a new policy or policy reversal. For instance, pamphlets discussing "excesses" in collectivization after Stalin called a halt to the winter 1930 campaign were intended to illustrate the culpability of local cadres and therefore abound with examples of the excesses of the times. The pamphlets also served an instructional or propaganda purpose. They are, therefore, useful in assessing the motives behind the actions of those for whom a pamphlet was intended. This is, in particular, the case regarding instruction pamphlets for 25,000ers.

The study has also drawn from both émigré and dissident memoirs and from workers' memoirs. Both types of memoirs are heavily slanted and reflect the social and political bias of their authors. In the case of the Soviet-published workers' memoirs, the bias of the censor is also reflected. However, the bias can be put to use once it is recognized. This is especially so for memoirs written by 25,000ers which reflect to some extent the opinions and perspectives of the workers and permit a glimpse at events through their eyes. This, moreover, is a glimpse which has been ignored or dismissed by most Western researchers, who traditionally have viewed the upheavals of this period from the perspective of the government, the intellectuals, or the peasants as observed by intellectuals. Memoirs, like pamphlets, can also serve as a source of sensitive information which might not ordinarily appear in a more scholarly or official source.

Published laws and directives are another category of source which can be put to a variety of uses. Their most obvious use is as a source of information on policy. They have another use, however, which is less obvious and which has been applied in this study. The "law of laws" is that the more frequently an almost identical law or directive is issued, the more likely the object of the law is not enforced or is unenforceable. The frequency of certain types of legislation in this period often implies continuing problems. In the case of the 25,000ers, there was a reverse correlation between the number of directives issued on particular problems and the degree of success in enforcement. This study has drawn on laws and directives from the Central Committee, regional party committees, the Central Council of Trade Unions, Kolkhoztsentr, and other administrative organs involved in the campaign.

Soviet newspapers and journals are perhaps the most important source used in the study. These relatively underutilized sources are the single most important available source for Western scholars. With the exception of newspapers from Moscow, Leningrad, the Urals, and the North Caucasus, the majority of the newspapers used are central newspapers. The journals used here are from central, regional, and *okrug* levels. These periodicals represent a range of institutional interests, including the party, the Komsomol, the trade unions, and Kolkhoztsentr.

Periodical publications have a variety of uses and contain rich material. There is good information in the press in this period on policy debates, the political mood of workers in the factories and in the countryside, and the method by which policy was implemented. To derive the most value from these sources, it is necessary to read in a detailed fashion, following chronology and differences in reporting between different organs of publication. In addition, it is necessary to be aware of the importance of journalistic campaigns centering around policy issues or problems. These often indicate the beginnings of a policy debate and serve to relax somewhat the ordinarily stringent control of information in the press, providing an occasion for descriptions of problems and mistakes.

Documents from Soviet government archives, the Smolensk Archive, and published archival materials constitute the final major source used in the study. The Soviet archival materials used are from the Central State Archive of the National Economy

(TsGANKh) and the Central State Archive of the October Revolution (TsGAOR). Documents from TsGANKh are derived from the holdings of Kolkhoztsentr; the documents from TsGAOR are from the rural departments of the central committees of the major industrial trade unions. The documents span the years 1929 through 1931, and include reports, resolutions, statistics, questionnaires, and letters written by 25,000ers. Needless to say, archives, like the other sources mentioned above, are not the repository of truth: they reflect the bias of the times, of the documents' authors, and of institutional recordkeeping. Nevertheless, the letters contained in the archives provide an extraordinary glimpse into the mind-set of the actors of this study, and the reports, questionnaires, statistics, and other archival documents used here provide a wealth of information unparalleled in detail and coverage of day-to-day events and policy implementation. This is the first time that these archives have been opened to a Western scholar; it is therefore hoped that the author's use of this new material, along with the other new data in the study, will provide further illumination on the events of the period.

BIBLIOGRAPHY

I. ARCHIVAL SOURCES*

Central State Archive of the National Economy of the USSR (TsGANKh SSSR)

fond 7446 *Kolkhoztsentr SSSR i RSFSR*
    opis' 11 *Upravlenie kadrov*
    opis' 12 *Gruppa 25-tysiachnikov*
    opis' 13 *Natsional'noe biuro*
fond 4108 *Khlebotsentr SSSR i RSFSR*

Central State Archive of the October Revolution and Socialist Construction of the USSR (TsGAOR SSSR)

fond 5452 *TsK soiuza gornorabochikh*
fond 5453 *TsK soiuza kozhevnikov*
fond 5457 *TsK soiuza sherstianoi, shelkovoi i*
        trikotazhnoi promyshlennosti
fond 5466 *TsK soiuza sel'skokhoziaistvennykh i lesnykh rabochikh*
fond 5469 *TsK soiuza rabochikh metallistov*
fond 5470 *TsK soiuza rabochikh khimikov*
fond 5475 *TsK soiuza stroitelei*
fond 5525 *TsK soiuza pechatnikov*
fond 7676 *TsK soiuza rabochikh mashinostroeniia*

Smolensk Archive

The records of the Western Regional Committee of the Communist party, available on microfilm from the National Archives of the United States. For further information, see *Records of the Smolensk Oblast of the All-Union Communist Party of the Soviet Union, 1917–41* (Washington: National Archives and Records Service, 1980).

*Citations of Soviet archival materials are by *fond /opis´ /delo / list* and abbreviated: f.#, op.#, d.#, l.#.

II. NEWSPAPERS

Bednota, published by the Central Committee of the Communist party from 1918; in January 1931 merged with and appeared under title *Sotsialisticheskoe zemledelie*

Izvestiia, organ of the Central Executive Committee of the USSR

Komsomolskaia pravda, organ of the Komsomol Central Committee

Krest'ianskaia gazeta, published by the Central Committee

Krest'ianskaia pravda, organ of the Leningrad regional committee of the party, the Leningrad regional soviet executive committee, and the Leningrad *okrug* committee of the party

Leningradskaia pravda, organ of the Leningrad regional committee of the party and the Leningrad regional soviet executive committee

Molot, organ of the North Caucasus regional committee of the party, the North Caucasus regional soviet executive committee, the North Caucasus regional council of trade unions, and the Rostov city soviet

Moskovskaia derevnia, published by the Moscow regional committee of the party and the Moscow regional soviet executive committee; from February 1930 appeared as *Za kollektivizatsiiu*

Pravda, organ of the Central Committee

Proletarii, published from October 1929 to January 1930 by the Moscow *okrug* committee of the party, the Moscow *okrug* soviet executive committee, and the Moscow *okrug* council of trade unions

Rabochaia gazeta, published by the Central Committee

Rabochaia Moskva, published by the Moscow regional committee of the party, the Moscow regional soviet executive committee, and the Moscow regional council of trade unions

Sel'skokhoziaistvennaia gazeta, published by the Council of People's Commissars; in January 1930 merged with and appeared as *Sotsialisticheskoe zemledelie*

Sotsialisticheskoe zemledelie, organ of the People's Commissariat of Agriculture RSFSR and USSR, Kolkhoztsentr, and Zernotrest; appeared from January 1930, superseding *Sel'skokhoziaistvennaia gazeta* at that time and superseding *Bednota* in January 1931

Trud, organ of the All-Union Central Council of Trade Unions

Ural'skii rabochii, organ of the Ural regional committee and Sverdlovsk *okrug* committee of the party, the Ural regional soviet executive committee, and the Ural council of trade unions

Vecherniaia Moskva, organ of the Moscow soviet

Za industrializatsiiu, organ of the Supreme Council of the National Economy from January 1930; earlier appeared as *Torgovo-promyshlennaia gazeta*

Za kollektivizatsiiu, organ of the Moscow regional committee of the party and the Moscow regional soviet executive committee; appeared from February 1930, superseding *Moskovskaia derevnia*

III. JOURNALS

Biulleten' Ural'skogo oblastnogo komiteta VKP (b)

Bol'shevik, theoretical journal of the Central Committee

Derevenskii kommunist, published by the Central Committee; in August 1930 merged with *Sputnik agitatora (dlia derevni)* to become *Sputnik kommunista v derevne*

Informatsionnaia svodka TsK Vsesoiuznogo soiuza rabochikh metallistov

Informatsionnyi biulleten' TsK Vsesoiuznogo profsoiuza tekstil'shchikov

Izvestiia Donskogo okruzhnogo komiteta VKP (b)

Izvestiia Moskovskogo komiteta VKP (b)

Izvestiia Nizhegorodskogo kraevogo komiteta VKP (b)

Izvestiia Nizhne-Volzhskogo kraevogo komiteta VKP (b)

Izvestiia oblastnogo komiteta VKP (b) TsChO

Izvestiia Severnogo Kavkazskogo kraevogo komiteta VKP (b)

Izvestiia Sibirskogo kraevogo komiteta VKP (b)

Izvestiia Stalingradskogo okruzhnogo komiteta VKP (b)

Kollektivist, organ of Kolkhoztsentr SSSR i RSFSR

Kontrol' mass. Biulleten' oblastnoi kontrol'noi komissii VKP (b) i RKI TsChO

Litsom k derevne, organ of the Department of Work in the Countryside under the Central Committee and Moscow Committee of the party; from no. 6 (1930), organ of the Department of Agitation and Mass Campaigns under the Central Committee and Moscow Committee of the party

Metallist, organ of the Central Committee of the Trade Union of Worker-Metalists

Na fronte kollektivizatsii, organ of the Union of Unions of Agricultural Cooperatives and Kolkhoztsentr

Na Leninskom puti, organ of the Ivanovo-Voznesensk regional committee of the party

Na putiakh kollektivizatsii, organ of the Lower Volga regional Kolkhoztsentr agency; beginning with no. 9/10 (1930), it merged with *Za urozhai* to become *Nizhnevolzhskii kolkhoznik*

Nizhnevolzhskii kolkhoznik, organ of the Lower Volga regional Kolkhoztsentr agency; superseded *Na putiakh kollektivizatsii* and *Za urozhai* in 1930

Partiinoe stroitel' stvo, organ of the Central Committee; earlier appeared as *Izvestiia TsK*

Put' sovetov, organ of the Middle Volga regional committee of the party and the Middle Volga regional soviet executive committee

Put' sovetov, organ of the North Caucasus regional soviet executive committee

Sel'skokhoziaistvennaia zhizn', organ of People's Commissariat of Agriculture RSFSR

Sel'skokhoziaistvennyi informatsionnyi biulleten', organ of the People's Commissariat of Agriculture USSR, All-Union Council of Agricultural Cooperatives, and Kolkhoztsentr

Sotsialisticheskaia rekonstruktsiia sel'skogo khoziaistva, organ of the People's Commissariat of Agriculture USSR

Sovetskaia iustitsiia, organ of the People's Commissariat of Justice RSFSR

Sovetskoe stroitel'stvo, organ of the Central Executive Committee of the USSR

Sputnik agitatora (dlia derevni), organ of the Department of Agitation and Mass Campaigns under the Central Committee and Moscow Committee of the party; in August 1930 it merged with *Derevenskii kommunist* to become *Sputnik kommunista v derevne*

Sputnik kommunista v derevne, published by the Central Committee and Moscow Committee of the party; superseded *Derevenskii kommunist* and *Sputnik agitatora (dlia derevni)* in August 1930

Sudebnaia praktika, supplement to *Sovetskaia iustitsiia*

Vlast' sovetov, organ of the Central Executive Committee of the USSR

Voprosy shefstva, organ of the Department of Agitation and Propaganda under the Central Committee and Moscow Committee of the party

Za urozhai, organ of the Lower Volga regional Kolkhoztsentr agency; superseded by *Nizhnevolzhskii kolkhoznik* in 1930

IV. COLLECTIONS OF LAWS;
PUBLISHED DOCUMENTS; STATISTICS

Belonosov, I. I., and Ivnitskii, N. A., eds. "Dokladnaia zapiska VTsSPS v TsK VKP (b) o rabote shefskikh obshchestv v derevne (1930–33 gg.)." *Istoricheskii arkhiv*, no. 1 (1959).

Bineman, Ia., and Kheinman, S. *Gosudarstvennyi apparat SSSR, 1924–28 gg.* Moscow: Statizdat, 1929.

———. *Kadry gosudarstvennogo i kooperativnogo apparata SSSR.* Moscow: Plankhozgiz, 1930.

Borisov, Iu. S., ed. "Iz istorii sozdaniia kolkhoznykh kadrov v pervyi god sotsialisticheskoi reorganizatsii sel'skogo khoziaistva (1930 g.)." *Istoricheskii arkhiv*, no. 2 (1956).

Bubnov, A. S. "Statisticheskie svedeniia o VKP (b)." *Bol'shaia Sovetskaia entsiklopediia.* 1st ed. Vol. 11. Moscow: Ogiz, 1930.

Chernomorskii, M. N., ed. "Rol' rabochikh brigad v bor'be za sploshnuiu kollektivizatsiiu v Tambovskoi derevne." *Materialy po istorii SSSR. Dokumenty po istorii Sovetskogo obshchestva.* Vyp. 1. Moscow: AN SSSR, 1955.

Gribkova, O. M., and Lepekhina, M. E., eds. "Uchastie rabochikh-metallistov v kolkhoznom stroitel'stve vesnoi 1930 g." *Istoricheskii arkhiv*, no. 2 (1955).

Isbach, A. *One of the 25,000.* Moscow: Cooperative Publishing Society of Foreign Workers in the USSR, 1931.

Isbakh, A. *1 iz 25 tysiach. (Povest' v tridtsati chetyrekh dokumentov).* Moscow and Leningrad, 1931.

Ivnitskii, N. A., ed. "Dvadtsatipiatitysiachniki-Moskvichi na kolkhoznoi rabote (1930 g.)." *Istoricheskii arkhiv*, no. 1 (1956).

Ivnitskii, N. A., and Ezerskii, D. M., eds. "Dvadtsatipiatitysiachniki i ikh rol' v kollektivizatsii sel'skogo khoziaistva v 1930 g." *Materialy po istorii SSSR. Dokumenty po istorii Sovetskogo obshchestva.* Vyp. 1. Moscow: AN SSSR, 1955.

K dvukhnedel'niku po massovoi proverke uslovii raboty 25-ti tysiachnikov i uluchsheniia sviazi s nimi. Baku: Azerbaidzh. SPS, 1930.

Kolkhozy nakanune XVI s''ezda VKP (b). Predvaritel'nye itogi. Moscow: Ekonomstatsektor gosplana SSSR i Kolkhoztsentr, 1930.

Kolkhozy vesnoi 1931 goda. Moscow and Leningrad: TsUNKhU, 1932.

Kolkhozy v 1930 g. Itogi raportov kolkhozov XVI s''ezdu VKP (b). Moscow: Ogiz, 1931.

Kollektivizatsiia sel'skogo khoziaistva. Vazhneishie postanovleniia Kommunisticheskoi partii i Sovetskogo pravitel'stva, 1927–35. Moscow: AN SSSR, 1957.

Kollektivizatsiia sel'skogo khoziaistva na Severnom Kavkaze (1927–37 gg.). Krasnodar: Krasnodarskoe knizhnoe izd-vo, 1972.

Kollektivizatsiia sel'skogo khoziaistva v Severo-Zapadnom raione (1927–37 gg.). Leningrad: LGAOR SS, LGU, Gos. i partiinye arkhivy Leningradskoi, Murmanskoi, Novgorodskoi, Pskovskoi oblastei, Karel'skoi ASSR, 1970.

Kollektivizatsiia sel'skogo khoziaistva v Srednem Povolzh'e. Kuibyshev: Kuibyshevskoe knizhnoe izd-vo, 1970.

Kollektivizatsiia sel'skogo khoziaistva v Zapadnom raione RSFSR (1927–37 gg.). Smolensk: Arkhivnye otdely, gos. i partiinye arkhivy Smolenskoi i Brianskoi oblastei, 1968.

Kollektivizatsiia sel'skogo khoziaistva Zapadnoi Sibiri (1927–37 gg.). Tomsk: Zapadno-Sibirskoe knizhnoe izd-vo, 1972.

KPSS v rezoliutsiiakh i resheniiakh s''ezdov, konferentsii i plenumov TsK. 7th ed. Part 2. Moscow: Gospolitizdat, 1953.

XV s''ezd VKP (b). Dekabr' 1927 goda. Sten. otchet. 2 vols. Moscow: Gospolitizdat, 1961–62.

Politicheskii i trudovoi pod''em rabochego klassa SSSR (1928–29 gg.). Sbornik dokumentov. Moscow: Gospolitizdat, 1956.

Rashin, A. G. *Sostav fabrichno-zavodskogo proletariata SSSR. Predvaritel'nye itogi perepisi metallistov, gornorabochikh i tekstil'shchikov v 1929 g.* Moscow: VTsSPS, 1930.

Rezoliutsii priniatye pervoi Ostrogozhskoi okruzhnoi konferentsii "25000." 28–30 iiulia 1930 goda. Ostrogozhsk: Ostrogozhsk. tip. poligraftresta TsChO, 1930.

Savel'ev, M., and Poskrebyshev, A., eds. *Direktivy VKP (b) po khoziaistvennym voprosam.* Moscow and Leningrad: Gos. sots.-ekon. izd-vo, 1931.

S''ezdy sovetov soiuza sovetskikh sotsialisticheskikh respublik. Sbornik dokumentov. Vol. 3. Moscow: Gosiurizdat, 1960.

XVI konferentsiia VKP (b). Sten. otchet. Moscow and Leningrad: Gosizdat, 1929.

XVI s''ezd VKP (b). Sten. otchet. Moscow and Leningrad: Gosizdat, 1930. This edition is used throughout most of my text.

XVI s''ezd VKP (b). Sten. otchet. 2 vols. Moscow: Partizdat, 1935.

Sobranie zakonov i rasporiazhenii raboche-krest'ianskogo pravitel'stva SSSR. Moscow: Sovnarkom SSSR i STO, 1929–30.

Sotsialnyi i natsional'nyi sostav VKP (b). Itogi Vsesoiuznoi partiinoi perepisi 1927 g. Moscow: Gosizdat, 1928.

Spravochnik partiinogo rabotnika. Vol. 8. Moscow: Partizdat, 1934.

Trud v SSSR. Spravochnik 1926–30. Moscow: Plankhozgiz, 1930.

Zapadnyi oblastnoi komitet VKP (b). Vtoraia oblastnaia partkonferentsiia. (5–12 iiunia 1930 gg.). Sten. otchet. Moscow and Smolensk: Zapadnoe oblastnoe otdelenie Ogiza, 1931.

Zharov, L. I., and Ovcharova, A. V., eds. "Mobilizatsiia 3000 kommunistov na rabotu v derevniu (1924 g.)." *Istoricheskii arkhiv*, no. 1 (1959).

Zvezdin, Z. K., ed. "Shefstvo tekstil'shchikov Moskovskoi, Leningradskoi i Ivanovo-Voznesenskoi oblastei nad khlopkorabami Srednei Azii (1929–30 gg.)." *Istoricheskii arkhiv*, no. 2 (1955).

V. POLITICAL PAMPHLETS AND CONTEMPORARY WORKS; SPEECHES; MEMOIRS AND EYEWITNESS ACCOUNTS; HANDBOOKS AND COURSE PROGRAMS; LITERARY WORKS

Anastasenko, F. I., and Krichevskii, A. O. *25-tysiachniki-Krasnoputilovtsy na kolkhoznoi stroike.* Leningrad: Sel'kolkhozgiz, 1931.

Belbei, R. *Dvadtsat' piat' tysiach rabochikh v kolkhozy.* Moscow: VTsSPS, 1930.

———. *Za ili protiv. Kak rabochii ispravliaet peregiby v derevne.* Moscow: VTsSPS, 1930.

Beregovoi, M. *Moskva-Khoper.* Saratov: Gosizdat, Nizhne-Volzhskoe kraevoe otdelenie, 1930.

Berson, L. *Vesna 1930 goda. Zapiski dvadtsatipiatitysiachnika.* Moscow: Ogiz, 1931.

Chto nuzhno znat' kazhdomu rabotniku kolkhoza? (Dlia 25000 tov., edushchikh v kolkhozy). Moscow: VTsIK, 1930.

Ciliga, Anton. *The Russian Enigma.* London: George Routledge and Sons, 1940.

Efimov, G. V., and Marmorshtein, I. B. *O 25-ti tysiachnikakh.* Leningrad: Leningradskoe oblastnoe izd-vo, 1931.

Efremov, A. *Uchastie metallistov v kollektivizatsii derevni. Doklad na VIII plenume TsK VSRM*. Moscow and Leningrad: VTsSPS, 1930.

Frenkel', S. M. *Rabochii v bor'be za urozhai i kollektivizatsiiu derevni*. Moscow and Leningrad, 1930.

Frolov, F., and Barchuk, V. *Kolkhoz "Krasnyi meliorator." (Kak kulak "vrastaet v sotsializm")*. Moscow: Knigosoiuz, 1930.

Furman, G. *Kak pomogali kolkhozam 25-tysiachniki*. Moscow: Knigosoiuz, 1930.

Gorky, M. "On the Russian Peasantry." *Journal of Peasant Studies*, vol. 4, no. 1 (Oct. 1976).

Grigorenko, Petro G. *Memoirs*. Translated by Thomas P. Whitney. New York: Norton, 1982.

——. *V podpol'e mozhno vstretit' tol'ko krys*. New York: Detinets, 1981.

Gurovich, E. N. *Proletariat na kolkhoznoi stroike*. Moscow: Moskovskii rabochii, 1931.

Hindus, Maurice. *Red Bread*. New York: Jonathan Cape and Harrison Smith, 1931.

Hoover, Calvin B. *The Economic Life of Soviet Russia*. New York: Macmillan, 1931.

Iakovlev, Ia. A. *V pokhod za organizatsiiu kollektivnogo proizvodstva. Doklad Moskovskim rabochim uezzhaiushchim na rabotu v kolkhozy*. Moscow and Leningrad: Gosizdat, 1930.

Iakubovskii, E. *Profsoiuzy v bor'be za kollektivizatsiiu derevni*. Moscow and Leningrad: VTsSPS, 1930.

Kats-Kagan, I. *25,000 proletariev u rulia kolkhozov*. Moscow: VTsSPS, 1930.

Khrushchev Memoirs Transcript. Lenta no. 1. Holdings of the Harriman Institute, Columbia University. New York.

Kirshon, V. *Khleb*. Moscow: Sovetskaia literatura, 1933.

Kolesnikova, G., and Kovanov, N. *Udarniki sotsialisticheskoi stroiki. (Dvadtsatipiatitysiachniki)*. Moscow: Krasnaia gazeta, 1931.

Kopelev, Lev. *I sotvoril sebe kumira*. Ann Arbor: Ardis, 1978.

——. *To be Preserved Forever*. Translated by Anthony Austin. New York: J. B. Lippincott, 1977.

Kureiko, M. *25-tysiachniki na kolkhoznoi stroike*. Moscow and Leningrad: Sel'khozgiz, 1931.

Kuz'min, N. *Sotsialisticheskaia perestroika sel'skogo khoziaistva i zadachi rabochikh edushchikh v derevniu. Rech' na sobranii rabochikh-dobrovol'tsev TsGR edushchikh v kolkhozy. 21 dekabria 1929 g.* Moscow and Leningrad: Sel'khozgiz, 1930.

Legran, Frederick. *16 let v SSSR*. Moscow: Profizdat, 1933.

Lenin, V. I. *Polnoe sobranie sochinenii*. 5th ed. 55 vols. Moscow: Gospolitizdat, 1958–65.

Levichev, T. *Pomoshch' goroda derevne. Rabochie brigady v derevne*. Moscow: Vlast' sovetov, 1930.

Maiakovskii, Vladimir. "Marsh dvadtsati piati tysiach." *Polnoe sobranie sochinenii*. Vol. 10. Moscow: Gosizlit, 1958.

Maksimov, A. *Dvadtsatipiatitysiachniki v kolkhozakh*. Leningrad, 1931.

Mel'kumov, A. *Proletariat i sotsialisticheskoe pereustroistvo derevni*. Moscow: Moskovskii rabochii, 1930.

Mirabo Iu. *Shchodennik dvadtsiatip'iatitisiachnika*. Kharkov: Ukrains'kii robitnik, 1931.

Molotov, V. *Stroitel'stvo sotsializma i protivorechiia rosta. Doklad o rabote TsK VKP (b) na I Moskovskoi oblastnoi partiinoi konferentsii. 14 sentiabria 1929 goda*. Moscow: Moskovski rabochii, n.d.

Nikolaievna, Galina. *Harvest*. Moscow: Foreign Language Publishing House, 1952.

Onipko, K. *Pervye shagi. Zapiski dvadtsatipiatitysiachnika*. Moscow: Krest'ianskaia pravda, 1931.

Ovechkin, Valentin. *Collective Farm Sidelights*. Moscow: Foreign Language Publishing House, n.d.

Pamiatka rabochemu dvadtsatipiatitysiachniku. Moscow: Kolkhoztsentr, 1930.

Panferov, F. *Brusski: A Story of Peasant Life in Soviet Russia*. Translated by Z. Mitrov and J. Tabrisky. New York: International Publishers, n.d.

———. *And Then the Harvest*. Translated by Stephen Garry. London: Putnam, 1939.

Platonov, Andrei. *Chevengur*. Translated by Anthony Olcott. Ann Arbor: Ardis, 1978.

———. "Vprok." In *Opal'nye povesti*, edited by V. A. Aleksandrova. New York: Chekhov Press, 1955.

Po zovu partii. Sbornik vospominanii i statei Leningradtsev-dvadtsatipiatitysiachnikov. Leningrad: Lenizdat, 1961.

Reswick, William. *I Dreamt Revolution*. Chicago: Henry Regnery, 1952.

Rudov, K. "Dvadtsatipiatitysiachniki." *Geroi Sibirskoi piatiletki*. Novosibirsk: Ogiz, 1931.

Rusakov, A. S. "Poslantsy russkogo rabochego klassa v Tadzhikistan." *Voprosy istorii*, no. 7 (1972).

Sholokhov, Mikhail. *Virgin Soil Upturned*. Translated by Robert Daglish. 2 vols. Moscow: Progress Publishers, 1980–81.

Shustov, G. *Kak organizovat' sdel'nye raboty v kolkhozakh*. Moscow: Sel'kolkhozgiz, 1931.

Simonov, N. V. *Kak my organizovali trud v kolkhoze. (Opyt kolkhoza im. Kalinina v vesnu 1930 g.)*. Moscow: Krest'ianskaia gazeta, 1930.

Stalin, I. *Sochineniia*. 13 vols. Moscow: Gospolitizdat, 1946–52.

Strong, Anna Louise. *I Change Worlds*. New York: Garden City Publishing Co., 1937.

———. *The Soviets Conquer Wheat*. New York: Henry Holt and Co., 1931.

Tarasov, I. "Po zovu partii." *Revoliutsionnyi derzhite shag*. Vyp. 1. Moscow: Molodaia gvardiia, 1968.

Uchebnyi plan i programmy kursov po podgotovke rukovodiashchikh kadrov v kolkhozakh. (V sviazi s napravleniem 25000 rabochikh v kolkhozy). Moscow: VTsSPS, 1930.

Vareikis, I. *O sploshnoi kollektivizatsii i likvidatsii kulachestva kak klassa*. Voronezh: Kommuna, 1930.

Vasileostrovtsy v bor'be za sotsialisticheskuiu derevniu, 1923–33. Leningrad: Raisovet, 1933.

Virin, D. *25,000 na fronti kolektivizatsi.* Kharkov and Kiev: Derzhavne vidavnitstvo Ukraini, 1930.

Vitolin, P. *Desiat' let rabochego shefstva.* Moscow: Mosoblshefbiuro i MOSPS, 1933.

Zamiatin, S. *Burnyi god. Opyt raboty piatitysiachnika v Rudnianskom raione na Nizhnei Volge.* Moscow: Krest'ianskaia gazeta, 1931.

VI. SECONDARY SOURCES ON THE 25,000ers

Alekseenko, I. I. "Rabochie-dvadtsatipiatitysiachniki—provodniki politiki kommunisticheskoi partii v kolkhoznom stroitel'stve." *K sorokaletiiu velikoi Oktiabr'skoi sotsialisticheskoi revoliutsii.* Krasnoiarsk: Knizhnoe izd-vo, 1957.

————. "Rabochie-dvadtsatipiatitysiachniki v kolkhoznom stroitel'stve Khakassi." *250 let vmeste s velikim russkim narodom.* Abakan: Khakknigizdat, 1959.

Amangaliev, Z. "Rol' rabochikh brigad i dvadtsatipiatitysiachnikov v ukreplenii soiuza rabochego klassa i trudiashchegosia krest'ianstva (1929–30 gg.) po materialam Kazakhstana." *Uch. zap. Alma-Atinskogo gos. zhen. pedinstituta,* vyp. 1 (1958).

Bitaev, K. A. "Rol' 25-tysiachnikov v provedenii kollektivizatsii sel'skogo khoziaistva v Severnoi Osctii." *Uch. zap. Severo-Osetinskogo gos. pedinstituta,* vol. 23, vyp. 3 (1958).

Bogomolova, K. A. "Dvadtsatipiatitysiachniki v Tadzhikistane." *Doklady AN Tadzh. SSR,* vyp. 9 (1953).

Borisov, Iu. S. *25-tysiachniki.* Moscow: Gospolitizdat, 1959.

Chesnokova, A. V. "Novye materialy o rabote Leningradskikh 25-tysiachnikov v Khakassi." *Uch. zap. Khakasskogo naucho-issledovatel'skogo instituta iazyka, literatury i istorii,* vyp. 15, no. 2 (1970).

Denisov, V. *Odin iz dvadtsatipiatitysiach.* Krasnoiarsk: Krasnoiarskoe knizhnoe izd-vo, 1967.

Diuvbanov, P. "Poslantsy rabochego klassa (25-tysiachniki)." *Kommunist Tatarii,* no. 3 (March 1958).

————. "Rol' rabochikh 25-tysiachnikov v kollektivizatsii sel'skogo khoziaistva i ukreplenii soiuza rabochego klassa i krest'ianstva Tatarii." *Uch. zap. Kazanskogo gos. universiteta,* vol. 120, kn. 5 (1960).

Duishemaliev, T. "Uchastie 25-tysiachnikov v kolkhoznom stroitel'stve Kirgizii." *Izvestiia AN KirgSSR,* vol. 5 (1963).

Efremenkov, N. V., and Mukhachev, V. I. "Dvadtsatipiatitysiachniki-Ural'tsy na kolkhoznoi rabote v 1930 g." *Trudy Ural'skogo politekhnicheskogo instituta. (Raboty kafedry Marksizma-Leninizma),* sb. 86 (1957).

Eroshkin, V. A. *Na ikh doliu vypalo schast'e.* *(O 25-tysiachnikakh).* Ioshkar-Ola: Mariisk. knizhnoe izd-vo, 1976.

————. "Rabochie-dvadtsatipiatitysiachniki v Mariiskoi ASSR." *Voprosy istorii rabochego klassa Mariiskoi ASSR.* Ioshkar-Ola: Kirovskii gos. pedinstitut im. V. I. Lenina, 1969.

Gel'berg, Ia. L. "Dvadtsatipiatitysiachniki Vitebsk-provodniki politiki partii v derevne." *Uch. zap. Vitebskogo veterinarnogo instituta,* vol. 16, vyp. 2 (1958).

German, K. K. *Dvadtsatipiatitysiachniki Belorussi.* Minsk: BGU, 1971.

Grigorchuk, P. S. "Iz istorii dvizheniia 25-tysiachnikov na Ukraine." *Sovetskie arkhivy,* no. 1 (1982).

Iakovlev, I. I. "Iz istorii dvadtsatipiatitysiachnikov na Altae v pervoi polovine 1930 goda." *Nekotorye voprosy istorii KPSS.* Barnaul: Barnaulskii gos. pedinstitut, 1973.

Iulina, A. I. "Kuzbasskie dvadtsatipiatitysiachniki na kolkhoznoi stroike Zapadnoi Sibiri (1929–30 gg.)." *Iz istorii rabochego klassa Sibiri.* Vyp. 3. Kemerovo: Kuzbas. politekh. institut, kafedra istorii KPSS, 1970.

Ivanov, N. I. "Rol' rabochikh brigad i dvadtsatipiatitysiachnikov v kollektivizatsii sel'skogo khoziaistva Chuvashskoi ASSR (1929–32 gg.)." *Uch. zap. NII pri Sov. Ministrov Chuvash. ASSR,* vyp. 40 (1968).

Khaliulin, G. G. "Rol' dvadtsatipiatitysiachnikov v ukreplenii rukovodiashchikh kolkhoznykh kadrov Sibiri." *Partiinye organizatsii Zapadnoi Sibiri v period stroitel'stva sotsializma i kommunizma.* Vyp. 7. Kemerovo: Kemerov. gos. pedinstitut, 1973.

Khodzhaev, Kh. K. "K voprosu o roli dvadtsatipiatitysiachnikov v kolkhoznom dvizhenii v Tadzhikistane." *Nekotorye voprosy istorii KPSS.* Leninabad: Leninabad. gos. pedinstitut im. Kirova, 1972.

Konoplia, A. N., and Zakharov, G. I. "Rol' 25-tysiachnikov Donbassa v sotsialisticheskoi preobrazovanii sel'skogo khoziaistva." *Nauchnye trudy po istorii KPSS.* Vyp. 51. Kiev: Kievskii universitet, 1972.

Larina, A. "Dvadtsatipiatitysiachniki-Leningradtsy na Altae." *Trudy Altaiskogo politekhn. instituta,* vyp. 6 (1968).

Liutvort, G. A., and Stepanenko, Iu. O. "Uchastie 25-tysiachnikov v provedenii sploshnoi kollektivizatsii v Vinnitskom raione (1929–30 gg.)." *Uch. zap. Vinnits. pedinstituta,* vol. 7 (1957).

Livshits, I. F. "Dvadtsatipiatitysiachniki na Ukraine." *Sbornik nauchno-issledovatel'skikh rabot kafedry obshch. nauk Tomskogo politekh. instituta.* Tomsk: Tomskii politekh. institut, 1958.

Machin, G. V. "Priezd rabochikh-dvadtsatipiatitysiachnikov v Uzbekistan." *Sbornik nauch. trudov Tashkentskogo gos. universiteta. (Materialy po istorii, istoriografii i arkheologii),* no. 556 (1978).

Madanov, Kh. M. *Dvadtsatipiatitysiachniki.* Alma-Ata: Kainar, 1972.

Meier, A. "Iz istorii deiatel'nosti partiinykh i profsoiuznykh organizatsii Srednei Azii po mobilizatsii rabochikh-dvadtsatipiatitysiachnikov i ikh ispol'zovaniiu v kolkhoznom stroitel'stve." *Iz istorii kommunisticheskoi partii Kirgizii.* Vyp. 3. Frunze: Mektep, 1967.

Moiseev, I. K. "Dvadtsatipiatitysiachniki v bor'be za sotsialisticheskoe preobrazovanie sel'skogo khoziaistva MASSR." *Aktual'nye problemy istorii sotsialisticheskogo stroitel'stve v Moldavii.* Kishinev: Shtiintsa, 1982.

Mukhachev, V. I. "Deiatel'nost' partiinykh organizatsii Urala po rukovodstvu dvadtsatipiatitysiachnikami (1930–32 gg.)." *Uch. zap. Ural'skogo gos. universiteta*, no. 81, sb. 2 (1968).

Nemakov, N., and Isakov, T. "Dvadtsatipiatitysiachniki v kollektivizatsii sel'skogo khoziaistva." *Iz istorii kommunisticheskoi partii Kirgizii.* Vyp. 2. Frunze: Mektep, 1965.

Nuritov, A., and Iunuskhodzhaev, A. "O roli 25-tysiachnikov v kollektivizatsii sel'skogo khoziaistva v Uzbekistane." *Nauchnye trudy Tashkentskogo gos. universiteta*, vyp. 373 (1970).

Pichugin, I. G. "Rol' 25-tysiachnikov v kollektivizatsii sel'skogo khoziaistva Kazakhstana." *Uch. zap. Kazakhskogo universiteta*, vol. 31, vyp. 3 (1957).

Poliakov, V. A. "K voprosu o 25-tysiachnikakh v Nizhnem Povolzh'e." *Agrarnaia revoliutsiia i sotsialisticheskaia preobrazovaniia v Sovetskoi derevne.* Gor'kii: Gorkii gos. universitet, 1980.

Portnoi, I. L. "Dvadtsatipiatitysiachniki i soiuz sel'khozrabochikh KazSSR v bor'be za kollektivizatsiiu sel'skogo khoziaistva respubliki (1930–32 gg.)." *Izvestiia AN Kazakhskoi SSR (Seriia obshch. nauka)*, no. 5 (1975).

Romanov, V. F. "Tverskie 25-tysiachniki-aktivnye boitsy za pobedu kolkhoznogo stroia v SSSR." *Uch. zap. Moskovskogo pedinstituta*, no. 250 (1967).

Rozenfel'd, V. Ia. *Dvadtsatipiatitysiachniki.* Moscow: Sel'khozgiz, 1957.

Selunskaia, V. M. *Rabochie-dvadtsatipiatitysiachniki.* Moscow: MGU, 1964.

———. "Rabochie-dvadtsatipiatitysiachniki provodniki politiki partii v kolkhoznom stroitel'stve (1929–30 gg.)." *Voprosy istorii*, no. 3 (1954).

Shalina, K. F. "Rol' 25-tysiachnikov v sotsialisticheskom pereustroistve sel'skogo khoziaistva." *Izvestiia Krymskogo pedinstituta*, vol. 36 (1961).

Suslikov, A. A. "Partiinye organizatsii Kuzbassa vo glave dvizheniia dvadtsatipiatitysiachnikov." *K istorii partiinykh organizatsii Kuzbassa.* Vyp. 1. Kemerovo: Kemerov. obkom KPSS, kafedra istorii Marksizma-Leninizma Novo-Kuznetskogo pedinstituta, 1962.

Sviridov, A. I. "Rol' rabochikh brigad i dvadtsatipiatitysiachnikov v provedenii sploshnoi kollektivizatsii sel'skogo khoziaistva (1929–32 gg.)." *Razvitie Sovetskogo sela v period stroitel'stva kommunizma.* Voronezh: Voronezhskii universitet, 1967.

Timofeev, A. N. "Dvadtsatipiatitysiachniki-provodniki politiki partii v kolkhoznom stroitel'stve na Ukraine (1929–30 gg.)." *Iz istorii bor'by kommunisticheskoi partii Ukrainy za sotsialisticheskoe pereustroistvo sel'skogo khoziaistva.* Kiev: Kievskii gos. universitet, 1961.

Tiushev, V. P. "Deiatel'nost' rabochikh-dvadtsatipiatitysiachnikov v kolkhozakh Irkutskoi oblasti." *Oktiabr' i Vostochnaia Sibir'.* Irkutsk: Irkutskii gos. pedinstitut, 1968.

———. "Dvadtsatipiatitysiachniki v Buriat-Mongol'skoi ASSR." *Zapiski Buriat-Mongol'skogo nauchno-issledovatel'skogo instituta kul'tury*, vol. 15 (1952).

_____. "Kommunisticheskaia partiia-organizator deiatel'nosti dvadtsatipiati-tysiachnikov. (Po materialam Vostochnoi Sibiri)." *Velikii Oktiabr' i Vostochnaia Sibir'*. Irkutsk: Irkutskii gos. universitet, 1968.

_____. "Novye dannye o rabote dvadtsatipiatitysiachnikov v Vostochnoi Sibiri. (Po materialam Krasnoiarskikh arkhivov)." *Uch. zap. Irkutskogo gos. pedinstituta. (Seriia istoricheskaia: Voprosy istorii Sibiri)*, vyp. 28 (1967).

_____. "Poslantsy partii i rabochego klassa-dvadtsatipiatitysiachniki-provodniki Leninskoi natsional'noi politiki." *Iz opyta partiinoi rukovodstva sotsialisti-cheskom stroitel'stvom v Vostochnoi Sibiri*. Irkutsk: Irkutskii gos. pedinstitut, 1972.

Ulanov, V. A. "Dvadtsatipiatitysiachniki na Stavropol'e." *Sbornik nauchnykh trudov Stavropol'skogo pedinstituta*, vyp. 9 (1955).

Viola, Lynne. "The Campaign of the 25,000ers: A Study of the Collectivization of Soviet Agriculture, 1929–31." Diss. Princeton University, 1984.

_____. "The '25,000ers': A Study in a Soviet Recruitment Campaign During the First Five Year Plan." *Russian History/Histoire Russe*, vol. 10, pt. 1 (1983).

Zakharov, S. M. "Rabochie-dvadtsatipiatitysiachniki-aktivnye uchastniki sotsialisti-cheskogo pereustroistva sel'skogo khoziaistva Uzbekistana." *Uch. zap. Karshinskogo pedinstituta*, vyp. 4, part 1 (1960).

Zombe, E. "Dvadtsatipiatitysiachniki." *Voprosy istorii*, no. 5 (1947).

VII. SELECTED SECONDARY SOURCES IN RUSSIAN

Abramov, B. A. "Kollektivizatsiia sel'skogo khoziaistva v RSFSR." In *Ocherki istorii kollektivizatsii sel'skogo khoziaistva v soiuznykh respublikakh*, edited by V. P. Danilov. Moscow: Gospolitizdat, 1963.

_____. "O rabote komissii Politbiuro TsK VKP (b) po voprosam sploshnoi kollektivizatsii." *Voprosy istorii KPSS*, no. 1 (1964).

Abramov, B. A.; Vaganov, F. M.; and Golikov, V. A. "O nekotorykh voprosakh istorii pervogo etapa sploshnoi kollektivizatsii sel'skogo khoziaistva." *Voprosy istorii KPSS*, no. 4 (1972).

Abramov, B. A.; Vaganov, F. M.; and Kulikov, V. I. "N. I. Nemakov. Kommu-nisticheskaia partiia—organizator massovogo kolkhoznogo dvizheniia (1929–32 gg.)." *Voprosy istorii KPSS*, no. 6 (1968).

Arsenov, G. I. *Lebedevka, selo kolkhoznoe*. Kursk: Knizhnoe izd-vo, 1964.

Arutiunian, Iu. V. "Kollektivizatsiia sel'skogo khoziaistva i vysvobozhdenie rabochei sily dlia promyshlennosti." *Formirovanie i razvitie Sovetskogo rabochego klassa (1917–61 gg.)*. Moscow: Nauka, 1964.

_____. *Mekhanizatory sel'skogo khoziaistva SSSR v 1929–57 gg*. Moscow: AN SSSR, 1960.

Bakst, E. I. "Uchastie Moskovskikh rabochikh brigad v kollektivizatsii sel'skogo khoziaistva osnovnykh zernovykh raionov strany (1929–31 gg.).'' *Ot Oktiabria k stroitel'stvu kommunizma.* Moscow: Nauka, 1967.

Bastiony revoliutsii. Stranitsy istorii Leningradskikh zavodov. Vyp. 3. Leningrad: Lenizdat, 1960.

Bogdenko, M. L. "K istorii nachal'nogo etapa sploshnoi kollektivizatsii sel'skogo khoziaistva SSSR.'' *Voprosy istorii,* no. 5 (1963).

_____. "Kolkhoznoe stroitel'stvo vesnoi i letom 1930 g." *Istoricheskie zapiski,* vol. 76 (1965).

_____. "Materialy sploshnogo ucheta kolkhozov 1930 g." *Istochnikovedenie istorii Sovetskogo obshchestva.* Vyp. 2. Moscow: Nauka, 1968.

Bogdenko, M. L., and Zelenin, I. E. "Osnovnye problemy istorii kollektivizatsii sel'skogo khoziaistva v sovremennoi Sovetskoi istoricheskoi literature.'' *Istoriia Sovetskogo krest'ianstva i kolkhoznogo stroitel'stva v SSSR.* Moscow: AN SSSR, 1963.

Bol'shaia Sovetskaia entsiklopediia. 3d ed. 30 vols. Moscow: Sovetskaia entsiklopediia, 1970–78.

Borisov, Iu. S. *Podgotovka proizvodstvennykh kadrov sel'skogo khoziaistva SSSR v rekonstruktivnyi period.* Moscow: AN SSSR, 1960.

Burkov, V. N. "Derevenskie partiinye organizatsii Zapadnoi Sibiri v bor'be za razvertyvanie sploshnoi kollektivizatsii i likvidatsiiu kulachestva kak klassa. (Konets 1929–vesna 1930 g.).'' *Uch. zap. Tomskogo gos. universiteta. (Sbornik rabot aspirantov kafedry istorii KPSS),* no. 56 (1965).

Chernopitskii, P. G. *Na velikom perelome. Sel'skie sovety Dona v period podgotovki i provedeniia massovoi kollektivizatsii (1928–31 gg.).* Rostov: Rostovskii universitet, 1965.

Danilov, V. P. "Dinamika naseleniia SSSR za 1917–29 gg." *Arkheograficheskii ezhegodnik za 1968 god.* Moscow: Nauka, 1970.

_____. "K kharakteristike obshchestvenno-politicheskoi obstanovki v Sovetskoi derevne nakanune kollektivizatsii.'' *Istoricheskie zapiski,* vol. 79 (1967).

_____. "Sotsial'no-ekonomicheskie otnosheniia v Sovetskoi derevne nakanune kollektivizatsii.'' *Istoricheskie zapiski,* vol. 55 (1956).

_____. *Sozdanie material'no-tekhnicheskikh predposylok kollektivizatsii sel'skogo khoziaistva v SSSR.* Moscow: AN SSSR, 1957.

Danilov, V. P., and Ivnitskii, N. A. "Leninskii kooperativnyi plan i ego osushchestvlenie v SSSR.'' In *Ocherki istorii kollektivizatsii sel'skogo khoziaistva v soiuznykh respublikakh,* edited by V. P. Danilov. Moscow: Gospolitizdat, 1963.

Danilov, V. P.; Kim, M. P.; and Tropkin, N. V., eds. *Sovetskoe krest'ianstvo. Kratkii ocherk istorii (1917–60).* 2d ed. Moscow: Gospolitizdat, 1973.

Diuvbanov, P. M. *Vedushchaia rol' rabochego klassa v sotsialisticheskom pereustroistve sel'skogo khoziaistva. (Na materialakh avtonomykh respublik Srednego Povolzh'ia).* Kazan: Kazanskii universitet, 1975.

Ezhegodnik Sovetskogo stroitel'stva i prava na 1931 god (za 1929/30 god). Moscow and Leningrad: Gos. sots.-ekon. izd-vo, 1931.

Finarov, A. P. "K voprosu o likvidatsii kulachestva kak klassa i sud'ba byvshikh kulakov v SSSR." *Istoriia Sovetskogo krest'ianstva i kolkhoznogo stroitel'stva v SSSR.* Moscow: AN SSSR, 1963.

Gel'berg, Ia. L. "K voprosu regulirovanii sostava partii v derevne v gody sploshnoi kollektivizatsii." *Uch. zap. Vitebskogo veterinarnogo instituta,* vol. 16, vyp. 2 (1958).

German, K. K. *Vedushchaia rol' rabochego klassa v sozdanii kolkhoznogo stroia v Belorussii (1926–35 gg.).* Minsk: BGU, 1968.

Gimpel'son, E. G. *"Voennyi kommunizm": politika, praktika, ideologiia.* Moscow: Mysl', 1973.

Gushchin, N. Ia. "Likvidatsiia kulachestva kak klassa v Sibirskoi derevne." *Sotsial'naia struktura naseleniia Sibiri.* Novosibirsk: Nauka, Sibirskoe otdelenie, 1970.

———. "Rabochie Leningrada i Moskvy v bor'be za kollektivizatsiiu sel'skogo khoziaistva Sibiri." *Istoriia SSSR,* no. 6 (1965).

———. *Rabochii klass Sibiri v bor'be za sozdanie kolkhoznogo stroia.* Novosibirsk: Nauka, Sibirskoe otdelenie, 1965.

———. *Sibirskaia derevnia na puti k sotsializmu.* Novosibirsk: Nauka, Sibirskoe otdelenie, 1973.

Gushchin, N. Ia.; Zhurov, Iu. V.; and Bozhenko, A. I. *Soiuz rabochego klassa i krest'ianstva Sibiri v period postroeniia sotsializma (1917–37 gg.).* Novosibirsk: Nauka, Sibirskoe otdelenie, 1978.

Iudin, I. N. *Sotsial'naia baza rosta KPSS.* Moscow: Politizdat, 1973.

Ivanov, I. A. "Pomoshch' Leningradskikh rabochikh v kollektivizatsii sel'skogo khoziaistva podshefnykh raionov." *Rabochie Leningrada v bor'be za pobedu sotsializma.* Moscow and Leningrad: AN SSSR, 1963.

———. "Uchastie rabochikh Leningrada v kollektivizatsii sel'skogo khoziaistva SSSR (1929–32 gg.)." *Istoriia rabochego klassa Leningrada.* Vyp. 1. Leningrad: LGU, 1962.

Ivnitskii, N. A. "Fond Kolkhoztsentra SSSR i RSFSR i ego znachenie dlia izucheniia istorii kolkhoznogo dvizheniia v SSSR (1927–32 gg.)." *Problemy istochnikovedeniia.* Vyp. 4. Moscow: AN SSSR, 1955.

———. "Istoriia podgotovki postanovleniia TsK VKP (b) o tempakh kollektivizatsii sel'skogo khoziaistva ot 5 ianvaria 1930 g." *Istochnikovedenie istorii Sovetskogo obshchestva.* Vyp. 1. Moscow: Nauka, 1964.

———. *Klassovaia bor'ba v derevne i likvidatsiia kulachestva kak klassa.* Moscow: Nauka, 1972.

———. "O kriticheskom analize istochnikov po istorii nachal'nogo etapa sploshnoi kollektivizatsii. (Osen' 1929–vesna 1930 gg.)." *Istoricheskii arkhiv,* no. 2 (1962).

———. "O nachal'nom etape sploshnoi kollektivizatsii. (Osen' 1929–vesna 1930 gg.)." *Voprosy istorii KPSS,* no. 4 (1962).

Karevskii, F. A. "Likvidatsiia kulachestva kak klassa v Srednem Povolzh'e." *Istoricheskie zapiski,* vol. 80 (1967).

Kostiuchenko, S.; Khrenov, I.; and Fedorov, Iu. *Istoriia Kirovskogo zavoda, 1917–45*. Moscow: Mysl', 1966.

Kozlova, L. *K pobedu kolkhoznogo stroia*. *Bor'ba Moskovskoi partiinoi organizatsii za podgotovku i provedenie kollektivizatsii*. Moscow: Moskovskii rabochii, 1971.

Kukushkin, Iu. S. *Sel'skie sovety i klassovaia bor'ba v derevne*. Moscow: MGU, 1968.

Kulyshev, Iu. S., and Tylik, S. F. *Bor'ba za khleb*. Leningrad: Lenizdat, 1972.

Lar'kina, E. I. *Podgotovka kolkhoznogo kadrov v period massovoi kollektivizatsii*. Moscow: Sotsekgiz, 1960.

Lel'chuk, V. S. "O nekotorykh sdivakh v riadakh rabochikh khimicheskoi promyshlennosti SSSR, 1917–37." *Formirovanie i razvitie Sovetskogo rabochego klassa (1917–61 gg.)*. Moscow: Nauka, 1964.

Lepeshkin, A. I. *Mestnye organy vlasti Sovetskogo gosudarstva*. Moscow: Gosiurizdat, 1959.

Levin, B., and Suvorov, I. "Sovety i stroitel'stvo sotsializma." In *15 let Sovetskogo stroitel'stva*, edited by E. Pashukanis. Moscow: Gosizdat, 1932.

Medvedev, V. K. *Krutoi povorot. Iz istorii kollektivizatsii sel'skogo khoziaistva Nizhnego Povolzh'ia*. Saratov: Knizhnoe izd-vo, 1961.

———. "Likvidatsiia kulachestva v Nizhne-Volzhskom krae." *Istoriia SSSR*, no. 6 (1958).

Morozov, B. M. *Sozdanie i ukreplenie Sovetskogo gosudarstvennogo apparata*. Moscow: Gospolitizdat, 1957.

Morozov, L. F. *Reshaiushchii etap bor'by s nepmanskoi burzhuaziei*. Moscow: Akad. obshchest. nauk pri TsK KPSS, 1960.

Moshkov, Iu. A. *Zernovaia problema v gody sploshnoi kollektivizatsii sel'skogo khoziaistva SSSR (1929–32 gg.)*. Moscow: MGU, 1966.

Nemakov, N. I. *Kommunisticheskaia partiia-organizator massovogo kolkhoznogo dvizheniia*. Moscow: MGU, 1966.

Nikolaievna, Galina. "Trebovanie zhizni." *Kommunist*, no. 3 (1958).

Panfilova, A. M. *Formirovanie rabochego klassa SSSR v gody pervoi piatiletki*. Moscow: MGU, 1964.

Rashin, A. G. "Dinamika promyshlennykh kadrov SSSR za 1917–58 gg." *Izmeneniia v chislennosti i sostave Sovetskogo rabochego klassa*. Moscow: AN SSSR, 1961.

———. "Rost gorodskogo naseleniia v SSSR (1926–59 gg.)." *Istoricheskie zapiski*, vol. 66 (1960).

Rogachevskaia, L. S. *Likvidatsiia bezrabotitsy v SSSR, 1917–30*. Moscow: Nauka, 1973.

Selunskaia, V. M. *Rabochii klass i Oktiabr' v derevne*. Moscow: Mysl', 1978.

Selunskaia, V. M., et al. *Izmeneniia sotsial'noi struktury Sovetskogo obshchestva 1921-seredine 30-kh godov*. Moscow: Mysl', 1979.

———. *Soiuz sozidatelei novogo obshchestva. Kratkii ocherk istorii soiuza rabochikh i krest'ian (1917–77)*. Moscow: Politizdat, 1979.

Semernin, P. V. "O likvidatsii kulachestva kak klassa." *Voprosy istorii KPSS*, no. 4 (1958).

Bibliography

Sharova, P. N. *Kollektivizatsiia sel'skogo khoziaistva v TsChO, 1928–32 gg.* Moscow: AN SSSR, 1963.

Sidorov, V. A. "Likvidatsiia v SSSR kulachestva kak klassa." *Voprosy istorii*, no. 7 (1968).

————. "Meropriiatiia po trudovomu perevospitaniiu byvshikh kulakov." *Voprosy istorii*, no. 11 (1964).

Smyshliaev, V. A. *Po Leninskim zavetam.* Leningrad: LGU, 1969.

————. "Uchastie Leningradskikh rabochikh v kollektivizatsii sel'skogo khoziaistva (1929–31 gg.)." *Vestnik LGU*, vyp. 1, no. 2 (1957).

Smyshliaev, V. A., and Solov'ev, P. V. "Na perednem krae bor'by za sotsialisticheskoe preobrazovanie derevni." *Leningradskie rabochie v bor'be za sotsializm, 1926–37.* Leningrad: Lenizdat, 1965.

Sovetskii rabochii klass. Kratkii istoricheskii ocherk (1917–73). Moscow: Politizdat, 1975.

Spektor, N. P. "Rabochie promyshlennykh tsentrov v bor'be za sozdanie i uprochenie kolkhoznogo stroia (1929–35 gg.)." *Ot Oktiabria k stroitel'stvu kommunizma.* Moscow: Nauka, 1967.

Strizhkov, Iu. K. *Prodovol'stvennye otriady v gody grazhdanskoi voiny i inostrannoi interventsii, 1917–21 gg.* Moscow: Nauka, 1973.

Stroitel'stvo sotsializma v SSSR i krakh opportunizma. Moscow: Politizdat, 1982.

Sultanova, E. A. "Leningradskie kommunisty v bor'be za sotsialisticheskoe pereustroistvo sel'skogo khoziaistva v 1925–30 gg. (Obzor fondov Leningradskogo partiinogo arkhiva)." *Voprosy istorii KPSS*, no. 5 (1964).

Turchaninova, E. I. *Podgotovka i provedenie sploshnoi kollektivizatsii sel'skogo khoziaistva v Stavropolskom krae.* Dushambei: Tadzhikskii gos. universitet, 1963.

Vdovin, A. I., and Drobizhev, V. Z. *Rost rabochego klassa SSSR, 1917–40 gg.* Moscow: Mysl', 1976.

Vyltsan, M. A. "Pobeda kolkhoznogo stroia i meropriiatii partii i gosudarstva po uluchsheniiu zhizni Sovetskogo krest'ianstva (1933–40 gg.)." *Voprosy istorii KPSS*, no. 6 (1968).

Vyltsan, M. A.; Ivnitskii, N. A.; and Poliakov, Iu. A. "Nekotorye problemy istorii kollektivizatsii v SSSR." *Voprosy istorii*, no. 3 (1965).

Zelenin, I. E. "Kolkhoznoe stroitel'stvo v SSSR v 1931–32 gg." *Istoriia SSSR*, no. 6 (1960).

VIII. SELECTED SECONDARY SOURCES IN ENGLISH

Atkinson, Dorothy. *The End of the Russian Land Commune, 1905–30.* Stanford, Calif.: Stanford Univ. Press, 1983.

Carr, E. H. *Socialism in One Country, 1924–26.* 3 vols. New York: Macmillan, 1958–64.

———. *What is History?* New York: Random House, Vintage Books, 1961.

Carr, E. H., and Davies, R. W. *Foundations of a Planned Economy, 1926–29.* 2 vols. New York: Macmillan, 1969–71.

Cell, Charles P. *Revolution at Work.* New York: Academic Press, 1977.

Chase, Wm. J. "Moscow and Its Working Class, 1918–28: A Social Analysis." Diss. Boston College, 1979.

Dale, Paddy. "The Instability of the Infant Vanguard: Worker Party Members, 1928–32." *Soviet Studies*, vol. 35, no. 4 (Oct. 1983).

Davies, R. W. *The Socialist Offensive: The Collectivization of Soviet Agriculture, 1929–30.* Cambridge, Mass.: Harvard Univ. Press, 1980.

———. *The Soviet Collective Farm, 1929–30.* Cambridge, Mass.: Harvard Univ. Press, 1980.

Fainsod, Merle. *Smolensk Under Soviet Rule.* Cambridge, Mass.: Harvard Univ. Press, 1958.

Fitzpatrick, Sheila. "Cultural Revolution as Class War." In *Cultural Revolution in Russia, 1928–31*, edited by Sheila Fitzpatrick. Bloomington, Ind.: Indiana Univ. Press, 1978.

———. *Education and Social Mobility in the Soviet Union, 1921–34.* Cambridge: Cambridge Univ. Press, 1979.

———. *The Russian Revolution.* Oxford and New York: Oxford Univ. Press, 1982.

Karcz, Jerzy F. "Thoughts on the Grain Problem." *Soviet Studies*, vol. 18, no. 4 (April 1967).

Kuromiya, Hiroaki. "The Crisis of Proletarian Identity in the Soviet Factory, 1928–29." *Slavic Review*, vol. 44, no. 2 (Summer 1985).

Kushner, P. I., ed. *The Village of Viriatino.* Translated and abridged by Sula Benet. Garden City, N.Y.: Anchor Books, 1970.

Lewin, M. *Lenin's Last Struggle.* New York: Random House, Vintage Books, 1970.

———. *The Making of the Soviet System.* New York: Pantheon, 1985. Collection of essays.

———. *Russian Peasants and Soviet Power: A Study of Collectivization.* Translated by Irene Nove. New York: Norton, 1975.

Male, D. J. *Russian Peasant Organisation Before Collectivization.* Cambridge: Cambridge Univ. Press, 1971.

Manning, Roberta Thompson. *The Crisis of the Old Order in Russia: Gentry and Government.* Princeton, N.J.: Princeton Univ. Press, 1982.

Medvedev, Roy A. *Let History Judge: The Origins and Consequences of Stalinism.* Translated by Colleen Taylor and edited by David Joravsky and Georges Haupt. New York: Random House, Vintage Books, 1973.

Millar, James R., and Nove, Alec. "A Debate on Collectivization: Was Stalin Really Necessary?" *Problems of Communism*, vol. 25 (July–Aug. 1976).

Miller, Robert F. *One Hundred Thousand Tractors: The MTS and the Development of Controls in Soviet Agriculture.* Cambridge, Mass.: Harvard Univ. Press, 1970.

Narkiewicz, Olga A. *The Making of the Soviet State Apparatus.* Manchester, Eng.: Manchester Univ. Press, 1970.

Olcott, Martha Brill. "The Collectivization Drive in Kazakhstan." *Russian Review*, vol. 40, no. 2 (April 1981).

Pethybridge, Roger. *The Social Prelude to Stalinism*. New York: St. Martin's Press, 1974.

Ribgy, T. H. *Communist Party Membership in the USSR, 1917–67*. Princeton, N.J.: Princeton Univ. Press, 1968.

Rosenberg, Wm. G. "Smolensk in the 1920s: Party-Worker Relations and the 'Vanguard' Problem." *Russian Review*, vol. 36, no. 2 (April 1977).

Schwarz, Solomon M. *Labor in the Soviet Union*. London: Cresset Press, 1953.

Service, Robert. *The Bolshevik Party in Revolution: A Study in Organisational Change, 1917–23*. New York: Macmillan, 1979.

Shanin, Teodor. *The Awkward Class*. Oxford: Oxford Univ. Press, 1972.

Taniuchi, Y. *The Village Gathering in Russia in the Mid-1920s*. Birmingham Univ. Soviet and East European Monographs, no. 1, Birmingham, Eng. 1968.

Tucker, Robert C. "Stalinism as Revolution from Above." In *Stalinism: Essays in Historical Interpretation*, edited by Robert C. Tucker. New York: Norton, 1977.

Viola, Lynne. "The Campaign to Eliminate the Kulak as a Class, Winter, 1930: A Note on the Legislation." *Slavic Review* (forthcoming).

―――. "Bab'i Bunty and Peasant Women's Protest During Collectivization." *Russian Review*, vol. 45, no. 1 (Jan. 1986).

―――. "Notes on the Background of Soviet Collectivization: Metal Worker Brigades in the Countryside, Autumn 1929." *Soviet Studies*, vol. 36, no. 2 (April 1984).

Yaney, George L. "Agricultural Administration in Russia from the Stolypin Land Reform to Forced Collectivization: An Interpretive Study." In *The Soviet Rural Community*, edited by James Millar. Urbana, Ill.: Univ. of Illinois Press, 1971.

―――. *The Urge to Mobilize: Agrarian Reform in Russia, 1861–1930*. Urbana, Ill.: Univ. of Illinois Press, 1982.

Index

281